Partners in Innovation

Partners in Innovation

Teaching Assistants in College Science Courses

Elaine Seymour
with
Ginger Melton, Douglas J. Wiese,
and Liane Pedersen-Gallegos

ROWMAN & LITTLEFIELD PUBLISHERS, INC.
Lanham • Boulder • New York • Toronto • Oxford

ROWMAN & LITTLEFIELD PUBLISHERS, INC.

Published in the United States of America
by Rowman & Littlefield Publishers, Inc.
A wholly owned subsidary of The Rowman & Littlefield Publishing Group, Inc.
4501 Forbes Boulevard, Suite 200, Lanham, Maryland 20706
www.rowmanlittlefield.com

P.O. Box 317, Oxford OX2 9RU, UK

British Library Cataloguing in Publication Information Available

Library of Congress Cataloging-in-Publication Data

Seymour, Elaine.
    Partners in innovation : teaching assistants in college science courses / Elaine
  Semour; with Ginger Melton, Douglas J. Wiese, and Laine Pedersen-Gallegos.
      p. cm.
    Includes bibliographical references and index.
    ISBN 0-7425-4020-0 (alk. paper) — ISBN 0-7425-4021-9 (pbk. : alk. paper)
    1. Science—Study and teaching (Higher)—United States. 2. Science—Vocational
  guidance—United States. 3. Graduate teaching assistants—United States. I. Title.
  Q183.3.A1S44 2005
  507'.1'1—dc22

                                                                                2005016517

Printed in the United States of America

∞™ The paper used in this publication meets the minimum requirements of
American National Standard for Information Sciences—Permanence of Paper
for Printed Library Materials, ANSI/NISO Z39.48-1992.

Contents

Tables

Acknowledgments

I am greatly indebted to the many people who have helped me with this project. First, my thanks go to the principal investigators and participants in the three initiatives that were the sources of data for this study. For the "Chemlinks Coalition: Making Chemical Connections," the principal investigators were Drs. Brock Spencer, James E. Swartz, Sandra L. Laursen, and David W. Oxtoby. For the ModularCHEM Consortium ("Sweeping Change in Manageable Units: A Modular Approach to Chemistry Curriculum Reform"), the principal investigators were Drs. C. Bradley Moore, Angelica M. Stacy, and Susan E. Kegley; and, at a later stage, Eileen L. Lewis as project director. Thanks also to the ModularCHEM evaluator, Joshua Gutwill-Wise, for his insights into student responses to innovation in modular chemistry classes, some of which are cited in this volume. Many faculty in both initiatives gave generously of their time as interviewees at different stages in project development, thus helping to set the background for this and other related studies. For the purpose of data gathering for this work, faculty at ten participating institutions gave us interviews and also helped us to arrange interviews and focus groups with the teaching assistants (TAs) and undergraduates in their modular chemistry classes and with some of their colleagues. Our particular thanks to everyone who gave us such good help at each of the following institutions: Evergreen College, Randolf-Macon College, University of St. Thomas, University of Michigan (Dearborn), Carleton College, University of California (Berkeley), American River College, New Mexico State College, Beloit College, and Rock County College, University of Wisconsin.

For "Educating Teaching Assistants in New Models for Teaching and Learning" at the University of California, Berkeley, my thanks go to the program designers, Drs. Angelica M. Stacy and Eileen L. Lewis, the course

x   *Acknowledgments*

coordinator Dr. Robert M. Bornick, and all of the TAs. For "Interactive Astronomy: Integrating Web-Based Curriculum into Introductory Classes
with Large Sections," at the University of Colorado at Boulder, my thanks
to Dr. Richard McCray, his head TAs, and the undergraduate coaches.

I offer special thanks to my three collaborators, beginning with Dr. Ginger
Melton, research associate at Ethnography and Evaluation Research, who undertook the difficult task of distilling, from a very large body of literature on
different facets of TA work and professional development, those studies with
most bearing for this project. Her careful work resulted in a thematic synthesis of aspects of the relevant literature that provide a useful commentary
on particular findings from this study. Her work indicates how little literature
is available in some of the areas addressed in this volume. However, she also
shows how the small body of research and evaluation on TAs in innovative
classrooms illuminates issues and needs, both in those contexts and in more
conventional classes that employ TAs. I am also grateful to Ginger Melton for
her excellent editing work on the manuscript overall and for constructing the
index.

My thanks also to Dr. Liane Pedersen-Gallegos, director of Ethnography
and Evaluation Research, Center to Advance Teaching and Research in the Social Sciences, the University of Colorado at Boulder. Together, Dr. Pedersen-
Gallegos and I undertook all of the on-site undergraduate interviews for the
second round of the modular chemistry evaluation project that are referenced
at points in this volume. She took the lead in coding the student text data and
played a major role in their analysis. As the formative evaluator for the Interactive Astronomy project, she also undertook most of the interviews and all
of the coding and analysis for the undergraduate interviews. She worked interactively with Dr. McCray and the coaches throughout the project, introducing issues arising from the analysis for discussion at their weekly meetings. These meetings were important in generating discussion among the
coaches about aspects of the innovation's progress and are often reflected in
my subsequent interviews with them. I am indebted to Dr. Pedersen-Gallegos
for our discussions over time on trends that emerged from the undergraduate
interview data in both projects.

Thanks to Dr. Douglas J. Weise, who undertook the initial analysis, for evaluation purposes, of the TA interviews for the Berkeley TA education initiative.
His two reports to the Berkeley principal investigators were valuable resources as I explored other aspects of the data sets and began the subsequent
cross-initiative analysis. He was also responsible for a good portion of the coding and analysis of student interviews for the modular chemistry evaluation.

Thanks to Graham Porter for help in organizing the cross-initiative analysis in its early stages.

Thanks also to our funders. The National Science Foundation, Division of
Undergraduate Education, provided funding for development and imple-

mentation for all three initiatives. The program officers were Susan H. Hixson, both for ChemLinks and ModularCHEM and for the Berkeley TA education initiative; and Herb Levitan and Joan Prival for Interactive Astronomy. These awards also made provision for data gathering and analysis for evaluation purposes and enabled me to include the modular chemistry TAs and the astronomy coaches in our samples. Additional funding was provided for both Interactive Astronomy and the ChemLinks Coalition by the Pew Grant Program. The funding required for the synthetic, cross-initiative analysis and writing that resulted in this volume was largely provided by an award from the National Science Foundation's program "Innovation and Organizational Change," directed by John Naiman. Aspects of the analysis that address issues of resistance to innovation in undergraduate science education were funded by a second National Science Foundation award, for which the program officer is Myles Boylan. My work on "resistance to innovation" is ongoing and is also supported by a matching grant from the University of Colorado at Boulder, at the instigation of the former vice chancellor for research Dr. Carol Lynch. An award from the Camille and Henry Dreyfus Foundation has allowed me to collect additional interviews and to do secondary analysis that addresses issues of change and resistance among faculty that have been exposed to chemistry modules through workshops and other means. Work on these topics is ongoing. However, I hope that the National Science Foundation, the Camille and Henry Dreyfus Foundation, the University of Colorado, and the program officers with whom I worked will be pleased with these first results and will see this volume as useful in their sustained efforts to encourage growth in quality and access in undergraduate and graduate science education.

I have been especially fortunate in the creative and fearless advice offered by a group of colleagues who undertook to review and critique the emergent manuscript and who have offered me suggestions as to the shape and style of the narrative. This group comprises Drs. Sandra Laursen (research associate in Ethnography and Evaluation Research and at the Cooperative Institute for Research in Environmental Sciences at the University of Colorado at Boulder), Susan B. Millar (former director and founder of the Learning by Evaluation, Adaptation, and Dissemination Center, now senior scientist at the Wisconsin Center for Education Research, both at the University of Wisconsin, Madison), Norman Fortenberry (director, Center for the Advancement of Scholarship on Engineering Education, National Academy of Engineering), Richard McCray (George Gamow Distinguished Professor of Astrophysics, University of Colorado at Boulder), Brock Spencer (Kohnstamm Professor of Chemistry, Beloit College), Eileen L. Lewis (professor of chemistry, Canada College; lecturer and specialist, Department of Chemistry, University of California, Berkeley), and Myles Boyan (lead program director, Division of Undergraduate Education, National Science Foundation).

My gratitude is especially expressed to Sandra Laursen and Susan Millar. Sandra has advised me on the project from an early stage. She tackled every chapter, initially in a rough form; worked with me through several iterations toward a readable draft; and saw the manuscript right through to its final version. In addition to her incisive critique of the manuscript's logic and style, reference to her own experience was invaluable—as a chemistry educator, as co–principal investigator of the ChemLinks Coalition, as a module author, and as a chemical education workshop leader. She was also able to advise on what findings would be of interest largely to the innovation participants and which would have relevance for a wider audience.

Dr. Susan Millar took on the whole manuscript as it stood in summer 2004. She offered a critical commentary on the flow of the narrative, the presentation of evidence, the argument, style, and level of detail needed (and not needed) to make a coherent, well-supported story. Her own role and experience at the center of the national movement for change in science education over the last fifteen or so years also made her a highly informed critic. One result of the combined editorial advice of these two reviewers and also that of Dr. Norman Fortenberry was to restructure the chapters to make what I hope is now a coherent storyline. Following the advice that the TAs and students gave to the innovators, I have sought to signpost the direction of the work and pay attention to building the story in a way that is useful to readers. My thanks to you all. A good editor is beyond price.

My last and warmest thanks go to all of the TAs and coaches who spoke with me about their experiences in so open and honest a manner. The detail of their observations, explanations, illustrations, and critique provide the substance of this account. In the ethnographic tradition, they are the expert witnesses, and their voices are the data in which my findings, explanations, and arguments are grounded. They were willing to share with me their doubts and sometimes their anger and frustrations, as well as their faith in the value of the innovations. Their analysis, examples, qualifications, and caveats are a trove of practical advice for faculty working in both innovating and more conventional modes. Collectively, they convince me that we have a national opportunity to engage and professionally develop a new generation of science faculty who can draw undergraduates into active, interactive, and responsible modes of learning that can change the ways in which educated people understand science and are enabled to use it in their everyday lives and work. My thanks to each of them. I hope that they will feel that this story offers a truthful and worthwhile account of their experiences and ideas.

Elaine Seymour
May 2005

1

Introduction

CONTEXT, SOURCES, AND SCOPE OF THIS WORK

Efforts to improve teaching and learning in science, technology, engineering, and mathematics (STEM) classes for undergraduates have been underway since the mid-1980s. Over that period there has grown an interconnected nationwide community of STEM faculty who are experimenting with alternative modes of curriculum, pedagogy, and learning assessments and discussing their discoveries with each other and the wider community. Their work is promoted and funded by public and private agencies, monitored by program evaluators, and grounded in a growing awareness of the relevance of educational theory and research to undergraduate science education. In the same time frame, this community's collective understanding of the task at hand, and how best to approach it, has widened—from an initial narrow focus on losses from the undergraduate and graduate STEM pipeline to a concern to promote the scientific and mathematical competence of all students (Seymour 2001). The processes of experimentation, refinement, and dissemination have produced many classroom-tested methods and materials that are accessible to STEM educators in published work, at conferences, on websites, and through workshops. However, a consistent challenge to the community of STEM educational reformers has been how best to infuse large university classes with more of the active and interactive learning methods that have flourished in the smaller classes typical of liberal arts and community colleges. The work of pioneers in this domain, such as that of Eric Mazur (1997), is imitated and adapted, while the search continues for more viable alternatives or supplements to lecturing as the dominant (and often sole) teaching method used in large university science classes.

Given the difficulties of addressing this issue, it is curious that relatively little attention has been given to exploring the collaborative potential of teaching assistants (TAs) who are employed as aids in recitation and lab sections in many, perhaps most, large university classes. There is an extensive literature on the "training" of largely graduate teaching assistants for work in more conventionally taught STEM classes and labs. However, there is relatively little written on the education and role of TAs who work with faculty who are using more innovative teaching approaches. Both bodies of work are reviewed in chapter 9.

The opportunity to offer some observations on this somewhat neglected resource arose in the course of four separate pieces of work—one in research and three as part of larger evaluations. Each of these, while focused largely on undergraduates in the STEM disciplines and their faculty, provided data on the contributions that TAs can make in both innovative and more traditional classrooms. Findings from the same data sets also address the conditions in which the TAs' potential to make such contributions is realized or constrained. The three evaluation studies were of two projects in chemistry and one in astronomy. However, there is nothing in the projects themselves or in the evaluation findings that would limit their wider application. Indeed, the goal of this volume is to distill from the patterns of experience described by participants in these three innovations principles that can usefully be applied across STEM disciplines.

Summarizing across these three initiatives, this account addresses what TAs can and do contribute as teachers and facilitators of interactive sessions with undergraduates, what they need by way of education and support to do this well, and what they may gain in the process. It also offers the TAs' critiques of the innovative classes in which they worked, examines the basis for these evaluations, and discusses their insights into the different reasons why both undergraduates and TAs may resist the work of classroom innovators. Finally, the account describes the role that TAs can play in helping to make faculty innovations work, the redefinition of the TA role that this involves, and the conditions under which TAs can make an optimal contribution to innovative teaching and learning for STEM undergraduates.

THE CHANGING ROLES AND RESPONSIBILITIES OF TEACHING ASSISTANTS IN UNDERGRADUATE SCIENCE COURSES

Institutions of higher education rely heavily on graduate students for the instruction of undergraduates. According to the National Center for Education Statistics (2000), across all disciplines, 46 percent of all graduate teaching assistants (GTAs), including those working in professional fields, carry full teaching responsibility for one or more courses, 26 percent lead discussion sections, and 37 percent supervise lab sections for faculty-taught courses. The use of graduate teaching assistants is particularly high in the disciplines of science, mathematics, and engineering. A 1989 survey of two thousand doctoral students in three STEM disciplines (chemistry, civil engineering, microbiology) plus sociology at major research universities found that two-thirds had been teaching assistants (Anderson and Swazey 1998). A national study of the top fifty public and private universities and sixty-nine regional state universities found that 93 percent of biology labs were taught primarily by GTAs (Sundberg and Armstrong 1993). Taking the life sciences and physical sciences together, 70 percent of lab sections are supervised by GTAs (National Center for Education Statistics 2000).

The work typically undertaken by graduate student TAs in more conventionally taught science courses includes supervising labs, leading discussion sections (also known as recitations or quiz sections), assisting faculty with specific tasks, or (in the case of some GTAs) assisting with aspects of the teaching. Within these broader role categories, graduate TA responsibilities include a wide range of duties. They lead discussions, review lecture content with students and answer their questions, supervise and work with students in lab sessions, distribute and collect assignments, grade student work and maintain their performance records, and hold office hours (Peterson 1990; Ford 1993; White 1993). Less frequently, graduate TAs design quizzes, proctor or grade exams, give substitute lectures, share presentation of new material with faculty, advise students, or supervise other TAs (Peterson 1990; White 1993).

Some institutions of higher education (such as liberal arts colleges) have always used undergraduates as teaching assistants. They are often recruited as students who have taken the course and performed well. Undergraduates have also begun to be employed as TAs in universities, where they share some of the functions of their graduate colleagues. In both settings, they facilitate small-group discussions, grade minor assignments, conduct homework or review sessions, and hold office hours. In addition, they often assist students with their projects (such as writing, research, and group presentations) and manage web-based discussion forums. Less commonly, they perform demonstrations and provide technology support (Eby and Gilbert 2000; Wood et al. 2001; Jacobs 2002).

With the shifts in STEM faculty thinking about their teaching role, the focus of undergraduate science education has been gradually changing from an exclusive focus on the production of majors to the broader goal of making science education available and relevant to more students. To this end, STEM faculty have led the way on their campuses in rethinking both the content and pedagogy of classes that are gateways into their disciplines. Their classroom innovations increasingly draw on a corpus of knowledge gleaned from education theory and research that have been made more accessible to

STEM faculty by national dissemination networks promoted by the National Science Foundation's systemic initiatives and by those sponsored by private foundations. The outcome has been a gradual shift in focus from teaching to learning and from passive teacher-dependent forms of learning to active student engagement in learning. The role of the teacher as lecturer is questioned and replaced by the role of teacher as facilitator of learning. Classrooms and labs have become more interactive, and course content is offered in greater depth, with more attention to conceptual and cross-disciplinary linkages, real-life relevance, writing, reading primary material, and learning retention (Seymour 2001). Although these changes have not, as yet, become the normal mode of teaching and learning for whole schools and departments, STEM faculty innovators can be found on most campuses, and their work is increasingly documented and discussed in disciplinary journals and at professional meetings.

All of these changes vitally affect the role of teaching assistants employed in innovative STEM classes. While TAs are likely to continue to lead recitations, supervise labs, hold office hours, and grade assignments, they must also support the new pedagogy as learning facilitators (Nurrenbern, Mickiewicz, and Francisco 1999; Sundberg et al. 2000). TAs may be redefined as "coaches" who help students work in teams as they explore new content, approach problems, and think about issues posed to them. French and Russell (2002) describe one revised TA lab role: "to socratically guide students to relevant information" as they explore new concepts in labs where the results are not predetermined. The extent to which innovating faculty are adjusting the work roles, preparation, and professional support of their TAs is, as yet, little documented.

A small number of studies explore the role of TAs in innovative classes outside of the sciences. TAs in a communication course at the University of Washington act as "research mentors" and model active modes of learning (Karasz, Reynolds, and Wall 1997). Sociology TAs at the University of Toledo serve as writing consultants and as intermediaries who amplify the students' perspectives to the professor and "translate" the professor's thinking for students. They model critical thinking by questioning the instructor, thus helping "to produce a more collective learning process, emphasize the role of experience in learning, integrate thought with experience, and empower students" (Stoecker et al. 1993, 335). In multidisciplinary courses at the University of California, Los Angeles, TAs are described as facilitating research, collaborative work, discussion and debate, critical thinking, quantitative reasoning, logical argumentation skills, and writing skills (University of California, Los Angeles 2000).

Finally, Wood and colleagues (2001) point to the consequences of innovations for graduate TAs in courses that simultaneously employ undergraduate TAs as learning facilitators. As GTAs in these classes no longer "teach," their traditional role may be reduced to holding office hours and grading. Their choice is to reinvent a role for themselves by exploring and building their expertise in the new pedagogy of collaborative learning and in mentoring, course and curriculum development, and cross-disciplinary teaching and learning.

None of the three STEM classroom innovations that are the focus of this volume employed TAs as "teachers." However, all of them employed some mixture of graduate and undergraduate TAs in proportions that reflect the nature of the participating institutions (research and state universities with graduate schools versus undergraduate liberal arts colleges), the size of their classes, and the educational philosophies of the innovators. As I describe in some detail, the educational goals of these innovations and the manner of their implementation had a profound impact on the work roles of their TAs. As I also discuss, the degree to which this impact was a planned, intentional aspect of the innovation was variable. Throughout this account, I use the term *teaching assistant* as a generic title to gloss the different job titles and work roles of the graduate and undergraduate students employed in each innovative class. However, in one of the courses included in the study, the innovating professor explicitly chose the title of "coach" for his undergraduate TAs, to emphasize their primary role as learning facilitators. I use this term wherever I wish to make a distinction between these coaches and other teaching assistants.

2

The Importance of Teaching Assistants to Undergraduates in the Sciences

I begin the discussion of how TA roles may be expected to change in innovative science courses with an account of what TAs in more conventionally taught science courses already contribute to undergraduate learning. The nature of this contribution is summarized from descriptions offered by undergraduates themselves. These data were a subset of findings from an intensive interview study whose overall purpose was to understand the factors that contributed to national field-switching losses of approximately 40 percent to 60 percent from among high-ability declared and intending majors in science, mathematics, and engineering (SME).[1] The sample of 335 SME "switchers" and "persisters" with mathematics SAT scores of 650 or greater were drawn from seven institutions that collectively represent the types of institution in which most undergraduates experience their SME education.[2] Findings were verified with a further sample of 125 SME majors in six other institutions. The full account of our findings appears in *Talking about Leaving: Why Undergraduates Leave the Sciences* (Seymour and Hewitt 1997).

From one part of our analysis of these interview data, we learned about the contributions that teaching assistants make both to undergraduate learning and to the support and survival of students in SME majors. We were also presented with evidence that counters faculty mythology that places on the shoulders of TAs some portion of blame for student losses from introductory SME classes. Across the sample, and in all seven institutions, complaints about poor teaching by TAs (largely in lab and recitation sections) came well down the list of the twenty-three concerns collectively offered by both switchers and persisters in the SME majors. Problems with the teaching or academic support of their TAs ranked seventeenth of all twenty-three concerns that were expressed both by switchers and by SME majors who had persisted to their senior years. Not one switcher reported poor teaching or lack of support by their TA as a factor in the decision to pursue a different major.

Faculty in the science commonly delegate more teaching responsibility to their largely graduate student teaching assistants for teaching the fundamentals of their disciplines than is customary in non-SME majors. As already noted, this is especially marked in lab teaching. Where undergraduates found it difficult to learn from faculty who taught poorly, they cited TAs as a critical resource in acquiring concepts and skills. For TAs assigned to assist with large classes early in their graduate school careers—commonly, in their first semesters—this is a weighty expectation. As I discuss in chapter 6, graduate TAs often receive little or no education in teaching methods. As a number of studies have noted (cf. Nyquist and Sprague 1998; McGivney-Burrelle et al. 2001; Wood et al. 2001; McManus 2002), and as I discuss further in chapter 4, TAs often see poor professional practices and attitudes toward teaching modeled for them by faculty and are given little incentive to take their teaching responsibilities seriously in face of the research priorities set for them by their dissertation supervisors.

Despite these common impediments, 84 percent of the undergraduates in this study reported that, overall, TAs demonstrated a higher level of interest in teaching and a greater willingness to meet the intellectual needs of undergraduates than did many of the faculty. Undergraduates were particularly appreciative of TAs who treated their questions seriously, found ways to explain material that they found difficult, offered applications of theoretical material, showed them alternative ways to work problems, shared their test-taking know-how, bolstered their confidence, and reinforced their enthusiasm for the discipline:

> They're usually more helpful than the professors. 'Cause they've been students more recently, and they know the professor's not making any sense. They'll tell you, "Here's a better way to explain it." (Female white engineering persister)

> They always knew where the tough spots on the problem sets were so we could focus on those. It was just very helpful. (Female white engineering nonswitcher)

> I've had TAs that were even better than professors, I felt, just because of their enthusiasm for teaching. And that made a big difference in us students wanting to learn the material. (Female white engineering persister)

Students often found their TAs more approachable than faculty, and some students (often women) who had looked, in vain, for a teacher–learner relationship with faculty were able to establish this with their TAs:

They are really the ones to go and see if you have a problem. They are easier to talk to and they don't put you down in the same way as the professors do sometimes. (Female white engineering persister)

They know how to talk to us really well; they're generally better at getting the point across. (Male white science persister)

TAs are the closest recourse that a student would have to a real teacher. (Male white engineering switcher)

When the system of TA teaching and support was working well, students expressed satisfaction with their classes, even when they saw the faculty who were teaching them as being inadequate:

The classes are a lot easier to handle when you have a good TA there to explain things to you when the professors can't. (Female black science persister)

There are classes where almost everyone out there is clueless, but no one will ask a question. Then you get with the TA in a smaller classroom situation and that's where the learning really goes on. Because we're not afraid to ask the TA what's going on, and they will explain things all the way down to every last step. (Male white mathematics persister)

Notwithstanding their high overall level of appreciation for the teaching support work of TAs, 16 percent of all students interviewed also expressed some level of dissatisfaction with their TAs.[3] In addition, some undergraduates who expressed appreciation of their TAs commented on the difficulties that their TAs appeared to face in seeking to do their jobs well. Taken together, these concerns and diagnostic observations suggest a number of unmet TA professional development needs and hint at their causes. They commonly point to their TAs' inexperience, lack of pedagogical training, or insufficient familiarity with the syllabus materials to teach them with confidence or in depth:

I haven't had much luck with chemistry or physics TAs. They seem very disorganized, and I feel like they're confused. I think they expect just to answer questions and don't prepare anything. I really like it when TAs prepare something to talk about, to try to incorporate the material. I don't like it when the TAs are sitting there ready to just tell you how to do problems. I mean, that's not what we need. (Female white engineering switcher)

He doesn't have the organizational skills that you need to direct a class. He obviously knows the material very well, but he's having a hard time relating it to the average student who doesn't know anything about it. (Male white science switcher)

For want of instruction on how to teach effectively, some TAs were portrayed as teaching in the same ways that they had been taught, thereby repeating the pedagogical errors of their own professors:

> The problem is that they don't have any education classes behind them. They don't know how to get people to learn. They do not know how to give information. They can't get their ideas across. It's a self-taught class. If you don't get what he does on the board, you go to the book. If you can't teach yourself from the book, you don't make it. (Female white mathematics switcher)

> My teaching assistant was really smart and tried to help, but, actually, she didn't. She was aiming more for everyone to get an A instead of everyone to understand. I mean, she would give us a lot of the answers, but she wouldn't really explain them very well. And I think that was partly because she just didn't know how to explain things. She would just *tell us* the answers, so you could memorize them, but never understand them. (Female white engineering switcher)

More seriously, the character of some undergraduate concerns suggest that not only were TAs learning poor teaching practices from faculty but they were also learning not to value teaching:

> They just toss the information at you and you have to learn it in your own way. The TAs just seem to be doing a job—getting through grad school. They're not qualified as teachers. (Male white engineering switcher)

Some undergraduates who saw their TAs' limited engagement in teaching as being prompted by a primary need to survive graduate school were not necessarily unsympathetic to their situations:

> They aren't interested in teaching you. They're doing it because they have to. They're grad students and this is part of their package. They have to teach this course. (From a focus group of women science persisters)

> Not very many of them plan to be teachers. This is just a job. I had one or two helpful TAs. But most of them are taking their own course load, which is very heavy, and they also have to do this just to make money. So, they have a bunch of pressures. (Female white engineering switcher)

However, some switchers who had found their TAs to be unhelpful were less forgiving. They saw many graduate students as having already assumed the same indifferent, uncaring attitudes toward undergraduate learners that they had already encountered in some faculty:

> I would say they are very similar to faculty. I think that people who have made it far enough to be TAs have the same sort of attitude. I had a TA teach me math,

and it was the same old thing as the professors—not exciting at all. He was already kind of on the same path. (Male white science switcher)

The section leaders were just kind of inept, but the head TA was really arrogant. He seemed much more interested in his own learning and advancement than anybody else's. (Male white engineering switcher)

Graduate assistants were also seen as mirroring their faculty mentors both in their professional priorities and in their constraints:

I got the impression she enjoyed doing the math rather than dealing with the students. (Male white engineering switcher)

I had a TA that was in engineering and he was so wrapped up in what he was doing that it was hard for him to teach. (Male white engineering switcher)

Finally, some undergraduates made unfavorable contrasts between the teaching they received from graduate assistants in SME majors with that experienced in other disciplines:

I've noticed in history or psychology, those TAs seem to be really good. And they will talk to you and help you. They're excited about what they're doing. But around chemistry or physics, they don't plan on teaching. They just want to make money so they can get through this. (Female white engineering switcher)

The absorption by graduate assistants of counterproductive faculty norms and practices with respect to teaching appeared, happily, to be incomplete. As already indicated, most undergraduates (i.e., 84 percent of this sample) reported more positive than negative experiences with TAs, while their experiences with faculty as teachers were more consistently disappointing. However, students who valued their TAs, as well as those who expressed some disappointment with them, pointed to structural limitations on the TAs' contribution to undergraduate learning. For example, some SME departments did not offer recitation sections in support of large lecture classes. Students also described recitation sections that were too large for the kind of interactive, interrogative learning they sought:

These recitation sections are enormous. They usually consist of just a smaller lecture where the TA will start working problems on the board, but it's not as though each student gets a chance to speak or ask them questions—not really. (Female white engineering switcher)

Some students reported that faculty delegated responsibility for teaching new material to graduate assistants rather than using recitations as an opportunity for TAs to help students clarify and consolidate material already presented in class:

> Our section probably had 40 people in it. That's bigger than a high school class. And a lot of times our prof. had our TAs teaching in the section. So, it's not even like we went over the old stuff. We actually did a lot of new stuff in recitations. (Female white engineering switcher)

Many students expressed their preference for small, well-organized TA-led recitations in support of all of their larger classes. Where this was provided, class size was not in and of itself reported to be a problem:

> We need to talk about and think through what we've learned—to see how the pieces fit together and how you can use them. And that's best done in a small group with a TA who knows how to help you understand the ideas. If you have that, it doesn't matter if the lecture class is two hundred or eight hundred.

Undergraduates were also aware that knowing how to help their students understand and relate concepts requires education. They expressed concern where their TAs appeared to receive little or no training for their teaching and tutoring work:

> At that school, graduate students are required to take a course in teaching and about the way their particular school requirements work. They're required to do that before they start TA-ing any courses. Someone who went there told me that it was really great, and they couldn't believe that this university didn't have something like that—that TAs just came in without any training at all. (Female white engineering switcher)

> The biggest thing about the TAs is they just don't have experience or training in teaching a class. I mean, they know all the stuff, but they just don't have any solid experience in how to explain the material or organize a discussion. (Male white science switcher)

As indicated at the outset, these accounts of undergraduate experiences with TAs came from seven institutions where science, mathematics, and engineering were taught largely by traditional methods using graduate students to work with undergraduates in recitation sections, labs, and office hours. The major theme that emerged from analysis of the data from both switchers and persisters is that undergraduates overwhelmingly value TAs as interactive and personally available teachers. However, many of those who expressed appreciation for their TAs' help also expressed awareness of the constraints that limit TA engagement with teaching as a valued professional activity and thus with their development of expertise as teachers. A small proportion (including some switchers) believed that these constraints had severely limited the capacity of particular TAs to help them. As already illustrated, some of these accounts reflect a concern that some aspects of graduate students' professional socialization serve to replicate in each new generation of faculty the pedagogical limitations and poor regard for teaching that undergraduates saw modeled by many SME faculty. Paramount among undergraduate recommendations was that TAs should be educated in teaching methods.

The engagement of TAs—both graduate and undergraduate—in three innovations intended to improve the learning and interest levels of undergraduates in introductory science classes offered an opportunity to discover what TAs could contribute when some of the limitations common to conventionally structured classes were addressed and TAs were enabled to become more active partners in the teaching, assessment, and curriculum development processes. The balance of this volume draws on a rich body of interview data gathered as part of the formative evaluation of these three initiatives and as extracts from the experiences and reflections of both graduate and undergraduate TAs. It paints a picture of the expanded role that TAs can play in innovative STEM classes, given some rethinking of their education and working relationships.

NOTES

1. In 1991, the year in which we began this study, the losses ranged from 38 percent in engineering, to 51 percent in the biological and physical sciences, to 63 percent in mathematics. The comparative field-switching figures for the humanities and social sciences averaged 30 percent, with a range of 15 percent in English to 34 percent in history and political science. Majors in computer science or technology were not included in this study; therefore, the SME abbreviation is used in discussing this study.

2. They included two prestigious research universities—one private and one public, both with strong engineering colleges; three large state universities—one with a high proportion of applied SME courses and a second with high race and ethnic diversity in its student population; and a private university and a liberal arts college—both with strong science departments. Six of the seven schools had engineering colleges, four of which were highly rated, by level of funding and national reputation.

3. Levels of undergraduate appreciation for the teaching and support work are also discussed in studies by Wagener (1991); Hatch and Farris (1989); McDowell (1993); and McGivney-Burrelle and colleagues (2001).

3

The Role of Teaching Assistants in Three Classroom Change Initiatives

The data that inform all subsequent observations in this volume were generated as part of the formative evaluation of three different projects, each of which sought to improve teaching and learning in undergraduate science. The design of evaluation strategies was negotiated with the principal investigators of each initiative and implemented between 1996 and 2002 by myself and members of my research group, Ethnography and Evaluation Research at the University of Colorado, Boulder. This chapter presents descriptions of these initiatives and an outline of the data sets gathered in the course of each evaluation.

THE THREE INITIATIVES

"Modular Chemistry: Learning Chemistry by Doing What Chemists Do," or ChemConnections: National Science Foundation

By far the largest of the three initiatives is ChemConnections, which is composed of two linked National Science Foundation–funded initiatives—the ChemLinks Coalition and the Modular Chemistry Consortium—both of which were established as part of the National Science Foundation's Systemic Change Initiative in Chemistry. The initiative began in 1995 with over one hundred participants in more than forty two-year and four-year institutions of different sizes and types across the country. It continues to grow through workshops and other outreach activities. ChemConnections approaches the enhancement of chemistry teaching and learning by the development, testing, and classroom use of topical modules that target the first two years of

15

college chemistry. Its two- to four-week modules all begin with questions of real-world relevance and develop the chemistry needed to answer them.[1] In the process, students model how chemistry is done, discover connections between concepts in chemistry and those with other sciences, and apply the chemistry learned to issues of significance for society. To develop critical thinking skills, the modules emphasize active, collaborative student-centered classroom activities and linked inquiry-based laboratory and media projects. Some lectures are retained but are not used as a primary teaching vehicle. Discovery and design experiences replace verification labs and emphasize conceptual connections between class and lab work. The innovators seek to promote a greater appreciation of chemistry and its importance in everyday life for an array of students and to encourage the process of educational reform in chemistry departments. The ChemConnections participants often refer to their approach and their products as "modular chemistry"—a label that I shall use throughout this account.

Teaching and learning with modules requires fundamental changes for those immediately involved—faculty, students, TAs, lab staff, and other support staff. It also has consequences for a wider group of departmental and disciplinary colleagues with varying degrees of interest in, or concern about, educational innovation. Central to the ongoing dissemination of the modular approach are regional workshops presented by a panel of volunteer faculty who have become skilled in the classroom use of modules. TAs were not initially invited to these workshops, although their participation has become more common in light of evaluation feedback that indicates benefits to participating faculty and TAs.

The use of teaching assistants is, however, neither an intrinsic nor a universal feature of the modular approach to undergraduate chemistry. TAs are incorporated into modular pedagogy in those same classes and sections where they have traditionally played a support role—that is, by teaching recitation sections, guiding students' lab work, and providing individual help in office hours. In modular courses, however, the nature of their duties often changes. They are expected to attend classes, sit with their own group of students, and may be called upon to facilitate small-group activities that are part of class sessions. In meetings with their own student sections, they are expected to lead discussions (some based on worksheets), enable group problem solving, and support the development of projects set as group assignments. They are also expected to learn how to work with unfamiliar labs—some with nontraditional equipment—to help students work on open-ended problems and to collect, analyze, interpret, and write about the resulting, often less predictable, data. The modular handbooks for instructors contain no special guidance for the training or monitoring of TAs. However, in the development and implementation of modular courses that employ TAs, individual faculty innovators have sought to engage their TAs and to offer informal education in the philosophy and methods of active and interactive learning.

As part of the formative evaluation, the second of two rounds of student interviews was conducted in the fifth year of consortium activities in a sample of modular chemistry classes at seven institutions of different types—four liberal arts schools, one research university, one comprehensive state university, and a junior college linked to a large state research university.[2] These classes were chosen because they exemplified the best-developed modules being taught by the most experienced module teachers. The faculty teaching modular classes were interviewed, along with samples of their students, their TAs, their departmental and more senior colleagues, and a variety of support staff. In addition to addressing program evaluation questions, the broader purpose of these interviews was to explore the context in which classroom innovation takes place and the factors that make it more or less difficult to establish, sustain, and spread innovative teaching and learning within chemistry departments. Single and focus-group interviews were conducted with all forty-two TAs who were assisting in classes and labs in seven of the ten modular classes. Because of the predominance of liberal arts institutions in this sample, more TAs were undergraduates (n = 28) than graduates (n = 14). Notably, in this initiative, both the graduate and undergraduate samples were evenly divided by sex.

"Educating Teaching Assistants in New Models for Teaching and Learning": University of California, Berkeley

The second initiative was developed between 2000 and 2002 by two members of the University of California, Berkeley, Chemistry Department— Professors Angelica Stacey and Eileen Lewis—who were also actively engaged with development, testing, and workshop dissemination of the Chem-Connections modules. Their difficulties in trying to introduce more interactive learning methods into classes of one thousand or more students prompted them to shift the focus of their efforts to smaller-sized undergraduate sessions with TAs. The overall goal of their initiative is to introduce interactive, reflective, and conceptual learning into large lecture-with-lab classes that are otherwise traditional in nature. In contrast with modular chemistry (where TA involvement varies depending on institutional type), TAs are the central focus of this innovation. The innovators have designed a set of worksheets that all of their TAs use to structure and guide their activities with students in their weekly recitation and lab sections. The worksheets are designed to explore and extend student understanding of the lecture and lab content by

- fostering discussion-oriented teaching by TAs and participatory learning among students and

- assessing student knowledge at the start and end of each recitation session.

In their discussion and lab sections, TAs work interactively with students in a series of activities—some designed for whole section use, some for small-group work. Doing this effectively requires TA education and support. The activities laid out in worksheets are discussed in weekly TA meetings, in advance of class section meetings. TAs also receive guidance in using different pedagogical techniques required by the worksheets and are introduced to the learning theories and research on which they are based and to group dynamics and classroom management.

In situations where it would be difficult to change a large traditionally taught class or where the introduction of interactive elements into a lecture class is limited by its size, this initiative offers a middle way. It is intended to address the limitations on student learning of large-class lectures and of recitations where TAs are neither trained nor monitored.

This innovation requires changes in the responsibilities and skills required of TAs. Rather than teaching selected topics in any way that individual TAs may choose—a common practice in many traditionally taught classes—all TA sections follow the preplanned common set of activities laid out in the worksheets. The program is run by a coordinator and has been developed and refined with the cooperation of the lecture and lab professors for the course. Students are expected to learn in new ways for some parts of the course, while lectures and labs continue in more traditional mode. Exams are modified by adding the types of problems that students encounter in the worksheet sessions with their TAs. Following normal departmental practice, TAs are assigned to the class rather than volunteering to work in it. They are expected to learn the new methods, use them in common across all sections, and attend weekly meetings to discuss progress and problems encountered. The innovation has relevance for other faculty who teach large classes, especially those who experience temporal, and perhaps conceptual, separation between class and lab. It is more broadly relevant to all faculty who seek ways to monitor and improve student understanding by encouraging them to be more actively engaged with their class materials and each other.

Two sets of interview data were gathered, early and later in the evolution of the Berkeley program. In the spring 2000 class, all seventeen TAs, working with approximately six hundred students, were interviewed. In late fall 2001, twenty-five of the forty-one TAs who were working in a much larger class (of approximately 1,250 students) were interviewed in focus groups based on shared characteristics—student status (graduate or undergraduate), major (chemistry, other science or engineering, and nonscience), and TA experience—with additional cross-cuts by sex and by race and ethnicity. The total sample for these two interview rounds was forty-two. By contrast with those of the other two innovations discussed, male graduate students formed a larger proportion of the Berkeley TA sample.[3]

"Interactive Astronomy: Integrating Web-Based Curriculum into Introductory Classes with Large Sections": University of Colorado, Boulder

The third innovation developed at the University of Colorado at Boulder over 2000 and 2001 has been taught and refined, first by its sole faculty developer (Professor Richard McCray) and subsequently by departmental colleagues. This web-based, introductory astronomy class uses undergraduate "coaches" in support of group-based learning and makes only limited use of lectures as part of interactive whole-class sessions. Course materials are available to students as hypertext that includes images; animations; linkages to astronomical websites; Java applets; and educational materials developed at other universities, by NASA, by the course developer, and by other members of the astronomy department. Materials are constantly updated to reflect new discoveries in the field. The intent is to encourage students to explore these resources and develop an active interest in the field.

Students work with their coach in "learning team" sessions in which the coach's role is to enable students to navigate the hypertext materials; help them address a weekly set of discussion questions that are later explored in whole-class sessions; work on group projects; help to prepare students for tests; and assist in general comprehension of the course content. The coach's role is not to teach but to facilitate learning. They are not subject experts and may only be one or two semesters ahead of their learning team members in their knowledge of astronomy. The coaches have to learn how to enable students' learning by means that are unfamiliar to both of them and how to exercise authority over same-level peers. This creates a potential for concerns and anxieties by both groups. Support for the online work of the coaches and their student groups is provided by a computer technician. For two of the semesters in which interview data were gathered, the innovator added a graduate student TA to assist in curriculum development and the generation of learning assessment materials.

Coaches are chosen for abilities shown in a prior astronomy classes, their high level of interest in the discipline, and their outgoing personalities.[4] They are not given any formal training in teaching methods, other than an orientation session that explains their role and the ways in which the class will operate. However, they discuss current course issues with each other, and with the professor, at their weekly meetings. The developer continues to reexamine his teaching strategies in light of this feedback and evaluation outcomes.

Focus group interviews included all twenty-four of the undergraduate coaches, plus the two graduate TAs, who were employed over three semesters—spring and fall 2000 and spring 2001. Eight coaches who had undertaken the job for a second time (the "experts") were interviewed separately from the sixteen "novices."

It is notable that seventeen of the twenty-four undergraduate coaches (71 percent) were female, as were fourteen of the twenty-eight ChemConnections undergraduate TAs and seven of the eleven undergraduate TAs in the Berkeley initiative. As table 3.2 indicates, across the three initiatives, women constituted 60 percent of all undergraduate TAs but only 32 percent of all graduate TAs. This pattern reflects some self-selection of undergraduate women into TA positions in these courses, as was evident in accounts of their experiences as learners in interactive courses in all three institutions. It also reflects institutional variations—notably, women's greater representation in STEM majors in the liberal arts colleges contributing to the ChemConnections sample, where women were half of both graduate and undergraduate TAs, contrasted with the continuing underrepresentation of women in STEM disciplines in graduate schools at research universities.

COMMON ELEMENTS IN THE THREE INITIATIVES

Although there are clear differences between these three course initiatives, there are also strong commonalities, both in their character and in the ways in which TAs, faculty, and undergraduates were engaged in them during the evaluation period. To varying degrees, each approach involves

- Innovations in learning objectives; materials; pedagogy; and use of resources for class, lab, and TA sections
- Strong emphasis on interactive learning, including small group work
- Use of web-based resources in support of learning
- Some revision of learning assessment methods in light of new or clarified learning objectives
- Evolution of the TA role in support of the innovation
- Appreciation of the need for appropriate TA education, support to new demands on TAs, and (variably) efforts to provide both
- Formative (and some summative) evaluation, including solicitation of responses to changes in learning methods from undergraduates, TAs, and departmental colleagues
- Some discussion or negotiation of methods, outcomes, and resources with departmental colleagues
- National dissemination and promotion of the philosophy, methods, materials, and outcomes of the innovation

Our data indicate that these similarities in the design and implementation of the initiatives make the experiences of both the TAs and their students highly comparable. TAs who were employed in different initiatives often responded in similar ways to aspects of their work role. Comparable responses were often evident in two, or all three, of the TA samples. It is these shared TA experiences and responses to experience—and some notable variants from them—that are the main focus of this account.

THE RESEARCH

The qualitative data discussed in this account were generated as part of the formative evaluation of the three innovative projects. All of the information was gathered between April 1998 and December 2001 by face-to-face interviews and focus groups at institutions participating in each project. The interview samples varied according to the nature of the projects and the needs of the evaluation. However, all of the data were collected and analyzed in the same manner. The proportionate contribution of each of the three sets of TAs to the overall TA sample is 38 percent from the Berkeley TA project, 38 percent from the modular chemistry classes, and 24 percent from the Interactive Astronomy classes. The sample distribution by project and the academic status of the TAs is shown in table 3.1, by sex and academic status in table 3.2, and by institutional type and academic status in table 3.3. Percentages are rounded to the nearest whole number.

Collecting the Data

A set of formative evaluation (and some summative) strategies was negotiated between the evaluator and each innovator or group of innovators early in the development of the three initiatives. Each formative evaluation design included interviews with salient groups involved in each initiative. By far the most extensive of the data sets, both in institutional types and in the numbers and categories of interviewees included in the total sample, was that collected as part of the ChemConnections evaluation. As part of the

Table 3.1.   Sample distribution of teaching assistants and coaches, by project and academic status

Project	PhD/MS Students		Undergraduate Students		Total	
	n	*%*	*n*	*%*	*N*	*%*
Interactive Astronomy	2	8	24	92	26	100
Modular chemistry	14	33	28	67	42	100
Berkeley TA initiative	31	74	11	26	42	100
Total	47	43	63	57	110	100

Table 3.2. Sample distribution of teaching assistants and coaches, by sex and academic status

	PhD/MS Students			Undergraduate Students			Total
	n	*% N*	*% sex*	*n*	*% N*	*% sex*	*N*
Female	15	14	32	38	35	60	53
Male	32	29	68	25	23	40	57
Total	47	43	100	63	57	100	110

Note: Totals adjusted for rounding.

formative work, the evaluation team tracked developmental processes and outcomes of these initiatives at different stages in the implementation of each initiative.

Data collection consisted of intensive, semistructured interviews and focus groups with intentional samples of those groups most engaged in, or affected by, these initiatives—undergraduates;, innovation developers and adapters; departmental colleagues, including some chair persons and administrators; faculty exposed to the ideas and methods of innovations, largely at workshops; and, as appropriate, TAs, lab staff, and support staff. Thus, the TA interview data form one part of a much wider data set.

The interviews were conducted as semistructured conversations that centered on the interviewees' experiences. Single interviews were typically sixty to ninety minutes long, with focus groups taking somewhat longer. All interviews were tape-recorded with the permission of the interviewees. Interview protocols were developed in light of what was already known about each initiative and what had already been learned from interviews with other groups.

Interviewees were asked to describe, and were prompted to explain, their array of responses to the innovation in which they were participating and the

Table 3.3. Sample distribution of teaching assistants and coaches, by institutional type and academic status

Type of Institution	PhD/MS Students		Undergraduate Students		Total	
	n	*%*	*n*	*%*	*N*	*%*
Research university[a]	47	43	37	34	84	76
Liberal arts college[b]	0	0	19	17	19	17
State university[c]	0	0	7	6	7	6
Total	47	43	63	57	110	100

Note: Totals adjusted for rounding.
[a]n = 2; three sets of interviews each.
[b]n = 4; one set of interviews each.
[c]n = 2; one set of interviews each.

responses that they observed in others. Issues were explored in an order guided by the natural structure of the discussion, with topics that were not spontaneously raised introduced at convenient points in the conversation. New issues pertinent to the evaluation questions that emerged in the course of discussion were always pursued, both as they arose and in subsequent interviews. Thus, from the outset, the tentative opening set of discussion questions was continuously refined and augmented by the emphases that informants placed on the factors that they introduced and discussed. As important themes emerged, they were explored in all subsequent interviews.

Processing and Analyzing the Data

Tape recordings of interviews and focus groups were transcribed verbatim into a word-processing program and submitted to the Ethnograph, a computer program that allows for the multiple, overlapping, and nested coding of a large volume of transcribed documents to a high degree of complexity. Each line-numbered transcript was searched for information bearing on the research questions. Lines or segments referencing issues of different types were tagged by code names. There were no preconceived codes; each new code name referenced a discrete idea not previously raised. Because answers to the same question were often not of the same character or did not cover the same set of issues, codes were developed not on the basis of the questions asked but by the nature of the responses given. Interviewees often made several points in the same sentence or speech segment, each of which was separately coded. Information was given both in answers to questions and in more spontaneously offered comments, narratives, and illustrations. Information was commonly embedded in speakers' accounts of their experience, rather than offered in abstract statements. This allows transcripts to be checked for internal consistency between the opinions or explanations offered by informants, their descriptions of events, and the reflections and feelings these evoke.

As hand-coding of the interview transcripts was completed, each code and its associated line numbers were entered into the Ethnograph, creating a data set for each group of interviewees. Groups of codes that clustered around particular themes were given domain names, and a branching and interconnected structure of codes and domains were gradually built into a code book that represented the current state of the analysis.

Frequencies with which particular codes occurred across the data set or in its subsets were counted. Conservative counting conventions were used to avoid overestimating the weight of opinion expressed on any issue. This is especially important in coding focus-group transcripts because it is not always possible for transcribers to identify each speaker during a group discussion. The frequencies offered in tables throughout this volume reflect a maximum of one observation on any particular point per interview for single interviews and two observations on the same point by different speakers for any focus group, regardless of the number participating in the group. However, other observations on the same point were logged separately and are sometimes referenced where they indicate a lively discussion of an issue and/or the expression of strong feelings.

The frequency counts enabled the construction of tables that describe the relative weighting of particular issues. As samples were not designed to be random, these numeric representations were not subjected to tests for statistical significance. Rather, they indicate the strength of particular variables and their relationships that may subsequently be tested by surveys or other means. In the analysis, not all data were subject to counting. For example, participants' explanatory theories for the behavior that they observed among members of their own, or other, groups have intrinsic value quite apart from their frequency. They often show how people see a situation and why they behave as they do. The participants' theories may also provide labels or explanations for commonly described behavior, and may also explain why people say one thing yet do another.

In the chapters that follow, some conclusions are drawn across two or all three initiatives, and some relate specifically to a single initiative. In direct quotations, where it is important for the reader to know the project for which TAs were working or personal details (such as sex, academic discipline, or whether the speaker is an undergraduate or a graduate student), this information is always indicated. Observations that apply across all three projects, or where personal details would identify the speaker or are not relevant to the point being made, are not so labeled. This convention is followed throughout.

NOTES

1. There are thirteen modules in widespread use (and several more close to completion) that are available from W. W. Norton (see subsequent web links). Their topical, question-focused character is indicated in their titles, for example, "Why Does the Ozone Hole Form?" "What Should We Do about Global Warming?" "Would You Like Fries with That: The Fuss about Fats in Our Diets," "How Can We Make Our Water Safe to Drink?" "What Happens to Acid Rain?" and "How Can We Reduce Air Pollution from Cars?" Additional information about teaching chemistry with modules is available at http://chemlinks.beloit.edu and http://chemconnections.llnl.gov. Information about workshops on using modules and other active learning methods for chemistry is available at www.cchem.berkeley.edu/~midp.

2. The first round of interviews are not discussed here. They were structured to answer a somewhat different set of research questions: the interviews were focused on comparison of student learning experiences in early modular chemistry classes with

those in more traditionally taught classes in the same institutions. Although some classes were taught with the assistance of TAs, they were not interviewed as part of the first interview sample study.

3. Data from the two Berkeley samples are described in two evaluation reports by Weise (2001, 2003) to the principal investigators and the National Science Foundation.

4. This is unusual. Most TAs at universities are assigned to particular courses.

4

The Benefits to Teaching Assistants of Working in Innovative Courses

One good place to begin to unpack the data provided by the TA interviews is to look at the ways in which TAs evaluated and explained aspects of their working experiences. In this chapter, I present what TAs saw as their gains from working in innovative classes; chapter 4 focuses on their evaluative observations on aspects of the innovations, the ideas that informed them, and their impact on students; and chapter 5 presents the TAs' explanations for common student responses to learning in unfamiliar ways. As will become apparent, the story embedded in the data moves very quickly from what TAs describe as their gains from involvement in these special courses to what they can and do contribute to them. Indeed, the subset of observations on TA "gains" from across all three initiatives is relatively small (seventy-six observations across the total sample of 110 TAs). Most observations on benefits ($n = 56$; 74 percent) came from the forty-two TAs (both graduate and undergraduate) who worked in modular chemistry classes. Of the balance of these statements, twenty (17 percent) were offered by the twenty-six undergraduate astronomy coaches and their two head TAs, and seven (9 percent) were spontaneously offered by the forty-two Berkeley TAs.[1]

Across the three initiatives taken together, the gains reported by TAs were of three types:

Gains in knowledge and understanding	33 percent
Gains related to teaching:	
• Gains in teaching skills and insights into teaching	22 percent
• Enjoyment of teaching and its intrinsic pleasures	21 percent
Appreciation of the personal impact and the career implications of participation	24 percent

GAINS IN KNOWLEDGE AND UNDERSTANDING

The discovery that teaching enables learning is commonly reported by undergraduates as a benefit of working in small groups. The TAs who highlighted this experience described how teaching had consolidated and extended their own understanding:

> I enjoy helping someone else figure it out because it really helps you. One of the other TAs and I are in the same math class, and we'll suddenly spot something in class that we just learned in teaching the modules. And you just start thinking about other ways to use it.

> It helps me remember all those little math problems with rationalizing that I had half forgotten. It's good reinforcement: it rolls it up and keeps it going.

Furthermore, nineteen of the modular chemistry TAs described how working together with students on the modules had helped them to acquire many of the same learning gains that the innovators sought for the undergraduates. Specifically mentioned were making connections; synthesizing ideas; transferring knowledge; employing familiar lines of reasoning to new problems; and learning by application, discussion, and reading original source materials. As learners with more experience in the discipline than their charges, the TAs found that working with the modules helped them to make better sense and wider use of the chemistry that they already knew:

> The best thing is that I learned a lot myself. Like some of the applications that I never thought could be explained by the chemistry I had learned a long time ago.

> Even when I was learning this chemistry, I always wondered what the applications were. I mean, I would just look at things and question and not really know the processes in real life. So I think that's part of what they accomplished—bring chemistry closer to home.

These TAs found that the modular materials and methods had stimulated them to reason, argue, and think about problems in new ways:

> I like the way they do individual labs, but then they all work together. It brought in all of their ideas. Like when we were working on thermodynamics and fats and learned how they all tied into the organic unit. We were using the same kinds of basic reasoning—even if they were new ideas. So we were learning skills that are not just about chemistry, but have everything to do with science.

The undergraduate TAs predicted that their new ways of thinking would be useful in their upcoming chemistry classes:

It will be extremely helpful when we actually get to start doing reactions and understanding how they work. . . . I think the fats module is going to be most useful just because it deals with proteins, and I think when I look back at that module, I'll understand more of the organic chemistry behind, say, the carbon chain.

The applied approach was seen as being particularly important to undergraduate TAs in consolidating and illuminating their existing knowledge, helping them to remember what they had learned, and prompting them to apply their chemistry to related problems in other fields or everyday life:

Years later, I'm not going to remember little equations, but I will remember through applications. I mean, in my chemistry classes right now, I remember examples and that hooks me to the concepts somehow.

I think it will give me an advantage in the long run because, you can tell me how to do something, but that's very different from asking me to apply what I know to a bunch of other things—some of them in other fields. . . . It just gives you a broader perspective, so later on, in whatever else I do, I think it will all make a lot more sense.

Contrary to the concern commonly expressed by students that chemistry learned in context will not meet their needs in preparing for the Medical College Admission Test (MCAT), four TAs who were preparing for, or who had just taken, these examinations found that the modules they were teaching were very helpful in addressing probing MCAT questions:

I took the MCATs last week, and a lot of the stuff I found very applicable—a lot of the logic questions they ask want you to apply what you know to the real world. So this has been a great preparation!

TAs also cited some very specific gains in practical know-how, especially those who had set up and tested new labs and those who had worked on computer-based projects with students.

Finally, eight of the modular chemistry TAs stressed how much they had enjoyed learning alongside the students and how they wished that they had learned the fundamentals of chemistry in this manner or could take another modular class—whether as students or as TAs:

TA 1: If there were a modular class for juniors and/or seniors, I would definitely be interested. I'm about to go into one in organics—a new module in carbohydrates—so I'm going to get to try it out soon.

TA 2: I'd definitely like it for this class. It would be so interesting. And I think for organic and biochemistry too—which I'm about to take—and it would be great to teach in them too.

GAINS IN TEACHING SKILLS AND INSIGHTS ABOUT TEACHING

Twenty-five TAs described what they had learned about teaching from their experiences in innovative classes. They offered an array of different insights and practical lessons learned with only a few dominant themes. These included the realization that good teaching requires good organization:

> I used to think that teaching was all about being able to explain things well. But, in my opinion, that's a very small fraction of what you need to do. Being effective is what matters and that makes organization so much more important.

A related insight is that teachers have to be organized because they cannot count on students getting as much from listening to a lecture, as they are apt to believe is the case:

> One time, I thought I gave my group a really good short lecture on quantum mechanics. So, I'm all pleased with myself. But I noticed one of the students looking at a sheet of notes after the session was over. And it was horrible. They had copied exactly what I had put on the board, and written nothing else. So the moral of the story is, I need to find a way to present things so that they'll listen. But if they're not going to write down anything I say, I need to get my board organized. Because if that's organized, then their notes will be too. I guess you have to structure ideas for people who don't yet know how to structure them for themselves.

A second theme was learning the importance of flexibility in teaching and being ready to rethink teaching strategies in light of student feedback about how well they work.

> I learned that some things won't work and some things will, and throughout the semester, you have to adapt your style and your skills to what you learned by trying things out. You have to harvest things that work well and build on them. . . . Since I came into this job, I've looked at my own classes with a different eye—looking at different teaching styles. And it doesn't matter whether you decide to teach more traditionally or more like the modules, you still have to respond to student feedback and make adjustments.

What works, as other TAs discovered, is highly related to the level at which the material is pitched. Four TAs observed that the material must reflect what students can handle at this particular stage in their preparation and level of comprehension:

> The toughest thing in designing labs is getting the level of difficulty right. If it's too easy, they turn off their brains, fill in the answers, and are happy to go home early. But it can't be so hard that they have no idea what the next step is, and they'll still turn their brains off. You have to find that middle ground where they're challenged, but not so much that they can't do it at all.

It seems the best thing you can do is to teach something several times, and that really kind of calibrates you to how much material and what level the students can take. Regardless whether I think this material or this lab is interesting, I need to know how a large fraction of my class will respond to it.

Watching innovative professors grapple with these issues and assisting in addressing them made three TAs more sophisticated consumers of the teaching that they subsequently received:

What I took away is that I look at classes a lot differently. I guess I learned a lot, but, in particular, when anyone starts lecturing, I find myself taking apart what they are saying, how they explain it, and what steps they leave out—especially that—I can see what you have to get people to understand before you can leap to the next idea.

A third theme was the importance of learning to deal with the limits of one's own knowledge—that is, how professionals respond when they have no immediate answer to a student's question and, even more, that it was *okay* not to know:

They ask a lot of questions and often they get straight to something I don't understand [*laughing*]. So now I know I can say, "I don't know, but these are a few ways that I might think about that problem." Sometimes I get a senior in the class and I ask them if they can help. Mostly I try to work through the problem with them. And the professor's got a really good attitude about not knowing. She tells you to be as prepared as you can be for the class—hit the books before you arrive—but be totally honest when you don't have the answer. I've really gotten the idea that it's okay not to know everything.

An enhanced awareness of responsibility was a theme that cut across several teaching-related gains reported by TAs. It appeared in accounts of how working in a class that stressed both personal and group responsibility for learning had shifted their own sense of responsibility as learners:

It changed how I approach being a student. I came away with a greater sense of my personal responsibility for my own performance. Although there are things in a class that might distract you or that you might not like, in the end, you're responsible for learning what you need to learn.

The theme of responsibility was also threaded through a long discussion in which one astronomy coach described his discoveries about how and when to exercise his authority to enforce course rules—for example, those governing attendance at coach-led sessions. He described his struggles to reach a set of workable principles: how he had learned to handle requests for assignment extensions, the nonattendance of group members, the effects of regular absence on group productivity and morale, how to support and encourage students who were experiencing problems, and when to hand over a problem to the professor. He concludes,

> It's more difficult for an undergraduate TA to handle authority well, but I got the opportunity to work out a system that was consistent but that took account of genuine difficulties and protected the group from breaking up. That was a great lesson to take away from this experience. And it applies not just in teaching, but in many other situations.

Finally, a focus group of modular TAs in a liberal arts college discussed the powerful influence of their professor in engendering in them a sense of professional identity and accountability and prompting their assumption of responsibility for student learning:

> TA 1: When we were in the lab together for these projects, she just divided everything up, so she took four students' projects, and I took four, and so on. And it was just like were all on equal standing in the lab.
>
> TA 2: Yeah, it was like we were the head research advisors for the students. And she and us, we were on an equal footing—except that we could still come to her with questions, and she'd help us out. But it was our job to make it work.
>
> Interviewer: How did that feel?
>
> TA 1: When I first started TA-ing with another prof, it wasn't that way, and it took me a while to come to terms with the fact that "Whoa! I guess I am accountable!" It's an odd feeling being a student, but then learning that you're in charge. I was expecting to be second-guessed as a TA when I first started. But, you know, now it's a really neat feeling.
>
> TA 3: Yeah, that's true for me too. It was frightening in the beginning. I wanted to say to the students, "I don't know any more than you do."
>
> TA 1: But she did such a good job of treating us respectfully, and being open with us—treating you like you're one of her colleagues. So you do your best to live up to that.
>
> TA 2: Yeah, that's so important. It changes everything. It gives you a whole new perspective on professors and yourself.
>
> TA 3: I agree. She does a really good job with that and it really makes you rise up to the job.

This was one of several places in the data set where we became aware of the powerful role that collegiality plays in determining how well TAs perform their role, how willing and active they become in enabling the optimal functioning of the innovative class, and how they gain from the experience a sense of identity as rising professionals.

ENJOYMENT OF TEACHING—ITS INTRINSIC PLEASURES

Aside from talking about gains in skills and insights about teaching and learning, sixteen TAs from all three initiatives wanted to emphasize how much they had enjoyed teaching in their innovative courses and why this experience had led them to want to continue teaching. The following was offered by two TAs in the Berkeley initiative:

Once in a while, you get a student who . . . you have helped expose to what is really neat about chemistry. . . . I'm definitely interested in teaching chemistry, particularly to people who [are] the real joys of teaching—when you finally get that spark of interest in someone and they're interested not merely for the sake of getting a grade . . . but that they're . . . interested [in chemistry] as an intellectual pursuit.

I thought [teaching] was the best experience. I love bonding with the students . . . talking to them, not just as a TA. You know, [giving] advice about other classes. And I think the most rewarding thing was . . . how much they enjoyed lab section.

In the modular chemistry and astronomy classes, some observations about the pleasures of teaching were made in response to the question "What was the best thing about being a TA in this class?" Nine TAs in institutions of different types cited as "the best thing" the satisfaction they derived from seeing their students become interested in the material and understand it:

The best thing is also the hardest thing—getting students' attention and sparking their interest. I think they achieved that through the modular system. For me, the pleasure was in helping them become interested and feeling that what they learned will stay in their heads as really long time.

The TAs described the pleasure of shared moments, such as when a student's question sparked curiosity in both the student and the TA and when the TAs saw that students understood an idea:

TA 1: The best thing is seeing that the kids like to do the work.

TA 2: Yeah. And seeing somebody get it.

TA 1: And then watching them tell somebody else how to do it, and then they're all working together at it. That's the teacher's main joy I think.

TA 2: Yeah, seeing them get it and then explain it to someone else, that's so neat! It's that flash of "Wow! I really get it. I feel like I really understand it: ask me anything!" That's where I get happy when I see that.

One astronomy coach described the experience thus:

When the student's sitting there and the shine in his eyes says, "Teach me"—
that's the best moment.

APPRECIATION OF THE INNOVATION'S
PERSONAL VALUE AND CAREER IMPLICATIONS

In addition to making observations about what they gained from their
teaching experiences, nine astronomy coaches and eight modular chemistry TAs described the impact of their teaching experiences in an innovative class on their interest in teaching and learning and their thinking
about academic and career paths. Of this group, three were first-timers
who wanted to sign up for another semester in the course; five were in
their second semesters as TAs or coaches; and one was in her third TA experience.

As a direct consequence of working as TAs in the innovative class, two
TAs were considering a change of major—one into chemistry, the other
astronomy—and two more had decided to add a postgraduate education
qualification. All together, ten TAs reported that the experience either confirmed or reinforced an interest in science teaching as a career—most at the
college level but some as K–12 teachers:

I used to think I would only teach at a college level but, because of this experience, I've started to think more and more that it would be really cool to help
younger kids understand more about the basic workings of their world.

I told [Professor X] that I wanted his job! He said I couldn't have it, but I think
that teaching is something I really could enjoy. And perhaps it's not going to be
at the college level. It's something I've been thinking about. In fact, I've been
having a bit of a midcollege crisis [*laughing*].

This group had also developed ideas about how they wanted to teach:

I definitely want to have the curriculum and the method of teaching be alive and
changing. I have picked up so many great ideas that I would like to try to incorporate into a class of my own. I kinda favor the lecture style, but I want to
vary it—give opportunities for questions and student dialogue, get students to
take more responsibility for their work and learn in small groups. I can see
there's a lot of different ways to make the mixture work.

Two TAs had developed or furthered an interest in education research as
a consequence of their work in the class:

I would like to look in more depth at how much these students actually learn. Are they learning more than in a lecture? And not just comparing test scores. I want to know, do they really understand the life cycle of a star? Could they really describe a black hole or explain how galaxies are formed? I want to explore that and, you know, pull a thesis from it. I also wonder if being interactive helps students retain knowledge.

I'm actually an English major, and I decided to write my thesis on education policy and some teaching improvements that can be made from the perspective of a student. So this was a perfect opportunity—seeing the teaching side of things and getting a better understanding of how that works technically. I have been studying a lot of theory about teaching and learning, but to actually experience it was a great opportunity.

The personal impact of working in innovative classes was also expressed by those who chose a second or third appointment to the class or who expressed a wish to act as TAs again if there were an opportunity to do so.[2] The most experienced repeater TA described her reasoning:

It's actually my third time. I just enjoy it. There's so much personal satisfaction, especially in the modular chemistry class. One of my profs suggested I switch to his class, which comes next in the sequence, but I really like this class because I think this is the way you should set the groundwork for the rest of their chemistry careers. I really enjoy helping to give them a good basic grounding and seeing them build on it. I just love the modular teaching.

Among the statements of personal value, some spoke of how the gains made in the innovative classes were already carrying forward into other classes—some in the same discipline, some not:

It got me used to working in the lab with computers. I noticed in my first zoology labs when we had to put our data into graph form, most people were pretty lost, but I knew how to make the computer do the work for me. I ended up helping quite a few of the other students. So you walk away with a lot of skills that are very transferable.

It permanently changes the way that you think—you find yourself always looking for the applications of what you are doing. I've also discovered that it's how I like to learn. And it's one of the things I look for in my other classes now, and it's part of how I'm thinking about what I want to do later on. I keep thinking, "How does this affect things in the world? And why is that important?"

Some were thinking ahead about the value of what they had learned for future careers. One of the two head TAs in astronomy described the experience as "the most demanding and the best" of their time as a graduate student. This TA reported learning many new skills—managerial, technical, and pedagogical—and felt better prepared for future teaching by the innovative class experience than "all the lab sections I have taught in the past." Along with three graduate TAs in other initiatives, this head TA especially appreciated the opportunity to learn what goes into curriculum development and testing:

> Curriculum development in and of itself is very challenging. I mean, it's usually the job of a tenured professor. And there should be a way to create this as an experience for all graduate students who are aiming for a career that will involve teaching. And it opens you up to important aspects of the professional world working alongside the professor and knowing that they really appreciate your contributions.

Again, we noted the powerful impact of working collegially with faculty to develop and test labs and to design student projects, computer applications, and assessment materials for the new class. It bonded TAs to the objectives of the class and its teacher, nurtured self-confidence, and helped to develop a sense of what a career in academe (including education) could be like.

We should not, perhaps, be surprised at the strength of the impact that a TA experience in a dynamic, creative class can have on the thinking and aspirations of TAs who work in it. However, unlike many other professions that build professional socialization experiences for their apprentices into a coherent program of education and career development—for example, nursing, medicine, law, the clergy, journalism, the police, the military—academe has been curiously casual in its approach toward the induction of recruits into teaching as an aspect of the academic profession. Socialization into the research role via undergraduate research experiences has received far more attention. This traditional disattention is illustrated clearly when we consider in the following chapter the TAs' assessments of their "training" as TAs.

RESEARCH ON THE BENEFITS TO TAs OF
WORKING IN INNOVATIVE COURSES

There is a limited body of recent research in which to look for comparisons to the benefits perceived by TAs of participating in innovative courses—some in the sciences, some not. This information is largely a facet of studies with a different focus that additionally solicited feedback from the TAs (or reflections by supervising faculty) on what TAs had gained from their participation. Broadly, the findings from these studies fall into the same categories as those that emerged from analysis of the data for the three innovations.

Several studies record that TAs reported gains in knowledge and understanding from their work in innovative classes. TAs at a Midwestern university perceived that their understanding of scientific method and their ability to explain it to others had improved as a result of teaching inquiry-based introductory biology laboratories. Although they began their TA work without expecting the experience to increase their understanding of the processes of science (including experimental design), a significant number of both new and experienced TAs reported that it had done so (French and Russell 2002). TAs teaching their own multidisciplinary, collaborative seminars at University of California, Los Angeles (2000), reported more general academic gains—that is, the opportunity to develop their intellectual skills. In their studies of TAs, Nurrenbern, Mickiewicz, and Francisco (1999) reported that not only did small student groups that worked effectively from the outset enjoy their work more and make cumulative and transferable gains in knowledge, but so too did their TAs. Eby and Gilbert's study (2000) of TAs who worked in George Mason University's innovative violence and gender course also reported gains in learning in their own specific fields of study. Upper-division physics TAs who worked closely with professors at Oregon State University reported a "much deeper and broader understanding of the material" (Manogue and Krane 2003). These personal assessments of the intellectual benefits of TA engagement were confirmed by Larson and colleagues (2001), who found that undergraduate TAs at the University of Arizona showed much higher academic performances than non-TA peers in the same class.

Studies that report gains in teaching skills record, as do the findings from the three innovations presented here, extensions of the TAs' teaching role as traditionally conceived. At Cornell University, the responsibility of training new engineering TAs was given to TA "fellows," who subsequently reported that the program's cofacilitation model, which included peer mentoring and teamwork-building skills, had significantly contributed to their personal and professional development. As cofacilitators, they reported learning to balance compromise with assertiveness, work through differences in learning and teaching styles, and improve their organizational skills as teachers (Hollar, Carlson, and Spencer 2000). Communication TAs at the University of Washington who served as role models and active-learning instructors in guiding undergraduates through a research project saw their new "teaching" role to be more interesting and satisfying than the traditional TA roles they had experienced (Karasz, Reynolds, and Wall 1997). Upper-division physics TAs at Oregon State University came to value innovative student-focused pedagogies and gained insights into the processes of learning: "The trial-and-error process of developing and teaching integrated labs and group activities convinced us of the value of actively engaging students. By observing students' behavior as they grappled with the physics and the curriculum, we developed a better understanding of how they interact with a curriculum to construct their own understanding of the material" (Manogue and Krane 2003, 57).

The TAs cited in Hollar, Carlson, and Spencer (2000) and Karasz, Reynolds, and Wall (1997) mingle enhancement of their teaching skills and their enjoyment of teaching with personal gains. Similarly, the TAs working in George Mason University's innovative violence and gender course found it to be a "tremendous and transformative learning experience." They were amazed at the sense of community that the faculty and the TAs developed as a teaching team and its contribution to the success of the class (Eby and Gilbert 2000). The supervising faculty also reported personal benefits from their involvement in the course. They particularly enjoyed their collaborative relationship with the TAs with whom they were in constant communication as well as in weekly three-hour meetings: "In effect, these energizing weekly seminars were a combination of learning from each other with respect to reviewing course content, discussing pedagogical strategies for approaching specific course content, debriefing the past week's classes, problem-solving any student or classroom issues, and team-building among the faculty and the TAs" (136). The intellectual stimulation and energy of the meetings surpassed their expectations, and their collaborative relationships with the TAs turned into lasting friendships.

Other personal impact gains reported by TAs were improved communication skills (French and Russell 2002) and appreciation by the UCLA (2000) TAs that their engagement in the multidisciplinary seminars offered them secure funding for an entire academic year. Undergraduate TAs at the University of Arizona reported improvements in their confidence, teamwork, leadership, organizational, and communication skills (Larson et al. 2001). Undergraduate TAs in peer-led team-learning chemistry workshops studied by Sarquis and colleagues (2001) gained understanding of different learning styles and became more interested in teaching as a career. Their faculty also reported enhanced confidence and a deeper understanding of the subject matter.

Although it is hard to judge from this relatively small group of studies, when combined with the evidence offered from the three innovations presented earlier, it would appear that TAs can and do benefit intellectually, professionally, and personally from their active involvement in innovative courses. How much they gain seems, as Eby and Gilbert also indicate, to depend on how appropriately and effectively they are prepared for their new roles and are supported in them. I discuss these issues, along with the broader need for professional development, in chapter 9.

NOTES

1. This issue was not included in the protocol questions.
2. Most of the TAs had more than one comment to make on these related issues.

5

The Nature and Consequences of Teaching Assistants' Evaluations of the Three Classroom Initiatives

In this chapter, I begin to show the range of contributions that TAs were making to the initiatives for which they worked. I begin with a digest of their formative feedback to faculty. Informed evaluative feedback is valuable to faculty in its own right. However, I found that it also vitally affected the degree to which TAs enabled or obstructed implementation of the innovative courses. I begin, therefore, with a discussion of the nature and consequences of TA evaluations of the three projects that were evident in the data. The TAs' evaluative observations—whether on broader aspects of the initiative for which they worked or on specific aspects of its implementation—were separated from all other types of observations for each of the initiatives; sorted into critiques of positive, negative, and mixed character; and counted. Evaluative observations were those that contained some element of course critique. Often they were combined with related observations, such as explanations for the speaker's viewpoint and pieces of advice. Examples of observations that were not evaluative include descriptions of the benefits of working as a TA, statements of educational needs in order to work effectively, and comments on the nature and source of students' difficulties with the course. However, as evaluative statements might also be attached to these or, indeed, to any particular TA observation, the evaluative portion of any statement was always included in the evaluation count.

As I will illustrate, evaluation statements reflect the TAs' views about the innovations' objectives and design, the teaching methods and materials used, and the ease or difficulty of their implementation. The statements also reflect TAs' experiences as teachers and learners and their observations on student learning in both innovative and more conventionally taught classes. I found that TAs varied in the degree to which they reached their opinions by drawing on beliefs about teaching and learning, making reference to their experiences, or reflecting on their direct observations. It was notable that the TAs who expressed greater openness to the innovator's approach were those who based their opinions on observations of student responses to new learning methods rather than on their beliefs about how introductory science classes should be taught. This was true even when TAs with largely pro-innovation views expressed reservations about some aspects of the course. Negative observations included fundamental objections to the philosophy that informed the class design as well as perceived flaws in its implementation. Negative observations that reflected the speaker's doubts about central features of the approach would be harder for the teacher to address than particular aspects of course implementation.

Mixed comments are always an important source of feedback for innovators because they often contain detailed observations on

- How well aspects of the course design or its implementation are working
- Aspects of the innovation that have been neglected and need attention
- Factors that limit success
- Situations where a strategy works better or worse
- Practical advice on what shifts in strategy could make aspects of the course work better

Mixed comments largely represent qualified approval: speakers express broad support for their teacher's goals and approach but point to aspects of the course that they see as needing adjustment. Mixed comments also include reserved judgments where speakers have not yet made up their minds about the value of the teacher's approach or some aspect of the class.

The TAs discussed in considerable detail the effectiveness of the innovations of which they were a part and the reasons for the evaluations that they offered. Overall, the three data sets reflect a high level of TA interest and engagement independent of the degree to which they supported or criticized particular aspects of these classes.

I begin the discussion by offering a broad answer to the question "How did the TAs in each of the three projects evaluate overall the innovations of which they were a part?" The question was approached by extracting TAs' evaluative observations from the three data sets and dividing them into three types—positive, negative, and mixed (see table 5.1). Divided thus, tables 5.2, 5.3, and 5.4 show the pattern of evaluative observations for each initiative and how frequently these were offered by particular subsets of TAs. Table 5.1 shows the patterns for all three initiatives. When all evaluative comments were combined, 44 percent were positive, 28 percent were negative, and 28 percent were mixed.

OVERALL EVALUATIONS OF THE THREE INITIATIVES

Interactive Astronomy

The Interactive Astronomy coaches were broadly supportive of the teacher's innovative approach to this class. As shown in table 5.1, positive observations were 42 percent of the evaluative observation totals. Mixed evaluations were slightly higher—that is, 44 percent of evaluative observations— and were largely (79 percent) of the qualified-approval-with-advice type. By contrast, the proportion of unqualified negative statements was 14 percent of all observations. It was evident that the large proportion of mixed evaluations arose because coaches were encouraged to discuss in their weekly meetings how well the course was working. They were also invited to offer detailed feedback, both directly with the professor and indirectly through the formative evaluation process.

Both of these feedback opportunities helped to establish a practice of regular collegial critique. As this initiative included eight TAs who worked as coaches for a second semester (the "experts"), we checked to see if the coaches' overall evaluation varied between these experts and the eighteen "novices." Novices were over double the number of experts and were interviewed as separate groups over three sequential semesters, while the experts were interviewed only in two groups. However, as the breakdown in table 5.2

Table 5.1. Summary of evaluative observations by teaching assistants and coaches

	Positive		Mixed		Negative		Total	
Project	n	%	n	%	n	%	N	%
Interactive Astronomy	120	42	126	44	40	14	286	100
Modular chemistry	231	52	120	27	95	21	446	100
Berkeley TA initiative	128	36	55	16	167	48	350	100
Total	479	44	301	28	302	28	1,082	100

Table 5.2. Summary of teaching assistants' evaluative observations for Interactive Astronomy, by level of interviewee experience

	Positive		Mixed		Negative		Total	
Level of experience	n	%	n	%	n	%	N	%
Experts[a]	90	42	93	44	31	14	214	100
Novices[b]	30	42	33	46	9	13	72	100
Total	120	42	126	44	40	14	286	100

Note: Totals adjusted for rounding.
[a]Evaluative observations from interviews with eight "experts" (teaching assistants who worked as coaches for a second semester).
[b]Evaluative observation from interviews with eighteen "novices" (first-semester coaches).

indicates, the experts had far more to say by way of detailed critique of the Interactive Astronomy classes in which they had worked than did the novices. Their evaluative observations (which accounted for 75 percent of all evaluative observations offered) were far more detailed and extensive than those of the novices. It became clear that their capacity to notice, explain, and analyze the effectiveness of the teacher's strategies and to suggest adjustments was greatly enhanced by the experience and confidence they had gained by a second term as coaches. That said, the novices and experts were almost identical in their overall distribution of evaluative comments: for both groups, 42 percent of the evaluations were positive, while 13 percent of the novices' and 14 percent of the experts' observations were negative. Both groups gave the

Table 5.3. Summary of teaching assistants' evaluative observations for modular chemistry, by type of institution

	Positive		Mixed		Negative		Total	
Type of institution	n	%	n	%	n	%	N	%
Research university[a]	69	37	61	33	55	30	185	100
Six other institutions[b]	162	62	59	23	40	15	261	100
Total	231	52	120	27	95	21	446	100

[a]The TA sample at the research university was 38 percent (16/42) of the whole modular chemistry TA sample.
[b]Four liberal arts colleges, one comprehensive state university, and one junior college.

Table 5.4. Summary of teaching assistants' evaluative observations for the Berkeley TA initiative: First- and second-round interviews

	Positive		Mixed		Negative		Total	
Interview round	n	%	n	%	n	%	N	%
First-round observations								
Innovative elements	60	36	21	13	84	51	165	100
Traditional elements	17	43	3	8	19	49	39	100
Subtotal	77	38	24	12	103	50	204	100
Second-round observations								
Innovative elements	43	39	24	22	43	39	110	100
Traditional elements	8	23	7	19	21	58	36	100
Subtotal	51	35	31	21	64	44	146	100
All evaluative elements								
Innovative course elements	103	38	45	16	127	46	275	100
Traditional course elements	25	34	10	13	40	53	75	100
Total	128	36	55	16	167	48	350	100

highest proportion of their evaluations to mixed comments that offered the teacher caveats and advice: mixed observations were 46 percent of the novices' evaluations and were 44 percent of the evaluative observations made by the expert group.

Modular Chemistry

Across the seven institutions that contributed to the modular chemistry TA sample, the overall level of approval for the modular approach was even stronger than for the Interactive Astronomy class: 52 percent of all evaluative codes and observations were positive. Mixed observations were a smaller proportion of all evaluative observations (27 percent) than were offered for the astronomy initiative (44 percent). This is not surprising. Difficulties that arose from the unfinished state of the modules, or from the teachers' lack of experience in working with them, were discussed in a first round of interviews with undergraduates who had experienced the modules during their development and classroom testing four years earlier. By the second round of interviews, both undergraduate and TA interview data indicate that many early problems had been worked through. Thus, the modular chemistry TAs experienced the materials and methods of their classes in a more polished form than did either the astronomy coaches or the Berkeley initiative TAs.

The modular chemistry TAs also offered a higher proportion of negative observations (21 percent) in their evaluative statements than did the astronomy coaches (14 percent). However, this finding requires some qualification. The research university with class numbers in excess of one thousand students and a high complement of graduate TAs composed 38 percent of the chemistry sample. Notwithstanding the high level of support for the modular approach overall, as table 5.2 indicates, the mostly graduate TAs at the research institution were far less positive about chemistry than the largely undergraduate TAs in the three other types of institutions represented in this sample. The evaluative observations for TAs at the research university was 37 percent positive, 33 percent mixed, and 30 percent negative, compared with 62 percent positive, 23 percent mixed, and 15 percent negative at the other six institutions combined. Later, I discuss the nature and sources of these differences in TA evaluations of the modular approach.

Berkeley TA Education

The evaluative observations offered by the Berkeley TAs in the two rounds of interviews (spring 2000 and fall 2001) differ from the other two initiatives because they address both the innovative and the unchanged, traditional parts of this very large chemistry course. Table 5.4 shows the TAs' evaluative observations for both aspects of the class. Because of the interview focus on the innovations, the numbers of TAs' evaluative comments on new aspects of the class are higher than those addressing traditional aspects. The Berkeley comments also referenced somewhat different issues than those of the other two initiatives. Evaluative observations on the innovation included the perceived utility of the worksheet methods in enabling student learning, the TAs' level of comfort in using them, and other interactive elements in the TAs' work with students (small-group learning, discussion). The Berkeley TAs also evaluated their teaching experiences, the quality of their education in the new teaching methods, and the opportunities for feedback to the faculty that this afforded. Evaluation observations on the traditional aspects of the class addressed a different set of issues: the value of the lectures, labs, and text for student learning; the quality of their contacts with the lectures and lab professors (including opportunities to offer feedback); and the utility of their office hours with students.

Where the two sets of evaluative observations intersect is on issues of coherence within and between the traditional and nontraditional parts of the class. Class coherence issues were commonly referred to by both undergraduates and TAs as "fit" problems. Over several studies, we have consistently found that issues of coherence (or fit) between the various parts of any class are always an issue for students. However, they become a central issue whenever classes are taught in more innovative ways because they change what students expect to experience in the structure and sequencing of more traditional classes. "Fit" issues are strongly featured in both the undergraduate and TA interview data for all three initiatives. In the case of the Berkeley initiative, TAs split the responsibility for attaining a rational relationship among class elements between the two groups of faculty responsible for the class—that is, the innovators working with the students via the TAs and the lecture and lab professors who were responsible for delivering class content. They offered praise or critique according to their sense of who was responsible for which aspects of overall class coherence. TAs saw it as the responsibility of the innovative faculty to make a working fit between the objectives, content, and activities of the new-style TA recitations and those of the lectures and labs that remained unchanged. However, they expected the traditional faculty contributing to the course to prevent the structural disjunctions that sometimes placed labs before related lectures. They also defined it as the responsibility of the lecture and lab professors to make a rational fit between the selection and emphases of particular content, their selection and use of the textbook, and the exams and quizzes that they devised.[1]

Despite the lower numbers of evaluative observations for traditional class elements as opposed to those for innovative elements, across both rounds of Berkeley interviews the percentages of TAs' positive, mixed, and negative observations for the two aspects of the class are quite similar. Across both interview rounds, negative evaluations overall average 48 percent, positive evaluations average 36 percent, and mixed observations average 16 percent. When the two interview rounds are considered separately, TAs in the first round were more negative than positive about both the innovative and the traditional aspects of the class, and their proportions of negative observations for each are similar—51 percent for the innovative aspects and 49 percent for the traditional aspects. They are a little more complimentary about the traditional class aspects (43 percent) than the innovative (36 percent) but offer more mixed evaluations of innovative class elements.

In the interval of eighteen months between the first and second interview rounds, the faculty innovators worked to address issues raised by TAs, drawing on both the formative evaluation and the direct personal feedback. Changes were made in the worksheet content and methods, in the TA education process, and in the conduct of the weekly meetings. One outcome of the faculty's response to TA feedback is clear in the drop, both in number and proportion, of negative evaluations for innovative class aspects—from 51 percent to 39 percent. Evaluations in the second group of TA interviews were also more positive about the innovative aspects of the class than were those offered by the first group. They were also less complimentary about traditional class elements. TAs offered a number of reasons for this position. They gave the innovative faculty considerable credit for trying to make this large lecture class more intellectually coherent for students despite the disjunctions in the traditional aspects of the class. These included a low level of collaboration between the class and lab professors, poor alignment between what is taught and what is tested, and sequencing problems between classes and labs for some student sections. The faculty innovators were also credited with listening to TA feedback and acting on it.

In our analysis of the modular chemistry undergraduate interview data, we also found that initial resistance to classroom innovations fades as faculty persevere with the new mode of teaching, as students become more accustomed to it, and as its benefits become apparent to them. Initial student resistance is exacerbated because faculty, in their early trials of new approaches, tend to be struggling with materials and methods that they have not completely worked out and are not yet fluent in using and with many practical issues of implementation and management. As both we, as the ChemConnections evaluators, and Allen, Weldman, and Folk (2001) have observed, resistance by undergraduates is commonly registered in lower end-of-course classroom evaluation scores in the first few semesters of an innovation. The experience of the Berkeley faculty innovators, with less than two years of experience in running their initiative, fits this pattern. As I later discuss, where they are successfully engaged, TAs can play a key role in helping innovative faculty to resolve implementation problems, smooth out imperfections, and establish a tone of "normality" about the way that the class is taught that enables undergraduates entering the class to accept it.

Finally, the contribution of mixed evaluative comments to the Berkeley innovation is constant in both interview rounds and, as in the other two initiatives, consists largely of ideas about how aspects of the course could be improved. As I will further discuss, qualified positive observations are a useful
indicator of both students' and TAs' active interest in any innovative approach and always contain valuable feedback for faculty. Also of note are the
consistently more positive views toward innovative aspects of the class from
the eleven undergraduate and five masters' students who worked as TAs
across the spring 2000 and fall 2001 classes compared with the consistently
more negative views of the doctoral TAs. Later I discuss why doctoral TAs
may be less open than undergraduates to engagement in innovative teaching and learning.

Character and Utility of TAs' Evaluations

Knowing the level of overall support offered by TAs for the innovations in
which they played a role is useful to the innovators. It may also be encouraging to faculty who are considering classroom changes. However, we can
obtain more specific guidance about the design and implementation of innovative courses by looking carefully at each of the three types of evaluative observations offered by TAs. From their positive evaluations, we learn
what TAs observed in the achievements and behavior of their undergraduates that disposed them to approve of the teacher's approach. From their
negative evaluations, we learn about sources of resistance to active modes
of learning for both TAs and undergraduates. We also learn what factors in
the implementation of innovations and in the working relationship between
faculty and TAs function to encourage or discourage TA engagement and
support. Finally, from the mixed evaluations, we learn what TAs notice
about what works and what does not—and why—and the kinds of adjustment that they advise to address particular problems. Most significantly, we
learn about the active role that TAs can and do play in making innovations
work. In what follows, we look at each of these groups of observations to
understand from the TAs' perspective what enables or limits the success of
innovations.

Taken together, what TAs valued or disliked about these innovations (or
saw as in need of improvement) and the rationales that they offered for their
judgments were found to be different in their nature and sources from those
of both faculty and undergraduates in our other related data sets. This is not
surprising: faculty, undergraduates, and TAs each bring to the situation different sets of expectations, goals, experiences, and concerns. This is important to clarify at the outset because faculty who, in their interviews, expressed reservations about the innovative teaching of their departmental
colleagues often cited negative student evaluations in support of their own

views as if they arose from a shared set of concerns. Our data do not support this assumption.

The rationales that TAs used to explain their positive, negative, and mixed evaluations were not of the same character. Indeed, each type of evaluation was grounded in distinctive forms of argument or reference to evidence. Most notably, many TAs who offered unqualified negative evaluations explained their opinions as disagreements of principle with the teaching methods used. By contrast, TAs who offered positive comments grounded them largely in direct observations of student responses in their section, lab, or the class overall. Negative and positive judgments also differed in how TAs used them to predict student performance outcomes. For example, those doctoral TAs who expressed low expectations for the outcome of the innovation used a rationale that is commonly offered by faculty—that innovations will not work because students are underprepared for the level of work required or because they have poor learning habits. By contrast, positive comments from TAs at every academic level reflected greater optimism about the possibilities of improving student attitudes and performance. As indicated, mixed comments were largely grounded in a creative, collaborative interest in making these innovative classes work more effectively.

An exception to the principle-versus-experience difference in the rationale for negative and positive evaluations was TAs' common reference to experience in more traditional classes (both as students and as TAs) as reasons for their judgments. TAs offering negative evaluations tended to ground their concerns in a preference for the traditional methods by which they had been taught and a view of the innovative classes as departures from correct practice. Those approving the innovative pedagogy often expressed the wish that they had been offered the opportunity to learn in these new ways. In the following sections, I show the contrast between the positive and negative evaluations, followed by a discussion of the character of mixed TA evaluations.

NATURE AND CONSEQUENCES OF POSITIVE EVALUATIONS

Overall Findings

This section explores the nature of positive evaluations that formed 44 percent of all evaluative observations. These were 52 percent of evaluative observations by TAs in late-stage modular classes at seven institutions, 42 percent of all evaluations by TAs in Interactive Astronomy classes across three semesters of the initiative, and 38 percent of TA evaluations of the innovative parts of the Berkeley TA education initiative across two semesters. As indicated earlier, TAs' positive evaluations were largely based on their direct observations of particular benefits to students. Their character was largely twofold: TAs described particular benefits and also explained them with reference to both general and specific attributes of the new courses. Positive evaluations clustered into the seven descriptive and explanatory categories shown here:

The contributions of small-group activity (and other forms of interaction) to student learning	21 percent
Improved learning in lab work and the significance of course–lab alignment	19 percent
Successes in motivating students to learn	15 percent
Learning gains related to course coherence and "signposting"	12 percent
Learning advantages derived from the innovative approach	12 percent
Evidence of improved learning, modes of learning, and learning retention	11 percent
The contribution of new class materials to student learning	10 percent

As is indicated, the dominant themes in all TAs' positive evaluative observations are reports of gains in student learning and discussion of their sources. At the broadest level, TAs cited learning advantages that arose directly from innovative approaches. TAs also described particular indicators of improved learning, modes of learning, and learning retention that prompted them to judge the course favorably. They pointed to successes in student motivation and improved attitudes toward learning. Other learning gains were attributed to faculty's attention to the coherence of related course elements and to making the flow of course ideas and their connections ("signposting") clear to students. The two largest categories of gains specifically cited were the contributions of small-group learning (and other forms of interactivity) and improvements in the learning objectives and organization of labs and in course–lab alignment. Both were seen as important factors in improved student learning. Finally, learning improvements are also ascribed to the quality of new class materials.

Each of the factors in student learning improvement reported by TAs is discussed in the sections that follow, beginning with broader categories of student gains and followed by gains ascribed to particular course attributes.

Learning Advantages Derived from the Innovative Approach

TA support for aspects of the innovative pedagogy and curriculum was commonly expressed as approval for class goals based on observations of their positive consequences for undergraduates. For example, in the astronomy classes, the coaches understood and supported the professor's intention to give undergraduates a small-group, honors-like experience within the context of a large class:

> They are trying to give a small-group experience in a rather large classroom. You get a very tight-knit group of people and the theory is that this brings about a better, more solid understanding of the material. Honors classes are usually limited to like eighteen people, so it's like giving an honors experience to a much broader array of people.

These coaches endorsed the professor's theory that, in a small well-functioning group, individual students can develop a deeper understanding of the class materials than they could achieve alone:

> They meet in the home group and get lecture and answer sessions, but then they get in a small group where they work as a team and get into the material in depth. . . . In lectures, you're learning all by yourself, and you are often scared to ask. With this, you have five to eight people who are always going to be your group and that you come closer to as the semester goes on, and you can go to them for help. And they do help each other.

Their support for the approach was grounded in their observations of these processes at work within their own learning teams. For example, as their learning team members rehearsed their draft answers to each week's discussion questions, coaches noted that students discovered how well (or imperfectly) they understood the ideas they sought to express. Thus, TA approval was often based on, or bolstered by, evidence from observing students that supported faculty hypotheses—in this instance, that explaining, answering questions, and arguing about ideas can indeed clarify and consolidate learning, force rethinking, and build deeper understanding:

> They say you don't fully understand something until you can explain it to someone else, and that's a big piece of the whole philosophy behind learning teams—the students have to come with their answers prepared and then rehearse them on each other. And when they're trying to explain what they have discovered, it's sort of pounding it into their own heads. They've already got an answer, but now they are explaining it to other people who are going to question them or say they don't understand. So, they've got to reword what they *think* they know until everyone understands it. And then they really get the concept—it finally sticks.

TAs also observed a decline especially in the instrumental preoccupations of engineering and other "serviced" majors who traditionally treat introductory chemistry classes largely as a means to collect a grade in a required subject:

> There's always a student who wants to know "When am I going to use this?" But the title of the module tells you what the point is to begin with, so those questions

went way, way down. Even people asking, "Am I ever going to need this for further classes?" I mean, they don't ask those questions any more.

Chemistry TAs also praised the modular approach as being valuable to nonscience majors, whose anxiety levels were observed to drop as the class progressed. They noted that students with limited experience with science were often surprised to find themselves taking an interest in chemistry and contributing to group projects by drawing on their writing, oral, and research skills. They gave much of the credit for these improvements to the real-world applications that are central to the modular approach:

> The best things about the modules is that it forces students to tie a lot of different concepts together into sort of big ideas. I think that's important in any class that you take, because tying ideas together, you're not learning abstract concepts but something that actually matters for something in the real world. And that really helps students, getting a clear way to make those links. I think that's the way learning should be. In another class I'm taking that isn't modular, I have to search for something to apply it all to.

> I think that what they do is more important than going over the book. The fact that they are in a process of applying chemistry, realizing what the chemistry means, and answering questions. Those are all more important skills than just learning things for tests. I think that practicing the chemistry the modular way helps them, prepares them better for learning in general than just knowing specific concepts.

The chemistry TAs also described the benefits created by the cross-disciplinary nature of the modules. The astronomy class coaches noted students' high level of engagement with the class content and hypertext material. The coaches cited instances of students who expressed interest in taking more science classes, including astronomy:

> Maybe this is a doorway to a major. Some of my group would definitely like to do more; some of them say that this stuff is fascinating. One guy who is an exchange student, he was like, "Man, I'd love to major in astronomy." And so I think that what they come away with you can't entirely measure by what they learn. The more important thing about this approach is that it spawns an interest in astronomy. And I can see, really see that it does.

Gains in Student Learning

TAs who offered positive evaluations most often described their support for innovative approaches in terms of their beneficial effects on student learning. Their observations focused on

- Evidence of improved learning, modes of learning, and learning retention attributed to both overall and specific attributes of the class
- The importance of all forms of small-group activity for improved student learning
- Learning gains specific to students' experiences in the innovative labs.

Observations of improved learning are discussed in this and the following two sections.

The TAs offered several kinds of evidence that students were making gains in understanding, and they described aspects of the courses that prompted this conclusion. For example, they noted (and were pleasantly surprised by) good oral presentations in poster sessions, the quality of the students' questions, and their ability to draw on their knowledge in class discussions:

It turns out the shampoo stuff we did was very appealing to a lot of my students— particularly when we got to the poster session at the end. It was just like, all of a sudden, they'd done all this work, and they knew what was going on. I was very surprised by their posters in that they'd spent a lot of time with all of the equilibrium stuff. When they started out, they were saying they didn't understand it and were having a lot of trouble understanding it. But when they got to the poster, they went all out, and they could tell me what all the pHs of their shampoos were and why it mattered. It was a very different picture when they were asked to apply the theory to something they were interested in. So that was very successful.

We were learning about boiling points, and one of my students asked me how sweat evaporates. . . . Just being able to understand things like that. When you are just taught the equations and the ideas, you don't really think about little things like that. And I sat there and explained it to her, which was just fine. But that's what the modules have provided them with—learning about computer chips and everyday things that you don't think about. They make you *really* want to know. Making students more curious—that's the biggest thing. That's what I liked about them too. It was just that interesting.

That students could and did talk about chemistry and that they were starting to ask more fundamental questions strongly suggested to TAs that they were also remembering more of what they learned:

I think they do have a better chance of remembering it because they have something to relate to. Every time they see an air bag or an article on the environment, they'll remember that lab we did. I wish there was some way to check it out, but my bet would be that they would remember it better. And it's interesting that they seem to think they will.

Maybe this way might be better for remembering things further along the road. They may not realize it now, but I think they will. Actually I'm teaching 1B this semester, so a lot of my students who took the modules as 1A are doing real well in 1B. And they are telling me how well they are understanding the new work because they really understood what they learned in 1A. And they're doing well.

Toward the end of their classes, TAs reported that it was common for students to express pleasure about how much they had learned and remembered. Students were often surprised by this discovery, and this reinforced the TAs' observation that students often shifted away from their incoming expectations that they would "hate the class," suffer their way through it, and forget most of it once they had survived the final test:

> After the debate, a lot of people said they were surprised at how much they knew. People may think that having memorized a chunk of something that they know it. But when they have to pull things together, they know it in a different, better sense. That was something they had to get over—that memorizing things isn't the only kind of knowing.

The TAs who described these gains were encouraged and motivated by them. They also took some credit for the signs of improvement that they saw in student learning.[2] As I illustrate later, they also tended to blame themselves when students showed poor progress.

Those TAs with experience in introductory classes also observed that the grades in these innovative classes "looked normal," and they saw no evidence of poorer student performances than in the more traditional classes with which they had worked:

> As far as the lab grading, it's mostly the same range of grades that I've had from other classes that aren't modular.

> It's about the same grades as other classes I've worked in—a few As, a reasonable number of Bs and a lot of Cs—just a normal spread for an intro chem class.

TAs credited some of these improvements—in comprehension, in the ways that students learned chemistry, and in their attitudes toward the discipline—to the various forms of interactive learning used by faculty and to their insistence that students read and write more. In modular chemistry, students worked from a wider array of sources than is customary in chemistry courses, and they wrote about chemistry as a way to learn it:

> They were definitely reading more than they are used to. I mean, they had a lot of questions in my office hours about specific areas of the reading. It was definitely making them read.

> Trust me: they write a *lot* more. And they put more effort into their work, and that means to me that they have more concern about it. You establish that early

in the semester; then, for the rest of the time, they'll be working hard and putting in the effort into chemistry. That's what you need to do. So, I'm a big supporter of writing more—although, speaking as a TA, it makes a lot more work for us!

TAs saw this combination of methods as pushing students to think about the material and making it much harder to reduce learning to rote short-term memorization for tests without any real engagement with course concepts:

> We had a debate on Olestra and had to write a paper to go along with it, so we had to write and get used to speaking about the topic and debating it with people. And I thought that was helpful in learning. And she graded on how well we could write and if we could back up our knowledge—you couldn't get away with copying facts—you had to be ready to defend what you wrote. (Modular TA who took the class the previous year)

The Contributions to Student Learning of Small-Group Activity and Other Forms of Interaction

A fundamental aspect of all of the innovative classes that TAs singled out as being particularly effective in promoting understanding—more so than had been the case in their own, more traditional learning experiences—was the interactive quality of innovative classes, labs, and recitation sections. Indeed, TAs saw the interactive nature of these classes as a critical contributor to the improved student learning that they reported:

> Most people learn through interaction—definitely. And when the class went back to being traditionally taught this semester, they lost the interaction that's critical for a good science course.

Across all three initiatives, the individual aspects of innovative course teaching that were most often singled out for positive TA comments were the various forms of small-group activity employed by innovative faculty. Some TAs who had reservations about other aspects of innovative pedagogy nevertheless expressed support for small-group learning methods. Commonly mentioned benefits of group work were those dealing with difficulties in comprehension as they arise, gains in confidence and independence to approach complex issues, and working out how to tackle new shared tasks:

> My intro chem was more traditionally taught, so the large lecture was the thing that overwhelmed me, without direct student-teacher interaction. I see the group work as a major positive in the modules, with students getting to work together.

> Yeah, I think the authors of the modules should definitely keep the group work in there, because it really does help the students.

I think they've learned how to work in groups better and use each other to help figure stuff out.

They noted that the students' confidence was built through the experience of success arising out of their group work and that this confidence building extended to the TAs as well as to the undergraduates:

> I think it was very interesting to get them to be responsible to each other and work in small groups to solve problems. I also think it was a good experience for the coaches. . . . I'd like to see undergraduates teaching other students more often. I've always known that the time I learn the material best is when I'm teaching it to someone else. It's always better than the first time I learned it. So, if everyone was teaching each other, they'd all be learning at the same time.

Groups that worked effectively from the outset were seen as enjoying their work more, and the benefits to members were seen as being cumulative and transferable. For example, some TAs noted that getting students to work effectively together in class had a positive effect on their efficiency as lab groups. Others noted that it encouraged students to form study groups and develop social ties:

> TA 1: In gen chem, we usually had lab partners, but these students worked together in groups in class as well, and they knew each other better than we did.
>
> TA 2: I think so too. They get together outside of class and form study groups, and that's really good.
>
> TA 1: Yeah, you tend to form study groups. And if you have a group of four people meeting outside of class, and you have subjects to go over and one person does each of them, then you can all learn each of them pretty quickly just by doing examples and problems.
>
> TA 2: And you're never going to learn everything in class.

> I could tell by the end of the first semester they were really helping each other a lot. At the beginning of the second semester, I had a lot of the same students in there, and they kept it going, and they just accepted the new people, and that new group just went right into it, so it kept it rolling along. (Undergraduate TA in two-semester modular chemistry sequence)

TAs from across all three initiatives endorsed and actively promoted the principle that students need to learn to work together because this is an important skill, both for many forms of professional work and for life in general:

> TA 1: A lot of the students who went through strenuous AP chemistry came here and they're like, "What's this, then?" Some of them had problems with it because

it didn't seem like classic chemistry to them. But those are the ones who I thought came around the most by the end and were helping the others.

TA 2: Yeah, I agree with that.

TA 1: I think it's very important. Most people aren't going to have a job where they're sitting at a desk by themselves and never interacting with anyone. You are going to have to make presentations and do projects where you work with other people, and you have to learn to work with them and assert yourself. Like she just said, this is teaching them skills that they are gonna need.

TA 2: I had one girl who's been really good about leading the team and getting them to come together. Maybe she's not realizing it, but she's developing valuable skills.

One TA, an engineer, impressed this on his students by explaining that learning to depend on one another to produce good work is key to success in his field. Because of the centrality of small-group learning to these and many other classroom innovations, TA advice about how to make groups function optimally is presented and discussed in more detail in chapter 6.

In the modular classes, debates and formal discussions were cited as being particularly effective in focusing learning, increasing work motivation, and giving students a way to check how much and how deeply they understood key ideas:

TA 1: Students should be talking to each other at points in the class and bouncing ideas off of each other. I think that can be very fruitful.

TA 2: And the teacher can do some things to stimulate that even in a big class. You have to find a way to elicit their input—just burst into their world.

TA 1: I think discussion is stimulating in itself. I know I was just amazed whenever they popped up a really good question.

Finally, TAs praised faculty use of all strategies based on dialogue—particularly group work and class breakout sessions—by which students were set up to teach each other. They noted the refining and consolidating effects on learning when students were pressed to explain what they thought they knew to peers; to find alternative ways to explain concepts that were difficult to grasp; and to respond to questions, caveats, and rebuttals:

It's a better way to help them understand, and it gets them to be responsible to each other. The whole philosophy of the learning teams is that they have to come with their answer prepared, then sort of rehearse possible answers on each other, and when they are doing that, it is sort of refining what they all know into an answer that they can explain to each other. And when someone says, "I still don't understand," they have to reword it and go on explaining all of the aspects of it until all of the questions get answered and they all get it. And that process helps it stick with them. And he's right—you don't know it until you can teach it.

TAs testified to the strengthening of their own conceptual understanding by precisely the same processes while working in these classes. One TA commented, "Being in the discussions with the students was also an important review for me." Another admitted, "I picked up on things that I hadn't really understood that well the first time around."

Improved Learning in Lab Work and the Significance of Course-Lab Alignment

Some of the improvements in student learning noted by TAs occurred specifically in labs. As we first documented in *Talking about Leaving* (Seymour and Hewitt 1997), the most commonly encountered source of student discontent with their lab work was failure to understand the purpose and significance of what they were asked to do. This problem has contributed perhaps more than any other single factor to student disinterest in labs and has reinforced a shared imperative to get through a series of seemingly meaningless processes as quickly as possible. One of the TAs described how this common student attitude was challenged by the nature of the modular labs:

> A lot of them have had labs in other classes, and they have got this mind-set of just doing the lab for the sake of it. They're not used to having this overarching goal like they do in the modular labs. And so that's been a brand new thing for lots of them. I think it irritates particular people who want to just get by and do the least amount of work. It's more real work because you're trying to tie ideas together and make a picture about what you see. And it forces them to think more about it. They don't want to think about chemistry that much.

Important objectives of the modular chemistry labs were to get students to see the connections between class and lab work and to answer open-ended questions rather than verify facts or laws. The TAs credited modular labs that are tightly and overtly connected to class learning objectives with breaking the pattern of conceptual disconnect between class and lab and with restoring the links between conceptual and experimental understanding:

> The module labs are quite different from intro classes I've TAed before. I was thinking about the stars lab with the atomic spectrum. Normally, you just kind of test and "Ooh that's orange—that's sodium." So then you write that down. But here, they give you the bigger picture—which isn't the objective I got a sense of in those other labs. They get you to understand what those lines are and why they would relate to the sun, and you go take a look at the lines from the sun. And you try to relate absorption and emission—instead of just saying, "This is sodium; this is lithium."

They have an idea of *why* you should be doing something. When we were in gen chem, they'd give us a procedure, you did the procedure, and then you left. You didn't really understand why you did it. So, I think these students understand. They often aren't science majors, and they are having a harder time actually doing the chemistry, but they understand why they are doing it.

TA 1: I think they all could tell you. I think they recognize the connections. The modular labs and the modular class—they're more interrelated. When they were doing CFCs [chlorofluorocarbons] and talking about their effects, they were doing a lab showing the actual chemical properties and why they were better than old refrigerator gases. The module helps link class and lab together.

TA 2: That's true. I heard one group talking while they were in the lab, you know, "We talked about this in class" or "Remember this from class?" So they do notice what they are bringing into lab from class and make those connections.

TAs praised the modules for directly addressing the common problem of low student interest in labs by restoring meaning to lab work. This was accomplished by conceptually connecting class and lab work and by addressing questions that were real for students:

I thought one of the best things was when we did the water hardness lab, and people would bring their own tap water from home. And they'd tell me that they told their mom or their roommate what they did, and they thought it was so neat to be applying what they directly to something in their own home.

The best aspect is linking the labs and class to real things. It's really important to explain why chemistry matters because there are some people who aren't superexcited about the periodic table, you know. I mean, there's some people who are going to be chemists. And then there's others that will use chemistry as a tool, and they really need to know why it's important and when it's applicable—maybe in medicine, dentistry, chemical engineering, or whatever. It's not just that it's fun to make something in a beaker like those of us who are chemists.

As indicated, the modular labs were seen as demanding more of students and making it harder to coast through the course with minimal effort. Again, I note that TAs often grounded their opinions in their own experiences as learners in introductory classes:

The big difference was that the labs were tied to real experiences. And it seemed more realistic that the students have to think about what does this mean. I thought about this in my freshman year. I learned equations and I'd do a lab, and I would have no idea how to apply it and there wasn't much explanation. But this year, the students had a lot of real-world experiences, and they talked about what they were doing a lot.

In addition to improvements in students' understanding of the meaning of their lab work, TAs reported gains in lab-related skills. These included learning to design experiments, collect and analyze one's own data, explain trends observed in data, make estimates, and develop particular skills in computing and statistical analysis:

> They were asked to observe, log, and interpret their own data. And once you kind of pushed them in the right direction, they could do it. There was just a first shock of having to look at it and analyze it. They know what direction to go in, but sometimes they are hesitant—not as confident. But they found it quite possible to understand and interpret. They didn't have too many real problems at all. And I didn't get many questions about "How do you do this?"

> These students are definitely going to leave with a good grasp of general computer skills—Internet searching, constructing webpages. I think that was vital. They had to know or to learn some HTML, and that's going to come in useful for a lot of them later.

Some TAs saw it as being more important than learning lab skills per se that their students were developing a responsible attitude toward the data they generated—that they were taking data seriously. This included learning to deal with error and becoming comfortable with the inherent ambivalence and the intellectual risks of authentic lab work:

> There's more design-your-own procedures than we had. That's good too. I mean, they might not design something that will work, but at least they tried and learned it won't work. And that's something everyone has to learn.

> Even when things went wrong, they seemed to know the direction they were going. They understood when something was wrong. That's really good. It's a good first step.

Learning Gains Related to Course Coherence

As briefly discussed in the section on TAs' evaluation of the Berkeley TA education initiative, issues of course coherence—expressed in the degree of alignment of important course elements—are central to explaining the effectiveness of any class, whether conventional or innovative, in enabling student learning. Achieving course coherence is often a target for course improvement, and the success of any innovation depends to a significant degree on the effectiveness with which this is achieved. TAs gave praise wherever they saw a good fit between the content and activities of classes and labs and between both of these and the nature and emphasis of learning assessments:

Everything else went real smooth—like a tight fit between the module stuff in class and what would be explained in the lab. And the students seemed to really know what they were doing.

And they do show you the application. One of the nice things about the modular labs is that they do really correlate well with what you're learning. So you're doing something that completely relates to what you're learning in the class.

They recognize the connections with class actually more with the modular stuff. Like we did this iodine clock reaction two weeks back, and it's not really related to the chemistry they're doing in class, but the teacher needed a good lab to model reaction kinetics. And a lot of them wrote in their notebooks something like "Okay, this isn't really about ozone, but the reason we are doing this is to understand that . . ." So they understood that this was something they needed to know how to make another link.

The efforts of modular chemistry faculty to align their learning assessments to class learning objectives, which they subsequently explained and reinforced in class, were also seen as promoting student learning. Discussing the process of learning with students and making them more aware of their learning methods, including meaningful test preparation, were seen as being important in getting students to take responsibility for their own learning. They contrasted this overt discussion of learning with students with the tacit, unspoken assumptions about learning that they had experienced in most traditional classes:

The general chemistry that I went through, we covered more, but I don't know if we had as good an understanding of it. Here, you're seeking it more—you seeing it in the lecture; you see it in the lab; and you talk about what you see and you make the links. I think they understand the concepts more and they *know* they do because they can talk about it.

I think they've learned more than I learned at this stage . . . just being forced to be prepared for the lecture with the idea that the prof might call on them. And then being forced to explain their answer and answer questions about it. It all helps them to understand and to think about their learning. And just hearing them talk to each other about their project, I hear comments like "Remember when we talked about such a thing?"

"Signposting"

However coherent the overall class structure, because of its unfamiliarity to students, TAs pointed to the additional need for "signposts" that allowed students to develop a sense of the direction in which their learning was going and an understanding of how elements of the class related and were complementary:[3]

> It's great for me—because it's focused. I can see where we're going a bit ahead of the day plan. I think it's probably better for the teachers too because it all starts at a certain point and then goes through highlighting important things, and you can see that it's leading up to something. When we're just working out of a book a lot of time, I'm not exactly sure where we're going or what we're doing. But I think that this method helps the students. They can actually see where we are going and why.

TAs praised faculty who signposted the flow of ideas by multiple means and by frequent repetition. They also endorsed their own role in reinforcing the students' sense of direction and progress in their learning. The need for signposting emerged in the development and early testing of the chemistry modular materials and, along with course coherence, appears to be a critical requirement for success in the introduction of new materials and learning methods to undergraduates. TAs constantly stressed the importance of signposting in their feedback to faculty, and I present a fuller account of their views on its importance in chapter 7.

The Contribution of New Class Materials to Student Learning

Both modular chemistry TAs and Interactive Astronomy coaches praised the quality of new curriculum materials—specifically, the module handbooks for students and the online astronomy hypertext. The astronomy coaches thought that the online materials had advantages even over what they saw as a good textbook:

> This class is introducing students to extraordinary things that are available on the web and then presenting class materials in the same way. He has some beautiful stuff in there. It's important for learning that kids can understand how to use the technology to find the material—and there's a basis for that already among them, so it's a fine way to go.

The module handbooks were described as containing up-to-date materials that explored "a lot" of chemistry and were praised as being well written with clearly explained concepts and good questions:

> I looked through the modules and thought, "Wow! These are really good questions." They're written in such an open-ended way that you can get a spectrum of ways that people could answer—even students who haven't got very far into the chemistry yet. I can see that there's layers of possible answers.

Berkeley TAs described the worksheets as being structured in a way that reinforced concepts presented in class and helped students to understand the course material conceptually:

> Some of the things on energy and thermochemistry have been really useful in supplementing the lecture material because the students have a hard time working through the concepts and thinking about the problems. And the worksheets have been helping them solidify the concepts and get a better feel for the material, instead of just memorizing.

These attributes of the worksheets were seen as being especially valuable for subsets of the class who had difficulties with the math involved or struggled with conceptual understanding. TAs appreciated the capacity of the worksheets and the discussions based on them to help students visualize an idea by encountering it other forms and to explore it in more detail and depth:

> The worksheets are certainly useful in the learning of the concepts. So, a concept may be presented one way in lecture, and using a worksheet, it may be presented three other different ways. So, if they've missed it in lecture and they couldn't quite visualize it . . . then certainly, after doing the worksheet, they might.

Like the modules, the worksheets also enriched students' understanding with good applications. Some TAs appreciated the capacity of the worksheets to encourage interactive learning, which one TA described as a necessary academic survival skill:

> I like the framework of how our labs are set up—that we do a discussion. In the upper-level classes that I'm taking now, you work with other students, and that's how you can bounce ideas off other people. And those are things my students have not learned yet. . . . One of the basics that you have to learn in your educational career is how to work with other students and how to learn from other people's strengths, and discussion is the perfect way to do it.[4]

Finally, in TA observations on new class materials and resources, TAs in both the modular chemistry and Interactive Astronomy classes offered positive comments (and some advice) about the value of introducing students to multiple-source multimedia learning.

Success in Motivating Students to Learn

TAs credited some portion of improvements in student learning to the faculty's success in promoting changes in student attitudes. The most important of these was a shift toward greater responsibility for their own learning. As bad learning habits became less effective in securing desired grades, and as demonstrations of comprehension and application were rewarded, TAs also noted an increase in the level of responsibility that students took for their own learning:

> Writing—that's a big part of it. Definitely. A lot of the quizzes were not just plug in the numbers and come up with an answer. There were a lot of multiple-choice questions that ended in "Explain your reasoning." It was difficult for some of the students because it's actually a lot easier to rely on doing equations. But they don't look at it and see whether it's a possible answer, and they weren't used to thinking about explaining what they got. So that was a definite advantage of the modules. They made them explain a lot of data—looking for trends—and always observing and predicting and always writing things down.

> We got strong positive feedback from students about the oral presentations at the end. They got a lot out of putting together their own data and having to explain it. They found that very helpful. I think they managed to explain what they know better. There's a lot of students who normally wouldn't open their mouths, but this time, they didn't just sit there and leave the answering to their lab partners.

> I think the great technology that we have and the software and hypertext, and getting them to work as a team and to learn the material themselves instead of just being lectured at all the time, having them teach themselves—it's all getting them more involved in their own education.

In modular chemistry classes, TAs cited as important outcomes of the overall approach its capacity to motivate students to learn by enabling them to make use of their chemistry knowledge. The TAs found it unusual and refreshing to hear students talking to each other, and to them, about chemistry:

> I saw a big difference from my first two times as a TA, just in the types of questions students asked. Both in open office hours and in general, they were asking more about what's fundamentally going on here, as opposed to "How do I do this problem?"

> One good thing you notice is when people are sitting in their groups, they're actually talking to each other and trying to figure stuff out. And they're actually working together. And I think the whole group gets more out of this than just sitting in rows saying, "I don't know how to do this problem."

Thus, in the view of these TAs and coaches, improving students' *attitudes toward learning* science, and also their *methods of learning*, were critical factors in improving their actual learning:

I think they learned more astronomy than I learned last year. 'Cause, just watching them in the lecture, being forced to be prepared for it and with the idea that the prof might call on them, and being forced to reiterate the information in the learning team and say it again for the people who haven't yet got it, I think all of that makes them understand it better. And just hearing them talk about their projects, I've heard comments like "Remember when we talked about X." It lets me know that they are remembering it.

Another source of positive motivational shifts reported by TAs was restoration of students' faith in the connection between effort and gain:

The most important thing is that they have to be willing to spend time reading and doing the homework. And I can look at my grades and those people who did the homework did well. It just took a lot of time and studying, and people who did that are doing well—people who took time to study on their own and then come to my office hours and ask questions, and go back and study some more. And those people who sort of ran through the work or did half the homework, unless they were incredibly gifted, they didn't do well.

Some TAs also noticed that effective group work encourages a spiral of positive reinforcement for effort and reward:

I think the people who enjoy it most are the ones who put most effort into it. I mean, the material is so cool, and the whole philosophy of the class is discussion. You're not going to enjoy discussing answers when you don't know what you are talking about. So the people who have done the work and are well prepared are real eager to give an answer in class for their team. It's a self-esteem kind of thing. It really gives them a little boost that sort of feeds on itself. If you work hard and you're getting the rewards, you also get little rewards for yourself: you're scoring team points and doing well on the quizzes, and that all keeps you working hard. It works!

Students began to see that working hard in the manner advocated by faculty and expressed in class activities brought rewards in both grades and personal satisfaction:

I mean, there's definitely those students who take the class just because they have an obligation, and whatever you do, they just learn it because they think they have to and don't really gain anything from it. But there are students—you know, when they did the poster session, I know they gained a lot from going through that. And they really worked hard and did great work, and they got a lot of satisfaction out of it.

It seems like the people who come in with a good attitude and are more open-minded, do a whole lot better. I think the ones who enjoy it most are also the ones who put most effort into it. The people who are well prepared, have done the work, and are eager and anxious to answer the questions: they are the ones who do well.

TAs also praised teachers who, by their own excitement about the course materials and their discipline, engaged students in the class content and motivated them by clear messages that they wanted students to understand and enjoy the material and do well:

> Some of my group tell me that this stuff is fascinating, and I can see that that part of that is how excited the prof is by it and how much he wants to share it with us all. Everyone is going to take different things away, but the important thing as that they all learn something and that they take away an interest in astronomy, and I think that's happening.

The ability and desire to engage and motivate undergraduates is not, of course, limited to innovative faculty. However, TAs thought it an especially important ingredient in innovative classes. They observed that students were willing to accommodate the imperfections in materials, methods, and class management that are endemic to new courses, because their teachers' enthusiasm and concern for their learning was so evident to them. As we have also found among undergraduates in innovative classes, winning trust is key to getting students to suspend their belief in the necessity, or inevitability, of "formulaic" learning.[5]

Finally, these TAs interpreted their observations of improved student learning and satisfaction with their classes as indications that the innovations were working well:

> They had some concrete suggestions about what to change but in context of a positive general attitude towards the class. There were not happy campers on every front by any means, but the level of enthusiasm and willingness to do the work was high. It was quite impressive.

In this section, we have explored the character of positive evaluations that formed 52 percent of all evaluative observations by TAs in late-stage modular classes at seven institutions, 42 percent of all evaluations by TAs in Interactive Astronomy classes across three semesters of the initiative, and 38 percent of TA evaluations of the innovative parts of the Berkeley TA education initiative across two semesters. Because of the contrasts I have drawn between the rationales underlying positive and negative evaluations, we consider next the character of their negative evaluations. In the final section of this chapter, I discuss the contribution to innovative class development made by TAs' mixed reviews.

NATURE AND CONSEQUENCES OF NEGATIVE EVALUATIONS

Of all evaluative observations, those that were critical of the innovations were 14 percent for Interactive Astronomy, 21 percent for chemistry, and 46 percent for the innovative parts of the Berkeley initiative. As indicated, TAs' negative evaluations were different in source and character from their positive evaluations in that they were less often based on direct observations of student responses and learning outcomes. However, the degree to which this was evident varied somewhat among the three innovations. Unlike positive observations, commonalities in TAs' negative observations across the initiatives were harder to see. Therefore, the nature and consequences of TAs' negative evaluations are largely described by initiative except where shared elements are evident.

Interactive Astronomy

In the Interactive Astronomy classes, the undergraduate coaches based more of their judgments—positive, negative, and (especially) mixed—on *observations* of how the students in their learning groups responded to the methods of teaching and learning used in the class than did either of the other TA groups. To wit, most of the forty negative evaluations offered by the astronomy coaches (62 percent) addressed limitations on student understanding created by insufficient guidance from the professor as to which aspects of class content were more or less important for students to focus on. Coaches identified insufficient clarity in communicating class learning goals and priorities to both coaches and students, leaving students struggling to place what they learned into a framework of ideas. This issue was exacerbated by the layered vastness of the hypertext created by the course innovator as the undergraduates' main source of course materials. Without clear learning objectives and navigational signposts, students were apt to get lost in the online materials. Three undergraduate coaches discussed this in a focus group:

> Coach 1: We need a general expectation of what [the professor] wants. Like he gives students these really open-ended questions, and we don't really have a sense of where they are going.
>
> Coach 2: Yeah. He shies away from telling us what he wants them to focus on.
>
> Coach 1: There's a discrepancy between that—which we need to know—and getting students to find the answers themselves—which I don't mind. But then finding there's several different answers, depending on which perspective you take—and it turns out there's only one right answer on the final.

Coach 3: And the students can get lost in the hypertext. They need a guide to sharpen up their search.

Coach 2: And we need a more solid grasp on the direction we are going, or we can't help the students.

Again, this dialogue highlights the need for clear signposting in classes where the pedagogy is unfamiliar both to students and TAs, where the syllabus and text are connected in a nonlinear way, where no text is used, or where multiple source materials are used with or without a text.

As the extract also indicates, even when they are criticizing the teacher's methods, the tone of the undergraduate coaches toward the innovation and the professor is courteous rather than critical or combative. The coaches' concerns center on the unmet learning needs of students and what they needed to do a good job. Achieving this level of appropriate collegial critique from TAs appears to be partly a function of employing only undergraduates as coaches. In the other two initiatives (where TAs included a mixture of doctoral, masters', and undergraduate students)[6] undergraduates were also found—both in the interview data and by faculty observation—to be more amenable than doctoral students to giving new methods a chance. Cadres of TAs composed largely of doctoral students were more likely to include one or two who expressed active hostility toward the innovation and some who were covertly noncompliant.

The explanation may lie in differences in the educational and professional agendas of undergraduates and graduate students. Many doctoral students have committed to a faculty career path, and I hypothesize that adoption of a more traditional interpretation of the faculty teaching role may seem the safest course in a situation where the good opinion of powerful senior colleagues is critical to success. Undergraduates are, as yet, not so constrained. Their career options remain more fluid, and they are not subject to faculty critique of their professional development. They may thus feel more at liberty to experiment with teaching methods. This issue is further discussed in the following section.

Modular Chemistry

By contrast with the undergraduate astronomy coaches, the character of negative TA observations for the two chemistry initiatives was more often expressed in terms of principles and presumptions that conflicted with those of the innovators rather than in observations of how students responded and performed in the new-style classes. Their negative observations may thus be as characterized as reflecting various degrees of 'resistance' to innovation. The two strongest features of negative TA responses in both chemistry initiatives were, first, a set of beliefs about the nature of science and the perceived necessity of particular modes of learning in order to acquire an understanding of science thus defined;[7] and, second, objections rooted in TAs' perceptions of their rights as teachers.

In the modular chemistry classes, the TAs' ninety-five negative observations followed the same pattern: fifty-seven observations reflected beliefs about science and science learning, and twenty-one expressed TAs' understanding of their teaching role. Of the remaining negative observations, thirteen were rooted in the TAs' own experiences and learning preferences, with only four grounded in observations of student performance or their responses to the new-style classes.

The most common issue of principle for modular chemistry TAs ($n = 36$) was that learning concepts through applications, and the questions that these raise, was thought to make it much more difficult for students to build a body of required knowledge in a systematic way. This concern was also evident in other ChemConnections interviews: it was an issue for some undergraduates and also for some colleagues of modular chemistry teachers. This group of TAs expressed a more limited vision than that of the faculty teaching modules of what was appropriate or doable in introductory classes. Students should, in their view, learn definitions, basic ideas, and problem-solving methods. Tackling issues of uncertainty in science and focusing on the application of concepts were seen as premature. The TAs expressed concern that time spent on "application" detracted from learning material that chemistry majors in the class would need in future classes:

> I guess I'm just a traditional science person. Give me the basics, and don't expect me to do anything with it until I understand it.

> It seems to me that some of the purpose of introductory chemistry had become a little lost—I mean, as a place to learn vocabulary and get these basic things in your mind—like the concept of a mole or doing conversions and solving problems—things that should have been part of the actual lectures and that you need to know them in order to understand something else.

> Explain the basis first, and then give examples, instead of going through these vague ideas—because the students don't know it's a concept yet—and then giving examples in class and making them go home and think about it without ever giving them the answer—and that's a thing I have problems with.

Some of this group of TAs used "applications" and "examples" interchangeably, as if applications were (or should be) "illustrations." Either they did not think it possible to teach conceptual understanding by asking fundamental questions, or they had not understood that this was what the modular faculty were seeking to accomplish.

A more ironic vote against "application before basics" came from TAs who found that the applications approach exposed holes in their own understanding of key concepts. Their confessions square with assertions from modular chemistry faculty at the research university (and sometimes elsewhere) that they could never take it for granted that graduate TAs had mastered the material they were asked to help introductory class students understand.

For some TAs, the chemistry modules opposed their beliefs about what science is and is not. The modules introduce students to the complexities of science and address the ambiguity and uncertainties inherent in all knowledge. However, some TAs shared with undergraduates the view that science is predominantly factual in nature and that teaching should be a presentation of "facts."

> I would say that there are some knowns, or facts. I mean, there's chemistry facts—this happens when that happens—so I don't think it needs to be explored. . . . I think it's nice if we can learn some of the theory behind it, but it's not a necessary component to learn if it's true or not.

Also shared with some faculty were concerns that modular lab work omitted or skimped on elements that they saw as necessary ingredients in any introductory class. Their list of omissions included particular lab techniques, and the purposes of particular pieces of lab equipment, and how and when to use them. In the following exchange, two differently minded TAs in a focus group discussed the utility of being introduced to particular techniques early:

> Interviewer: What were they missing from these labs that you would have liked to have seen?
>
> TA 1: Let's see—just basic techniques. Like I can't remember some of the stuff we were doing. You know, creating a vacuum or distilling stuff. They didn't do a whole lot of that like we did. They didn't do a synthetic organic lab at all. Remember? We did a Palmer's lab.
>
> TA 2: But I guess we get a lot of that in organic later.
>
> TA 1: Well, yeah, you do, but you're *supposed* to get it in the intro classes first.

For some TAs (as for some faculty and students), the variety and nontraditional sequence of class and lab content entailed in a semester of three to five modules frustrated a sense that all introductory class students should be exposed to particular elements of the canon and evoked a concern that this was not happening. These TAs also proposed that undergraduates should follow the order of topics given by the text in order to build learning in a particular sequential way. They disapproved of what they glossed as "skipping around" in the text and did not like using multiple sources, with the text being treated as one of several resources or used for reference. While this was agreed to be an appropriate learning strategy in economics, psychology, or English classes, chemistry was seen as requiring one primary source:

> We did use a textbook with the module, and the textbook was just a reference. . . . We'd take like one page from this chapter and then three pages from another, and like skip around, so you never knew where you were.

> I believe sciences are totally building upon each other, and you have to start with chapter 1 before you can do chapter 5, because there's always going to be referring back.

> Is the module supplementing the textbook, or is the textbook supplementing the module? I wondered why we ever needed a textbook if the module's supposed to be our new book. I mean, why did we need two?

For these speakers (as with some of the undergraduates that we interviewed), the idea that only one book should be used in a course seemed almost self-evident. As this is a strongly socialized view, built up and reinforced since high school, innovative faculty need to help both TAs and undergraduates navigate the alternative story line through conceptual material by the kind of careful signposting described earlier.

TA beliefs about what was flawed about the modular approach were sometimes held in contradiction to their observations of what students were learning. This is nicely illustrated in a conversation in which, early in their focus group, two TAs discussed their belief that the modular approach did not give students a sufficient grounding in basic knowledge. Later in the same focus-group interview, the TAs acknowledged that their students were demonstrating reasonable conceptual mastery. The TAs were puzzled by that apparent contradiction between their a priori belief and their own observations:

> *Earlier statement:* To me, the modules seem to be going beyond general chemistry—and that's what they're trying to do—but they're missing the basic chemistry parts.
> *Later statement:* I noticed that the students were coming to me less to ask about conceptual questions. They seemed to be getting those because both instructors closed with lengthy postlabs where they clarified anything in the course that was not clear. I don't know if they got the basics, you know, from the modules, but they seemed to be getting where they could understand some of the basic ideas.

Other objections to the modular approach focused on its impact on TAs rather than on their students—namely, that modules make more work for

TAs (especially the emphasis on writing, which requires more grading and individual help for students) and that TAs disliked using for themselves particular modes of learning emphasized in the modules. Although, as already reported, the majority of TAs favored various forms of small-group learning for their students, some TAs preferred not to use them for their own learning:

> Personally, if I took the class, I'd like to answer my own questions and, you know, not work with other people. So, make it more individual. That's my preference.

They also referenced the high volume of reading and writing required by the modules. Four TAs complained about the discursive nature of the modular handbooks and looked for greater brevity; two more wanted a format that highlighted definitions and key sentences:

> Well, some modules were worse than others, but they would always come with pages and pages of useless writing about "Let's examine this" and, you know, try to make it like a conversation and very down to earth. And that made a few students, and myself included, discount what they were saying in some places. And I'd have to page through all these paragraphs of, like, really exposition— transitional things. It would have been nice if I could have gone straight to the source—right to the learning part of it.

> And it was very difficult to pull out like the important points. I knew what I was looking for because I'm a senior and I know the basic concepts now. But it was hard to see because there weren't any highlighted sections that said, "Here's the definition of a mole." It was all gibberish and didn't relate to the fundamentals of chemistry. You can't understand the central issue if there's too much to read.

Finally, there was a small group of negative observations that defined the modules as being suitable for nonscience students in introductory classes but not for chemistry or engineering majors or anyone beyond the introductory level.

Stronger Forms of Negative Evaluation among Doctoral TAs in the Chemistry Initiatives

A strongly expressed, although minority, form of opposition focused on the impact of the innovation on TAs' understandings about their teaching role. It was expressed by eight modular chemistry TAs at the research university and by nine TAs from the Berkeley TA education initiative (over two interview rounds).[8] It is important to note that all of these TAs were graduate students. Although these TAs were a minority among their course peers, the strength and persistence with which they expressed their concerns made their impact on the innovating faculty, their undergraduates, and the other TAs greater than their number would suggest. It is important to understand and address the negative opinions of these TAs because all course innovators are likely to encounter some TAs with similar views and find them as difficult to accommodate or convince as did the faculty in these two initiatives.

The objections of these TAs were rooted neither in the specifics of the innovative approach, nor in observations of student responses to them, but in the requirement that TAs teach their recitation and lab sections using a common approach defined by the nature of the innovation. Their fundamental concern was that these innovative approaches undercut what they saw as their professional prerogative as teachers to teach as they saw fit. In the Berkeley initiative, the materials and methods to be used by all TAs were laid out in the worksheets and discussed both before and after each class in meetings with the faculty innovators or course coordinator. The approach was also explored in sessions on learning theory and research. The same type of objections was raised by the eight doctoral TAs assisting with modules, where preparation sessions were often more informal. All of these TAs objected to having to teach and grade in the same manner as all other TAs who worked for their class:

> We were told, "You have a lot of control." Well, NO. We don't! We don't choose how we grade. That has to be across the board. We have to do this like a team. And we all have to be brought up to speed. Well, "Go team!"

> I prefer the traditional classes: there's more independence for the TAs in the way things are run.

The TAs contrasted the requirement of a shared approach with a common traditional arrangement by which course professors give their TAs a list of topics or problems to address in recitation sections and then leave it to each of them to decide how to do so. Some TAs treated this custom as an extension of the faculty's prerogative to choose their own pedagogy (though not necessarily their own curriculum). They also expressed pride in their abilities as fledgling professional teachers and felt affronted that their expertise seemed to be discounted:

> It was just the type of training that we got. I mean, I was a TA for a lab class before. And the reason that I was good at teaching that class is because I set up the lab. I went in and got all the lasers and the other stuff together, set it up, and made it *work*! Then the students would come in, but I already knew everything about it. And so this time, we come in, and we had to read a sheet about the lab. What I'm saying is that I could have taught the labs more effectively. Take away the boring TA meetings and some of the other things we did.

Developing one's own teaching style may be seen as part of the professional socialization of graduate students into the faculty teaching role as traditionally conceived. For TAs who are seeking to establish their professional identity in this way, the requirement that they work as a team using common pedagogical and assessment methods was seen by this subset of graduate students as undermining their growth in expertise and their status as teachers.

These TAs were also very distrustful of the motives of the faculty innovators, tended to define them rule breakers, and portrayed themselves as holding firmly to more appropriate professional norms. Two TAs discussed the dilemma that, because they endorsed the faculty's right to teach a class any way that they liked, perhaps they should accept their choice of teaching methods. They explained that their decision to suspend this norm was reasonable because the innovating faculty had failed to select their pedagogy from within a conventional range. Another TA could not quite believe that the teacher's overt goal of improving students' understanding of scientific ideas was their "true" purpose: they suspected that the students were the subject of an experiment in which the real goal was to resocialize students into learning in an incorrect manner:

> It's not about teaching; it's an educational experiment. I got the feeling that the priority wasn't teaching science; it was doing this new idea. They said they wanted to resocialize the students as to the way they learned. What an affront! I got the impression that the main goal of the class was to learn how to teach this new thing. It's sort of advocating a new way of teaching, and it put down the old way. I think they were selling a way of teaching—to the TAs as well as the students.

Some of this group were vocal in their anger: they disrupted TA meetings by their objections to particular teaching strategies, were rude to the course faculty or coordinator, wrote them abusive e-mails, complained to other members of the department, and encouraged disaffection among students in their recitation sections. Two TAs allied themselves with faculty who disliked the innovations and colluded with them in running labs in ways other than those designated by the class teacher:

> TA: We kinda got together, me and the other TA and the two professors who weren't teaching with modules, and made our own little changes to the lab.
>
> Interviewer: You were smiling as you said that. How little were the changes?
>
> TA: Oh well, I had TAed with one of the professors before, so we had a really good time figuring out the lab experiments ourselves.
>
> Interviewer: Did the professor teaching the modular classes know that you were making changes from the modular labs she had planned?
>
> TA: Oh, I guess so, because I heard that she and the lab profs had an argument about it.

My lab instructor was totally unfamiliar with the modules. He didn't want to give his opinion about them to me, but I was aware of how he felt—he wasn't convinced. He wasn't sold on the idea. And, as some of the module labs were new and there were still things to be worked out in them, it was just easier to give the students something a bit more standard. So, no, we didn't really follow the modules.

The number of graduate TAs in both initiatives who directly opposed or sabotaged innovative classes in these ways was small. However, their behavior had a disproportionately disruptive effect and was distressing to innovative faculty, other TAs, and (by their report) some undergraduates:

Some of the TAs, they just wouldn't do what they were asked. And some of them were giving their opinions to their students—that they just didn't agree with the approach. And that affected their students—which is bad because I think that the students are open to trying it this way.

These TAs' attitudes ended up affecting me because I thought, "If they don't want to do it this way, why am I pushing it?" And it became hard for me to believe in the method and stick with it.

The impact of TA negative attitudes toward an innovative course was clearly demonstrated by Gutwill-Wise (2001) as part of the evaluation of chemistry modules at two sample institutions, one of which was the University of California at Berkeley. The attitudes of TAs on a scale of positive to negative correlated closely with those of their students. Indeed, the attitude of their TAs toward learning via the chemistry modules was one of three main factors determining the nature of students' responses to them.

Because of institutional rules that assign graduate TAs to particular classes for a semester, some faculty discovered that they were not in a position to request the dismissal or transfer of highly disruptive TAs. One of the dissenting TAs was, however, able to move to a more traditional class at his own request.

Not all of the TAs who disagreed with the innovation or with the expectation that TAs should use a common approach were vocal in their dissent. Though all of the TAs expressing strong vocal objections were graduate students, three undergraduate TAs at one institution kept quiet during the TA meetings and then taught their recitation sections as they wished. The resulting variations in what and how they taught generated student complaints that they felt free to discount. The three passive dissenters discussed this in a focus group:

TA 1: We all do different things. There is supposed to be a common pattern, but I take some liberties in how I have the students do things. I mean, the instructor's very innovative [*laughing*].

TA 2: Yeah, we do things differently.

Interviewer: And how do the students respond when they learn that what they are doing is different in each section? Aren't they expecting it to be the same across all groups?

TA 3: Oh, I hear some grumbling about that.

TA 1: Yeah, but it depends on why they are coming to class. If they are interested enough, they accept the situation.

Other TAs who watched these subversive behaviors urged the importance of finding ways to bring all TAs on board from the outset—to avoid the erosion of trust in the teacher and in the goals and methods of the innovation, as well as the escalation of opposition among TAs and students. Later, I discuss their recommendations in some detail, but the principle was clearly laid down by one TA:

> I felt that the beginning of the class kind of lost it. Maybe it was disorganization, or just whatever reason, the professors didn't get some of the TAs on board. And there was a bit of animosity there that trickled down to the students. And I think that was one of the fundamental problems that there was always a kind of tension there and the students picked up on it. There were obviously a lot of issues that need to be addressed, but I think if the TAs and the professors were in lockstep, the students wouldn't have gone down that road.

Explanations for TA Resistance to
Course Innovation Offered in the Literature

Very little research has been conducted on TAs' observations on student resistance to, or learning difficulties within, innovative courses. However, there are a few exceptions. Millar and colleagues (1997) studied TAs' evaluations of an innovative chemistry course at the University of Wisconsin, Madison. The TAs credited a combination of innovative learning activities—learning through visualization, group work, discussion sections, "challenge problems," and inquiry-based labs—with helping students to connect course concepts, clear up misconceptions, discuss practical applications, become more confident and self-reliant, and make fewer mistakes. The sources of resistance they cited arose from students' actual difficulties in using some of the new learning methods rather than reluctance to try them. In group work, some students with stronger backgrounds "felt used" by weaker students; in working challenge problems, students became frustrated if they ran out of time or if problems were given before the relevant material had been discussed; students who focused on individual steps in lab work did not see the discovery focus of the labs, did not understand the purpose of the lab, or did not relate the lab activities to course concepts until they reached the phase of data analysis.

Also at the University of Wisconsin, Madison, Alexander and colleagues (1996) studied TAs' perspectives on chemistry and mathematics courses that used active and interactive teaching and learning methods. Issues of both TA and undergraduate resistance were documented. Some TAs reported that they were drawn back into traditional lecturing methods by time pressures that seemed to force a choice between covering content and, for example, fostering connections between disciplines or facilitating group work. In their new role as "guides on the side," they encountered resistance from students who expressed the opinion that TAs were being lazy or not performing their job adequately. Some TAs responded by returning to their old role as knowledge experts, where it seemed easier and more rewarding to give students answers rather than push them to take more responsibility for their own learning.

There is also a small body of work that can be drawn on to address questions of why graduate student TAs in particular may resist the innovating faculty's learning theories and methods and their efforts to get TAs to work together in an agreed manner rather than according to their individual views of how particular materials should be taught. Hammrich (1996) found that traditionalist views of teaching predominate among TAs who primarily define teaching in terms of "knowing your subject matter and having good organizational skills." Menges and Rando (1989) report a primary interest among TAs in the transmission of content, with lectures as the most commonly preferred teaching method. McGivney-Burelle and colleagues (2001) found that TAs resisted the introduction of group-based learning because they believed that lecturing was the only way to efficiently cover the material. These TAs did not understand how mathematics could be taught interactively and were concerned that giving time to group work prevented them from covering the required material. They believed that effective instructors were those who delivered well-organized lectures and were knowledgeable about their subject matter. Hatch and Farris (1989) also found that TAs were concerned that, by using innovative techniques rather than lecturing, they jeopardized adequate cover of course materials. McDowell (1993) similarly reports that 70 percent of the TAs sampled believed that students learned more from lectures than by any other method and ranked the idea of "the teacher as facilitator" fifth out of seven approaches to teaching.

Some authors have sought to explain these conservative tendencies in TAs. Hatch and Farris (1989) point out that TAs are rarely exposed to pedagogical information about their discipline. As a result, they "rely on their awareness of how they acquired their own knowledge and on their skill in translating this awareness into activities that help new learners acquire this knowledge" (90). Lawrenz and colleagues (1992) argue that, where TAs have not experienced cooperative learning or other pedagogical alternatives to lecturing, they are unsure of their value. McGivney-Burelle and colleagues (2001) add that this is particularly true for international graduate students. McGinnis (1991) found that, although TAs adopted ideas about teaching from the professors for whom they worked, they also exhibited "career-prompted" behavior. This, as Nyquist and Sprague (1998) also found, is a conservative response to the mixed messages that they receive from other departmental faculty about the value of teaching. Both studies portray TAs as bringing to the task their own, largely traditionalist set of beliefs, theories, and attitudes about their role and its responsibilities. Some of these preconceptions were based on their own learning experiences; others reflected their career concerns. Nyquist and Sprague also found that TAs relied heavily on their peers as primary information sources. This tendency can also reinforce conservative views, whether overly or covertly expressed in departments where conservative views about teaching predominate. By contrast, Hatch and Farris (1989) found that, where TAs are ready to try or actively engage in new pedagogies, they may do so in the face of resistance from their own supervisors who favor traditional teaching methods.

Four studies focus less on the social context in which graduate TAs commonly work and more on the psychology of TAs. Nyquist and Wulff (1996), Nyquist and Sprague (1998), and Robinson (2000) argue that the nature of TAs' resistance to teaching and learning other than by lecturing depends on their own developmental stage as learners. Many graduate TAs are first-year students in their programs, and their primary concern is with their own survival. They are also influenced by their students' opinions of them as people. New TAs, argues Robinson, are especially concerned with age differentials, authority and control issues, being liked for their personality, being admired for their knowledge, and being seen as competent in that they can answer students' questions. From their research on the subconscious theories that TAs develop to manage their thoughts, feelings, and experiences in the classroom, Menges and Rando (1989) found three main orientations among TAs toward their teaching work. The first is interest in content, which leads TAs to emphasize dissemination of a body of information through lecturing. This supports the lecture orientation that remains the dominant mode for most TAs. However, two other orientations open TAs to change. The TAs' second focus is on process, which leads them to help students learn to think about information, often through the use of discussion. The third is motivation, which encourages TAs to engage their students in interesting discussions on content that they find engaging as a means to stimulate their interest in the material.

Nurrenbern, Mickiewicz, and Francisco (1999), however, found that it was difficult to get TAs to "change their ideas of themselves as teachers—ideas that, in large part, are modeled on personal classroom experiences" (119). They observed that it was four to five weeks into the term before the chemistry TAs in their study were committed to the process of interactive teaching and learning. Even then, some maintained passive resistance by signing the mandatory workshop attendance sheet then leaving or doing other tasks during that time. Others showed active resistance during both the workshops and the weekly meetings. Hatch and Farris (1989) report similar forms of TA resistance. However, they found that reframing the course goals as the acquisition of concepts and analytical approaches helped to reduce the TAs' level of resistance.

Thus, for graduate TAs especially, these studies document some of the conservative pressures that help to explain some TA attitudes and behaviors when working in innovative science classes.

Changes over Time in Levels of Resistance in the Berkeley TA Initiative

Notwithstanding these contextual difficulties, there was a notable shift in graduate TA perceptions of their prerogatives as independent teachers between the first and second rounds of the Berkeley TA interviews. In the first semester, the two innovative faculty and their course coordinator struggled with the disruptive consequences of the actions of two highly vocal opponents to the worksheet–discussion method and those of a small group of passive dissenters who covertly avoided using the sheets. Eighteen months later, although four graduate TAs expressed negative views about teaching their sections by the common worksheet method, and although some clearly augmented this approach with other teaching techniques, everyone used the worksheets and no one opposed their use openly or angrily. Indeed, as one dissenter explained it,

> I already had some teaching experience as an undergraduate TA, so I was used to my way of explaining things and my particular way of working with students. And sometimes it feels a little forced to have to present these discussions by teaching with someone else's method. . . . I know a couple of TAs who say they don't always use a discussion. But I feel I need to stick with the discussion [sheets] because [the faculty are] expecting everyone to be getting the same thing.

The same point was made by a TA who actually liked the worksheets but who added the following disclosure:

> I don't stick rigidly to the worksheets. I go through everything that's there, but I often add stuff. So . . . I make sure to do everything that's on the discussion sheet because that's often tested on, and it's not fair to my students not to do it.

This shift echoes the lowered level of resistance to innovation over several sequential semesters of implementation that was also observed in students taking modules over time. As faculty become more skilled and relaxed in the use of the method, and as they addressed imperfections and missing elements in light of observation and feedback, student concerns diminished, and the innovation began to acquire an established place in departmental course offerings.

For all types of negative evaluations in the Berkeley TA initiative, the most striking feature is a sharp drop between the first and second rounds in both their overall number (from 127 to 40) and their percentages (from 62 percent to 27 percent) of all evaluative comments. As indicated, both vocal opposition by a disruptive minority and covert noncompliance fell away sharply. Negative observations about the quality or adequacy of TA education and support also dropped, from sixteen to zero, by the second round.[9] As with the modular chemistry initiative, most negative evaluations focused on ways in which central features of the initiative ran contrary to TAs' views about how chemistry should be taught and what their own role in the teaching process should be. However, in the second round, TAs began to offer negative evaluations based on observations of student learning using the worksheet method rather than on preconceived ideas of appropriate pedagogy— a development that may be seen as progress by the faculty innovators.

Negative evaluations across both sets of Berkeley interviews largely centered on three issues: problems with course coherence ("fit" issues; $n = 59$); concerns about the fairness of tests and exams, including (again) perceptions of insufficient fit between questions asked and curriculum emphases ($n = 20$); and critiques of the worksheets ($n = 40$). A smaller group focused on its dislike of, or its problems in teaching via, small-group work or discussions ($n = 15$). Low evaluations of their overall teaching experience (except for one sole comment) were offered in the first, but not in the second, round. As indicated, negative evaluations addressed either aspects of the innovation or traditional class features with remarkably little crossover. However, responsibility for course coherence was an exception. Negative evaluations for fit-related problems were almost evenly distributed between the innovative and traditional faculty who contributed to the course ($n = 32$ and $n = 27$, respectively). However, each group of faculty was faulted for different aspects of coherence problems.

Course coherence problems, which TAs and students alike commonly referred to as issues of fit, arose in all three initiatives and may be viewed as a key structural issue for all courses, whether conventional or innovative. However, in innovative courses, students and TAs are apt to become especially aware of coherence issues as the new course developers work to find the right balance and timing for course activities. For example, in Interactive Astronomy, fifteen of the coaches commented on practical problems, confusion, and lowered moral that resulted from the developer's midcourse adjustments in aspects of class organization, timetable, and assessment pattern. These changes were arguably useful in the longer term and were made in light of good formative feedback from his evaluator and the coaches themselves. However, active course experimentation while a course is continuing tends to undermine its cohesion.

The coherence issues of the Berkeley TAs arose from another type of innovation where innovators insert new elements into a preexisting, otherwise conventional, course. In this case, the TAs had to cope with a formal course structure that was conventional, while the recitation sections, TA activities, and preparation conveyed the innovative elements to students. As indicated, the TAs divided responsibility for course coherence between the two sets of faculty: innovative faculty were seen as being responsible for fit issues arising from the design and implementation of the worksheets. TAs criticized the innovative faculty for not achieving a good fit between the focus or content of the worksheet discussion sessions and that of the traditional lectures and labs:

> The discussion sheets are very conceptual. . . . I don't think we should teach only for the tests, but at the same time it's good that students have practice working the types of problems that you're going to ask them to do [on the tests], and I don't think the discussion sheets [and] the test questions . . . supported one another.

Some TAs thought it was too early to expect conceptual understanding of students; some were pragmatic and thought there was no point in their teaching conceptually if the lecture professor continued to focus exclusively on quantitative problem-solving exam questions. Although the innovators had made it clear to the TAs in their orientation, education, and weekly meetings that they were overtly seeking to address an apparent lack of conceptual understanding among students, some TAs saw it as the role of the lecture professor to determine the nature of course content and tests, and the role of the TA educators to fit in with that schema:

> I think they should work on getting the worksheets more integrated into the lecture material. So, the lecture may introduce a concept, and what the worksheet should do is build off of that concept.

However, two major coherence issues for which the Berkeley TAs faulted the lecture and lab professors were structural disjunctions that placed labs before some related lectures, and misfits between emphasis on particular content in class and an emphasis on different content in tests.[10] These were defined as critical issues because of the essential link between course coherence and students' learning—a link that becomes especially evident in the design of course assessments. Most of the TAs' negative comments about exams or tests referenced a criterion that we have found to be universal in interviews with both students and TAs, namely, whether exams and the grading system were considered "fair." Fairness, is determined by students and TAs by the following attributes:

- the proportionality between effort required and the numeric worth of the grades given,
- the amount of mental "stretch" required of students beyond what is taught, and
- the number and spacing of tests over the semester.

However, their dominant determinant of fairness is

- how closely the exam, test, or quiz questions reflect the emphases placed by the lecturer on particular content or skills.

In our efforts to assist chemistry faculty to devise forms of assessment that addressed the learning objectives of the modules, we often encountered what appears to be a long-standing faculty habit of writing tests and other assessments virtually the night before they are due to be taken by students. Evidence from faculty interviews also confirmed this observation. This common practice helps to explain why TAs found that many test instruments fitted poorly with course content and why their level and quality were often inconsistent:

> The first thing I should say is that one of the tests was extremely poorly written. . . . [It wasn't] proofread, and a lot of students didn't do very well, and they were upset about it. . . . One question had missing data. Another was worded in such a way that it led you to one type of answer, while, in reality, you could only give another sort of answer.

Modular chemistry developers and adapters reported that they now gave increasingly more time and thought than in their previous, more conventional teaching mode to designing assessments that explored the effects of their new methods on student learning. However, some modular TAs observed that the habit of producing hastily written tests and assignments was still a feature of some professors' approach to learning assessment:

> And he did give two homework assignments that, to me, just seemed thrown in there. It was something they read about three weeks later. And I don't think very much came out of it—they turned it in and they got it back, and that was that. There was no real discussion about it. The applicability of the assignment— what you were learning—it wasn't right there.

Coach: The big complaint about quizzes is that many of the questions are obscure—they ask for little bits of information which don't seem central to the understanding of the big concepts.

In their negative comments on the quality and coherence of learning assessments, Berkeley TAs also ascribed incoherence in assessment design to insufficient discussion between the two groups of faculty contributing to the course overall. However, they placed responsibility for leading these conversations largely on the lecture professor:

I wish they would run the class quantitatively, but since they don't seem to be doing that, I think the tests should move further towards a conceptual standpoint. I don't think it's fair to prepare the students for the conceptual questions, which are the short answers, and not for the multiple-choice questions where they actually have to get the right answer numerically. The lecture prof needs to pay attention to what we are trying to do here.

In the first-round interviews, TAs were polarized in their opinions about the worksheet–discussion method of teaching. Either they really liked them—thought that they helped the students understand important class concepts and weaned students away from rote learning and the plug-and-chug approach to problems—or they really disliked them. There was no middle ground. Negative responses were of four kinds: the worksheets reflected inflated expectations for students at this level; they contained design flaws (e.g., questions were too general, tricky, confusing, easy, or hard or were vague, unclear, or ambiguous);[11] the TAs did not approve of the method; and using it usurped their right to teach by methods of their choice. Again, critiques of the approach to the methods used and their implementation were dominant: only one TA criticized the worksheets on the grounds that his students did not gain much from working with them.

In the second interview round, TAs evaluative comments were roughly divided into thirds, between positive, negative, and mixed views of the worksheets. In the positive and mixed comments, more TAs than in the first round discussed the value of the worksheets in terms of benefits that they saw in their students. These notably included encouraging students to take more responsibility for their own learning, reinforcing their understanding of important concepts, providing good applications of scientific ideas, and increasing student interest in chemistry. By contrast, as in the first round, negative evaluations continued to focus on the constraints that the worksheets placed on their teaching options, on expecting too much from students at this stage, and on students' resistance to learning by unfamiliar methods.

There was also some fusion (and confusion) of the TAs' negative opinions with those of their students—in this case, that it would waste less time if the TAs lectured to the students. This alignment occurred when TAs who expressed dislike for the required teaching method did what was asked of them reluctantly and poorly and thereby encouraged a negative response in their students. In these instances, the students' resistance served to legitimate that of the TAs:

> I asked them like the fourth week of school, "Tell me what things you like, what things you don't like." Almost *every* single person in the class said, "Don't spend so much time on the worksheets." Almost everyone. I knew from the start it wouldn't work—that the students wouldn't go with it. It's not what they are used to. They think it would be more efficient for me to talk to all of them at once.

TAs' evaluative comments—both positive and negative—should be seen in light of a set of additional observations that were a recurring theme in both rounds of interviews. In these comments, TAs described sharp differentials in the students' preparation for the course that caused difficulties for the TAs in teaching their sections and, by implication, limited the impact of the worksheet–discussion method on student learning. Two-thirds of TAs in the first round and almost half in the second described many of their students as lacking basic knowledge and skills, while a significant number of students in their sections were overprepared for this level of course. The TAs cited wide variations in students' skills in, and knowledge of, math and science and in their ability to write clearly. They also noted that basic academic skills and habits were inadequate or missing in many of their students.

Discussions and small-group work were complicated for both students and TAs by this wide range of understanding and skills. TAs reported difficulty in working effectively with students, whether using the worksheets or an array of other teaching methods that they employed to cope with the problem:

> The worksheets seemed to identify what the major topics are pretty well, but I think the way they do it is not as productive as it could be, because a lot of these students have problems not just with math but with basic algebra and with manipulating equations to get things in the right form and so on. And the class assumes that they know how to do that kind of thing . . . and when they do these discussion sheets, they're expected to work through them without a lot of prior preparation for dealing with this kind of material.

Few of the TAs offered suggestions about how to solve this problem, but TAs did not fault the innovative teachers or their methods for these difficulties and their consequences for student learning:

> You can't solve this problem in a single course. It's up to the high schools and middle schools to teach this stuff. They come in thinking they are A students, but they haven't got enough of the basics to work with. It's pretty frustrating for the professors and for us.

I think the faculty who wrote the worksheets were trying to make sure that the students got more out of the lectures and labs. The lecture prof, he has no clue what students walk away with. He just lays it out there. But they are trying to get them to understand it better. But some of them just know too little to benefit from it, and we just can't catch them up. And then the others who know it all get bored, and you have to deal with them being a pain. The worksheet idea could work quite well. But you have to solve this other problem first.

As illustrated, TAs' negative evaluations reflect a wide span of opinions. At one end are expressions of strong dislike of the course approach or teaching methods and, for a small group of doctoral TAs, a sense of affront in being asked to teach by unconventional methods in concert with the other TAs. This group of negative evaluations, which may properly be labeled "resistance," was found in both active and passive forms. Some resistance appears to derive from perceptions of usurpation by the innovators of TAs' customary teaching prerogatives. At the other end of the range are the astronomy coaches whose notably courteous critiques were centered on the unmet needs of their students and what changes they needed from the professor to do a good job.

In both the Berkeley and modular chemistry courses, a larger number of concerns was derived from beliefs about the nature of science and science learning and from prior experience and personal learning preferences. In contrast with their positive observations, fewer of their criticisms and concerns were based on observations of student performance. However, the shift of opinion between the first and second interview rounds in the Berkeley TA education initiative points to an encouraging phenomenon that was also noted in interviews with participating undergraduates in the modular chemistry classes—that resistance to the fundamental principles and practices of innovative classes is apt to fade as both students and TAs become more familiar with them and as faculty become more confident and adept in using them.

Finally, the inherent value of some forms of negative TA feedback is evident in observations that highlight the need for good signposting and in their critique of structural disjunctions in the organization and timing of classes and labs, and other problems of course incoherence—especially those of poor fit between emphases made in class and those presented in tests.

NATURE AND CONSEQUENCES OF MIXED EVALUATIONS

Mixed evaluations by TAs largely supported the work of their innovative professors and offered information or advice intended to improve the innovations. For the most part, these may be regarded as qualified positive

evaluations. Unlike negative evaluations, mixed comments were comparable across the three initiatives and fell broadly into five types of issues arising from:

The innovation's approach, design, and structure	49 percent
Its implementation (especially with group work)	15 percent
The TAs' role in the innovation	21 percent
The departmental context	9 percent
The TAs' beliefs about aspects of the innovation	6 percent

The majority of mixed comments addressed issues arising from the conceptual basis, design, or structure of the innovative courses. They were offered by TAs and coaches across all three initiatives. This group of observations (which is discussed in the next sections) included issues of alignment
of course elements, level and volume of course work, and the use of technology.

Issues Arising from the Innovative Approach and Design

In many ways, the modular chemistry courses presented the students and
their TAs with the most clearly articulated, radical departure from conventional ways of teaching and learning science. In eleven focus-group conversations, modular chemistry TAs debated but did not always reach agreement on issues arising from the philosophy of the modular approach.
Unlike negative evaluations of course philosophies (which focused on objections of principle), these conversations focused on whether and how
students could benefit from the modular focus on learning chemistry by addressing questions of real-world significance. Some TAs thought that students needed more background knowledge before they could understand
the fundamental questions contained in the modules; others thought that
students could acquire the necessary knowledge and understandings as
they went along:

TA 1: I think what the modules miss is that chemists ask very well-defined, specific questions. And a lot of the questions the students were asked to deal with
seemed vague, and they're asked to think about them with insufficient knowledge.

TA 2: I don't agree. I think part of what they had to learn was how to take a
broad question and figure out what the little questions were that they had to ask
themselves. 'Cause chemists don't start out with specific questions; they start out
with a bigger problem.

TA 3: Yeah, but the course didn't really show them how to do that.

TA 2: I think that was partly my job—to work on that with them in my office hours. But I do agree they need more guidance about "What do I need to know to begin? What questions do I have to ask to get a grasp on this one?"

TA 1: But is that too much real science for students at this level? That's my question.

TA 3: Mine too. 'Cause it's great to approach things in a discovery manner. But intro students often know the very least about science, and you are putting all of science right in their face—how scientists approach problems. How do you help them to weed out things that are less important? It's okay for the well-prepared student but not for the novices.

The questioning but open-minded tone of this discussion stands in contrast with the rather despairing views of Berkeley TAs in the early interview round who saw the underpreparation of many of their students as a bar to the gains in conceptual understanding that were intended by the worksheet method.

Also dividing the modular TAs was a related issue: the open-ended character of the modular pedagogy in which students must work through reading, lab experiences, class activities, and discussion to reach reasoned answers to questions posed by the modules. While it was thought beneficial to wean students away from accepting ideas without thinking about how they were derived, some TAs thought that expecting first-year (especially nonscience) students to think and act like researchers was premature. Some TAs wondered if all or most students could derive a necessary understanding of key concepts by working backward into the chemistry from real-world questions:

TA 1: It seems like you are putting the cart before the horse—trying to apply the concepts before you have learned them. It's like reading a book while you are still learning the alphabet. Although I really appreciate the fact that you should apply it—that's such a good idea, but I think it's too soon.

TA 2: I'm going to agree with that. I mean the really nice thing about the labs is that they totally correlated with what you are learning in the lecture. So, that part's good. But there were always a lot of questions on the concepts—because some of them weren't understanding the point of doing the lab. I mean, I could see it, but some of the students didn't.

This is not to say that these TAs disliked the applications—quite the contrary. What some found difficult, however, was going beyond using applications as illustrations and making them a vehicle by which to invoke conceptual grasp.

By contrast, some astronomy coaches wanted to see the professor make far more use of real-life applications. They argued that teachers need to get nonscience students to see their discipline as being interesting in its real-world applications, as well as something that is of intrinsic interest within a particular discipline:

> When professors assume that their field is, in and of itself, its own motivation and reward and doesn't need to be explained, it can be coldly received by people who don't consider themselves to be scientists. But when the teacher realizes why it's interesting beyond this field, and can communicate this to students, it opens up a wider response. I realize why this class is taught to business and English majors—why this is a field of human study.

The chemistry modules were described as being open-ended in that students are discouraged from moving to a "right" answer too quickly, that is, before they have seriously discussed the alternatives. Some TAs were divided about the value of downplaying the idea that there are right and wrong answers in science. Although some students were reported to reach "good" answers out of the discussion process, students with poorer conceptual grasp often did not:

> I think about half of my students could figure it out, but the other half didn't really have a grasp of the concepts well enough to root out the information, and, for them, it was extremely detrimental. I mean, it frustrated them to the point where they didn't want to go to lecture.

Thus, in these well-developed modular classes, where the modular approach was clear and consistently applied over the semester, this group of TAs debated broadly the same issues as some skeptical faculty colleagues. However, as the foregoing examples illustrate, their arguments are thoughtful, often supportive of many facets of the modules, and based largely on direct observation rather than contrary beliefs. As many of these extracts also illustrate, the discussants had not necessarily made up their minds and were watching to see how the modular ideas worked out in practice.

Issues of Course Structure and Alignment

The astronomy coaches worked with a course whose design was at an earlier stage of development than that of the chemistry modules. Thus their mixed reviews on course design focused on the primary need for a structure that was well articulated by the innovator and clearly understood by the students and themselves. At this point in its development, the course structure was described as being vague, informal, and changing. It was based on principles that the coaches largely approved, such as placing high responsibility on students for their own learning. However, TAs warned that an insufficiently structured learning framework promoted anxiety, rather than independence, among their students:

> His enthusiasm is infectious, and he definitely kept their attention, but they could also tell that it was unstructured—that it hadn't really been planned out. And they didn't want to be part of a "we'll figure it out together" sort of process. They wanted a class that was laid out and to know that the method was actually going to work for them—that they would understand the material and do okay. Students aren't democrats. They want the prof to take the lead.

> They were unhappy that the course was proceeding without enough structure—that it wasn't worked out enough beforehand. It seemed inappropriate to them to play it by ear—to be developing the curriculum as we went along. Right now, it's a little too heavy on the "it's what you make of it" approach.

The coaches advocated development of a set of prioritized learning objectives as the most critical element in achieving structural cohesion. Without this, they saw their professor trying to address too much material and their students becoming confused about what was of greater and lesser importance:

> In my opinion, he should take the time to sit down and ask, "What do I really want the students to learn in this class?" Because they can't learn everything. And then he should tell the students what they are going to learn—that would help them a lot to see where things fit in.

Across all three initiatives, TAs who approved of the innovative approach discussed the same critical design issue that was raised by some TAs in more negative terms—namely, problems caused by misfits between class learning objectives and class assessment methods. However, the central focus of mixed evaluations on this issue was insufficient thought about assignments and the problems this created for students:

> It was neat that the first project focused on just one area, because last semester the students got to pick whatever they wanted. And that was a lot harder because, not only did you have to decide what you were going to do, you had to make sure it was feasible and you could find enough information. It helped a lot having that direction. The second project involved a lot of data analysis. And I could see how it applied in understanding the processes that scientists go through. But a lot of students didn't know what they were looking for.

The Berkeley TAs also described misalignments between class emphases and subsequent tests. These misfits created problems for students that neither the worksheet writers nor the TAs could resolve. In all three initiatives, TAs cited examples of faculty giving assignments whose purpose was obscure.

Level and Volume of Course Work

In another group of discussions about course design, TAs addressed the level at which content was presented to students and the amount of work that faculty expected of them. Issues of level and volume of work were seen as being highly connected to the degree to which faculty had laid out their student learning goals and had built their selection of materials and activities upon them. The issue of pitching materials at an appropriate level was raised in both groups of chemistry TAs—in the case of the modular TAs, those in larger classes:

> There were three main problems. One was that they didn't have sufficient chemistry background; another was they were freshmen and don't have sufficient intellectual development to sit and think about things and arrive at the knowledge on their own. And thirdly, the class was just too big, with too many people in a lab group and not enough time to interact with the TA and their peers in order to construct the understanding in their own minds. They simply did not have the tools, the time, or the structure in order to do that. Those were the things that made the modules difficult to teach and difficult to learn from.

Problems in setting an appropriate and consistent conceptual level were also discussed by astronomy coaches:

> Coach 1: There's this inconsistent depth and breadth, and I can see why students are confused about the level they are supposed to focus their understanding on.

> Coach 2: We told him that it would be good for him to spend his time just dealing with one theme—one related chunk of issues. But I think it's hard for him to figure what size chunk to offer, and students don't know how big that chunk is in relation to everything else.

Berkeley TAs who noted the care taken by the innovators to structure the worksheets in ways that helped students get optimal understanding from the lecture material also reported that this was not always sufficient to address the wide range of preparation and aptitude among their students. The underprepared were often confused while the well prepared were bored:

> Some of the worksheets have been very effective, but the students who don't have as much background still have difficulty. The faculty definitely assume that you already know a certain amount of stuff.

> Some students know how to think about problems. They come to a conclusion much faster; they're able to accomplish tasks really quickly. The extra time that it

takes with the students that haven't gotten it and are still trying to work with the problem seems like a waste of time to them. So, for some students, the discussions are a really beneficial way to get an understanding. But with well-prepared students, it's less beneficial, because they already know how to work with the problems.

TAs often described the faculty with whom they worked as being highly energized by their enthusiasm for the materials and by new ideas about how to present them to students. However, the TAs noted that this trait could encourage a tendency for the faculty to set their expectations of introductory class students at unrealistic levels. Student overload also occurred when class goals were poorly articulated and faculty expected more of students than seemed appropriate for the class level. The TAs described faculty who included too much material in the course, moved too quickly into difficult conceptual areas, or did not take into account how much time students could give to their course, given the demands of other courses:

It's only a three-credit-hour class. You come to that discussion period, and you come to your team meeting for two hours, and those are your three hours; yet, the prof is asking for more, and he expects the students to give it to him. But they're intro students, you know. It's not like it's their major.

Most of these observations came from the astronomy class, where the materials and student activities had been worked out in less detail than had the chemistry modules:

Coach 1: He knows so much and is so in touch with all the current research and so excited by it all. But some of them have difficulty because they wish he'd start a bit lower down the scale of human knowledge—a little closer to the ground floor.

Coach 2: Last semester, not being a science major myself, I had to study every detail over and over, and eventually certain things would knock into place.

Coach 3: It's the first time they've dealt with anything like it.

These observations are valuable precisely because some of the coaches offering them were themselves nonscience majors, and all of the coaches worked with students whose places they had occupied only one or two semesters previously.

Some astronomy TAs further noted that pitching assessment questions beyond first-year students' level of science or mathematics preparation has the unfortunate effect of provoking answers that are copied from source material, or other responses that give insufficient indication of whether and what students have learned. Where most students are not science majors, these

TAs thought that establishing an appropriate level and amount of work was critical to success.

Working with Technology

Increasingly, innovative courses require students to explore class materials and undertake assignments by computer. Although the astronomy coaches broadly applauded this approach, they also offered some caveats. Learning new computer skills to do the work of the class can be a bonus to students. However, it may also take too much time—both the students' time in learning how to use a program and the coaches' time in troubleshooting software so that students can do assigned work. Although many students appreciated the chance to learn valuable computer skills, they could also become discouraged when the time and trouble involved seemed to outweigh the benefits:

> I definitely feel we're losing time—one of the homeworks involved an Excel spreadsheet, and about 80 percent of the kids didn't know how to use Excel. And I spent hours trying to help them, which means that they might have a better grasp of how Excel works, but I guarantee they don't remember what they learned on the homework.

> My best girl in the group threatened to drop because of the technical difficulties. She wasn't uncomfortable with the technology, but the software wasn't working correctly. So, she would enter her answer and it would disappear. You need to work the bugs out of any software before you ask student to use it.

Some coaches argued that universities and colleges should offer basic computer skills courses to all students so that commonly required skills do not have to be taught in subject classes.

The emphasis of the Interactive Astronomy course on specially developed hypertext as the central learning resource for the course also raised the issue of how well students adapt to getting most of their course materials from electronic sources. Coaches observed that the ability to learn from hypertext varied: some students seemed to work better with printed text and liked to write notes as they read. TAs saw these students at a disadvantage: they could print out text—which is cumbersome—but not Java applets. TAs who worked on this course for more than one semester noted, however, that more of their students had become accustomed to reading on-screen, and thought that it was no longer a problem for most students.

A more intractable problem was that of navigating the layers and branches of so large a resource. Students experienced difficulty in finding information sources for a second time—often they could not track down their original sources of information when they needed to reference them. Another fundamental difficulty for professors wanting to combine greater student exploration of electronic source material with interactive group-based learning was the problem of finding ways to translate the inherently solitary activity of web searching into a relevant collective endeavor. As indicated, the astronomy coaches saw that their professor was grappling with the problem of how to design group work (including that based on hypertext exploration) that could only be done collaboratively. Finally, making hypertext the students' primary source of information places more pressure on faculty to use their class time as an occasion to explain, clarify, and point out connections; give information searches a theoretical framework and direction; and offer students a sense of what is more or less important. The TAs were encouraged that the astronomy professor had sought to respond to each of these expressed needs by rethinking his class-time strategy several times before arriving at its current format. He used part of class time to link materials that students were exploring online into a conceptual framework, and part to discuss the results of students' efforts to answer questions set for that week.

Implementation Issues

Of the 25 percent of mixed evaluations that focused on the implementation of innovations, by far the most commonly discussed issues were how best to structure group membership and how to run groups so that they produced genuine collaborative effort. However, as almost all TAs had observations to offer about group work as a central feature of the TA role, the smaller number of observations made in the context of mixed course evaluations is considered in a broader discussion of group work in chapter 6.

Other implementation issues referenced the TAs' own participation in class work. Both the chemistry and astronomy TAs discussed the importance of knowing what their students were experiencing in their lecture or class sessions in light of what the professor was emphasizing. They thought this need was best met where TAs went to class and sat with their students. Doing this allows TAs to know what materials are introduced, what the assignments require, how class and labs are conceptually connected, and what problems in comprehension students are experiencing. TAs can also be active in class discussions and activities and act as monitors for in-class quizzes (TAs noted some problems of cheating where students in larger classes were supervised only by the professor). Whether TAs can attend classes depends on their own schedules, but some TAs thought that going to class should be a requirement of undertaking the job.

Issues with the TAs' Role in Innovative Classes

One-fifth (21 percent) of TAs' mixed evaluations referenced the enhanced role of TAs in innovative classes and its consequences for them. As I discuss in chapters 6 and 7, a large number of nonevaluative TA observations also addressed these issues. The most basic need of TAs in a nonfamiliar class structure was to have their role defined in some detail at the outset. Where innovators changed the nature of the TAs' contribution as they went along, TAs experienced confusion and stress. Friction also developed between themselves and the innovators, and the lowered morale that resulted was quickly communicated to students.

TAs argued that defining their work role very clearly is incumbent on innovative professors in part because new courses invariably create more work for TAs. TAs with experience of working for more traditional classes described their innovative classes as "a lot more work":

> It's very ambitious. It's really hard to do. It's a lot of work, and you need a lot of time. And I think what it makes it that way is the new structure.

> Just knowing the material makes things run smoother, so I can cue into whether the students are understanding, but it's finding the time to do that background work.

> I had more training this time than I had in the past. But we had more to do than I did in the past too.

The extra role demands that were reported in mixed comments included more time spent

- Helping individual students during office hours
- Reading new materials
- Attending class sessions
- Leading student group work (for which both training and troubleshooting sessions were seen as needed)
- Assisting in the development, implementation, and grading of new types of learning assessments and helping students understand how to approach them
- Learning new labs, helping in their development and testing, and helping students to engage in the more active lab role required of them

TAs also described the extra work created by their collaborations with faculty—for example, in testing and adding pieces to labs; piloting new materials and methods for use in labs, group work, and recitations; and giving faculty feedback:

> There were so many meetings, and it was too many hours to attend them all. It was supposed to be a ten-hour commitment, but sometimes I would spend

the ten hours just developing the lab material. Then there was the time spent in the lab—which was the best part of it. It was always eye-opening to think that everyone will know what this is, and then find out that 90 percent of them didn't.

That innovative classes demand more from both TAs and students is often an intentional element in new course goals. However, it also may arise because professors have not yet figured out how much effort will be required by either group to make their ideas work:

> He's not used to assessment or the amount of time it takes to do it right. So you are trying to juggle this job—which is very ill-defined or undefined—with your own work. And it's such a time suck. So what does he need us to do as TAs? I think the problem is that he doesn't quite know yet. His main concern is with the students, and he wants to make sure that they're taken care of. But he changes his mind about how to get there, and that puts more work and stress on us.

As I discuss in some detail in chapter 6, extensions of traditional TA roles were found in these innovative courses. Some were generated by the character of the course; others, by its stage of development, the expectations of its instructors, or as TAs' responses to perceived course needs.

A second basic need of TAs is to be appropriately prepared for the redefined role they are asked to play (all TAs' observations on their education and support needs—both met and unmet—are discussed in chapter 9). Here we note that TAs offered mixed evaluations where they wished to stress that adequate TA training is critical for the success of aspects of new-style courses. Picking TAs because they seem to have the right personality, level of interest and disciplinary background, or the potential to organize small-group work is not enough; neither is casual, informal guidance offered without regular, planned meetings. TAs expressed concern when the training offered to them seemed inadequate to the tasks they were asked perform. For undergraduate TAs, this need is especially acute because, in addition to teaching preparation, they may also need intellectual support. Undergraduate TAs are also more vulnerable and have less knowledge and experience than graduate TAs in how to establish order in their groups or enforce class rules about attendance, assignments, or grading. For all of these reasons, TAs sought appropriate formal training and feedback sessions with faculty.

Mixed evaluations also document several sources of stress that can undermine the TAs' effectiveness in a demanding new class. Teaching is seen as inherently time consuming, and TAs can feel challenged to do well both in their academic work and in their work as a TA. Because of this demand, undergraduate TAs thought that working for an innovative teacher was more

suitable for sophomores than for upper-class students; graduate TAs cited
the first two years in graduate school as the best time to learn to teach:

> Coach 1: Last semester, I had time for it. I could devote all the time I wanted.
> Now I'm a junior, I have to cram it into a really heavy load.

> Coach 2: As passionate as I am about astronomy, it really hurt me to see that it
> had slipped so far on my priority list because my learning and GPA have to
> come first. Last semester I handed out my phone number and e-mail address so
> the students could contact me twenty-four/seven, but this semester, I just
> couldn't do that.

Other studies also report that TAs' dual role as teachers of undergraduates
and as students often leads to time-related role conflicts. Freyberg and
Ponarin (1993) found that TAs face tremendous time pressures and have to
balance the risks to their own academic progress of giving too much time to
their students' learning. A significant number of TAs decide to focus their
limited time on their own work. In a survey of 120 randomly selected graduate TAs from twenty disciplines at a Midwestern university, McDowell
(1993) found that 40 percent of TAs saw their own work as their primary responsibility.

Both in these three studies and in universities in general, teaching assistantships for graduate students appear to be offered largely in the early years
of graduate programs, before TAs begin their own research work. We encountered only two senior graduate TAs, both of whom had chosen head TA
positions because of their interest in science education as a field of research
and as a future career. Following graduation, both gained assistant professor
positions in university science departments. One head TA described the time
and mental energy involved in curriculum or lab development and in supporting the other TAs. The competition thus created between graduate teaching and thesis work explains why many graduate students take less interest
in teaching than did this TA:

> It's much harder mental work to be asked to create new material than to simply
> grade exams. It's not necessarily more hours, but it's far more challenging, and
> grad students might not be TA-ing with the desire to be challenged. They feel
> that they don't need that—they're taking classes and attempting a thesis, and
> they don't need more to expend their mental energy on. Grading exams doesn't
> tax the soul that much.

The TA role in innovative classes may also be stressful because innovators ask more of their TAs than do professors in a traditional class. As indicated, this obligation often includes helping to troubleshoot aspects of their
classes that are working less well. Success in the innovation may also depend on the TAs' effectiveness in working with groups. As I discuss in chap-

ter 6, for both undergraduate and graduate TAs, managing groups can be stressful.

In addition to finding the stresses of innovative teaching, we found that graduate TAs were prone to other stresses that made their role more difficult. For first-year graduate students, TA orientation, training, and their first teaching experiences are likely to happen in their first weeks of graduate school, when they are also undergoing stressful adjustments in many other aspects of their lives:

> TA 1: For most of the TAs, it was also our first week of graduate school, and for the rest, it was the first week of college. And nobody knew what they were supposed to be doing. I mean, you're trying to adapt to a new environment. Some of us are still looking for places to live—or moving into them. And then there's the big pressure of having to find a research group within six weeks—which was the overriding one for me. . . . And all of a sudden, you're thrown up in front of thirty people and are expected to be coherent and intelligent.
>
> TA 2: And usually you have course work too.
>
> TA 3: I wasn't doing that [*laughter*]. Something had to give!
>
> TA 2: Also, you're in a new environment—finding people, making friends, sort of finding a niche.
>
> TA 1: And for some people, teaching for the first time.

As I discuss in chapters 6 and 7, many TAs become willing collaborators in enabling the success of new courses. However, they ask innovative faculty to be aware of the extra demands placed on their TAs, the departmental constraints and expectations pressing on them, and their need for adequate work-role definition and professional development.

The Departmental Context of Innovation

In this small group of mixed comments (9 percent), TAs qualified their otherwise positive evaluations with considerations of the departmental climate in which the new classes were set up. Graduate TAs who discussed the new courses' chances of acceptance or uptake in their departments reported the same barriers to greater interest in teaching that innovative faculty themselves identify. One TA lamented "as a sad fact" the lower value that many faculty in her department placed on teaching. Another offered,

> The majority of my faculty are, sadly, unconcerned about the quality of undergraduate teaching. They would probably not regard it as a wise expenditure to put out too much effort into a brand new experimental course.

A third TA thought it fortunate that the innovator was a senior member of his department:

> I am sure our course cost a great deal—we all had to be paid, so did a programmer, and we bought new computers. I think any of the professors would not have seen that there was insufficient return on that investment. . . . But he's such a senior member of the department, no one is going to question him. If he thinks it's great idea and can get the grant to do it, then there's nothing standing in his way. Had he been a junior faculty member, I think that the department would have seen this as spending too much time on teaching instead of research.

The same view was expressed in our interviews with junior faculty engaged in modular chemistry teaching who were concerned that the possibilities for teaching experimentation that were available to their senior colleagues were not open to them.

Among graduate TAs who commented on the chances of success for teaching innovations in departments where prevailing attitudes undervalued teaching, none were optimistic:

> [The faculty] know that learning to teach is a pretty separate set of skills than research—which I think is a central pillar of the great failure of academe. Teaching and research don't help each other, although they should.

> The biggest source of inertia is the constant need to write grants. It saps [the professors'] energy to do other than the minimum as teachers.

Two university-based TAs observed that their fellow graduate students were highly aware of the low level of interest in teaching among many or most faculty in their departments. This awareness made it difficult for them to do anything other than follow dominant faculty preoccupations with research, grants, and publication. Among their peers, the TAs saw themselves as part of a minority that was interested in science education. However, six other TAs thought they saw a break in this pattern and reported growing support among graduate students for improvement in science teaching:

> I don't feel that nearly as many faculty are interested in improving their teaching as the graduate students. Although it's the faculty who can affect the most change, it's the grad students that I meet who are much more interested in improving teaching.

Finally, TAs discussed the transferability of innovations to other faculty in the department. As noted, innovative classes tend to be offered by highly enthusiastic and energetic faculty whose passion for the material communicates well to students and attracts TAs to the philosophy and methods of the class. TAs warned, however, that enthusiasm and the ability to use discussion creatively are insufficient to ensure the longevity of the class or its uptake by other faculty. From my observations of these and other classroom innovations, I might add that the prospect of colleagues taking up a new course methods or materials may also be poorer when these are developed by a lone innovator who lacks the benefit of discussing and refining the experiment with similarly minded colleagues. Lone innovators also have a harder time selling new teaching ideas to those colleagues who are focused on research and are unaccustomed to spending time learning new teaching methods.

TA Beliefs about Teaching and Learning

Finally, 6 percent of evaluations were classified as mixed because TAs tempered their judgments of the courses with their own beliefs about how undergraduates ought to be taught. As with that of both positive and negative evaluations, the familiarity and comfort of "how I was taught myself" is a reference point for some TAs. However, unlike negative evaluations based on this rationale, these mixed reviews reflected a willingness to work with innovative methods that were seen to benefit students. The caveats expressed in this group of observations include the following:

- Well-conducted lectures have merits, including the chance to hear ideas presented and discussed by professors who bring great depth of knowledge and enthusiasm for their discipline to the class. Giving too much of the interactive teaching role to TAs, or a professor's insistence that students undertake much of their own material gathering, deprives students of exposure to teaching by fine scholars.
- New teaching practices may also deprive students of these learning opportunities by handing over to TAs too much responsibility for teaching fundamental material.
- It is unnecessary to "dress up" the material to secure interest for an intrinsically interesting subject. A concession was, however, made for nonmajors; discussions and applications could be important in their securing interest. Traditional teachers were similarly faulted for "trying to make chemistry look flashy—blowing things up and making fifteen things change color." While lectures with demonstrations can be extremely entertaining, important conceptual content may not be adequately explained.

Also tying together this small group of mixed observations is TA ambivalence about some traditional modes of teaching as well as aspects of the innovators' approaches. Some chemistry TAs were looking for a modified approach that could not only generate interest, illustrate real-world relevance, and demand more active engagement of students but also keep alive the tradition of good lecturing as a means to present fundamental concepts:

> The concept behind the modular teaching—which is teaching more of the fundamental ideas behind chemistry—I think that's a good idea. But it's not necessarily a good idea with fifteen hundred freshmen who have been brought up with the traditional way. On the other hand, I know there's a lot that future chem and biochem majors don't get out of the big survey classes—things they are going to need later on. So, there's got to be some sort of mix between the totally modular and traditional way that makes sure they don't go forward not understanding important things.

The nature of TA observations that comprise all of their mixed evaluations also strongly points to a theme that I will elaborate from other aspects of the TA interview data, namely, the TAs' potential as enablers and collegial commentators on the innovative teaching work of faculty.

NOTES

1. Karasz, Reynolds, and Wall (1997) also report that disparities between traditional course lectures and innovative recitation sections with TAs can be confusing. Students feel as though they are attending two distinct courses.

2. Similarly, the researchers in the University of California, Los Angeles, study (2000) reported that over two-thirds of the students in an innovative course based on multidisciplinary clusters felt as though their TAs challenged them to think more critically in this course than they did in other, more traditional courses.

3. *Signposting* was not a term used by the TAs or the undergraduates. It is a term that I coined to describe a particular student learning need that I communicated early in the evaluation process to the chemistry faculty who were developing and testing modular materials and methods. The group quickly adopted the concept and made extensive use of it in subsequent module development and refinement.

4. The Berkeley TAs referred to their sessions with undergraduates as "labs" rather than "recitations" because the sessions were attached to lab work that the TAs also supervised.

5. I discuss the issues arising from students' overdependence on memorization and on other passive forms of learning in some detail in chapter 6.

6. One-third of the TAs in the modular classes and three-quarters in the Berkeley TA education initiative were graduate students.

7. It is also possible that differences in the ways in which astronomy and chemistry are sometimes perceived by students—the former as a "softer science" that attracts nonmajors, the latter as a "real science"—affect both students' and TAs' perceptions of teaching methods that are "appropriate" for each discipline. As I have no data that might clarify this point, this is merely speculation.

8. See Weise (2001, 2003).

9. Critiques by all TAs of the education that they received are discussed in chapter 9.

10. Other criticisms of traditional course aspects that were unrelated to coherence issues were, critiques of lecture content and presentation, the poor quality of the TAs' working relationships with the lecture faculty, and problems with choice or use of the text. TAs noted the dominant role taken by the lecture professors who seemed distanced from both their work and what the innovators were seeking to accomplish.

11. Some TAs with a positive view of the worksheets specifically praised the ways in which they addressed the issue of ambiguity in science.

6

Teaching Assistants' Explanations for Undergraduate Responses to Innovative Teaching and Learning: Student Learning Difficulties versus Student Resistance

In the previous chapter, we considered some of the concerns of TAs about the innovative courses for which they worked as part of their array of evaluative observations. The interview data also revealed the TAs and coaches as being able to diagnose the different types of problems that students commonly encounter in innovative science classes, and to identify and distinguish between the different sources of these problems. These distinctions are of particular consequence to faculty innovators who may be concerned that end-of-semester student evaluation scores for their innovative class are lower than those to which they are accustomed when teaching in a more traditional mode. What the TAs clarify is that students' resistance to the new learning approach and their learning difficulties related to the demands of innovative classes are different phenomena, with different origins that require different remedies. In this chapter, I lay out the TAs' and coaches' explanations for the array of responses that they observed in students and the various ways in which TAs sought to address them.

PREPARATION ISSUES

Across the three initiatives, TAs and coaches identified a set of problems with student readiness to undertake the work of the class. Their accounts of student readiness and their explanations for both learning difficulties and resistance to innovation are connected because they are all grounded in observations about what students do, and do not, bring to class.

Diversity of Academic Preparation within Classes

Both the modular chemistry and Interactive Astronomy classes target a wider range of students (by intended major) than do the large introductory chemistry classes served by the Berkeley initiative. Given that many of their students intended to pursue science or engineering majors, the Berkeley TAs expressed higher expectations of their incoming students in terms of preparation, skills, and abilities than did their counterparts in the other two initiatives. The Berkley TAs expected undergraduates to enter the class with sufficient knowledge and skills in chemistry and mathematics to undertake the class work, and they assumed that students would know how to solve problems, operate in the lab, write lab reports, and tackle unfamiliar problems by making use of what they already knew. In all of these expectations, they were disappointed: across both rounds of interviews, more than two-thirds of the Berkeley TAs reported that many students in their lab sections arrived in the class underprepared in the fundamental knowledge and skills required to perform at least adequately. Direct experience with students in their own sections led them to conclude that many did not possess an understanding of the methods and principles of science and that some were incapable of doing elementary algebra (in a course that demanded no mathematical skills above this level.) TAs also noted that the writing and study skills of some students were below what they would expect at the college level. Less than one-third of the TAs in this large introductory class felt as though most of their students entered the course with the requisite knowledge and skills to undertake introductory chemistry:

> A lot of these students have problems not just with math but with basic algebra and with manipulating equations to get things in the right form and so on. And the class assumes that they know how to do that kind of thing . . . and when they do these discussion sheets, they're expected to work through [them] without a lot of prior preparation for dealing with this kind of material.

> Their writing skills are not good. Horrible. The writing is a lot lower than I would've hoped for. I corrected grammar, spelling, contractions, completed sentences, fragments, *everything*. You should know when to make a word plural or how to conjugate your verbs correctly. . . . I see students who speak fine, perfect English but will write a sentence that's five lines long and has 10 commas in it.

Berkeley TAs reported that many of their students also lacked basic academic skills:

> When I talk at the board, a lot of them don't write down anything I say. So I wonder how they manage. Then later when they don't write about whatever I talked about in their lab report, I say, "Well, I said that in class." But they just,

they don't take notes on any [of] the things that I talk about. . . . Some of them aren't writing down what I say when I lecture about the concept of what's behind the lab and why we're doing this. I guess they're confident that they understand, but if I say [what] things to include in the lab report, they don't write that down.

Concern that first- and second-year students enter their classes underprepared for the work was also documented in a survey of 314 U.S. and international TAs in forty-five science and nonscience classes taught by conventional methods at the University of Nebraska, Lincoln. Two-thirds of the TAs thought that their students were underprepared (Luo, Bellows, and Grady 2000). No parallel studies in innovative science classes have been located.

By contrast, the Berkeley TAs noted that other students were overprepared for this introductory class:

I think they should encourage more people to take Chem X even if they're not chemistry majors. Some of my students should definitely be in Chem X, which is the chemistry for chemistry majors. They're *way* overprepared for this class.

Indeed, the largest single teaching difficulty reported by the TAs who serviced this large introductory university chemistry class was the wide variation that they encountered in the levels of preparation in math, science, writing, and study skills that students had received from their precollege education:

It's very diverse. And that's one thing that makes it difficult—that some of these people took a lot of AP chem and are super well prepared. And they're the ones that won't really pay attention when you're talking 'cause they're like, "I know all this." I don't even know why they're in this class. That just makes it really hard. And then there's some people that have hardly seen chemistry at all. And you're trying to cater to both those groups at the same time.

However, even among nominally well-prepared students, TAs encountered many who were unable to tackle problems that they had never encountered. One modular chemistry TA commented,

I had one student who had taken three years of high school chemistry, and she felt she really knew chemistry. . . . But, she has not scored above the mean on a single exam in the class. One of the things I've been trying to help her with is . . . she knows how to execute basic problems . . . but as soon as she is exposed to a new situation, she has trouble with what to do with the numbers that are before her. And I find the same problem in many of the students who . . . know how to do the basics. As soon as they're hit with a new situation, they lose all grounding and they're simply not able to do the problem.

The Berkeley TAs similarly complained that their students were often unable to transfer knowledge they had just learned to problems of comparable types. This observation reinforced their perceptions that students habitually focus on "the numbers" as opposed to learning and understanding the concepts underlying the problems:

> They've got this one idea down very well, but there are all these other topics that they haven't covered. So, they know this one idea very well and they should be able to apply it to these other topics, but they can't. . . . I realized that because they had several worksheets on equilibrium, and they were getting pretty good at those. Then I just had another worksheet on acid-base equilibriums, and I thought, "Oh this will be no problem for them, because it's just an extension of what they've been doing and they were doing so well at it." And they had no idea. That really showed me that they can't make the carryover.

TAs in the modular chemistry and Interactive Astronomy also encountered wide variations in their students' preparation and grappled with the problem of getting them to apply what they knew. However, these problems seemed less acute because both of these initiatives assumed less prior knowledge and because faculty designed these courses so as to build student competence from a wider range of starting points. By contrast, the Berkeley TAs, working with a large unremediated lecture class, could not, by their best efforts as interactive intermediaries between lecturer and students, overcome this fundamental problem. What is clear, however, is that the Berkeley TAs were taking most of the strain in seeking to bring many underprepared students up to a level of working competence.

That said, TAs across all three initiatives reported a different kind of preparation problem that arose directly from the ways in which students had learned how to learn. They saw their courses as demanding far more from students than what many of them were accustomed to giving—more responsibility for their own and each others' learning, more reading and writing, more application and transfer of knowledge, and more initiative in generating ideas and working through unfamiliar problems. These demands, which were seen by TAs as essential features of these innovative classes, had the effect of exposing a linked set of habits and attitudes to learning that hitherto had served to insulate students from active engagement with their own education. TAs saw their students as having learned during high school or earlier to be overdependent on their teachers for their learning.[1] In classes composed largely of first-year students, this expectation was quickly transferred to their TAs. The following extracts were offered by TAs in modular chemistry at two different institutions:

> TA 1: At the beginning of every single lab, "How do you do this?" I mean, they don't want to do anything on their own. And if you're willing to help them on it, then they don't learn it at all.

TA2: Thinking of things on their own. That's hard. They don't like doing that—like designing their own experiments.

TA1: I don't want them to just sit there. I don't want them to give up so easily. . . . They're not willing to go to the book and try the examples and figure it out. They're just waiting for me to give them the answers.

TA2: They don't have the confidence to do it. . . . That's a big one I think. Sometimes a problem looks complex, but if you break it down, you can figure it out. A lot of my students don't have the confidence to begin the problem. But, once you show them a few steps, they can figure it out.

TA1: Yeah, it's part of our job to help them to understand that this is doable.

As the last two speakers deduced, students who had not been exposed to the expectation that they should think some things out for themselves were the ones who failed to develop the confidence to do so. By giving them some practice in a supportive context, TAs took on the task of building student confidence to work independently, and they discovered in the process that they could improve both confidence and competence in their students.

Instrumental Attitudes

TAs discovered several different reasons for their students' dependence on teachers. One cause was a highly instrumental attitude toward introductory chemistry found among students who were taking it to fulfill a requirement:

There's definitely those students who take the class because they have an obligation and they just learn it for the sake of having to learn it and just don't let themselves gain anything from it: "Let's just get through this and get out."

We have a lot of biology majors that we teach that aren't necessarily in it for the class. They're just taking it because they have to. It seems like they don't really care. They just want to get out of there.

Some of it depends on where the students are headed. This guy wanted to be a premed, and he didn't put any effort into the class at all. He just hated it, and he complained a lot. He just wanted to do it and get out. There are some students who just don't want to be bothered because it's a means to an end.

TAs saw the innovative classes as being demanding more in time and effort than some students had learned to give in previous science classes. For some students, the demands of innovative classes thwart a learned habit of getting through school with the least amount of time and effort that will produce grades that are sufficient for graduation. One senior in the *Talking about Leaving* study (Seymour and Hewitt 1997) described this kind of

student behavior as "calculating the profit-to-grief ratio." Student instrumentalism is sometimes career-goal related, sometimes part of a generalized attitude to getting through an undergraduate program. In discussing
this phenomenon, three modular chemistry TAs observed:

> TA 1: I was just thinking about student attitudes toward the modular labs as op-
> posed to the normal labs. A lot of them who have done labs before; they've
> learned this mind-set of just going to do the lab for the sake of it. They're not
> used to having an overall goal like they do in the modular labs. It's a new thing
> for a lot, and some of them get irritated.

> TA 2: And there's particular people that I see who want to do the least amount
> of work and just get by in the class—who take chemistry because they have to
> for some reason and want to work as little as possible—just kinda coast through.
> I think it forces them to do more, and they don't like that.

> TA 3: I think it's more actual work because you are trying to tie ideas together
> and make a bigger picture out of them, and it forces them to think more about
> it. So that's what irritates them: they don't want to think about chemistry all that
> much. And it demands more time from them than labs normally do.

When the teacher or the TAs set up assignments that force such students
to work harder and become more engaged than what they have bargained
for, this new expectation becomes a source of resistance. TAs observed that
student resistance to the innovator's demand for more effort took a number
of forms. Students complained that they had to work harder for the level of
grade that they had come to expect. Some with good science and math
preparation developed the habit of not doing assigned work because they
did not appreciate its value until they encountered unfamiliar material. These
students ran the risk of getting conceptually lost and losing ground to students who worked more steadily. Resistance to the innovation was also
made evident in complaints during the class and in negative class evaluations at its end.

The two modular TAs discussing why they lost five of the original twenty-five
students in their class confirmed what we had learned in the earlier study
(Seymour and Hewitt 1997)—that considerations of effort and reward contribute both to minimalist class performances by some able students and to
field switching by others. This group of field switchers moved into majors
that appeared to afford them a more cost-effective distribution of their time.
TAs described the calculations that students made in deciding how much
time they could afford to give to any particular class or assignment. The TAs
were not unsympathetic to their students' time-juggling dilemmas:

> TA 1: I think it relates directly to the amount of work they have to do for the
> class. I mean, those people who have the chemistry background can get by
> without having to do something every day. The question of the day is intended

as a motivation to get people to read, but it may not work because people get too busy with all their classes and stuff gets pushed back.

TA 2: And if you are a freshman trying to get a required class out of the way and you get off to a bad start, there's no reason not to drop the class—you have seven more semesters to get that science class.

TA 1: So it's really a matter of hedging your bets and deciding how best to portion out your time. And if this class looks like more work that you really bargained for, you may decide to take it some other time or do some other class. It's really a betting matter.[2]

Astronomy coaches also noted minimalist behavior toward learning tasks. They recounted examples of students who answered their groups' set questions but then gambled on not being asked to respond to the professor's questions for some time thereafter. They did not, therefore, do the background reading for questions assigned to other groups. The coaches ascribed this behavior to what one coach called a "survivalist approach to getting through school," the success of which depended partly on being able to count on a high degree of passive engagement with their classes. The TAs saw this attitude as contributing to students' rejection of the expectation that they take responsibility for their own learning. The coaches lamented this response but understood it as a common way of adjusting to college work demands:

Some of them hate the fact that they actually have to learn the stuff themselves. Some of them are, you know, the continual slackers throughout all of school. It's not just this class. They wanna slide through the education system with the lowest grade that will do the trick. The fact that they are having to actually do some work in this class and that there's no way to avoid it, that's what upsets them.

One of the things students figure out in college is how to distribute their time, you know, how much time you have to put in, just enough to be competent. For some students that's shorter, and for others longer. And I can see why some students won't hang in with a class that begins to look like a time suck.

The coaches cited the steps that their professor took to warn students from the outset that they could not expect to "just coast through":

He's trying to let them know that you're going to be active in this class. It's the whole point of the class. You have to come to every class—it's required, and attendance is taken. And you have to get involved in your own learning experience.

Another modular TA observed that most instances of students' dropping the class occurred before the modules had really gotten underway—that is, early in the course when students were weighing whether the payback would be worth the effort that seemed to be required:

> It just looked like a lot of work for those who were looking for an easy science course. We started with quite a bit of book work, and they stopped showing up to class when we were still mostly reading. They didn't really encounter the modules yet.

The Berkeley TAs discussed whether faculty warnings—"heard in every one of our classes that 'you're expected to work twice the amount of time out of class as you do in class'"—had any effect on this approach to getting through school. The TAs concluded that for a consistent subset of their students the warnings had no effect. Across both rounds of Berkeley TA interviews, the most common observation about the ways in which students learned was that most students did not work unless they were required to do so, that is, only if it was graded:

> I think the people in my class, I don't know if they're premed students or *what.* . . . They are extremely grade greedy and grade driven, and that's their motivation.

Indeed, "grades" was the only answer offered by the Berkeley TAs to the interview question "What motivates your students to learn?" Grades were seen not only as the students' primary source of learning motivation but also as affecting their learning methods. The TAs saw many of their students as being obsessed with "getting the right answer" to the detriment of understanding the purpose or concepts behind the problems they were trying to solve. The TAs saw the students' apparent inability to transfer knowledge between contexts as an extension of their overfocus on the mechanics of solving problems. This preoccupation often overrode reason in that students did not stop to check whether their answers were within the realm of possibility:

> TA 1: They're just starting college, and I don't think they have the kind of problem-solving skills that they'll develop later on. . . . Some of them tend to obsess about the numbers, and that drives me crazy. Like in discussion this week, I was showing them how to do this problem, and this girl was like, "I just punched the numbers into my calculator." (They're so obsessed with their calculators.) And she's like, "I didn't get that number"—the number that they gave on the discussion sheet as the answer. And I was like, "Well, what I'm really trying to teach you here is *how* to do this problem." A lot of people are still obsessed with the number or just what's the right answer.
>
> TA 2: I get *so* frustrated with my students when they give me answers that are absurd. One of the first labs we did with dropping a monolayer of stearic acid

on a little watch glass. They had to determine the volume of water in the watch glass, right? And they had to do all these calculations to do it. One girl said in her lab report, she had 1×10^{26} liters of volume of water in her watch glass. And one guy on the test got a –74 for his equilibrium constant. . . . And that frustrates me so much . . .

TA 1: I know.

TA2: . . . because they're so obsessed with the numbers: they go through the whole problem, get the number, and they're like, "Oh! Well, you know, that must be right. I must have had ten to the twenty-sixth liters in this little thing."

TAs saw an overpreoccupation with grades as being counterproductive. The modular TAs reported that those students who benefited most from the chemistry modules were those who were most open-minded and unconstrained by instrumental attitudes:

I think the modules help students who are open to becoming excited about chemistry—the ones who don't come in at the beginning with a mind-set that "I'm just here to pass the class and that's all I want to do." Those are the students that will be disappointed and will complain because they just want to get the concepts and get out of the class. But the ones that are willing to get excited about it really do benefit from the modules, and it doesn't seem to depend on how much chemistry they have done before.

An astronomy coach similarly observed,

It's not a matter of how much they know before they start the class. It seems like the people who come in with an open sort of attitude do a lot better in the whole class. Those are the ones who enjoy it most. I mean, the material is so cool and the whole philosophy of the class. And you are not going to enjoy the discussion when you haven't read the material and sound like a fool in front of the whole class. The ones who have done the work, put in the time, and get real interested do well, but they also get self-esteem in the process.

Some students who had already become engaged were observed to sanction lab peers who grumbled about labs being too much work:

I had somebody in my lab last semester who just complained and complained about doing it. And the students around him started to say things like, "Come on. Get over it. This is way more interesting." I mean, he just wanted us to give him a recipe that said, "Mix 0.5 ml of this with 10 ml of that, stir, and heat it." But I think that most of the students really got into it and learned more from doing it this way.

TAs also identified as a broader form of instrumentalism the fear of being unable to complete a task among those students who were more focused on performance rather than on learning. TAs noticed that these students were reluctant to attempt anything that appeared to carry the risk of performance failure. TAs became frustrated when students gave up too soon or sought to get assignment answers out of them:[3]

> TA 1: What they want is the right answer.
>
> TA 2: That's right, always.
>
> TA 1: I always say at the beginning of the lab, "Today, I am not going to give them the answer" [*laughing*]. Well, I start off the day saying, "Well, think about this, and think about that, and how they are related to each other." At the end of the lab, I look at the board, and I'm like, "I just gave them every answer."

Fearing a low grade, such students ignored the approaches to an assignment advocated by the teacher and the TAs and fell back on following familiar procedures or relying on others for answers:

> TA 1: There were always questions on the last page of the test that were applied questions. Most students would avoid those, and most could not get them.
>
> TA 2: I think they are more comfortable in teamwork when someone tells them what to do—some routine thing. But, if they had to come up with something themselves, they either avoided it or just couldn't do it.

Aversion to risk taking was not confined to weaker or less-prepared students. Some modular chemistry TAs noted that modules can be something of a leveling experience for students with a strong chemistry background who have never had the experience of working things out on their own:

> Students that have taken a lot of chemistry and are used to one method of teaching may not like the modules, because it makes them think about chemistry in a different way. It's confusing to them not to follow their tried and true formula, and it puts them more on a level with the rest of the class. There's a sort of status in having done AP chemistry, but you won't know anything about ozone kinetics, and you have to learn it same as everyone else. So, that can throw people and make them reluctant to get involved.

Again, we noted that TAs undertook the task of breaking down this syndrome of fear, avoidance, and teacher dependence:

> I think that, overall, the project went well in the end. It took then a while to get going, and first they had to understand what they were doing. But, at the end, after a lot of prodding from me, they started to think and found they could actually do it.

TAs commonly concluded that the origins of risk-averse behavior were that students had left high school with a history of being rewarded for following procedures (such as working equations) in a mechanical way and had not been required to think for themselves. Many TAs saw it as part of their job to help students to break the performance-only habit and begin to experience success in more active modes of learning.

Expectations of Limited Reading and Writing

By demanding far more reading and writing than students had learned to expect in science courses, all three innovative classes flouted some students' expectations of what teachers and TAs can reasonably or legitimately expect of them:

> I've never had to take a chemistry class where there was a lot of writing, and I can understand them being a bit weirded out by having to write a paper rather than do a midterm. Before I came to work in this class, I'd never had any experience with that at all. So I can understand why the students get so anxious.

> Some of the people who go into the sciences might be trying to get away from trying to write so much [*laughing*]. I know some people who are like that in this class.

> They need to get on the ball, figure out how to use spell check and learn that you've got to read over everything once, at least *once*, before you turn it in.

Across all three initiatives, the TAs and coaches noted a legacy of low teacher expectations and of limited tutoring in writing technique, resulting in poor competence and avoidance of writing. TAs also noticed that the more extensive academic writing experience of liberal arts students allowed them to do better in innovative classes than they would have expected to do in a more traditional science classes:

> TA 1: Usually three times a week students have a few in-depth questions where they have to analyze some materials and write a paragraph about it. They do a lot of writing. Most of the homework assignments have a writing component.

> TA 2: And the liberal arts students find they can do quite well in this aspect, although they often have to adjust their writing style. But it's a hard sell with the science majors who winge [*sic*] about it—a lot! They don't think they should have to write, and many of them have quite a struggle to pull together a few clear sentences.

Modular TAs also understood that writing in the formal, passive voice of science reporting is inherently difficult, and it may be particularly awkward for students from the humanities:

> I think it's very difficult for everyone to learn to write scientifically. It's just a weird format. And the passive voice is so nontraditional, even bizarre, for nonscience

majors. I've helped a lot of students start to learn to write in scientific format. Even those, like the English majors, who write correctly find it hard to convert to scientific language. It's especially hard for them.

Some TAs who appreciated the help that they had received in learning to write well recounted their experiences of having to unlearn their diffidence toward writing:

> I remember when I hit the modular course on the ozone hole. I wasn't expecting to write so much. I remember that we had to write a paper instead of taking a midterm exam, and I thought it was ludicrous that you have to write a paper for a chemistry class. I had no idea what to do. And, looking back on it, it was a good experience because you do have to write in science—in fact, you have to write in just about anything—but, at the time, I was frustrated and confused and had no idea what to do.

The astronomy coaches whose students worked with hypertext also observed that the expanding accessibility of computer text has exacerbated the student practice of avoiding writing by cutting and pasting material available on websites. One coach called this "passive writing" because it is possible for students to present what looks like written work without showing any evidence of understanding. The coaches were trying to address this problem in their groups by forcing their students to explain, discuss, and then draft short answers to the professor's weekly questions.

Across all initiatives, TAs reported that reluctance to read is also common. Asked to put a figure on what their students believed was a reasonable amount of time to spend on reading, TAs reported that requests to spend more than about two hours per week on reading provoked protest. They complained that some students did not prepare for classes, even when the professor and TAs specifically directed them to do so. They also had difficulty in getting students to read materials that were not in the textbook, such as short scientific articles.[4] Again, TAs noted that the structure and expectations of these innovative classes exposed the students' minimalist attitude toward reading and their reluctance to undertake independent study:

> They were kinda taken aback that they had to look up stuff that they had never seen before. And I explained it to them the week before, "From now until next week, you need to look at your handout, look at the CD-ROM, and at some of the websites it tells you about." And, to begin with, I don't think that too many people did that. Then they were kind of surprised and shocked when they came into the class and hadn't a clue what was going on.

A minimalist reading habit also included a reluctance to look up sources needed to do assignments:

If there's a concept in the module that they don't understand, they're not going to their textbook and looking in the index, reading that section, and practicing some of the problems. So they just tolerate not understanding it and complain.

Most of their problems go back to them not reading their textbook. After their tests, they complain that we didn't go over this or that in class. But they just didn't read their book. They say to me, "Oh, I don't know exactly what pages to read." Seems like almost every complaint after tests comes right back to that.

Some TAs interpreted complaints about the text or the modular handbook as reading avoidance, which one TA characterized thus:

They don't want to read anything, so they're probably not reading the module, and they're probably not reading the textbook either. I think they feel like— even if they don't say it outright—"If it's not on the board, it shouldn't be on the test."

Effective group work was also undermined where the astronomy coaches had difficulty in motivating students to do the reading on which group assignments were based:

I think that my group has done the least amount of work—like, we hardly ever had anyone do the readings—like three people maybe. And everyone just looks at each other and they are stuck. It's not about the groups; it's about getting the reading assignments done. And that reluctance to read is making the group work less effective.

Again, TAs clearly understood the history of these learned attitudes and behaviors and took professional responsibility for trying to change them:

Coach 1: They wouldn't read it. They just wanted the answers. "Tell me what to do next. Just tell me the basics." And it's like, "No. You have to read the paper. It's just four pages with some graphics, so not a big deal." I just know they would have understood it better if they had read it.

Coach 2: They are still clinging to a passive way of learning—"You just tell me, and I'll do anything you say so long as you don't ask me to read, or write, or think, or, you know, get active in any way." And some of the irritation—and worse—that we get from them is coming from that place. Some of them never get over it.

Coach 3: We have to push and pull them into getting them to do it. Some people do read, but the maximum I've found is two hours.

Coach 2: Yeah, just the bare minimum. Like, "Gee, my question is on binaries, so I am going to the hypertext to the tab that says 'binaries,' and I'm gonna read this page, and that's all I'm gonna read. And I'm saying, "You could read the page before and the page after, God forbid. Because you're sitting at this keyboard that's connected to every piece of information that you could possibly ever desire." But not once in all of my coaxing did any one of them do a Yahoo! search. It's still, "Show me where I find this. Where do I look?"

Coach 1: It's frustrating to watch them clinging to the same old ways of getting through a class, even when they are doing things that are not particularly useful to them, even when it's making them miserable that they don't seem to be getting anywhere. It's "I'm not going to read anything, and I'll just cheat on this quiz"—I know there's cheating going on.

Coach 3: "And I am going to come to the learning teams as late as I can and get out as quick as I possibly can." I mean, what's the way forward for [Professor X] and us in dealing with all this foot dragging, this trudging kind of passive resistance?

I have included this rather long conversational extract because it shows how well the coaches understand both the sources of the problem and the difficulty of changing students' deeply learned, if counterproductive, attitudes and behaviors.[5] It also illustrates their high degree of collegial investment and professional responsibility in engaging with the problem of passivity and inertia among their students.

Unlearning Performance-Focused Learning Methods

In all three types of innovative classes, faculty wanted to see their students develop a qualitative understanding of concepts and be able to apply them. TAs reported that implementation of this learning goal exposed weaknesses in some students' customary learning methods, including a dominant (or exclusive) reliance on memorization as an approach to both learning and test preparation. Although each initiative gave students guidance in how to think about class materials and connect their knowledge into a framework, TAs found that many students ignored this guidance and clung to memorization, particularly as they approached tests:

Probably from high school they just did not know how to approach studying. They tried to memorize something—even applications—so they didn't work on applying what they knew to other areas. I think they were just grasping at something to memorize. To them, study means memorizing stuff, and they just couldn't let go of that.

Failure to build a conceptual map of their understanding, or to otherwise structure their learning process, left some students behind. TAs met with complaints from students who tried to get good grades by memorization alone and who could not understand why this did not produce the outcomes to which they were accustomed, either in high school or in more traditionally taught colleges science classes:

Most of my students were frankly terrified of tests of their understanding of concepts. They were just uncomfortable, as all they had learned to do was memorize and spit things out on the tests. So they couldn't figure out how well prepared they were. When they saw the questions, they just didn't know what to do.

Two modular TAs explained the problem this way:

TA 1: Students who claimed they studied very hard come to office hours and
complain that they are getting Cs. They didn't seem to understand anything from
the looks of their papers. One girl was in tears. She was saying, "Oh, I studied
so hard for my midterm." But I wasn't surprised. She deserved her C in my opinion. I think the problem is that the emphasis in this class is on qualitative understanding not memorization.

TA 2: Yeah, I guess they know something about the pieces of the puzzle, but
they don't know how to link them together and then apply the ideas to a problem. They just didn't have the kind of structure to their learning that would allow them to think about problems.

TA 1: That's right. Sticking at trying to memorize everything just can't get them
to that kind of thinking.

TAs understood why students who come into the class with so limited an
experience of how to study in a productive way find it difficult to break with
their prior experience of what "learning" or "studying" mean. They understood how hard it was for some students to begin to think about the class
material conceptually and to apply it:

It's a good approach, but it's really hard for them to start thinking. . . . They're
just not used to thinking and applying concepts. I know it's really hard. They've
just never been asked to do this before.

TAs also understood that students became frustrated because they had
learned to see grades as essentially being related to effort rather than to performance:

TA 1: Grades were a big source of frustration because most of them felt like the
grades they got were not proportional to the amount of work they put in.

TA 2: Absolutely. It's not how much time; it's how effectively they use it.

TA 1: And the fact that they were mostly freshmen and hadn't yet learned how
to work at the college level. But what was constantly frustrating to them was that
now they found they did not know how to prepare for quizzes or answer questions in the labs. Worst, they did not know how to prepare for exams.

The TAs understood, perhaps better than their faculty, how and why their
students' had acquired a mechanical approach to learning, and did not

blame them for this. They sought to help their students learn how to learn in more productive ways, but they became frustrated when students refused to try the approach they were explaining:

> TA 1: And I told them to look at the exam they just took and think where the questions came from—things from the class, the book, the homework, and combinations of all three. "What's the focus of the questions? Read the questions again. Start the test problem, and if you get stuck in the middle, go back to the question. Make sure you are answering it. When you get to the end, does your answer address the question?"

> TA 2: These steps take more time, and that's also an issue for them. But if they did their homework this way, they would be in good practice, and the test would just be an extension of how they are pulling together what they learn from all of these sources.

> TA 1: You really learn by practice. That's right.

> TA 2: But I know many of them just weren't hearing it.

TAs who taught students how to prepare themselves for tests by doing the homework, asking questions, working collaboratively to understand the material, and otherwise following the learning methods advocated and modeled by the teacher reported that those who made these adjustments were able to do the tests. Indeed, TAs from both the modular chemistry and Interactive Astronomy classes noted that students of all preparation levels could do well if they did the work from the outset. They also saw this as an intentional aspect of these classes. However, many students who clung to memorization, continued to be afraid of the tests and to do poorly.

Along with memorization, TAs saw students holding onto a learned habit of mindlessly carrying out tasks—most commonly, solving equations or working problems without reference to what they represent and going through lab procedures without understanding the reason for the inquiry or making a serious effort to interpret the data they generated. TAs observed confusion, resistance, and resentment when students were pressed to move beyond task performance:

> I've taught chemistry more traditionally too, and I know this is much more demanding for students. Because they can't coast along not really understanding, just relying on memory and mechanical performing. So, that's why they are resisting the prof. They are not thinking, because they don't really understand the material. If you give them an equation where they can just pop in a number, they would get the answer right away. But if you ask them to explain something, they may not be able to do that. Then if you ask them to apply the material to something else, they get confused.

Especially in their lab work, TAs appreciated how hard it was for students to break the learned habit of "just performing." Resistance to labs is traditional, and, as we reported in *Talking about Leaving* (Seymour and Hewitt 1997), students have learned to place normative limits on the amount of time they think it appropriate to devote to labs. The modular teachers seek to integrate the work of classes and labs, and labs are designed to reinforce and extend students' conceptual understanding, encourage discovery, the framing of research questions, and engagement with authentic data. Consequently, students often need all of the lab time available to accomplish lab objectives. Some students behave resentfully—as if these faculty have not understood the established custom of completing labs mechanically and as quickly as possible. Three modular chemistry TAs who discussed this issue sensed that their students were engaged in a silent battle with their lab teacher:

TA 1: The students say that she gives them all these little activities to do that are designed to keep them there the entire four hours [*laughing*].

TA 2: Yeah, they say, "All she's trying to do is get us to stay the whole time."

TA 3: Well, maybe the modular lab approach doesn't facilitate the students' leaving early because there's always more questions to ask and things to find out. And if you just have this goal and make this reaction go, then answer the postlab questions, then it's just like for its own sake—you know, a short-term objective that they can just race through as fast as they can.

TA 1: Yeah, it's really unfair of these modular teachers to try to make the labs meaningful [*all laughing*].

One of the astronomy coaches described parallel behavior in the learning groups:

I kinda get frustrated with them when they come here and do their discussion question in twenty minutes and say, "Can I go now?" And I'm like, "No, you are here for an hour because we have other things we need to do."

Modular TAs reported that some students respond to additional demands by minimal lab attendance. Their absence increased the difficulty of the TAs' task of helping the group through a whole experiment. TAs understood the dynamics of this situation because many of them had also experienced (and moved beyond) the same norms and behavior at an earlier stage in their own education.

In addition to thwarting learned expectations that task performance was (or should be) "enough," the TAs and coaches across all three initiatives acknowledged that it was intrinsically hard for students to engage in the independent thinking that was asked of them. Often, little of their prior education in the sciences had prepared them to rise to this challenge:

> I think the most important thing—the thing I wasn't ready for—something I didn't expect, was how hard it would be to motivate the students to think. They just had a lot of trouble thinking.

> Students were very resistant to the idea that the teachers wanted to make them think about what they were doing. And that's hard. It's hard to think. And I see it in my labs. They just go and do the lab mindlessly, and then they go home and try to put it all together. And they end up e-mailing me the day before the report is due, and they're still trying to figure out what they should have been thinking about when they were actually doing the lab. Thinking is hard work. It's a lot easier just to follow something out of a manual and leave early.

> TA 1: The method they used for all of the labs was "predict, observe, and explain." And a lot of them didn't understand why that sequence was important. They are not good at making observations in the labs.

> TA 2: Maybe they observe it, but they don't take any notes on what they see.

> TA 1: But they don't take observing seriously either. Some students would always ask me what they should write down for their observations, and I'd say, "Anything that you can see. Do you see any changes happening?"

> TA 2: And it's very hard to make them think about why something happens. Most of them just don't think. They mostly just work on the equations in the manual.

INNOVATOR AND TA RESPONSES

The Innovator's Contribution to Student Difficulties and Their Resolution

As I have described, TAs' explanations for students' difficulties with and resistance to new learning methods derived from their observations of inadequacies in students' preparation for the class—whether in academic background, learning methods, or attitudes to learning. However, TAs also observed that student receptivity to new learning methods was mediated by the innovators' responses to the challenge of restructuring students' learned behaviors, beliefs, and attitudes. Students' difficulties and their level of resistance were compounded where faculty failed to take students' learned limitations sufficiently into account in their implementation of new learning methods. Conversely, the faculty's chances of success in getting students to learn actively, responsibly, and effectively were increased where they understood the source of students' difficulties and directly addressed them in their materials and methods. As the TAs and coaches also made clear in many of their evaluative observations, the dominant student need was help in the unfamiliar intellectual task of actively ordering their knowledge in coherent ways.

It was clear, for example, to the modular chemistry TAs and astronomy coaches that many of their students had little experience of working with multiple sources, whether written or electronic. Where the text was one of several learning resources that they were expected to use, students needed help in ordering and organizing what they read. TAs and coaches who approved of students learning to read more widely also warned that, unless the teacher constantly clarified the links between class material and particular sources, some students got lost:

> Modular chemistry TA: They have to know where to go looking for the reading material that will explain or illustrate a particular idea to them. They are only used to working with a textbook, so they need to be helped to learn how to get an understanding from several different sources. It's a very new thing for them. That means starting by giving them a sheet that lays out all the sources for learning about different concepts. And then they need reminding as they go along that they need to read particular chapters or articles to really understand something. You really have to teach they how to do this and get them comfortable with it.

A related difficulty for students was to understand the progression of ideas that defined the class syllabus and how any new piece of learning fit into this structure:

> Coach 1: It's not supposed to be a lecture. It's supposed to be an introduction—like an outline.

> Coach 2: But a lot of the students don't get out of it as much as they should because the class format doesn't convey to them a sense of the direction they should go or give them ways to explain and connect difficult ideas.

In the previous chapter, I discuss the TAs' evaluative comments in support of more "signposting" of the intellectual direction taken by the course. In more conventionally taught science classes that work sequentially through a single text, the chapter headings and subheadings of the text act as a road map that order students' learning of individual pieces of knowledge. In any class that uses an array of sources (which may include a textbook, articles, and Internet resources), students have an immediate and pressing need to know where the teacher is taking them and how what they are currently learning fits into the structure of the class story line. They also need regular reminders of what they have already learned and how those pieces of knowledge connect with new work. Sources that illuminate particular ideas need to be made explicit in written guidelines that are reinforced by frequent reviews and reminders.[6] Where innovative teachers failed to sufficiently meet these needs, TAs were pressed to do so:

> The biggest pain is the fact that they have all of these modules plus the textbook, and they don't have somebody saying, "Well this chapter goes along with this section in your module, and these problems relate to that," instead of flipping through the book trying to find the right kind of problems. So maybe if there was some way to incorporate the textbook materials, questions, and problems with the modular materials so students could track their way around them. They need a sort of resource guide that you can give them at the start.

> My students would come to me pretty stressed out. They often wondered where the class was going and what they were supposed to get out of it. I was always trying to get them to see how different pieces hung together.

Concern that students need a framework in which to locate their learning prompted two astronomy coaches to question the presumption that students can understand everything by reading alone. They stressed how important explanation and discussion of material were in achieving comprehension and chafed at the limitations of their work role, which precluded them from meeting students' needs and reducing their level of frustration:

> Coach 1: You can't learn everything by reading. For me, I'm kind of half-and-half verbal and online reader. So, to me, hearing [Professor X] talk about it after I've already read it reinforces it. But I'm not sure that's the way a lot of the students feel. A lot of them want him to explain more so they can understand what they are reading.

> Coach 2: And they get so frustrated. They want me to explain the things they read but are just confused about. And we're not supposed to do that. We're not teaching TAs—we're coaches.

Like the modular chemistry TAs, they argued that students need the help of the teacher and their coaches (or TAs) in building a knowledge framework into which to set what they learn by reading:

> Coach 1: The hypertext has a lot of facts—beautiful animations, um, but it's hard to get the big picture from it. And the textbook is a marvelous book and has very good explanations. So, if people need to know what's going on, they just need to read it. The problem seems to be to tie the two resources together, you know, to actually point people to the pieces in the text that are going to help them explain what they are seeing on the hypertext.

> Coach 2: If he made the class questions more general and then said, "You can find this in hypertext section 2 or in book section 4 . . ."

Coach 3: Yes, exactly, double referencing! And that would allow the people who like to work with the book do that and those who like the hypertext go to that first.

Coach 1: Many of these students are freshmen, and they are not used to using a reference book. We have to help them learn to do that. You know, having a sheet showing the linkages would be a good help with that.

The prof needs to build that scaffolding in his class sessions so students can see where to hang the information and ideas that they are reading about. Freshmen can't build it on their own. I'm not sure I can either.

A contributory factor in determining both the degree of student difficulty with, or their level of resistance to, new learning methods—namely, class size—is one that innovators may or may not be able to address in any direct way. The group of astronomy coaches who worked in the class for more than one semester identified class size as a structural determinant of student learning attitudes and behavior. They noticed that it was possible to change unproductive student learning behavior and attitudes when both the professor and the coaches worked interactively with a fairly small class. However, in a later semester, when the class size was substantially increased, coaches saw that students were, again, depending on learned bad habits:

Coach 1: In a way you have to break the traditions again because of the problems created by going back to the big lecture. People fall back into bad old habits.

Coach 2: Yeah, we got people coming to office hours and working well on their group assignments. But now they've stopped coming, and the old bad lab habit of doing the least work in the fastest possible time has come right back again.

Thus, these more experienced coaches made a causal connection between large lecture format, as a structural aspect of the class, and the perpetuation of unproductive student behavior. In most universities, innovators may have little choice but to work with large classes. Indeed, it was precisely this situation that prompted the Berkeley innovators to seek to interrupt the pattern of passive learning encouraged by large lecture classes by developing the interactive potential of smaller groups led by TAs. As I argue throughout the remainder of this book, innovators who seek to move students to more active modes of learning within the structural limitations imposed by large classes must inevitably learn to work with and through their TAs in order to create small group learning environments. As I discuss in chapter 9, the structural reality of large classes will make the professional development of TAs one of the next major imperatives in the national effort to improve the teaching of undergraduate science.

TA Responses to Student Learning Problems

TAs explained students' problems by sympathetic reference to what it is like to be a a first-year student with limited experience by which to navigate early college classes. TAs are much closer to the students than are faculty, so TAs become more aware of common undergraduate difficulties. They may discover, for example, how easy it is to misperceive the level at which many incoming undergraduates can work:

> It took me a while to figure out how much help my students needed. Maybe I've just forgotten what it's like to be a freshman in college, but it seemed there were some ways in which they were quite unprepared for answering questions at all. And it didn't occur to me until I had been grading their stuff for a couple of weeks that this was a problem.

Looking back, they could also see how scared they had been as first- and second-year students, to ask questions and thereby risk exposure of their ignorance to the professor and other students:

> TA 1: I think a lot of them feel intimidated.

> TA 2: I think that changes with your time at school. I remember, I would never ask questions as a freshman, but as a junior, I began to stick my hand up all the time [*laughing*]. They say there's no such thing as a dumb question, but when you're sitting in a big lecture hall full of students, you learn that there *are* some dumb questions by seeing the look in the eyes of the professor and the students around you.

> TA 1: And in this class, the professor is pushing them to ask questions, and they are really very scared about that.

They also understood why learning in peer groups can seem risky to incoming students:

> It's their first year in college, and they can feel intimidated learning from one of their peers—"Why would they know it, and why don't I know it? They can understand it, so why can't I?" And it makes them feel dumb.

Thus, as the TAs were clearly aware, some student resistance in innovative classes arises because certain teaching strategies (such as question-and-answer sessions in class, and group learning) provoke fear of exposure among students, especially those who are underprepared. Students may be just as intimidated in a traditional class, but they have a better chance of avoiding such exposure. This observation by TAs was, again, supported by student interview data. In the first round of interviews with students in matched modular chemistry and more traditional chemistry classes, students offered evaluations of their small-group learning experiences.[7] Negative evaluations were 17 percent of all evaluations across both class types. We discovered that almost one-quarter (24 percent) of students' negative responses to small-group learning methods across both the modular and the more traditional classes arose from fear of exposing inadequacies in their knowledge or understanding. This was one of three types of negative evaluations. The other two were expressions of a preference for working alone (28 percent of all negative evaluations) and unsatisfactory experiences in groups that, in the students' view, had been inadequately designed or managed by faculty (48 percent of all negative evaluations). I discuss these issues in more detail in the next chapter.

TAs also saw the vulnerability of male first-year students (more so than that of women) who had not yet unlearned a disinclination to seek academic help when appropriate—an attitude that is reinforced in young male peer culture:

TA 1: I try to convey to my students, "Hey, I'm here, you know. Come ask me lots of questions." I get through to some, but a lot of freshmen are really hesitant.

TA 2: It's somewhat gender-related too. The women are generally more willing to come and ask questions or come to office hours. The men kinda find out later on that it would have been a good idea to do that [*laughing*], but they don't seem to know it at the time.

TA 1: Well, it's just young men. We're are all a bit cocky in the way we think, you know. We think we can figure it all out—hence all the jokes about men refusing to ask for directions.

This observation by the two TAs in modular chemistry reflects very accurately another finding in *Talking about Leaving* (Seymour and Hewitt 1997), that young men are especially vulnerable to failure in introductory science and mathematics classes when they do not understand how important it is to ask for help in a timely way or to seek out study groups.

TAs also understood that some part of help avoidance arises from the stigma of being seen as someone who needs help or as someone who gets "too friendly" with the TA. Those TAs who were sensitive to this issue worked around it in a variety of ways:

If they're like coming to office hours, nobody else knows about it. But if they talk to me in recitation, everybody sees, and then they are stuck with "Oh she's liked by the TA" sort of thing. So I try to sit every class in a different place, and I purposely sit next to somebody who never talked to me before.

The people who aren't talking to you in office hours or discussion, those are the people you need to talk to. And the lecture hall isn't the place to start those conversations. So I try to catch them in the lab sometimes, like when they're waiting for something or catch them just after lab.

TAs varied in the degree to which they sympathized with students (particularly first-year students) who struggled with a legacy of counterproductive learning behaviors and attitudes, inadequate academic preparation, and the difficulties of adjusting to the unfamiliar demands of college. At one extreme of empathy was this Berkeley TA:

> As we got later into the term, they got more and more tired. I mean, I felt really sorry for some of my students as I sat there watching them struggle to stay awake. I ended up bringing them cookies for midterm reviews: I gave them a cookie if they could answer a question.

By contrast, although TAs clearly understood that "formulaic" learning methods had been acquired and reinforced via teaching methods for which their students were not responsible, some TAs blamed students who clung to dysfunctional learning methods and attitudes. These TAs were impatient with students who were unwilling to let go of passive dependence on the teacher and take more responsibility for their own learning. One head TA observed,

> Many of them appreciated that this class wasn't just the same old thing, although part of them wanted the comfort of the old tried-and-true process, even if it did make them fall asleep from boredom. I see them responding positively to an interactive session in class or to group work where they can get a misconception clarified, and they don't have to sit mutely and miserably not understanding. But then some of them slip back into wanting not to have to make an effort to read and understand things for themselves.

This TA was one of a number who commented on the ambivalence or inconsistency of students caught between old and new ways of learning:

> As much as they complain about how dry so many lectures are and how boring, and then they are offered an alternative, you think they'd respond more positively—like get off their asses and do something for themselves—like go to the library, read the book. Perhaps it's our sound-bite culture that teaches them to want the information prepackaged—just one piece of paper with an outline of what's to be on the test, with the TA supposed to fill in the details. Our prof just refuses to buy into that.

SOURCES OF RESISTANCE TO NEW MODES OF LEARNING

TAs and coaches in all three initiatives found themselves confronted by a subset of students who expressed strong resistance to change in the traditional teacher–learner relationship. As indicated, the expectation that students become active thinkers was identified as a major trigger for resistance.

TAs could clearly identify several types of resistance to the class approach or methods by their different sources, as, for example, in this exchange:

> TA 1: There's a few types of students who won't like this kind of a class. There's a smallish number who just like to work on their own, answer everything on their own, and don't like any part of their grade to depend on getting the whole group to do a good piece of work.
>
> TA 2: Then there's a larger number who are just the opposite. They just want to be lectured to, and they don't want to do anything for themselves.

They distinguished between the resistance of students who struggled because they were underprepared and that of students with strong high school science backgrounds who had succeeded thus far by more traditional learning methods and were not open to the new learning approach:

> It's kind of a problem with students whose attitude is "This isn't what my high school chemistry class was like. This shouldn't be how a chemistry class is!" And their brain shuts off right there. In my lab section there were some students who thought, because they'd had AP chemistry, they were too good for this. And they just wouldn't do the work. In the end, they didn't do all that well, and, I mean, they would have gotten so much more out of it—'cause they were bright kids—if they had just been open to trying to learn it this way.
>
> TA 1: Some of the students with a strong chemistry background, I don't see them liking it as much. They would be like, "Just teach me the chemistry, or . . ."
>
> TA 2: "Forget the fluff."
>
> TA 1: I think the class splits that way—maybe half and half.
>
> TA 2: Definitely.
>
> TA 1: Because some people really do love it and they do very well.
>
> TA 2: Yeah, the ones who are prepared to give it a try end up doing really well.

TAs also distinguished between what they saw as an understandable level of frustration or anxiety among students who were trying but found the material or mode of learning difficult and those students who did not try, either because (as indicated above) they disapproved of the teacher's approach or because the method demanded so much more of them than did a traditional lecture class. As the following discussion illustrates, the astronomy coaches had no patience with students who sought to get through the course by making little effort:

> Coach 1: I think we have to dispel the rumor that you pay to be taught, and that means just sitting there are absorbing prepackaged material. Some people say that they could just have sat in a library and learned it by themselves. But that's

not true. There's a whole lot of thought and structure that has gone into developing the hypertext, organizing the work with the coaches, and preparing all of this stuff for them to work on in groups. And the professor is far more accessible than lecture profs often are. He goes out of his way to be there in person and to answer their e-mails.

Coach 2: I think this sort of protest is often a cop-out. You know, "I just want to sort of sit here and slide through. I want to sit in the lecture half awake and then buy class notes." Some of the people in my group continually don't show up, don't do their work. They don't apologize for not being there, and they really don't care if they are letting the rest of the group down by not preparing their work. I have been working with them all semester so you really get to know pretty well whose concerns you need to attend to and who is making a fuss but no effort.

Coach 1: Yeah, there's a world of difference between that sort of protest and the people I want to spend my time helping—the ones who are trying but are hitting up against some difficulties.

Coach 3: And when the prof said right away that he was going to take attendance, that alone scared off a lot of people who aren't very diligent about their college work. They make a big thing about it interfering with their freedom of choice. But, we could see right off that those students were going to be the slackers in our groups. And that's how it panned out.

Modular chemistry TAs defined some student protests about the learning methods required by the class as being dishonest:

TA 1: They knew this course was taught differently from some other semesters, but some of them were still resentful at having to be "the teacher's lab rats." But I say they could easily have taken it another semester if it was bothering them that much that it gets in the way of doing the work. They liked to use that as a scapegoat for everything, and I don't buy it.

TA 2: I think a number of people used that excuse—to complain about the course structure. It was a convenient way to rationalize why they weren't doing well. There were two like that in my group, and the truth is, they weren't doing the work.

One of the Berkeley TAs observed that it was not necessarily important that students liked or approved particular class methods. She agreed with the course designers that some things that students did not like had desirable outcomes:

Sticking strictly to the class policy of not giving students answers to questions set as assignments annoyed all of the students. And sometimes it annoyed all of the TAs because it was very hard to stick to. But the one thing it definitely did was to keep all of those student hungry. They wanted to know and were frustrated, so they actually dug in and kept working because it was the only way to get their work done.

As some of the observations cited in this discussion suggest, TAs can be a moral force in the service of course goals—particularly those that emphasize students' taking an active role in their own learning progress. They are not necessarily dismayed at or swayed by student protest, and often make moral distinctions between student concerns that they define as making legitimate claims on their help and support and those that do not.

Across all three initiatives, some TAs and coaches, especially those who had worked in their innovative classes for two semesters, offered a longer view of students' difficulties with the shifts in learning required. They observed that, with time, students get used to the new modes of learning and that both their problems and their protests tend to fade:

> Just at the beginning of the year, there was a negative attitude among the freshmen talking to one another about doing the chemistry modules. But that faded after a while, and I don't hear it at all now.

> In the midsemester evaluations, the students did seem to be kind of down on everything, but, by the end of the semester, they tended to be kind of getting into the groove. I think it was really just overwhelming for a lot of people in the beginning.

> We lost a few students in the first two weeks but not after that. There's the initial shock, and then things settle down. I think that as time went on, the students got used to it, and they knew how to apply what they were learning in class to the lab work.

This group of TAs took a balanced view of student protest. They directly addressed what they saw as flaws in class design or the implementation of particular strategies, but they also distinguished between student concerns that seemed to warrant their attention and those that did not:

> TA 1: It's my impression that there will be a few people who will come out of this class still unhappy.

> TA 2: But there's always people who come out of classes unhappy.

> TA 1: Yeah, they sort of won't settle down and enjoy the class. There'll be a few. You just have to expect that.

SUMMARY AND IMPLICATIONS

The diagnosis of student difficulties and negative responses offered by the TAs and coaches speaks to a set of concerns shared by innovative and more traditional teachers. We have learned something about how student resistance to faculty teaching is perceived and explained from our interviews with modular chemistry innovators and their departmental colleagues. This faculty sample reflected a wide spectrum of opinion and practice—from interest and engagement in innovation at one end to angry objection to the innovative approach at the other. Many faculty between these extremes supported the innovators' professional right to change their classroom methods; some were making small changes to their own courses; and many departments were rethinking aspects of their curriculum. However, with notable exceptions, most innovators formed a small subgroup within more traditionally minded departments.

Both from interviews with the colleagues of modular chemistry participants and from the modular faculty's characterization of attitudes that they encountered in their departments and discipline, we learned that student resistance to science learning is commonly identified as being normative and intractable. This is especially the case in large lecture classes and their associated labs where student dropout rates are high, class attendance is low, and student distancing behavior is commonplace. Students indicate their disengagement from the class by arriving late, sitting at the back, talking, reading nonclass material, doing work for other classes, eating, sleeping, and failing to ask or answer questions; and, in lab, by perfunctory performances completed in the shortest possible time. In a study at the University of Nebraska, Lincoln, two-thirds of the TAs in conventional lecture classes in the forty-five disciplines surveyed reported instances of what I have defined as "normative resistance." Students were described as coming to class unprepared, arriving late, frequently missing class, looking bored or disinterested, yawning during the lecture, and failing to respond to their TAs' questions. Over half of the TAs were bothered by students who ate or drank during class; socialized while they were teaching; challenged, questioned, or contradicted them during class; and packed up their books before the class session was due to end (Luo, Bellows, and Grady 2000).

As do TAs in these interviews, faculty comment on students' overreliance on memorization and their focus on grades rather than comprehension or effort. They lament students' poor ability to transfer knowledge and regard cheating as endemic. Faculty explanations for this state of affairs are often focused on the perceived moral and intellectual flaws of students as a group: students are lazy, do not want to learn, will not take responsibility for their own learning, are ill-prepared by their high schools, are of lower intellectual caliber than hitherto, and are not to be trusted. In studies of TA work in conventional classes, Worthen (1992) reports that TAs are frustrated by what they perceive to be unmotivated students. Similarly, Peterson (1990) found that anthropology TAs were frustrated by student disinterest, lack of preparedness, and resistance to intellectual challenge. Faculty tend to cope with these student characteristics in a somewhat fatalistic manner—by ignoring them or defining them as regrettable but normal student behavior. Their explanations largely focus on perceived flaws in the K–12 school system and on the personal inadequacies of the students themselves. In the four studies of TAs working in conventional classes already cited (i.e., Peterson 1990; Worthen 1992; Hesse 1993; and Luo, Bellows, and Grady 2000), TA perceptions of their students' shortcomings echo the tendency of faculty to blame these behaviors on students' moral and intellectual defects. In light of this fatalism, it is perhaps not surprising that little research effort has been expended on understanding the causes of student resistance to traditional modes of science teaching and learning.

However, the community of science innovators chooses not to ignore or normalize the dysfunctional aspects of science teaching and learning and defines them as system induced. They argue that students do not learn science well by traditional teaching methods. Innovators also ascribe a wider range of outcomes to the inadequacies of more traditional science teaching: many potential science majors are lost, including students of color and women of all ethnicities; the shortage of trained science and mathematics teachers continues to grow; and science illiteracy is widespread. These related concerns have driven the national effort for improved undergraduate science teaching for over a decade (Seymour 2001).

Classroom innovators, such as those whose work is showcased here, are like fish who become aware of the water in which they swim. They have taken the position that disengaged student behaviors are system effects rather than part of the intrinsic nature of students as a species. As innovators start to change the environment in their own classrooms and labs, students, TAs, and their colleagues take notice, and some of them resist. As the TAs have clarified, students who have learned how to swim in traditional science classes find that their techniques no longer work well and may feel that they are drowning. Their resistance to learning in new ways is noted by the innovators' colleagues who may suspend their normal practice of blaming students and instead blame innovative teachers for churning up the water. Understandably, in the face of student discontent and collegial disapproval, faculty innovators are concerned both to demonstrate and to disseminate the successful outcomes of their work while bringing to wider attention the dysfunctions of the forms of teaching and learning that their efforts are designed to address.

In this context, the TAs' analysis is particularly valuable, grounded as it is in close observation of students and faculty in classrooms and labs with changed learning objectives. As described, TAs make the point that innovative courses demand greater student engagement with, and responsibility for, their own learning. This expectation inevitably exposes inadequacies in some students' customary learning practices—insofar as these are passive and teacher dependent—and thereby provoke student protest at the discomfort this creates. The TAs' portrayal of learned attitudes and behaviors that inhibit active student engagement with their own learning is, as I have indicated, built from many observations of particular facets of the syndrome. No single TA laid out all of its elements and connected them into an explanatory model. However, the composite picture that emerges is clear. TAs collectively explain many of their students' problems and protests as arising from inadequacies in their preparation as learners that are exposed by the demands made on them by innovative college science classes. The methods of the innovative teachers thwart a set of expectations and habits that amount to a formula for learning science. The formulaic approach is learned in high school or earlier but may remain undisturbed or become reinforced in college science classes. Because it may serve students over a period of years without being called into question, these expectations and behaviors acquire the character of an implicit contract between teachers and their students. Resistance to faculty teaching methods in traditional science classes may be viewed as an effort by students to draw faculty attention to parts of the contract that are not, in the students' view, being upheld.

The fundamental elements of the traditional implied contract as identified by the TAs are the teacher as the active giver of information and the learner as its passive receiver. "Learning" entails memorizing parts of the information and carrying out tasks. Rewards (in the form of grades) are given both for making an effort and for performing well. Grades become desirable in their own right, detached from the learning or skill they represent. The teacher's power to compel work from the student derives largely from his or her monopoly of grade distribution. In a situation where the learner is dependent on the teacher both for information and for grades, the student learns to focus on performance rather than on learning, for fear of receiving an unacceptable grade—that is, a grade that is thought insufficient to secure the next stage in acquiring desired credentials. Students often express wheedling, bargaining, or even aggressive behavior in seeking to obtain better grades. These behaviors reflect an instrumental attitude in which "education" is seen as a means to obtain the grades and other success markers required to achieve particular career or income goals. Some students develop a cost-effective approach to their progress through high school or college in which the amount of time and effort expended in acquiring any course grade is weighed against that required for a grade of similar numeric weight in other courses. The peer culture reinforces this commodified view of education by offering admiration to students who gain high grades with minimal effort (or who successfully project the appearance of doing so). Spending longer on homework, labs, projects, reading, or writing than what seems necessary to achieve a particular grade is to be avoided.

Accustomed to being rewarded for mechanical performances, students are often bored in class. However, they may respond with anxiety or protest when teachers break from their role as knowledge distributors by using strategies that refocus attention on comprehension, exploration, discovery, or the connection and application of ideas. Students may react angrily to such breaches of the implied classroom contract. They may respond with anxiety about the risk that activities with uncertain outcomes pose to their grades, and cling to memorization as their dominant mode of "study." They may express frustration because they have not acquired the skills to learn actively and independently. They therefore find it difficult to discuss an idea, make an argument, write (and edit) in discursive or formal modes, approach a novel problem, make a synthesis from multiple reading sources, or analyze authentic lab data. Or they may simply not comply— by not reading in preparation for class or not pulling their weight in a group task.

Thus, the longer-term outcomes of learning how to learn by formula and of seeking to uphold the classroom contract include difficulties in developing independence and responsibility as learners, constructing a personal learning framework, and acquiring the skills and habits of mind required for more advanced work. Depending on the quality of the learning experiences that first-year students bring from their high school classes and encounter in their early college classes, they may be challenged to bridge a gap between passive, teacher-dependent learning and active, self-directed learning.[8] Or, they may be enabled to continue in accustomed mode by college courses that reinforce giver–receiver role behavior until they are confronted by teachers who are ready to redraft the contract.

In this chapter, I have focused on the ability of the TAs and coaches to collectively diagnose the nature and sources of student problems and of resistance to innovation, and to identify strategies (whether by faculty or themselves) that can ameliorate both types of difficulty. Learning to address student concerns without taking the students' critique personally depends on developing shared understandings of the different sources of student problems and how to respond appropriately to them. As noted, many TAs clearly have insights into particular dimensions of student dissent and difficulty, but none put this information together into an explanatory framework that they could articulate as such. Thus, only by group discussion could their individual understandings become a shared body of experience and reflection on which all TAs and their faculty can draw. Similarly, a set of strategies by which TAs can address student problems and protest needs to be collectively developed by TAs and faculty in regular working conversations. These processes are part of professional development for TAs or coaches (and, indeed, for faculty), and they are perhaps best undertaken as part of formal weekly meetings. These and other issues of professional development for TAs are discussed in chapter 9.

In the next two chapters, I consider how some of the TAs respond to these and other challenges of working in innovative courses and how, in this process, TAs and coaches effectively redefine their roles. The distinctions that TAs and coaches make between student difficulties arising from their efforts to adjust to new ways of learning and their resistance based on attitudes and behaviors derived from past learning experience, are translated into ad hoc TA coping strategies. Because many aspects of the new classroom are novel to faculty and their TAs, both groups often find themselves flying by the seat of their pants. However, out of experimentation and discussion, some strategies emerge that offer the promise of more stable solutions.

NOTES

1. Streveler and King (2000) found that engineering students at the Colorado School of Mines were overdependent on their TAs and treated them as an "absolute authority" on class material. They resisted TAs' attempts to guide them through the discovery process; some students interpreted their TAs' efforts as trying to trick them or withhold information. This finding is confirmed in the work of Alexander, Penberthy, Millar, and Standifer (1996).

2. This question-of-the-day strategy was used in the modular courses of one participating college but is not necessarily found in other modular chemistry classes.

3. This finding is also confirmed in Millar and colleagues (1997). Additionally, Nurrenbern, Mickiewicz, and Francisco (1999) found that when TAs refused to supply their students with the answers to set problems, the undergraduates became frustrated. They sometimes defined their TAs as being incompetent, or accused them of not doing their job.

4. Hesse (1993) found that TAs teaching in conventional classes were also frustrated by their undergraduates' resistance to reading materials that were perceived as being difficult. When students claimed that the material was poorly or obscurely written, the TAs interpreted this as evidence of the students' intellectual laziness.

5. In a study of inexperienced TAs working in an inquiry-based nonmajor biology course at Arizona State University, Lawson (2000) found that the TAs' most serious problems were their students' passivity and lack of participation. Students did not appear to know how to get started on the inquiries, did not see them as being relevant to their lives, did not want to think for themselves, were disruptive, and wanted the "right" answers given to them. Similarly, in a study by McManus (2002), TAs using active learning techniques in an oceanography course reported problems in motivating and engaging students in their learning.

6. A fuller discussion of signposting and TAs' awareness of its importance is offered in chapter 9.

7. Findings from the analysis of these student interviews (outlined in chapter 2) are reported in Seymour, Pedersen-Gallegos, Laursen, and Weise (n.d.).

8. The dominance of formulaic forms of learning in high schools has begun to change; increasingly, high school teachers are using active learning methods. Thus, some entering undergraduates will be obliged to adjust to the more passive pedagogical approach of science faculty in higher education.

7

Redefining the Teaching Assistants' Role in Innovative Courses: Expansion of Traditional Work Roles

What may already have become apparent to the reader is that working in innovative courses prompts changes in the ways in which the TAs and coaches define their work roles and respond to their challenges. The most basic and universal change is that working for innovators (especially those who are continuing to rethink and refine elements of their new courses) requires more time and effort from teaching assistants than does teaching the same course in a more traditional manner.[1] Across the three different initiatives, this extra work included keeping abreast of, and sometimes helping to develop, new class and lab materials; learning to work with new forms of learning activities and assessments; dealing with student responses to theses; and helping to resolve unforeseen implementation problems. As the following observation indicates, TAs who approved of the innovative class approach were willing to do this:

> There's definitely a lot more work required and constant work too because there's new labs to work through, discussion questions every week to prepare, and constantly persuading students to work this way and put in the effort for themselves. In other classes I've worked in, you have far less responsibility. Here, you're always fixing things that aren't quite worked out yet. I actually think it's a good class because of that, because you always have to keep on top of things. It's a lot of work, but it's always interesting.

However, beyond the additional time and effort required, the challenges and opportunities that arise for TAs and coaches in their innovation support work prompt changes in their work role and in how they perceive it. While some formal responsibilities are the same as those for conventional courses, they are expanded and enhanced to serve new course goals. This broadening is partly instigated by the innovators, but, as the data indicate, it is also an inventive response by TAs themselves. In addition, whole new dimensions to the TAs' role emerge that have only slight precedents.

In this and the following chapter, I discuss the role expansions and emergent new role functions that are evident in the accounts of TAs and coaches. Some of these role redefinitions are, as in the Berkeley project, an intentional part of the innovation. However, most arose spontaneously as TAs and coaches responded to the daily need to make aspects of the innovation work in accordance with the new course goals. I found that, depending on the nature of the professional development provided to their TAs, the innovators were somewhat aware of the expanded contribution that their TAs were making. However, its extent will, I think, surprise them. The colleagues of faculty innovators may also be surprised to learn how much more graduate and undergraduate teaching assistants, as colleagues, can contribute in support of student learning than what they may have assumed.

The challenge of dealing with student responses to new courses falls heavily on TAs. Both the students' problems with new learning methods and their resistance to them arise in many facets of the TAs' work.[2] I discuss the ways in which TAs approach both of these in context rather than as separate issues. As in the last chapter, I attempt to draw a composite picture: not every TA or coach experienced all of the changes described. Most information was embedded in descriptions and discussions of their work; only a few (including some head TAs) were able to abstract from these details the overall changes that they observed in their role.

TAs' accounts of their work reference five traditional responsibilities of their work roles. Three of these responsibilities involve interactive work with undergraduates—namely, their work in small groups; their laboratory roles; and their academic support for students, largely in office hours. The fourth involves some degree of responsibility for grading and test setting; and the fifth, some exercise of delegated authority.[3] The nature of this authority varies but may include checking on nonattenders, securing submission of work for grading, or negotiating grade disputes.

In all three initiatives, the ways in which TAs were expected to perform their responsibilities in each of these five areas were somewhat prescribed by the innovating faculty or the course design (e.g., in the discovery-focused labs of modular chemistry and in the worksheet sessions in the Berkeley initiative). However, the data strongly indicate the presence of an organic process of interpretation and expansion of these traditional areas of responsibility. This arose as a function of TAs' and coaches' figuring out as they went along how best to implement aspects of their faculty's broadly conceived, but often incompletely operationalized, learning goals.

This process of TA improvisation did not, however, expand the overall TA role in random directions. Indeed, the process of role redefinition was remarkably consistent across the institutions, courses, and types of innovation represented in the interview sample. Three forms of behavior and attitudes emerged as a response to the challenges of meeting course goals, faculty expectations, and class logistics. These shaped the ways in which the TAs and coaches defined the boundaries of their work and approached their responsibilities. Expressed in behavioral terms, TA assistants became

Creative troubleshooters, who spotted and addressed day-to-day problems, sought to resolve those that lay within their skills and knowledge, and alerted faculty to difficulties beyond their provenance

Consultants, who offered faculty feedback, analysis, and advice grounded in their experiences

Collegial collaborators, who shouldered responsibility for student learning alongside the faculty and with each other, took ownership of their work, and thought creatively about facilitating learning in their interactions with students

These forms of behavior and their accompanying attitudes were evident in how TAs undertook their more traditional responsibilities and engaged in new ways with students, faculty, each other, and with the materials and methods of the courses.

Across the initiatives, these three forms of response emerged partly as a consequence of TAs' and coaches' seeking to implement innovation goals in situations where the teachers' methods were still in flux and where unforeseen issues arose day to day. They were also a response to fundamental changes in teaching and learning relationships. The essence of all of these innovations was to redefine what it means to be teachers, learners, and teaching assistants. Where innovations achieve a steady state, some TA role improvisations will fade; others may be incorporated as regular features of the course. If the course is perceived as being successful enough to be incorporated as a regular departmental offering, or if courses with a similar philosophy and methods are developed, it will become imperative to rethink what is offered by way of TA preparation and support. The TAs and coaches in these three initiatives clarify the educational needs they evoke and offer pointers to the kinds of role preparation that will meet them.

Individual TAs and coaches varied in the degree to which they responded to the challenges of working in innovative classes by infusing their more traditional responsibilities with troubleshooting, consulting, and collegial attitudes and behaviors. Similarly, not all TAs and coaches extended their role by undertaking new responsibilities that reflected these same three forms of engagement, nor did they do so to the same degree. Developing collegial collaborative working relationships with the professor and with each other, and a sense of responsibility for student learning and the success of the innovative class, was the highest level on a spectrum of work-role extensions. How far TAs and coaches progressed in developing their role in these ways varied across the three initiatives and, in the case of modular chemistry, among participating classes in different institutions.

As indicated in table 7.1, taking the three initiatives together, approximately 84 percent (92 out of the 110 interviewees) offered observations on what they were doing and how they were thinking about their work in which it was evident that to various degrees they were voluntarily extending the limits of their formal responsibilities. By "voluntarily extending," I mean being actively engaged in support of course goals in ways that transcended what they were required to do. This count comprised that majority of teaching assistants who approved of their faculty's learning objectives, including those who offered caveats about the methods used to achieve them. It also included three TAs who expressed reservations about course goals or methods but who nevertheless were engaged in troubleshooting to make the day-to-day details of the innovation work. Thus, as in all professional life, expressions of critique and dissent do not necessarily betoken unwillingness to make a good contribution.

Table 7.1 shows the number and percentage of TAs and coaches in the three initiatives whose commentaries on their work reflected active engagement in troubleshooting, communication with their faculty about ways to make the course work better, and collegial collaboration with faculty to facilitate student learning. The count includes TAs and coaches who applied one or more of these three forms of engagement in the way that they performed their more traditional functions. It also counts those who applied them as part of new forms of engagement with students, faculty, and each other and with the materials and methods of their courses. Inherently, troubleshooting and collegial collaboration are categories that reflect active engagement. In the consulting category, however, TAs and coaches were not counted if they offered advice during the interview but gave no indication that they were also offering this feedback to their faculty. The most common form of work role expansion was troubleshooting. Across the three initia-

Table 7.1. Number and percentage of teaching assistants and coaches demonstrating engagement as troubleshooters, consultants, and collegial collaborators, by project

	Trouble-shooters		Consultants		Collegial Collaborators		Total	
Project	n	%	n	%	n	%	N	%
Interactive Astronomy	26	100	22	85	18	69	26	100
Modular chemistry	39	93	34	81	28	67	42	100
Berkeley TA initiative	27	64	25	60	18	43	42	100
Total	92	84	81	74	64	58	110	100

tives, most TAs and coaches (84 percent) were actively seeking to address the day-to-day problems that they encountered. This was highly evident among the twenty-six undergraduate coaches working in Interactive Astronomy, all of whom engaged in troubleshooting course-implementation problems, both individually and in discussion with each other. This was the most loosely structured of the three initiatives and was still evolving when the second round of interviews were conducted. The coaches clearly saw themselves as having useful roles to play in shaping the ultimate form of the course.

Their willingness both to expand their responsibilities and to undertake new ones reflect their high degree of buy-in to the course goals, the weekly opportunities to discuss and resolve emergent issues, a good level of rapport with the faculty innovator, and a strong sense that their input was valued by him. These factors also contribute to their high level of engagement as consultants who offered feedback, analysis, and advice (twenty-two of twenty-six) and their strong sense of collaborative co-responsibility for student learning with their professor (eighteen of twenty-six).

The high degree of active engagement among the forty-two TAs working in the modular chemistry courses is perhaps the most remarkable of the three initiatives because it is not the outcome of an interacting TA group working for a single professor (as with Interactive Astronomy) or for a small group of innovators (as in the Berkeley initiative). The undergraduate modular TAs worked in seven different institutions, often with two or more faculty contributing to the modular courses. The similarity of the TAs' responses across these more variable situations is quite remarkable—thirty-nine acting as troubleshooters and thirty-four acting as consultants to faculty. Collegial collaboration by twenty-eight TAs spread across seven institutions is as high as that demonstrated by the twenty-six coaches in the single-class astronomy initiative.

The Berkeley counts reflect the difficult early days of the initiative followed by considerable improvement in TA morale, buy-in, and engagement by the time of the second interviews. As discussed in chapter 3, the Berkeley initiative faced more difficulties in getting TA support for the initiative. The high proportion of graduate TAs included a subset whose opposition to the goals and methods of the course reflected some of the professional identity problems found among graduate students but not normally among undergraduates. Notwithstanding these constraints, what is impressive is that two-thirds of the forty-two TAs showed active engagement in troubleshooting and consulting with faculty and the course coordinator and that eighteen saw themselves as making collegial contributions to the course.

The TAs and coaches described three factors that determined their degree of willingness to contribute to the success of the course: professional development, regular meetings with each other and with the faculty, and the experience of faculty openness to critique and suggestion. No teaching assistant in this sample experienced all three, but many reported two. As discussed in chapter 9, adequate professional development was the most advocated and least experienced of these variables. A collegial attitude by faculty was seen as the most significant factor in prompting a high degree of engagement in the innovation.

In this chapter, I discuss how the five more traditional areas of the teaching assistants' work role were augmented by their active engagement as troubleshooters, consultants, and active collaborators. To repeat, these traditional roles are as follows: work in small groups; laboratory support roles; academic support for students, largely in office hours; some degree of responsibility for grading and test setting; and some exercise of delegated authority. These five formal areas of work are retained as part of each innovation. However, their scope is enlarged, partly by the character of the innovation but also by the creative response of TAs and coaches to course goals. I discuss each augmentation of the TAs' traditional role responsibilities in an order that reflects the relative emphasis given to them by TAs. In the following chapter, I discuss how TAs and coaches developed as troubleshooters, consultants, and collaborators in ways that transcended the boundaries of their formal role responsibilities and thereby increased the chances of success for these innovative classes.

SMALL-GROUP WORK WITH UNDERGRADUATES

Across the three initiatives, the coaches provide the most complete case study of the development of an enhanced TA or coach role in small group work with undergraduates. Both the worksheets in the Berkeley initiative and the modular chemistry handbooks provided guidelines for the conduct of group activities that structured the TAs' contributions. However, the Interactive Astronomy coaches were engaged with their professor in discovering what were more and less effective ways to put his ideas about peer learning into practice. Their experience is offered as an illustration of what issues innovators and their TAs (or in this case, coaches) are likely to encounter when making small-group learning a central feature of a new course and how TAs can contribute to its development and, in the process, augment their own role.

The astronomy professor made "learning teams," each led by a coach, a major vehicle by which students learned and discussed course material. The process of students' learning in these teams was established in principle more than in operational detail, and coaches experimented with ways to make their teams operate effectively. In the process, they learned something about dealing with difficult group members and reached conclusions about how groups should be structured and managed and how group tasks should be set up. The professor encouraged them to share their observations and recommendations and discussed their feedback in weekly meetings. They were confirmed in their emergent roles as consultants and collaborators because he heeded their advice. In the process of trying out the professor's initial ideas about running the learning groups, the TAs made fundamental discoveries that they offered to him as active troubleshooters and collaborating consultants. Their discoveries and consequent advice to their professor are reviewed in the following sections.

Discoveries in the Essentials of Group Setup and Management

The coaches discovered that the most critical requirement in getting a team to work together at all is that they be given something meaningful to do:

Coach 1: And you can't just expect people sitting in a room to be a team all at once and figure out what to do. You have to force them together somehow.

Coach 2: Yeah, you have to plan something that makes them gel.

Coach 1: By now, a lot of the groups have gelled, but he could have had that happen a whole lot sooner. It's a matter of knowing what to ask them to do.

They also discovered, and conveyed to their professor, how important it is to give groups assignments that can be done *only* as a group:[4]

The aim is to read it, learn it, and then explain it to each other, and my groups have really been doing that. They sit together, and, if somebody has trouble, they help each other out. But they still do most of the work independently. That's what we needed to fix.

The prof and I have had some discussions about some learning teams that aren't acting like a team. In my opinion, it comes down to the fact that you're assigned four questions, and you have to do them. That's an individual assignment, yet you're in a group. It's not really a group activity.

Group assignments also need to be sufficiently capacious and complex to require a division of labor, a synthesis of what is learned, and ways to make individuals accountable to the enterprise:

Coach 1: When you set a question to answer, it has to be complex enough for people to go off in twos and investigate pieces of it. And they have to come back and report to each other because there's some big decisions to make. And they need an assignment that has to be turned in and that needs everyone's input. They've all got to be accountable for doing some of it and then putting the results together.

Coach 2: That's why we saw more unity with the projects—just because they had to split up the work—no one person could do it all. People won't necessarily work together as a group unless you give them a real group job to do—even small things that actually require them to talk to each other.

The coaches advised their professor that projects need to be tractable, attainable in the time available, and should address central themes of the course:

The projects were great for getting people to work, but the students didn't necessarily think they were well designed. They enjoyed coming together and doing something, but they wanted something that was more central, less offside. We told him that the students thought the projects were not well correlated with the class material.

They also advised their professor to begin project work early in the course because doing so helps the groups to coalesce around their first task and quickly get down to work:

Coach 1: It's valuable, I think, to do projects early. A lot of the teams worked better after we started the projects, but that was about one month into the course. We explained that it would help to do them earlier.

Coach 2: That's right. Everyone has certain tasks, and it comes together as a whole. I mean, they just work together so unbelievably better than when they are answering class discussion questions.

The coaches also gave a lot of thought to group size and composition and discussed with each other and with their professor alternative ways to set up the groups.[5] Each coach had two learning groups to run, and these varied from four or five students to ten or eleven. The coaches came to a consensus that a group of seven or eight was best. They offered two main reasons: first, such a group is large enough to accommodate variations in personality, levels of knowledge, and learning styles; second, it can tolerate the absence of one or two members each week and still be functional. Groups of four or five were seen as being risky because, with absence, they could easily becomes nonfunctioning pairs or trios. (By contrast, the Berkeley TAs, who already had student sections of twenty-eight to thirty, hypothesized that groups of around ten would work best. However, they did not get the chance to discover how smaller groups worked.)[6]

Regarding group composition, the coaches were both experimenters and consultants as the professor tried various ways to balance the makeup of the learning groups. They described how, in one semester, the professor had used SAT scores to try to cluster students with others in broadly the same performance range. However, the coaches preferred to see in their groups a balance of academic backgrounds and other characteristics. They reported that class schedules can conspire to place students from the same group of majors together and that simple random mixing can also produce unhappy lopsided groups with, for example, too many science majors or only one woman. The coaches cited unbalanced groups as being among their less-successful groups—for example, a group exclusively composed of arts majors who all struggled together and a group of science majors who never saw the point of discussing the material. They advocated sufficient tinkering with group composition to produce groups that were balanced by sex and academic background.

The coaches discussed these observations and conclusions with each other and with the professor and seemed confident that their information and advice would be taken into account in adjusting the course. The weekly meetings were the main forum for feedback and discussion and, where the professor made changes that incorporated their input, this forced the coaches' self-image as his active consultants.

Using Small Groups to Meet Course Learning Goals

Becoming collaboratively and creatively engaged in their work with learning teams was contingent on the coaches' understanding and approving the goals of the course and on an awareness of how much the innovator depended on them to make his strategies effective. In the following examples, the coaches used the groups as a vehicle to make their students more independent, responsible, and collaborative learners:

> One thing the prof is real clear about is, "I don't want you to give them the answers or tell them where to look." So, I say, "Ask your teammate. See if they know." I always try that. And, "Ask your backup and get them to help you find the answer." I try to be very consistent, and I think my kids aren't having a problem with it now. They know this is how we are learning the material, and they need to work at it on their own or with a peer.[7]

They brainstormed together what strategies might better serve the learning goals—sometimes to resolve a problem, sometimes to add an improvement:

> The prof's discussion questions are really thought provoking. And I think we should suggest having them talk about what the question means in group and do some outside work on it using the web and an array of source books. He could call on perhaps two groups each class to present what they have discovered. So everyone has to be down there in the front of the entire class to present it together—throw up some transparencies and say, "This is what we've found." It would distribute the work and make everyone take it seriously and be responsible for offering a decent answer.

The coaches were good observers of the dynamics of their groups and were quick to make use of whatever strategy seemed to work:

> At the start of the semester, we didn't have enough laptops for everyone so, in group 5, we had to have two or three students working together on the questions. Even though they each had their own computer in a few weeks, that group still worked well together compared with other groups. So, this semester, I started them all off two to a computer, and, guess what, same result!

They reported great satisfaction when their efforts bore fruit and they were able to harness the talents of more diffident members for the benefit of the whole group:

> I have one person in each group that doesn't like to work in groups. At first, they really sort of resisted it, but they've both come around. [Student A] especially would get in there real fast so she could have her own computer, but she's become a great resource. She's a bio major and is very bright, and the physics and other stuff that a lot of people don't understand, she already knows. I encouraged the others to ask her questions, and she's really been able to help people. And that's the point—that's the whole point of this philosophy—knowing it because you can explain to someone else. And I think it's helped her. Seeing how hesitant she was before, now she'll sit with the group and talk to people.

Building Morale and Addressing Resistance

In a class where the mechanics of the learning teams were still under construction and review, not only did the coaches work to make the students collaborate more effectively, but they also used their work with groups to address student resistance to aspects of the class. The coaches took primary responsibility for establishing and sustaining group cohesion and morale and saw this as a good way to preempt disengagement:

> In both of my teams, I began by sitting them down and explaining as much as I could about how the course operated and how we would work in the team. And then I encouraged them just to talk about themselves, and it actually got quite personal. And I always check in with them every week to see how they are doing. I think that's important. You need to build ties across the group before anything comes up that's going to test them.

The coaches supported the professor's practice of visiting each learning team once during the semester and applauded him for soliciting students' concerns and for acting on them:

> Coach 1: They definitely got to interact with him on a personal level. They like the fact that he's actually taking the time to come and visit them. And I'm pretty sure he got around to everybody.

Coach 2: When he came to one of my groups, he asked them, "What are your concerns about the class? Are you having any problems?" And this one girl told him, "I just don't see the bigger picture." And the group agreed with her. I think that kind of helped him to see that they needed some lectures.

However, the coaches saw the main responsibility for building group morale as lying with them, rather than with their professor:

I'd definitely support him coming into the learning teams. Maybe not the first ones because I need time to get to know my team and get them going on the style of work they're doing. But maybe after that.

The expert coaches advised that the best way to get students to take ownership of the group's work was to set meaningful assignments right at the outset, get straight into the work, and establish a tone of enjoyable active engagement:

I think that if you get the work started straight away and set the norm, people pick it up and start doing it themselves. Then the more ownership they take, the more they enjoy it. I've got some people in my groups who are awesome—they have just decided that they want to get the most out of this.

Some coaches who had struggled to get a good level of group engagement also advocated being clear with students about their expectations, enforcing the rules consistently, and sticking to whatever procedures were established at the outset. They were pleased that the professor had come to the same conclusions:

Coach 1: It really was like pulling teeth to have them turn from the computer, let go of the keyboard, and sit together and have a conversation. I'd say, "Okay, let's discuss this. Don't read it off your printout. Explain what you have learned to the rest of us." And it was so difficult to get them into that mode. So I think [Professor X] has the right idea about enforcing the method. Starting next semester, "You will have these answers prepared by the time you show up in group."

Coach 2: Yeah, there are a number of things that absolutely have to be laid down in the beginning and stuck to consistently in order to stop the drift.

Coach 1: And we threatened to grade them on having their answer done, but then we didn't do it, so they never saw anything happen. That was a big mistake.

The coaches agreed on the need to act together as a group in setting standards for the conduct of their learning teams, using their authority to get students to participate, establishing consequences for noncompliance, being consistent, and supporting each other:

Coach 1: It would be really useful for us to decide how we're gonna run things and set some standards. I think it's really important for the TAs to be consistent among themselves so we don't have anyone claiming that their TA lets them off. We should make a syllabus for learning teams that's classwide and that lays out the rules—you must come with your work prepared; if not, we all take off points. If you say that at the beginning, then it's expected and they will do it.

Coach 2: I think the confusion is our fault, and my biggest mistake is not having made a syllabus for what's going to happen. But the professor mustn't go changing things in the middle either. The syllabus needs to be set up the way it's gonna be. Then we can help each other to make it stick.

Some of the coaches capitulated under student pressure. When a significant portion of their groups did not prepare their material and were thus unready to discuss it, they gave the students the first portion of group time to prepare their answers. Once they had allowed this, they were never able to reverse the practice.

Given the reluctance of some Berkeley TAs to agree that consistency across groups in their activities and management was important, the contrast with the undergraduate coaches is interesting. As indicated, most of the Berkeley TAs were graduate students, some of whom expressed an emergent sense of professional independence as teachers—an interpretation of their role that they used to counter the idea of acting in concert. That the undergraduate coaches reached agreement on the value of common group methods and policies without any prompting from their professor and that they felt free to act on their decisions appear to be important factors in their support for a coherent shared approach to their group work with the learning teams:

The professor doesn't necessarily have to be there, because we have the most information on what works and what doesn't work in learning teams. The coaches can get together and say, "Let's design how the learning teams should work next semester." That should include our roles and what the students are gonna do. Then we can take that to [Professor X] and turn it into a learning team syllabus.

Securing Participation and Addressing Bad Behavior

Like most people who organize group work, the coaches grappled with two related problems—what to do about group members who avoid taking an active part in their group and how to assuage the frustrations that this creates among group members who are pulling their weight. Resolving these issues involved methods highly related to group cohesion, engagement, and morale:[8]

I think there's three people who consistently do their work, and there's some kids that come in late and don't really pull their weight in the group at all. The kids who are working are frustrated, and I think they feel that no one is really looking out for them.

The coaches were successful in persuading the professor to adjust the weighting of points for group products such that individual students who did good work got credit for it. They also developed a system in discussion with the professor whereby group members awarded extra points to other group members according to their assessed level of contributions to group work. Some coaches also exerted moral pressure to co-opt the help of disengaged but talented group members:

> She's a second-semester senior, and her attitude was that "I don't have to put up with all of this—this was supposed to be a fun class." So I could see she was frustrated, but I saw that she could do so much for the team—she was really the team leader—and I tried to pull her back in. I said, "You're free to drop or just go to the lecture class, but it's really gonna let the rest of this team down because they need you." And we didn't talk for two or three days, and then I saw her in class, and I said, "What did you decide?" And she said, "I got to thinking about it, and, yeah, you're right, like, I'm gonna stay." So that made me feel pretty good. It was so powerful to find you could make that happen.

Some coaches had discovered that the assertiveness of active group members could be harnessed to confront a noncontributing member:

> They are a really good group. They talk and enjoy themselves and get their work done. But there's one slacker, and I've tried to engage her and prod her along, but with no success, and that frustrates them a lot. But there's one girl in the group who's very outspoken, and she asked if I minded if the group said something to her as well. I said, "Go ahead. It's your group, and she's spoiling it." So, the next time she came, they all told her how they were feeling. She was pretty shaken by that, and she did start coming. She was never a good member, but she did start contributing.

Whether these strategies were successful depended on the composition of the group. The coaches might successfully exert moral pressure on a single resister, but several resisters in a group may be more than any coach can handle:

> Maybe when you have one person who's dragging, you can say, "You know, this is really fun. Get involved with someone; have them take you through the steps as you do them." Perhaps with one person you can inspire something. But when you have three people who don't show up, who don't really want to be there, it's hard to get anywhere.

The coaches observed that the same problem sometimes overwhelmed the professor. They recounted particular class sessions where several groups in a row were unprepared to answer their assigned questions, and neither the designated respondents nor their backups were in attendance to present their group's answer. This brought home to the coaches how much the professor was depending on them to make the class work in the ways that he intended:

> Despite all the things we do to try to prevent something like this happening, when it gets dysfunctional, it really gets dysfunctional. I mean, it really collapses; it doesn't work at all. And it affects everyone.

Although it was the coaches' job to help students prepare for the question-and-answer sessions in class, the coaches were not required to attend. Some coaches came to the conclusion that it would be good for them to attend when their own class schedules allowed it. As well as supporting their groups when it was their turn to answer class questions, they found that sitting with their groups curbed some of the bad behavior that was identified in the previous chapter as a "traditional" form of student disengagement in larger classes:

> Coach 1: It seems to me that the analogue of a coach doesn't work as well when we're not there supporting our team. This is one of their performances, and so I think we should be there.
>
> Coach 2: And I think two or three TAs should be there for the quiz. And I always stay for the lecture if I haven't a class. And, you know, I get sick of seeing people talk during lecture. It really upsets me.
>
> Coach 3: Quite often there are people in the back doing all kinds of things—newspapers, chatting, coffee, sleeping. I suppose the coffee's fair enough. It's almost as though people feel they have the right to behave like that. And they don't do it in group, because we don't tolerate it and neither do other group members.
>
> Coach 1: I don't think they would do that if we sat together with our teams.
>
> Coach 2: I agree. We should organize a schedule so some of us are there every week.

With good support from the professor, some coaches were ready to confront the "slackers" in their groups. However, they found this hard to do with fellow undergraduates:

> Coach 1: She would come late, and her cell phone would ring, and she would talk to whoever was calling. And it was very shocking to me. So I said to the professor, "I don't know how to deal with it." And he said, "You know, if you have problems with people, you need to pull them aside and talk to them, because you have the authority." Well, it's intimidating to pull someone aside because you know the rest of the group knows you are doing this and why.

Coach 2: It's difficult because you're the same age as them. But he's right, we do have the authority to do it.

Coach 3: We don't really want to do it, but when you know that the prof will back you, I was able to say to her, "If you keep coming late and not joining in the work of the group, your grade is gonna be affected. And I am not going to tolerate your bad behavior."

Coach 2: Yeah, you have to assert yourself, although it is intimidating.[9]

Three female coaches discussed how they exercised authority with both male and female group members who were behaving badly or not doing their work:

Coach 1: I have one guy that just didn't show up for a couple of times and I e-mailed him. That worked. He started coming.

Coach 2: Yeah, that's what I always do. At least that way, it's completely private.

Coach 3: I do that too, but it may not be as effective as direct in-your-face confrontation when it's another girl. I e-mailed that girl who was constantly late and not pulling her weight—in fact, I did it several times. Then I forwarded a follow-up letter I was thinking of sending to the prof to ask his advice, and he suggested I tone it down a bit. So I did, and she wrote back all apologetic. But I'm thinking, it might have been more effective to confront her straight away. It's us I think. We shy away from speaking up when we really should get up the courage to do it.

The coaches also discussed the problem of students who were completely disengaged. Having experienced this once, a coach who was returning the following semester felt as though he now understood what had to be done and set himself the task of tackling the problem head on:

It's like people want to get out of the group sessions so bad, they don't care, they just sit there. They're not engaged. And that's something I want to facilitate next semester is people asking each other, "I don't understand; would you explain that to me again?" I want people taking notes when others are giving their answers. I want them concentrating. I want eye contact. I want them to ask lots of questions. I want them to probe the mind of the person giving the answer to find the weaker spots in what they are arguing. And that's hard, but I am determined to do it now I know what I'm up against.

Other Sources of Resistance

The coaches discussed at great length why groups varied so much in how well members got along and worked together. Despite the best efforts of the professor and the coaches, some groups contained members who remained disaffected. The coaches saw some patterns in this behavior. They found resistance in some upper-class students who had expected to coast through this three-credit class on their way to graduation, and among lower-level students who were taking the class to meet a science requirement and expected it to be an easier option than other science classes. In class, they noticed some forms of resistance that they had encountered in traditional lecture courses, including disattentive behavior and truculence about being obliged to attend. Their learning teams included some students who tried to spend as little time, and give as little effort, as possible—behavior that parallels traditional forms of resistance to lab work. They also learned that assessment drove the behavior of some students. As one coach observed,

> I had all nine people showing up for the first half of the semester, and then as soon as the web-based project was done, two of them disappeared and never came back.

This did not, however, alter this coach's opinion of the importance of building cohesion around meaningful work. He added,

> Despite this, the cohesion that was developed in doing the project stayed strong, and they remained a friendly productive group even though the other two were completely gone.

In addition to addressing these more patterned reasons for resistance—largely in the form of absenteeism and failure to do assigned work or to work effectively with their group—the coaches pondered with each other how to explain or address the apparently more unpredictable variables that disturbed the dynamics of their groups. They concluded that a group that has got into working stride and has become focused on projects that interest them can function despite individual members who are disruptive, absent, unreliable, reclusive, surly, lazy, or uncommunicative. However, more than two such members were reported to disturb group cohesion and functioning beyond the coping capacities of the coach or other group members. As discussed, these realizations prompted the coaches to ask their professor to rethink the character and timing of group work and assignments, and the balance between individual and group grades for assignments. Although they advised keeping group size to that of around seven or eight students and seeking to balance the members by sex, majors, and background in the sciences, they appreciated that this was difficult to accomplish for a raft of practical reasons.

This case study is instructive because, as I observed earlier, although success in working with small groups was a key feature of this innovation, the coaches received little preparation for this work, possibly because group work was new to the innovator. Nevertheless, they accepted this responsibility and became creatively engaged in figuring out the best ways to make their learning groups work well. For faculty innovators to secure this level of collaborative effort requires the kind of collegial openness to critique and suggestion that was evident in this class. The sense that the professor needed them, trusted them, and had confidence in their ability to do the job encouraged in the coaches a high degree of buy-in to the class approach and a strong sense of responsibility for making it work. Looking back on the experience, some of the more experienced ("expert") coaches counted the experienced gained with the learning teams as one of the personal and professional gains of being a coach:

> Coach 1: It was very interesting—getting them to be responsible to each other and to work in small groups to solve problems.

> Coach 2: It was a good experience being an undergraduate coach—the experience of teaching in the small group and dealing with a certain amount of authority. We really got brought to the other side of the lectern, and that was a very valuable experience.

By contrast, although the TAs in the Berkeley initiative were, as a group, less supportive of the innovation with which they were working than were the astronomy coaches, they reported very little difficulty in getting their groups to work together. Both in the first and the second round of interviews, statements about difficulty in getting students to work together are almost absent. The most frequent statement made by the TAs was that the students generally behaved well and did their assigned work without protest or undue socializing. The TAs found some students more passive than others and struggled to manage students who liked to dominate discussions, but most students were reported to respond well to the array of group activities set for them in the worksheets. A likely explanation for this difference in the two experiences is that the Berkeley worksheets were built on the group-work experience of their authors in an earlier initiative and were specifically designed to address the requirements for effective group collaboration that the astronomy coaches identified as being necessary, but missing or imperfectly established, in their course.

What is clear in the case of the astronomy coaches is that, given the high degree of trust and support given to the coaches by their professor, the coaches developed their work role with the learning teams in active and inventive ways. They discussed their problems and shared solutions with each other, independent of the professor and as collaborating professionals, and offered him their observations in a direct, courteous manner. They clearly saw themselves as collaborators with him and with each other and took their role as course development consultants seriously.

LABORATORY ROLES

The modular chemistry and Berkeley TA initiative employed TAs in revised forms of lab work, while in Interactive Astronomy most "lab" time was spent in the learning teams working on discussion questions and group projects. What was new about the TAs' work in the Berkeley labs was not the labs themselves but the use of the worksheets to clarify and reinforce students' understanding of lab and class work. Thus, these two initiatives offered less clear case studies of expanded TA lab roles than did the chemistry modules, which offered the most radical departure from traditional TA lab work. Modular labs were reconceived and structured in ways that complemented and reinforced the conceptual focus of the class work. I found modular TAs acting as troubleshooters, consultants, and collaborators in performing their lab support role and, again, confronting resistance issues. For this section, therefore, the work of the TAs in modular chemistry classes is offered as a case study, with some additional observations from Interactive Astronomy.

Preparation and Design Issues

TAs reported that the success of the modular labs depended on good pre-planning and preparation. Teachers also needed to be sure that TAs understood the purposes and procedures of the lab, as they depended on their TAs to reinforce in students the connection between lab experiments and what they had learned in class:

> She lays out everything really well ahead of time. We do some prelab testing with her, and we make sure that the students have read the lab and understood the procedure. We have to get across to them more of why they need to do the lab so they can understand what they are looking for and learn how to apply what they've learned in class. They have to get the point of the lab when they're done with it—so they don't come away thinking the lab and class are totally separate things.

Some professors, and also some of the lab staff, observed that it could not be taken for granted that all TAs were prepared for the labs they were to supervise. One of the head TAs for Interactive Astronomy who helped to develop some of the labs also commented on the underpreparation of students for their lab work:

> The best part of it was working with the students and finding out what it was like when they worked my labs. It was so eye-opening. I would think, "Oh, everybody will know what this is," and then find out that 90 percent of the students did not know.

A modular chemistry TA who recognized that she needed some lab preparation suggested to the professor that they hold a prelab session for students and TAs to discuss lab goals, procedures, and technical aspects:

> If none of the groups in the class know what's going on, it really slows things down and the students get frustrated. I think doing the prelab is a really good idea. It gives me a chance to catch up, you know, get some reading done in case I need to review basic material. And the students get a chance to ask questions right at the beginning before the whole class. And the whole class learns from the answer.

Modular TAs also offered their observations to their faculty on how well aspects of the lab experiments worked. One head TA saw that success depended on setting the students' activities at an appropriate level of difficulty and disequilibrium. She offered the following advice from her point of view as a participant in the lab design process:

> The toughest thing for us with the modular labs has been getting the level of difficulty right—such that it wasn't so easy that they turned their brains off, filled out the answers, and were happy to go home early, nor so hard that they had no idea what was the next step and still turned their brains off. They'll do it either way [*laughing*]. We had to find that middle ground where they are challenged, but not so much that they can't do it.

Pitching the lab at the right level was an important ingredient in heading off traditional forms of student resistance to lab work:

> You know there's this tradition of students expecting to come in and do something fairly boring and get out as fast as they can. It's unfortunate, but it's a long tradition. And we were working to break that up front by making the labs doable as well as interesting and relevant.

One head astronomy TA found the coaches to be as active in giving him good information about the level of the experiments that he designed as they were in giving feedback to the professor:

> I got a lot of valuable feedback from the coaches who had seen the class taught a year before—"That material is too advanced," "You've put too much into it," or "You made the assignment too long." So, as I developed the labs, I tested them on the coaches. And we got better and more efficient at our feedback loop. We were piloting it within a week of my drafting it. And I think the material improved significantly for the students.

Working with Students in Labs and Dealing with Resistance

Beyond these issues of design and preparation, the role of TAs in modular chemistry labs contained traditional aspects—TAs worked with the faculty or lab coordinator to set up the labs, then acted as a roving resource for students. However, they were also more likely to be helping students collect and analyze data from experiments whose outcomes were variable, and they were expected to help students to do this without providing them with answers. The open-ended character of the labs that accompanied modular courses increased the TAs' work in dealing with student resistance. This, as already discussed, includes a deeply socialized expectation that, after completing a lab in the shortest possible time, the students see themselves as being entitled to leave. TAs looked for ways to preempt this problem and advised professors to make lab attendance compulsory for the whole period. That made it easier for TAs to exercise their authority with respect to nonattendance, lateness, or attempts to leave early:

TA 1: It's a three-credit hour class, and we say that you have to spend the whole two hours.

TA 2: When I found they were wanting to get done quickly and leave, I started making it that they had to be there the whole time, and once I'd laid it down a few times, it started getting better.

Interviewer: Does it bother you to have to do that?

TA 2: No. I think that we're in an authoritative position. They sort of know that we're in charge, and I think most of the students respect that it's our job.

TA 3: I know my group appreciates it when I come down on somebody for being late, because they want them there too. Part of their grade depends on that person.

TA 2: I think as long as you go about it in a good way, they understand why you're doing it.

I say more about TAs' use of their delegated authority in a following section.

Troubleshooting Labs

The role of TAs as troubleshooters was especially emphasized in their lab role. TAs reported that they worked interactively with the professor and each other to sort out practical problems in running new labs. In both the modular chemistry and Interactive Astronomy classes, this collaboration included helping to make computer applications work as intended and teaching students how to use them. Those who had been TAs during the early stages of module development and implementation worked to resolve glitches in the instructions, edit the supporting reading material, and make sure that the lab experiments would work as intended:

The earlier modules needed editing, and the errors got the students confused— like referring to something as an acid on one place and an acidic solution somewhere else. So we had to proofread them, especially lab instructions.

We didn't really mind working with the prototypes. It made it interesting. But some of the early modules were clearer and better put together than others. There were some that left you guessing what you were supposed to do.

As labs were spread out over the week, with new labs introduced early in the week, both the modular and the Berkeley TAs developed information-sharing systems to get the labs debugged in time for sections held later in the week:

I think that, next year, they'll be able to tell the TAs beforehand what's likely to be a problem. Like last fall, the Monday lab would have awful results, and then [*laughing*] for the rest of the week, we'd be spending late night with the profs trying to figure out what the heck to do with the rest of the sections. So, by Thursday and Friday, we were getting good results.

I had a Thursday lab, and I would always talk to everyone I could from Monday through Wednesday to find out what they did. And it always took us a much shorter time because we had talked to the students who had done it and had figured out what was wrong. And I had a friend who ran the Tuesday lab, and she would cross out parts of the module lab and say, "You don't have to worry about this bit."

As these extracts suggest, the TAs seemed to enjoy and take pride this aspect of their role. After all, there is always something highly satisfactory to an apprentice about being able to fix something designed by a superior. This kind of troubleshooting may not, however, be an entirely new role. As two modular TAs explained,

TA 1: I had Mondays too. That was why we were working out all kind of bugs.

Interviewer: Was it worse working Monday labs for the modules than it would be in another class?

TA 2: No. It's always that way. Unless you have a lab that you've done for five or six years. Any time you're doing the first year of a lab. It was the same in gen chem labs.

TA 1: Yeah. Last year, I TAed for gen chem and they didn't have modules, and it was the same thing. They had the same kinds of problems. And we were helping them fix them.

However, in innovative classes, every lab is likely to be new or adapted to meet particular learning goals, and as innovators continue to update and refine labs, a willingness to be flexible, mentally agile, tolerant of experiments, and ready to give practical feedback will continue to be valued capacities in TAs.

RESPONSIBILITY FOR TESTING AND GRADING

That TAs and coaches took on collaborative, consulting, and troubleshooting roles is, again, evident in their work in support of testing and grading. Evidence of role expansions in this area of TA activity occurred across all three initiatives, and data from each of them are drawn on to illustrate TAs' active engagement in diagnosing the sources of problems they encountered and suggesting remedies.

Alignment of Assessments with Course Learning Goals

The particular piece of TA feedback about learning assessment issues with most significance for the success of these innovations was that test and exam questions did not always match course learning goals. This problem arose, for example, in one semester of the Berkeley initiative:

TA 1: I felt that the testing style didn't necessarily match the teaching style, which is where I think the students had a *lot* of trouble. The tests were extremely quantitative.

TA 2: That's right.

TA 1: Whereas what we taught them was extremely qualitative.

TA 2: And it drove them nuts.

TA 1: They hadn't had a whole lot of practice with numbers questions.

TA 2: We took a lot of the flak about that. On my evaluations from students, they said over and over, "Prepare us for the exams better." And, honestly, I thought I'd done a really good job at giving a review session for every exam. But a lot of it was their frustration about not knowing how to get ready for the exams, based on how the class was structured.

TA 1: I was surprised about that in the first exam. It actually shocked me.

TA 2: I was surprised in every exam.

What is notable in this exchange is that, although they were the immediate target of the students' anger, the TAs understood that the cause of the problem lay not in the quality of their own work but in collaboration and coordination difficulties among the course faculty. In a similar case, modular chemistry TAs observed that it was unreasonable to expect that students demonstrate in their assessment answers an ability to transfer knowledge unless they had been given some practice in doing this. Again, the substantive issue was consistency in connecting qualitative with quantitative expressions of a concept:

> What would really have helped is if they had followed up some of the good examples that kept students interested with thorough quantitative explanations of why whatever happened qualitatively. So, then, if the student was given a problem which involved a similar idea, they would know how to address it. Because, like the others just said, everything was really qualitative except for the exams.

Another example of misalignment of emphases in course and exam content arose where standard tests were employed that did not reflect the material taught:

> TA 1: When they got to the final exam and thought they knew what to expect, they made this switch on us, and, all of a sudden, they had this big multiple-choice section that the teachers didn't even write.
>
> TA 2: Yeah. That was bad. It was so inconsistent—just a standard exam pulled off the shelf.
>
> TA 3: And it was very unsettling to a lot of my students.

A different form of the same problem arose when students were tested on matters that seemed trivial or at odds with broader ideas stressed in class:

> Coach 1: The big complaint about the quizzes that I'm getting from the students is that some of the questions are obscure, or they're factoids—little bits of information which don't seem to be central to the theme of understanding the big concepts.
>
> Coach 2: What the students are saying is "I've been trying to understand the theories and the big ideas and then I get an assignment or a test on who discovered what in which year."

Both TAs and their students were aware of failures to align assessment with emphases in class content, and TAs reported that such misfits undermined student confidence in the value of their grades:

> And homework instructions were kind of hard to figure out so when you were finished, it was still, "So what?" The work didn't really tie to anything that we were doing at the time. People were really upset and they got very frustrated.

> The one thing that matters tremendously to students is that projects, assignments, homework, or any kind of tests is that they make sense in terms of what they are doing in the rest of the course so they can see where they fit. They have

to seem relevant rather than off the wall. And that's really a general principle I think.

We also encountered the problem of misalignment between aspects of new courses in the initial round of interviews with students taking early modular chemistry classes and with the comparative sample of students taking matched, but more traditionally taught, classes.[10] What students labeled "poor fit" was identified in both types of class. However, in the traditional classes, failure by students to see connections between the content of classes and lab sessions was reported far more often than in the modular classes. Failure to understand why they were doing what they were doing in labs was consistently the most often-mentioned problem in relation to labs by students in the traditional science classes sampled across seven institutions in the *Talking about Leaving* study (Seymour and Hewitt 1997). Indeed, resolving students' difficulties in conceptually connecting these two forms of activity was a cardinal aim of the modular chemistry initiative. Students' "fit" problems in the early modular classes were more commonly caused by the faculty's efforts to get students to draw on materials from different sources or by the faculty's difficulties in rethinking their exams and other assignments in light of their changed learning objectives. Faculty often found this to be a difficult new task.

Both the TAs and the coaches gave examples of misalignment between course learning goals and learning assessments in the more traditional classes that they had taken. However, they expected the innovating faculty to be closer to resolving these difficulties than in fact they were:

> Coach 1: I mean, I take tests, you know, in calculus, and I think, "This is trivial. Who cares? This is a theory that I'm never going to need again after this test." But you know, you are hoping for something better from this class.
>
> Coach 2: Right. You hope that this time, it will be different.
>
> Berkeley TA: I had an instructor in my sophomore year who gave you absolutely no guidance about how you got from here to there and what was important in between. And his exams were the same—totally inconsistent in terms of depth and breadth. When faculty teach and test like that, how can students be other than incredibly confused about what level they are supposed to focus their understanding on.

The modular chemistry TAs were, overall, happier with the high degree of coherence between course content and course learning assessments that were built into the modules as an essential element in their design than were the TAs and coaches in the other two initiatives. The Berkeley TAs appreciated that the lectures, labs, and recitations—and the tests associated with each—were the product of different faculty designers who did not necessarily collaborate with each other. The astronomy coaches were working with a single professor who was experimenting with various ideas in developing his assessment strategy. In modular chemistry, interviews with the module developers at various stages in their work documented their struggles to make the assessments reflect key learning goals in their class and lab work. Feedback from the formative evaluation data alerted faculty to students' difficulties with these and other fit issues. As a result, the well-developed modules with which the modular chemistry TAs were working by these later-stage interviews contained suggestions for assessment based on key content, and the TAs commented positively on their use:

TA 1: The fit between the tests and what they are doing in class is very good.

TA 2: It's very applicable.

TA 1: Sometimes, it's amazing how they'll go over problems in class or lab, and when I go over the problems after the test, many of them are very similar to what they have already experienced—just with a different angle to stretch them a bit—to make them think.

TA 2: In the airbag module, you could definitely see how the tests questions linked with what we had been talking and reading about.

TA 3: There are some real chemistry questions in the tests—like the electron configurations. They may have been taught it through the module, but they were clearly taught this stuff and should be able to apply it.

In summary, TAs offered collegial commentary and practical advice on the extent to which faculty were successful in aligning their course learning goals and assessments. Because of the criticality of this issue to the success of classroom innovations, TA monitoring of this issue is particularly valuable to innovating faculty.

Choice of Assessment Methods

TAs discovered that faculty decisions about learning assessment methods affected student responses to other aspects of the class. For example, in one modular chemistry class, the lack of regular tests or a final exam reinforced a common student disinclination to read class material on a regular basis:

TA 1: They should put in more exams.

TA 2: Yes.

TA 1: So people know it's important.

TA 2: More emphasis on exams.

TA 3: And on the homework too.

TA 1: And I'd like some of the qualitative questions on the exams. I really liked the real-world questions on the tests.

TA 3: Yes, some of them are very good. I think a lot of thought went into those tests.

TA 1: I think it would go fine with the modules if we had tests. But my people have stopped reading because they don't have anything to memorize for a final or a monthly test. With the module that we are doing right now, I don't think that anyone in my group has done any reading, so a lot of times, in the first hour of the group, we'll spend time going over stuff they should have read the night before. And it's because people are used to being motivated to read because there's a test structure in place that gives them some benchmarks.

TA 2: In chemistry, you're usually evaluated every other day, so you have to do your homework. And they don't do well in this class because they fall behind when they don't do their work because the tests are much less frequent.

Thus, these two groups of TAs had discovered that resistance to keeping up with course reading can be reinforced when an innovation departs from the students' learned work stimuli of frequent tests and graded homework assignments.

In addition to their observations about overall assessment strategy, TAs and coaches also offered advice about the particular methods of assessment used in these courses. The utility and thoughtfulness of their comments underscore not only the TAs' willingness to make a larger contribution to course assessment but also the value to faculty of setting up a regular feedback mechanism to further engage them in the assessment process. Some examples of the TAs' feedback and collaborative thinking about assessment methods are offered in the following section.

Both TAs and coaches favored the use of quizzes as an inherently useful way for students to learn to what degree they understood class content. However, this was thought to work well only if faculty thought through their objectives for each quiz and selected questions that explored recent topics. If carelessly done, quizzes could become counterproductive: students failed to get useful feedback, and their morale was undermined. The TAs and coaches understood that students look to quizzes and tests as ways to confirm whether they really understand the material that they think they understand. For students to find quizzes meaningful, their content needs to explore recently presented material in proportion to the emphasis it was given:

Coach 1: Badly designed quizzes and tests can be kind of demoralizing to students. It's nice to know how you're doing; it's immediate feedback. It's like, "I've done the work. I go in and take my quiz, and I find I knew what I was talking about. So, now I know I'm doing the right thing." But if the test doesn't correlate well with the material—and like we said, some of them are ridiculously hard—you lose that.

Coach 2: After the quiz, all the members of my team came into group, and they were like, "We had no idea how to answer this quiz. We all failed. We had no idea how to study for it." Some of the stuff was so obscure.

TA: If students feel that the questions are obscure or tangential or they seem like little facts that don't really hit the main ideas that they are trying to understand, or they are impossibly hard, then, even if they get a decent grade, they don't think that they achieved it or know that they understood it so that they can feel good about it.

The TAs and coaches viewed well-designed quizzes as a good learning reinforcement tool—as a way to tie content together in the student's mind and as a wasted opportunity if poorly designed.

TAs and coaches broadly favored projects as a means of assessment and offered some ideas about their optimal use. The modular chemistry TAs praised the culminating projects that were a common feature of the modules. They saw them as a valuable way to get students to pull together different aspects of their work across the module. Projects also allowed both the students and TAs to see how much they had learned:

I was very surprised by the students' posters in that they spent a lot of time on the equilibrium stuff. It's comic seeing how much they said they didn't understand the material and how they were having awful trouble doing the work. Then they got to the poster, and most of them chose to do it on the shampoo topic. They had all gone out and done their investigations, and they could all tell me what the pH of their shampoos was and why that mattered. So it was a very different picture that I got from them. They were working hard; they understood the chemistry, and they were very motivated by working on an application that meant something to them. They got the equations right, but they could attach them to what they were presenting. Best of all, the whining stopped.

Projects were largely designed by the module authors who worked to make project topics address important modular themes. However, the authors also modeled for the faculty who used the modules an array of methods that they could adapt for projects of their own. TAs thought that good projects were more difficult to design than good tests or exams. Like other learning assessments, exams needed to be aligned with significant course goals. However, because of their duration, it was harder to align them temporally with relevant class content. They needed to be thought through so that the purpose and scope of the project were transparent to students, the instructions were clear, the work was within their level of expertise and was doable in the time frame. TAs advised that students did not know enough about any new topic to choose their own projects and suggested that faculty should give clear guidelines in which they built student choice into the project design. A number of these caveats about project design are represented in the following observations, from four different astronomy coaches:

> One of the things I heard from my students was, the projects were great for getting people working together as a group, but they didn't think the projects themselves were well designed. They liked the idea of coming together and doing something based on what they were reading, but they wanted topics that were more central, less off on the side.

> It was a lot harder than set assignments. Not only did you have to decide what you were going to do, but you had to make sure it was feasible and whether you had enough information. I think students need more direction.

> The second project had a lot of data analysis. I could see that it applied, but a lot of the students just didn't understand what they had to see—which was what thinking processes scientists go through.

TAs and coaches also favored oral presentations of students' work. As already illustrated, the coaches advocated projects that ended in presentation as a good way to focus group effort. The modular TAs reported a number of other advantages: students worked with their own data and read and synthesized source materials. Where project work was presented to the class, students had to compile in a coherent way what they had learned. They also gained confidence by explaining and discussing what they knew and by answering questions about their work:[11]

> TA 1: We got strong positive feedback from students about the presentations at the end of the courses. They seemed to have got a lot out of it—putting together your our data, doing your own bit of online research, and then having to explain what you've learned.

> TA 2: I also think they are happier with an oral interrogation than with the written tests. I saw they were a lot less nervous about it, and I think they managed to demonstrate what they knew better—or what they didn't know in some cases. I think the vast majority of students got a lot out of it.

Both modular chemistry TAs and astronomy coaches also approved the effort to introduce more writing into assignments. However, two expert coaches struggled to think of a way to do this once the class size increased:

> Coach 1: I noticed a complaint last year that people had trouble tying it all together. We should try to use the quizzes to help them with that, but using Scantron makes that hard. It largely gives you true-false options—which opens it up

to a lot of guessing—or multiple choice, and it's hard to get at someone's understanding. For that, all you need is a blank sheet of paper, and ask them to say, "Describe the life of a star." But with a class this big, you'd need a lot of graders, and you'd have to decide what you give points for, as opposed to a Scantron test where the machine just rips through it. The other problem with grading a lot of writing is that it's hard to get it back to the students quickly enough for us to use it to be a real debriefing experience.

Coach 2: Yeah, it's finding something which can be coped with in a timely way. What's good is you can ask questions which are central to what you want the students to show that they know. But we haven't figured it all out yet.

Again, it is notable that this coach uses the collaborative "we" and assumes that he and the other coaches will contribute to resolution of these problems.

Teaching Students How to Study for Tests

Another traditional aspect of the TA role that was expanded by working in innovative classes was the job of preparing students for tests and exams. TAs who supported the modular approach undertook the task of teaching students how to prepare for tests in ways that stood in contrast to some students' learned habit of generating answers without understanding:

TA 1: Writing. Definitely. They had a lot of quizzes in the lecture, and there was a lot of "Explain your reasoning" or "Explain your answer." It's a lot easier to rely on doing equations.

TA 2: I think that's so important because a lot of people try to plug-and-chug it into an equation and come up with some sort of answer. And if they had actually sat back and looked at it, they'd see they had produced an impossible answer.

TA 1: They say, "But we used the right numbers." And never think about explaining their answer and what it means. We have to get them to see beyond that.

TA 2: Exactly. That's a definite advantage of this class. They made the students explain trends in the data and insisted that they always writing things down.

They also approved of using the exams as part of an overall strategy to teach students how to think about the material. Some modular TAs advised, however, that students (especially first-year students) need more time for exams that require them to write and to explain their answers.

Some of the Berkeley TAs described how they sought to teach students to study for tests and how to prepare for them through homework and by asking questions. They observed that students who followed their advice were better able to do the tests; those who clung to memorization and an uncritical approach to solving equations did not:

> TA 1: After the first exam, a lot of them complained, "We never learned this." And my attitude was "You need to go through and look at the exam. Look at where the questions came from. Did they come from something in the class? Was it something from the book combined with something from the homework?" Try to figure it out. Then, next time you study, you really know where to focus. And I also explain some basic problem-solving methods, like "Read the question. Read it again. Start the problem. If you get struck in the middle, go back to the question and make sure you're answering it. When you get to the end, does your answer match the question?"

> TA 2: I tell them, "If you do the homework that way too, it's the way to practice. You can do it on the test the same way."

> TA 1: I agree with that.

> TA 2: But they're not listening yet!

By taking an active role in teaching students how to study and thus prepare themselves for tests, these TAs were tackling head-on one important source of student resistance to new learning methods that was discussed in the previous chapter.

Engagement in Assessment Issues

Many TAs and coaches showed a capacity to share with faculty the responsibility for helping students to learn and perform effectively and were creatively engaged in addressing assessment issues.[12] For example, the astronomy coaches brainstormed how they could give students both individual and group credit for their work:

> Coach 1: Even if they're one of the good students and are really enjoying the class, they don't like rating each other.

> Coach 2: But they also don't like it that people who don't do the work could bring them down.

> Coach 3: But this is what grading each other is supposed to fix. And then some groups act like a set of individuals—they're always seeing the backs of the others at the computer.

> Coach 1: But that's mostly our fault. It's our job to resolve that.

> Coach 3: But, with the software, it's hard even for us to tell without some digging who's been answering question and who hasn't. It would be better if we could see those individual scores.

Coach 1: Well, I think we should suggest the idea that we discussed on Friday. There needs to be a short-answer homework that they can hand in individually, and follow it up with a related discussion question that they have two weeks to research and prepare. Then they present it as a group and are graded on that.

Coach 2: If the professor went with our idea, they would have to work together, and we would all have a much more accurate idea of how much any person does in relation to the group.

Coach 3: And if they all worked on that question, the group members could tell for sure who's doing what amount of work for the presentation.

Coach 1: Yes, yes. Because now they don't know how much more than the bare minimum that someone is doing.

Coach 2: It's a good idea. We should suggest it. But we would still have to deal with how group members feel about the others knowing their individual grades. I guess we start by asking our groups how they would feel about that—just run it by them as an idea.

I have included the whole of this discussion because it illustrates several important themes. First, the coaches clearly viewed this set of related problems as something that they could and should help to resolve. The conversation also shows their assumption of responsibility for group effectiveness and morale. In offering their critique of course assessments, it is (again) notable that as the coaches debated how to best to address these problems, they also took some responsibility for aspects of the assessments that they saw as being flawed. This is even more strongly stated in the following exchange:

Coach 1: I blame myself for some of this because I didn't get around to making up good homework questions. The project went quite well, but I could see where it was lacking—making its purpose more clear.

Coach 2: And when we got them talking it through, they started to think, and I think they got it. That's what's key.

Coach 1: But I failed to put good questions into the homework that would have helped them make connections.

The experience of the astronomy coaches with learning assessment issues stands in contrast to that of the TAs in both the modular chemistry and the Berkeley initiative, where the nature of the assessments was more settled and TAs had less (or no) input into their development. The coaches again offer a good example of how much thought and effort TAs may be willing to put into assessment design and testing when they have an open working relationship with the professor and with each other. The coaches expressed a high level of good will toward their professor and support for the aims of his course and were quick to offer him compliments as well as critique. However, collegiality issues arose around assessment issues for TAs in other initiatives. The most fundamental of these was the need to be briefed about the character and format of tests or exams for the good professional reason that they needed to appropriately prepare their students. This point is illustrated in a discussion among the Berkeley TAs:

> TA 1: We should have had some information about the exams before they are given. We don't need hints about what they are going to test, and we don't have to see any of the problems. That wouldn't be appropriate. But the type of questions and problems and the format in which questions will be asked.

> TA 2: Like, "We are going to give quantitative exams this time"—which they haven't been teaching to. Then we can do a review and make sure all of our students know how to do these. Just give us a general idea. The first exam surprised everybody, and the second one was still very different from what they were teaching.

> TA 3: You know, the faculty could take us into their confidence more as far as telling us what we need to do.

> TA 1: To do our job properly.

Extending Grading Responsibilities

TAs and coaches discussed their responsibilities for grading and for dealing with student concerns and complaints about grades and grading systems. They discussed grading criteria with each other and sought to reconcile their grading scales:

> TA 1: We grade them on their answers to discussion questions and whether they are prepared. If they're not prepared, we grade them down, and if it's a good answer—as opposed to one that's just thrown out there and they're not really sure of the material.

> TA 2: It's a numeric, one-through-three grade. And if they don't have an answer at all, it's a negative grade.

> TA 1: Some students don't like that there's such a short scale and they argue with us, but I think it would be made fine distinctions for so many answers with a more complex scheme. But we can sort them into four piles quite well.

More experienced TAs were sometimes given the task of keeping track of grades, compiling scores from individual or group grades, or posting grades for students. Especially in larger classes, it proved harder to give students useful feedback on how they were performing. In the less-structured but small-class context of the astronomy course, the coaches sought ways to ensure that grades were meaningful to students. They discussed different ways to distribute grading responsibilities in order to give students prompt feed-back:

> Coach 1: This semester and last I've been in charge of entering the grades. I'm a computer science major, and I can see that we could develop a system that would do a better job of keeping track of the grades. And that would take some of the workload off us. This semester, it's harder to grade with such big groups, and I don't ever see any of the raw data—just an end number. So it's hard for me to get a feel for how my teams are doing and give them feedback. Last semester, it was easy for me to go to my team and say, "Okay, you guys did awesome. You ripped it up in the discussion questions." Without the raw data, I have no idea.

> Coach 2: And half of them don't know what the number means.

> Coach 3: I think it could be part of the TA's role when they are grading ques-tions to put in a written comment, like "This was a good answer overall, but you are missing a piece here."

> Coach 2: I think you could split up the grading responsibility so more of us got involved. Or you could have two specialist coaches who didn't work with the groups but who did the grading and included comments to students.

> Coach 1: You could have them giving office hours, but it would be like a dis-cussion session hosted by one of the TAs who did the grading to talk about what's a good answer and what the grades mean.

> Coach 3: The thing would be to share the responsibility for grading among us more widely and made sure the system gave students feedback. We are missing that and it's important.

> Coach 2: Exactly. And give it to them quickly.

Both TAs and coaches saw it as an important part of their job to give their students detailed, live feedback on the quality of their answers and to use this as a basis for discussion that would further stimulate interest. They wanted students to be sure they were answering questions as asked, reading their answers more critically, and learning to spot flaws in their argument:

> TA 1: Their answers are sometime half there; they're not complete. So they like it when I go through what they wrote and say things like "You're not really an-swering this question but a related one. You need to be sure that you are an-swering what's asked."

> TA 2: And I think it's good to give that feedback orally. You can tell them, "This is pretty good, but I think you're missing a piece."

TAs also offered examples of difficulties that arose where communication with faculty was inadequate. Where TAs were asked to grade student home-work or other assessments, it was important to them that the criteria for grad-ing were agreed on and clear and that an appropriate ratio was established between the amount of work required to grade particular pieces of work and the value of the grade for that work to the student. TAs were distressed where they had given a good deal of time and effort to grading homework that they subsequently found was contributing to a small proportion of the students' overall grade. TAs were also distressed when efforts to discuss and resolve grading issues with their professor were brushed aside:

> He had one quiz with short answers, and I really looked forward to the chance to grade it. I had some expertise in scaling to share, and I wanted to contribute that. But he didn't like how I graded them. He didn't discuss it with me. He just regraded the questions. And at the beginning of the semester, he asked us all to look at his homework assignments and make suggestions for improvements. And I did that in an e-mail, but he never got back to me.

As I discuss in greater detail in chapter 10, where other aspects of the innovation have led TAs to believe that the innovating faculty wish them to approach their work as colleagues, failure or withdrawal of collegiality is more damaging to morale than it would be if no such expectation had been developed.

The emergent role of TAs both as consultants and as collaborators is, again, highly evident in their testing and grading work, and as I have indicated, they are often ready and able to contribute more than is formally asked of them. They identified one of the most critical issues that classroom innovators have to address—alignment of their learning objectives with learning assessment methods. The TAs and coaches also showed a capacity to give faculty thoughtful feedback about the efficacy of particular assessment methods, undertake collective and individual responsibility for preparing students for tests, and give them feedback on their performance. Their ownership of these role aspects is increased where faculty are experimenting with various forms of assessment and where faculty are open to discussing these methods and their outcomes with their TAs or coaches.

EXERCISING DELEGATED AUTHORITY

Exercising some degree of authority on behalf of the class teacher is a traditional TA role. However, it takes on additional dimensions in an innovative class because faculty look to their TAs to ensure that students understand and comply with new and unfamiliar procedures, resolve problems arising from class policies that are still in flux, and help in dealing with negative student responses. In these three innovations, authority was given to TAs and coaches to deal with problematic student behavior in the conduct of exams, submission of work, attendance, and in the level of group-work participation.

Conduct of Exams

A traditional exercise of delegated authority is that of helping to limit the extent of cheating in quizzes, test, and exams. Cheating is, as we discovered in our 1997 study (Seymour and Hewitt), normative in large science classes, especially those that grade on a curve. Because it is important to innovators to get students to focus less exclusively on their grades and more on what they take from the class in comprehension and mastery, the persistence of a high level of cheating in tests is one indicator that this goal is unrealized. Again, we see TAs and coaches coming forward to address problems where the innovating professor has yet to develop disciplinary policy and procedures. For example, in Interactive Astronomy, because the professor had not directly addressed cheating in class quizzes, the coaches took the initiative to deal with the problem themselves. Class attendance was voluntary for the coaches, so few or none of them might be there on any particular day. Those who had attended during quizzes observed that the professor was not paying enough attention to notice either talking or cheating. The coaches discussed the situation among themselves and (as described in an earlier section) decided to set up a rotation system so that some coaches would always be present in class to invigilate during quizzes. Their search for solutions was spontaneously generated; they added this dimension to their work role from a sense of responsibility for the conduct and morale of their students:

Coach 1: A couple of times, I've been the only TA there, and the professor wasn't paying attention—he's preparing his lecture or whatnot. And people are blatantly cheating—talking to their neighbors, showing their work. I've had to go up to people and say, "Please do not discuss the quiz." I didn't take the quiz away because I didn't know if it was my place. But it blew me away, and I felt I had every right to go and tell them to stop. So after that, I would stand in the middle of the classroom and just watch everybody, and I think they're not used to that. Because we are not there consistently, they are used to the prof not watching them and being able to cheat.

Coach 2: I was talking to one of the other coaches this morning, and she has noticed quite a high level of cheating in quizzes. And it may be getting worse because there's quite a big subset of the class that's demoralized and resorting to cheating as a means to survive. And part of it is there's nobody there, and the prof's not paying attention to what people are doing. So she started attending and going round between the rows like the enforcer. But part of this is how you deal with demoralized people who are stuck and desperate. What about us all going to class on a rotational basis?

Coach 3: I think we should try that. Last year we could all get to class—and we had a really good time because it was a small close-knit lecture and discussion. I think the problem started when the class got big.

Coach 2: We have to nip that behavior in the bud because it has a negative effect that spreads. With a couple of us there each time, that would stop it. We
don't need all eight of us there all of the time.

Coach 1: I agree. We need to do this. Letting it ride undermines everyone's
morale, and the prof can't handle this all on his own.

TAs' and Students' Need for Guidelines

All professors, whether traditional or innovative in their teaching methods,
depend on their TAs to exercise sufficient authority to make certain aspects
of their class work effectively—particularly in large classes where greater division of labor is needed. This role often includes monitoring attendance and
the completion of work. Where, as in these three initiatives, active student
participation in group discussion and collective work projects were an essential part of the class, TAs and coaches shouldered most of the day-to-day
responsibility for making this pedagogy work. To do this effectively, TAs
need faculty to lay down the rules and expectations for students early in the
class, give TAs clear guidelines for dealing with breaches, and help them deal
with persistent offenders. They found it difficult to get active compliance
from their group members when faculty failed to do this:

Modular chemistry TA: I don't think that our professor has done a very good job
of telling them what they are expected to do as work outside of class. And when
they don't do it, there's no real consequences because then she gives them class
time to get the work done.

Coach 1: I think he has the right idea about enforcing that rule and starting off
with that next semester—that this is going to be how it's done: "You will have
this work prepared before you come to class."

Coach 2: We threatened to grade them on that, but we haven't tried enforcing it
just yet.

Coaches and other undergraduate TAs described it as being difficult to assert authority with other undergraduates but, with advice and backing from
their faculty, were variably able to do this.[13] As discussed in the previous
chapter, they felt uncomfortable in asserting their delegated authority but
understood the necessity and saw it as a step forward in their professional
growth:

Berkeley TA: I had one person in each of my groups that would show up an
hour late to class or didn't come to group. And their excuses just weren't ex-
cusable—like "I couldn't wake up to my alarm." I was trying to deal with people that were always absent and weren't contributing to the class. And I got
quite a bit of help from other group members in dealing with them—they

backed me up when I tackled them, because their bad behavior affected them all. They've actually improved a lot. And the experience has helped me a lot in learning how to deal with difficult people.

Coach 1: I took the problem to the prof, and he told me what to do and assured me he would back me up. But it's still intimidating to confront someone, particularly someone of about the same age.

Coach 2: We shrink a bit from doing it, but, if you don't, you know, students like that are going to fail and they drag the group down too.

Dealing with Difficult People

In all three innovations, making the dynamics of their groups work well enough to keep them functioning fell largely to the TAs and coaches. The task involved dealing not only with students who did not attend class or hand in their work but also with those who were surly or unproductive or who otherwise undermined the working effectiveness of the group. Undergraduate TAs and coaches expressed uncertainty about how they were supposed to address problems of these kinds:

Coach 1: There was friction between some members and a couple of blowups that blew everybody back. And in that case, I thought, "I'm not getting involved."

Coach 2: Yeah. It's difficult to know what to do when you get someone who's kind of noisy and raucous.

Coach 1: And then there was the problem child who didn't show up at the beginning of the semester, and that really affected the dynamics of the whole group. You know, "We're supposed to be a group, but this guy never shows up and never pulls his weight."

Coach 2: Right. So that was affecting the rest of them.

Coach 1: I think we could do with some guidance about how to handle these situations.

The astronomy coaches were relieved when their professor took a firm line with their nonproductive group members, especially students who were senior to them—for example, upper-class students trying to coast through the course. Making it clear that he expected all students to work for their grades and backing it through his grading policy relieved coaches from trying to handle this problem student by student:

With a lower-division class that satisfies arts and sciences core, you get everybody, including the upper-division types. And I think the prof does a pretty good job of letting slackers know that they may screw up the group dynamics but they will get Fs. I mean, first set of assignments, people got Fs left and right. Doing that made our job a whole lot easier.

As noted earlier, it can be especially hard when a female TA or coach has to confront a male student, particularly where they are both undergraduates. However, those who had dealt with a "slacker" of either sex were somewhat surprised to find that their intervention could have good effects on both the person they confronted and the group:

> Modular chemistry TA: They sort of know that we are in charge, and I think most of the students here respect that, you know, it's our job, and most of them appreciate that we do it. I know that my group appreciates it when I come down on somebody for being late, because they want them there too, especially when part of their grade depends on that person.

> Berkeley TA: His behavior actually improved a lot after I tackled him. I was so nervous beforehand, but I thought it would work better to talk to him rather than just to e-mail, and it turns out that was right. He is really turned off school—and that seems to be the core problem—and he was actually surprised that anyone took an interest in him—even a negative interest. And I don't think I will be so anxious next time I have to do it. It definitely gets easier.

One of the head TAs observed that undergraduate coaches almost always found it difficult to exercise authority appropriately. They were apt to swing between finding it hard to tell students what to do, or stop doing, and being over-friendly with them. Anxiety about tackling a difficult group member tended to produce a delay in dealing with any matter, followed by an exaggerated style of intervention. The head TA estimated that the coaches managed their authority successfully about half of the time, but he also observed that, with support from the professor, they were learning how to do this. He strongly suggested that teaching undergraduates how to handle authority over other undergraduates should be an aspect of formal preparation for any course that depends heavily on their assistance.

ACADEMIC SUPPORT FOR STUDENTS

The fifth aspect of the traditional TA role is that of providing academic support to students, whether as individuals or small groups. In some of the institutions represented in the sample, TAs offered formal office hours. In others, TAs and coaches gave support on an as-needed basis during their normal contact time with students. For those providing office hours per se, TAs struggled with the same question as their faculty—namely, why students did not make good use of this tutorial opportunity. Some TAs echoed a common faculty explanation—that many students do not care about their level of understanding, only about their grades. However, the focus-group discussions also revealed TAs' efforts to understand more dimensions of the problem, their sense of responsibility for changing student behavior, and their experiments with ways to get students to come and discuss their academic difficulties.

Taking Responsibility to Avert Student Failure

TAs and coaches included in their role a responsibility to monitor their students and intervene where they seemed to be in danger of failing. They understood that students were unlikely to recover if they got into academic difficulties and did not get timely help—perhaps because of the perceived stigma of doing this. They sought ways to prevent their students from falling into a downward spiral:

> Coach 1: We need to provide resources for the students who are starting to fail—something that works for them before they fail miserably. There's an adjustment period to a class like this, and by the time some people have adjusted to the way this class works, they are already failing. Maybe this is another place we need a grad TA to help them with the content ideas. We can identify them quite quickly, but we need to point them to a good resource.

> Coach 2: That's right. And you have to be a bit careful how you handle this. You can make a student who's not so strong in the subject feel really worthless if you constantly mobilize others in the group to help them. They can walk away from the help if you hurt their feelings.

> Coach 1: Like you stigmatize them

> Coach 2: Right, right. Exactly.

The dominant pattern encountered by those TAs who gave formal office hours was that that students whom they identified as being in greatest need of help either did not come at all or did so only before tests or when assignments were due—that is, when it might already be too late to deal with fundamental difficulties:

> TA: There's the people I see all the time at the TA sessions, and I have come to know them pretty well. Then there's students who are just along for the ride. They show up just before they get a big assignment. There's a big separation between them. This group has something they just want to get done. Worst case, they just want the answers. The people who come all the time—they are often confused, but they come willing to work.

> TA: The regular students that came were struggling hard. And, in an hour or two a week, I couldn't really teach them too much, so I focused on trying to get them

to see where their weaknesses in understanding were. And usually, it was from some weeks past—something that they never got straight.

The TAs also reported groups of regular attenders with whom they worked as teachers rather than in triage mode:

> I have a list of about twelve people that I see on a regular basis—they all have different types of problems—some in the content of the modules, some with writing the equations and getting them balanced. Some of them don't understand the concepts. But they all come regularly to work on these things. And that's just fine. I'm glad they do.

Encouraging Rational Use of Office Hours

The TAs recognized some other patterns in student use of their office hours: more of the students who attended regularly were women. Two modular chemistry TAs (in the research university) expressed the same disapproving view toward nonattenders that faculty often take—but a third TA was thinking about what she could do to change this pattern:

> TA 1: We always say that it seems like the students that come are the ones who don't need it. Also, there are definitely regular students—always the same group.

> TA 2: And it's the women more than the men that come. And I've tried to talk to some of them that I know are struggling—just based on their midterm scores.

> TA 3: A few of mine came almost every time. But I got the same impression that the ones who could have used it most didn't come and didn't care very much. They weren't going to come and see me unless they found something wrong with what I had done.

> TA 1: I know. I know. But I'd like to think we could change that. I wish I'd stressed in my class right from the start of the semester why it's important to come, and that it's not some kind of admission of failure.

Another modular chemistry TA defined students' failure to make appropriate use of office hours as a gender-linked phenomenon. Like the preceding TA, he wondered about its cause and took responsibility for trying to break the pattern:

> I will say, "If you can't make my office hours, I'm here right now. Come ask me a lot of questions." I think I got through to some, but some are still really hesitant. And I noticed that there were some students who got defensive very quickly. Maybe they're worried about me finding out what they don't know [*laughing*]. I wish I knew how to crack this attitude. I mean, I take so much advantage of all my TAs' office time. I suspect they just want to learn it all of their

own—especially the men—but when they are struggling, I would say, "Get some help." But when I would ask them, "Do you understand this?" they would all go, "Yeah, yeah, yeah." It's worrying when the males especially need help and they just won't take it. The women come. I'm not worried about them at all.

In *Talking about Leaving* (1997), we found that the perceived stigma of asking for help did indeed prevent a significant number of young men from seeking it. Even among apparently well-prepared male students, reluctance to seek help with academic problems was a serious contributory cause of failing grades in the science, mathematics, and engineering majors that they had chosen to enter. That undergraduate TAs should understand some of the causes of this problem is impressive, given that many faculty wonder why students who should seek help do not do so.

Two modular chemistry TAs noticed additional patterns—that students in the middle of the performance range also made poor use of office hours. Again, they took responsibility for trying to get their students to come and for getting them to understand how to use the time most usefully. In the process, they made some discoveries about other dimensions of the problem:

> TA 1: I had a hard time getting people who are in the middle as far as grades go to come and talk to me. And some that I persuaded to come sort of sat there, just waiting for enlightenment [*laughing*]. And I don't think I delivered that. So I tried to explain to them all the importance of asking questions. And then it dawned on me that some of them haven't learned to express their problems in the form of questions. They just don't know how to do that. So that's what I'm working on now.

> TA 2: And the other thing I've noticed is that the ones who need most help don't come prepared. In fact, it hasn't occurred to them to bring the things they have been working on so we can talk about it. So now I'm stressing that as well.

Other discoveries included the realization that undergraduates can be just as scared to approach graduate students for help as they are to approach faculty.

As they discussed these issues with each other, the TAs and coaches were revealed as people who personally valued the opportunity to work one-on-one with a tutor. They lamented that failures in understanding could be resolved if brought to them early but not if they were left unresolved for days or weeks. Regular attenders who came prepared by reading and trying to do their homework were seen as gaining most, because TAs developed a sense of their progress, could see why they were stuck, and took a continuing interest in them. These sessions were also described as a safety net for particular users, for example, those who enter underprepared in science or mathematics. In larger classes, office hours could also be the student's only opportunity to ask questions. Because they saw the value of making good use of this time, TAs were often frustrated—with their students and sometimes with themselves:

> TA 1: A lot of times people come in, and I ask if they did the reading, and they'll say, "No." So they expect me to help them through whatever homework task they have—even reading the chapter. It's almost like they want to come in for half an hour and do all of their chemistry stuff. And they don't do any of it themselves. It irritates me.

> TA 2: Me too. I'll ask them, "Could you show me how you started this?" Or I'll offer, "I can help you get going and then you can work on this." And if it just takes that to get up their confidence and point them in the right direction, I think that's fine. But if they don't want to put in the two hours, if they come in just for fifteen minutes and want me to work it out on the board for them and then leave, I feel used.

> TA 1: I can understand it when people have trouble getting started because that happens to me too. So I don't mind helping with that. But it's frustrating when they're not willing to make the effort. I'm glad to help them when they need help, but I don't want them to just sit there. I don't want them to give up so easily.

Some TAs identified in their students' behavior a fear of failing in an unfamiliar task—a fear that they saw as rooted in a preoccupation with grades rather than comprehension. As discussed in chapter 5, TAs defined this as a type of risk aversion that they also identified as a source of student resistance:

> The first time they meet this, they don't know what's going on. And they are not willing to go to the book and try the examples and figure it out. They are afraid to do that in case they fail. So they want me to lead them through it, or, worse, they just wait in hopes I will give them the answers.

TAs' Learning Strategies for Office Hours

TAs responded with some creativity in face of these challenges. Some decided to keep their office hours unstructured in order to accommodate students who learned in different ways and to encourage students to take more responsibility for tackling things that they did not understand. Two modular chemistry TAs explained their strategies thus:

> TA 1: I kept it completely, deliberately, and explicitly unstructured, telling those that came, "This is your time. If you have questions, I am happy to help you to find ways to answer them." Over time, they learned that they got most when they came in with good questions. But to begin with, I had to help them to see what the questions were.

> Interviewer: Why did you decide to approach your sessions this way?

TA 2: Couple of reasons. One is that the classes are very structured and not everyone learns in the same way and sometimes the structure leaves some people out. So, leaving people a chance to learn how to ask for things in their own way, and helping them think through problems in a way that makes sense to them, is valuable. Two, it forces them to be more independent as learners—to pinpoint what they need to understand—what bits are missing, and not to be afraid to ask for help with that.

One astronomy coach developed a similar strategy. He began by getting students to explain to him what they knew about an area of particular difficulty, guiding them to finding the pieces they were missing on the hypertext, and helping them to tie together the old and new elements of their knowledge. He wanted his tutoring strategy to reflect the spirit of the course philosophy by which students take primary responsibility for finding information. Once he was satisfied that the students had done all the investigation to find all of the necessary pieces, he was happy to work them through more difficult conceptual areas:

Once they have found it all, I have no problem explaining things to my team. I can say, "Okay, you found all the answers, let's try and tie it all together. Let's go through it step by step and see how it works." I'm getting more comfortable doing this after a couple of semesters with the material. My job is to help them get a sense of coherence—"Here's some things that I know, but how do they fit together?"

Other TAs experimented with changing the venue or the label of "office hours" in an attempt to change their students' expectations and behavior. Working on the presumption that undergraduates would find it easier to approach him in a more informal atmosphere, one TA shifted his office hours from the office space he shared with other graduate students to a corner table at a local coffee shop:

I started to hold my office hours at a cafe over on [X Street], as it was a much more laid back kind of an atmosphere. Although it was hard sometimes talking over the espresso machine. But it seemed that the students were more willing to come, and I started to get more regulars—more of a working club atmosphere. I could take up to eight at a time—so long as we kept buying coffee!

Two of the undergraduate modular chemistry TAs in a liberal arts college made their office hours and recitation the same thing—a voluntarily attended hour of preplanned activities that focused on increasing student understanding of the class and lab work. Activities were worked out each week in discussion with their faculty:

TA 1: We plan our own activities with help from [Professor X] that are built up around what they should be reading, what their homework is. And then we might think up some questions, make a handout and put them in pairs to work together.

TA 2: Then we might get them to go to the board and explain it to each other—or open it up to everyone. It depends on the question.

TA 1: We're getting more and more of them coming. It's partly because we advertise in every lab what we are going to do in the next session, and partly by word of mouth from people who have found it useful.

TAs also tried to change the image of office hours as a purely remedial experience for strugglers by offering knowledge extension opportunities for enthusiastic chemistry majors in the class:

TA 1: There are two types of students who tend to come, and one is those who are really excited about chemistry. They're going to do fine in the class, but they want just want to talk for an hour about chemistry because they like it. So we want to encourage that. We want to stimulate their interest—although they do also come for help with homework problems. And that is good for the others in the group to see—that anyone can use some help.

TA 2: And, of course, once you have got a regular little group of the good students there, you can start to rope them in to give a hand explaining things to some of the others who are finding it tough. You almost have to make the whole thing feel a bit like a club.

Another group of modular chemistry TAs at the research university worked with a system of open office hours that they arranged in the same room for eight hours every day, with one TA always available. Each TA gave one hour a week, so this arrangement actually reduced their office time. Students could arrange to meet a particular TA or drop in at a convenient time and see whomever was on duty:

I thought the open office hours were a great idea. You could either go at a time that was convenient or go to a TA that you liked. If they had a problem with their own TA, they could shop around and find someone they worked with better. I thought that was really an advantage.

This was not an idea developed as part of modular chemistry, and TAs discussed where else they had encountered the system within this and other universities. In a variant of this system at another school, some fixed office hours were retained, but two open sessions were also offered for any student to attend. The TAs judged both systems as being successful and particularly appropriate for classes that emphasized students' responsibility for their own learning:

I'd definitely say that the best part of the class were the open office hours when you could get down to a couple of students having a discussion. One-on-one discussions can be very intense for learning. Maybe I just focus on that because it's the way I learn best, but I thought it was just incredible.

Probably the best thing this semester was running into a student that I met in open office hours. And she thanked me over and over again, saying, "Oh, I really got so much out of your open office hours." And I thought, "People are really getting something out of this." And it wasn't always the students with whom I'd spend the greatest amount of time.

One modular chemistry TA in a school that retained closed office hours envisaged an open office system:

I don't know if it solves all of these problems, but it would be nice if students who could only go to seek help at one particular time when there's normally no TAs available could go and find a TA they could interact with—someone who could help them pound this concept into their head so that, by the time they leave, they could explain it to that other person. So that's a goal. We need a more flexible system to make that happen.

Turning their office hours into an active seminar gave the TAs who experienced it a taste of real interactive teaching and learning with gains for both their students and themselves. The only critique of the open office system came from one TA who, in a focus-group discussion, questioned whether students would not gain more by coming serially to closed sessions with their own TA, who knew each student's level of understanding and could help each of them to build mastery over time. However, as a colleague in this focus group wryly observed, "If they don't show up, you can't teach them anything."

The office hours system is one aspect of the TA role that, having been defined as an official part of the TA's job description, is thereafter pretty much left to the TAs themselves to organize. TAs and coaches spoke less about this aspect of their work with their professors than they did any other aspect of their work and clearly felt at liberty to organize their office hours sessions in any way that got students to attend. It was also clear that many TAs assumed the same disapproving attitudes as their faculty toward student underuse of their office hours. However, as illustrated, TAs were also open to figuring out why students may not make good use of their help. Individually and together, they sought ways to change that behavior. Thus, troubleshooting, the assumption of professional responsibility, and creative extension are all apparent in the ways in which TAs and coaches developed this traditional aspect of their role.

In this chapter, I have sought to illustrate from the data some ways in which the traditional roles that teaching assistants perform are extended by their work in innovative classes. These role extensions occur partly because of additional demands that the innovative faculty make of them. They also

occur because a high proportion of the TAs and coaches responded positively to the challenges of working with these new approaches and, on their
own initiative, sought ways to make them work as their faculty intended.
Thus, these traditional role functions became infused with three kinds of activity that extended their scope—namely, troubleshooting, consulting, and
collegial collaboration—both with their faculty and each other. All three extensions entailed extra thought, as well as action, and reflected some assumption of professional responsibility for student learning and the success
of the class overall. Indeed, one way to look at these data is to see them as
indications that working in innovative classes has the potential to encourage
teaching assistants to take ownership of aspects of the class and to develop
a sense of professionalism about their work. As stressed at the outset, the degree to which troubleshooting, assumption of professional responsibility,
and creative extension of their five traditional work roles developed was
variable, but, as indicated in table 7.1, three-quarters of the TAs and coaches
showed evidence of some degree of role expansion in descriptions of their
work.

There is a small amount of evidence from other studies that indicate that
working in innovative classes can promote changes in the ways that TAs
think about and practice their role responsibilities. For example, chemistry
and math TAs at the University of Wisconsin, Madison, believed that their
role (defined as "coach" or "cheerleader") took on greater importance as
they worked to facilitate students' adjustment to the innovative pedagogy
and curriculum. These TAs also expanded their role by acting as mediators
between the professor and students. The professor and other TAs drew on
their feedback on students' reactions to the innovations in modifying and improving the course (Alexander et al. 1996).

Several researchers report a critical shift in the way that TAs view themselves and their role—from (potentially at least) all-knowing lecturers to facilitators of learning (see, for example, Sundberg et al. 2000; Nurrenbern,
Mickiewicz, and Francisco 1999; Millar et al. 1997; Alexander et al. 1996). As
in the three initiatives I have described, TAs have been found to develop
coaching roles that include helping students to work together in order to explore, problem solve, and critically think their way through the topics and issues presented to them. This change has been noted in several disciplines.
In a study at the University of Washington, communication TAs were acting
as "research mentors," who modeled active, rather than passive, learning
(Karasz, Reynolds, and Wall 1997). French and Russell (2002) found that TAs
in an innovative science class understood their task as being to "socratically
guide students to the information they need" as they explore new concepts
in labs where the results are unknown beforehand (1037). Engineering TAs
at the Colorado School of Mines showed that they could help students to develop open-ended problem-solving skills, recognize alternative ways of de-

signing an experiment, and select procedures based on evidence (Streveler and King 2000).

As I have also reported, not all TAs are ready to make such changes. For example, Robinson (2000) found that some of the chemistry TAs that they studied embraced the active-learning pedagogy and were concerned to improve their teaching and lab work within this paradigm, while others continued to interact little with their students and showed little awareness of them throughout the lab. In the face of student resistance to active learning, Alexander and colleagues (1996) reported that some chemistry and mathematics TAs reverted to their traditional role as knowledge expert and "provider of answers" while other TAs de-emphasized group learning.

None of this is to argue that teaching assistants working in more traditional classes do not, or may not, also develop a high degree of professional engagement in any of the activities discussed in this chapter. By extrapolation from these data, the combination of an open and collegial attitude by faculty, good preparation for the work, and regular meetings to discuss emergent issues all seem likely to encourage a high degree of TA engagement regardless of the character of the class. However, the higher demands that innovative classes place on teaching assistants bring into sharp relief their potential to lift TA work to a higher level of professional engagement than is expected of them in less-challenging circumstances. It also illustrates what teaching assistants are capable of contributing in optimal circumstances.

NOTES

1. This finding as confirmed in Penberthy and Millar (2002).

2. Alexander and colleagues (1996) found that chemistry and mathematics TAs at the University of Wisconsin, Madison, were key players in implementing active learning startegies because they had greatest direct contact with students.

3. Studies that include descriptions of TAs' duties in traditional classes also report these five types of responsibility (see, for example, Peterson 1990; Ford 1993; White 1993).

4. The same advice was offered by undergraduates who were interviewed as part of the ChemConnections formative evaluation.

5. Millar and colleagues (1997) found that TAs in an innovative chemistry course at the University of Wisconsin, Madison, were concerned about issues of group composition and their effects on student learning.

6. However, the "expert" coaches who saw the class size increase after the pilot phase of the course advised the professor that the large class was a more critical factor than the size of their learning groups in determining the success of the course's interactive learning goals.

7. Each student who was designated to discuss the group's answer to the weekly question in class had a backup respondent from his or her own group.

8. Students at the University of Southern California who had taken courses that used collaborative learning methods had more positive opinions about these methods and were less concerned about group grading issues than were students without such experiences (Hagedorn et al. 2000).

9. Jacobs (2002) found that when students resist the authority of an undergraduate TA, faculty can handle this quite effectively by clearly articulating the TAs' responsibilities and powers to the students.

10. These first-round interviews held early in the classroom-testing phase of modules are described in Chapter 3.

11. The value of oral presentation was also strongly endorsed by undergraduates in our recent study concerned with the benefits of undergraduate research experience. Gains arising from the experience of preparing and presenting their research work were among the most highly valued outcomes of undergraduate research described by participating students. These and other gains are discussed in Elaine Seymour, Anne-Barrie Hunter, Sandra L. Laursen, and Tracee DeAntoni, "Establishing the Benefits of Research Experiences for Undergraduates in the Sciences: First Findings from a Three-Year Study," *Science Education* 88, no. 4 (2004): 493–534.

12. I do not claim that responsibility sharing is exclusive to TAs working in innovative classes. Earlier in this chapter, I describe a study by Kirk and Todd-Mancillas (1991) of graduate TAs working in conventionally taught courses. They too found that TAs judged their competence by how well their students learned. The TAs also blamed themselves and questioned their abilities as teachers when their students did poorly.

13. Robinson (2000) reports that new TAs in conventional classes are concerned with issues of age difference, authority, and control and that they struggle with wanting to be liked, admired, and able to answer students' questions. This was also found in studies by Jacobs (2002), Eby and Gilbert (2000), and Wood and colleagues (2001).

8

Redefining the Teaching Assistants' Role in Innovative Courses: New Facets of the Teaching Assistants' Role

In this chapter, I illustrate how the same three dimensions of troubleshooting, consultation, and collaborative engagement are evident in the ways in which teaching assistants voluntarily extended the boundaries and scope of their formal role in ways that helped to make these innovations work or work better. These are not new roles in the formal sense of defined areas of responsibility. They are, rather, a set of attitudes and behaviors that lift the total role of the TA to a higher level of engagement, responsibility, and professionalism. This shift is prompted in part because the innovative faculty both ask more and get more from their TAs than they might in more conventional faculty–TA relationships in more conventional courses. Both direct and implied invitations by faculty to contribute provoked an active response from the TAs. The level of collegial engagement represented in the examples that follow shows, I would argue, the TAs' potential to play a greater formative and collaborative role in course development and implementation that has traditionally been their lot. What emerges is a picture of TAs and faculty reinventing together what the role of TAs can become. The shape that a reconceptualized TA role may take is, as yet, fluid. However, data from these three innovations offer good indications of what this might include.

As in the last chapter, I gather examples of TAs who push their work role beyond traditional formal role responsibilities into three broad categories: troubleshooting, consultation, and collaborative engagement. Doing this allows me to show some of the TAs' substantive contributions to their faculty's thinking about fundamental aspects of their course structure and approach. These contributions are especially evident in the section describing TAs as "course consultants." The issues raised by TAs are also important in their own right because TAs identify and, within the limitations of their powers, seek to address areas of difficulty that are apt to be generic for all or most STEM course innovators. An overarching theme of enhanced TA–faculty collegiality and shared professional responsibility for course outcomes is also evident across the categories and in examples offered throughout this chapter.

The literature on TAs' expanded role as partners in innovation is, as yet, slight. However, from the small number of studies of TA observations on their innovative course involvement come indications that TAs have insights to offer from which all faculty benefit (Millar et al. 1997). In their study of "graduates-through-faculty" in STEM fields at the University of Wisconsin, Madison, Millar, Clifford, and Connolly (2004) found that educators welcome partners who can discuss teaching strategies and practices and can offer feedback based in observation. In an initiative at the University of Miami, faculty partner with one or two students who provide them with feedback on their teaching and curriculum throughout the year and, in some cases, undertake team teaching (Cox 2001). The Center for the Advancement of Engineering Education at the University of Washington, Seattle, has set up a research agenda to track its efforts in increasing the use of effective pedagogies in engineering classrooms, including an expanded involvement of TAs. No published work is, as yet, available from this initiative (see www.engr .washington.edu/caee).

TROUBLESHOOTING AS BOTH A TEMPORARY AND A LONGER-TERM RESPONSIBILITY

In each innovation, TAs and coaches worked to troubleshoot unforeseen problems, including those raised by student difficulties with and resistance to the new-style classes. The need for TAs to step forward to help innovating teachers resolve particular problems often arose because of the newness of the materials and methods, the inexperience of the teachers in using them, or both. However, some troubleshooting work promises to become a regular feature of the teaching assistants' role in innovative classes. For example, the ongoing use of formulaic learning in many high schools and introductory science classes will continue to create learning adjustment problems for students and prompt resistance when students are faced with learning methods requiring active engagement. Most examples of troubleshooting specifically related to course content were provided by the modular chemistry TAs and Interactive Astronomy coaches where the class content or its implementation were still evolving. However, the content and use of the Berkeley worksheets, although narrower in scope, were also under continual review in light of feedback from TAs, the undergraduates, and the evaluator.

Working with New or Incomplete Course Materials

In modular chemistry, some troubleshooting work arose because of variations that TAs discovered in the quality of the modular handbooks, particularly the degree of clarity with which they conveyed the connections between ideas. Where these were incomplete or obscure, TAs found themselves working to close conceptual gaps:

> Some things made more sense to my students in terms of how well connected the modules were with the chemistry. It was very uneven because they were not quite finished and ideas weren't equally well worked through. So students got confused about what one thing had to do with something else they were talking about. So we had to work quite hard to make those connections for the students.

Modular TAs also coped with problems that may be generic to the introduction of new materials that have received limited classroom testing. Some modules were seen as giving students too much depth too soon or presenting material in a sequence that made it harder for students to understand:

> TA 1: The module that I didn't like went into so much depth with the Ksp stuff, and it was so confusing, even for me.

> TA 2: And they need to look at the order in which they present things—like basic stoichiometry. If you learned it step by step and follow the rules for solving equations, you can get it. But the students were coming to us for help because they couldn't get it this way. There were still some people in the second semester that were having a hard time with stoichiometry, which they needed to understand early on.

> TA 1: And there were some other basics that needed to be hammered in place earlier, like electron transfer. If you don't get things laid out in a sensible sequence and back it up with the homework, we end up backpedaling with the students all the time.

TAs reported that the module handbooks varied in their capacity to help students to see how principles that they learned in the context of specific applications could be applied in other situations. Where this arose, TAs undertook the task of helping students derive the basic concept from the applied material:

> They're having a hard time understanding some things that shouldn't be that difficult to understand because the material was too specialized. Instead of having two labs on copper, it would be better to have one and then to use different metals in the other so they don't get the idea that these ideas are only useful in relation to copper. Same with the ozone module, a lot of that chemistry is widely useful, not just for environmental chemistry—even though that's an important field. If you get too specialized and too applied, there's a risk they'll lose the

whole picture. So, I found myself trying to get them to extract from these particular applications back to the general idea.

Some problems that TAs addressed arose simply because of the unfinished, unpolished, or incompletely edited character of new materials:

TA 1: I guess every new textbook or, in this case, module has to be tried out in a developmental stage somewhere. Of course, you'd rather get the final product so students don't come across something called by one name in one place and by another a few pages later.

TA 2: It does need editing, which is an inconvenience.

TA 1: And that's really confusing for the students. Like, we know when different terms are used for the same thing. But they don't. So we have to edit and interpret for them as we go along.

TAs also worked alongside their professor to figure out as they went along how best to conduct modular labs that were new to the teacher:

My instructor was probably just as confused as I was. I had labs later in the week so the professor could tell me before my lab what went wrong earlier in the week and how she and the other TAs had worked around these. We discussed this before she started talking about it to my group of students so I knew what points to watch out for. And I gave her my own ideas about how to make things work better after the lab. I think that next year, they'll be able to tell the TAs beforehand about how the lab works and what's likely to be a problem.

The unfamiliarity of modular labs was compounded in the early tests of the modules when incomplete, underedited, and sometimes unfinished or untried labs arrived at the last minute. However, even at this more mature stage in module development and use, some TAs still scrambled to get new labs organized and avoid student confusion:

TA 1: The second semester was more in disarray because the professor didn't have the lecture material until the last minute.

TA 2: Yeah, the last module got there like the day before they started it. So it was tough for us all to figure out what the students were supposed to do in the labs. But we managed, and actually it didn't go all that badly.

Interestingly, this was not necessarily a source of irritation for those TAs who described a good working relationship with their faculty and who portrayed themselves as taking these emergencies in stride. However, TAs and coaches thought it inappropriate to do this kind of troubleshooting work in a regular way because they needed the chance to plan ahead and prepare their sessions with students:

We worked on a module for three weeks or so, and then there was another brand new one. It was always catch-up. But, the second semester, they gave us the one for the beginning of the year in advance, so I could actually spend some time every week reading and figuring out exactly what they were going to do— which was nice. I could actually be prepared when I came to class [*laughing*]! It's important to get to read all of the labs before you start.

Preparation of unfamiliar lab materials, and readiness to spot and deal with student difficulties with them, is likely to be an ongoing aspect of the work role for each succeeding group of TAs in classes with innovative labs.

Resolving Computer System Problems

Another common form of TA troubleshooting was trying to make the computer systems or software used in new courses work as intended. Although this is not documented in the literature, TAs in conventional courses that employ technology in support of class goals and methods are likely struggling with the same issues. In the following example, one of the astronomy coaches had sufficient know-how to enable fellow coaches to get all of their students onto the system. Without his intervention, the start of the students' hypertext exploration work would have been delayed:

Coach 1: A lot of my background knowledge came into play because I can work in UNIX, which the others hadn't used before, so I knew how to manipulate things.

Coach 2: It was the first time we had seen this.

Coach 1: Yeah, the different platform was disconcerting to some people, and I know that this is the coolest, newest thing, but, man, the first meeting with the setup and trying to get everybody logged in, and changing passwords and then getting back into CITRIX and setting that up—it was such a headache.

Coach 2: True, but we would have been in a greater mess without you. I had the first team meeting, and we fought it through and finally got everybody logged in and operating.

Coach 1: It will be a whole lot smoother next time—no need for the seventh cavalry!

As the TAs testified, web-based courses and materials are often vulnerable to setup problems and are apt to need TA intervention or (better still, in their view) assistance from a computer technician who is assigned to the course. Although innovative courses are likely to include some use of computers as an intrinsic part of class or lab work, none of these TAs or coaches had been recruited for or trained in the computer skills that their classes required. The availability of at least one TA in the group with technical expertise proved significant in getting this part of the class to work as intended. However, in this case, the TA was a serendipitously available resource.

The TAs also observed that student tolerance for computer glitches is extremely limited. Initial problems encountered in using computer software provoked student anxiety:

> My best student threatened to drop because she couldn't handle the computer difficulties. It wasn't that she was uncomfortable with the technology but the software didn't work correctly—she had problems entering her answers, and when she had managed that, the answers would disappear. A new course like this needs the bugs to be worked out.

When hardware or software does not work as envisaged and has to be manipulated, TAs found that student confidence in the new course was quickly undermined:

> When the students came to the first meeting, nothing was working right—none of the web software. And that really discouraged the students. Most of them are very worried if the tools they are going to be using don't work. They tend to want technical things to be hammered down even more than other aspects of a course.

TAs and coaches found that their students had highly variable backgrounds in computing. They advised that faculty cannot assume that all students will be able to use the computer as a tool to work on particular projects. Some TAs diverted time and effort that they would have preferred to spend on class materials to teaching use of computer operations to their students. They also lost group time while they or a technician were troubleshooting technical problems:

> The students' unfamiliarity with the system made it a real hassle, and the first three weeks I had to get everyone together and go, "Click here, type this in, and then do this." If we had just had a PC setup from the outset, we could have got moving the first day because everyone knows how to use a PC desktop. But it took eight weeks to get everyone up and running, and that's more than half the course.

Astronomy coaches noted that student unfamiliarity with the structure and methods of a new course exaggerates common negative responses to the use of computers for class work. Fast and effective response by the TA or the technician prevents loss of motivation and morale. Web-based courses also need computer equipment that is up to the intended task. Student frustration sets in quickly if machines are slow or there are problems loading programs. The astronomy coaches who had worked for two semesters reported good progress in students' work engagement once the computer problems that bedeviled the class at the outset were resolved. They found student attitudes to be much more positive when the use of computer in labs, communication systems, and organizational functions all worked well:

> I think every semester it's going to get a little better—like this semester was ten times better than last. The lab is beautiful—and it worked almost flawlessly. There were just a few little glitches left for us to attend to. But even stopping to deal with those can really make a difference in a class like this, especially with people being so impatient the way they are.

One head TA (whose role included the design of computer labs) observed that students are no longer excited or motivated by the idea of working on computers in lab because they have become accustomed to using computers for many purposes in their lives. Students also belong to a generation that is accustomed to a high quality of visual imagery in computer material from commercial sources. This throws back onto the professor (or onto a TA who is assisting with this aspect of curriculum development) the challenge of designing or adapting computer-based materials that are visually attractive and operate reliably. Several TAs described the value of computers in presenting material that is otherwise difficult to illustrate and of doing so in ways that appeal to students with different learning styles. However, they also observed that to do this well takes a lot of work and skill.

TAs and coaches viewed their work in troubleshooting computer problems as being important in making particular innovative classes work as intended. However, they tended to see this as a temporary responsibility that was better done by a technician. They looked to the innovator to resolve problems with equipment or software, rethink its format or use, and consider how to train students to use required systems other than in class time.

Innovative courses may temporarily undertake the role of educating students in computer techniques that they also need for many aspects of their education and future work. TAs observed the benefits to their students but questioned whether innovative classes (and they) should continue to perform a function that, in their view, belonged to the university at large:

> The computer skills that they are learning are relevant across their education and for life in general. And it's a way for them to take away something practical as well as what they learn in the discipline. . . . And looking at their stuff, it's pretty good quality—some of it's quite beautiful. But, I think they should have been learning how to do this in a general computer education class—all students should learn how to write webpages and work with Excel. We shouldn't have to teach them those things.

Except in periods of initial course development, testing, and adjustment or in emergencies, the role of computer troubleshooting does not appear to be a role that this sample of TAs and coaches wished to incorporate into their regular job descriptions. However, insofar as innovating faculty take a lead in the creative use of technology, TAs may continue to find themselves involved in a troubleshooting role with information technology in innovative courses.

Communicating Directly with Students

E-mail had clearly become an important tool for TAs and coaches in managing day-to-day tasks and dealing with problems—all of which allowed the course to proceed more smoothly. These advantages included sending out information about assignments and answering related questions; checking on students who missed classes or group meetings or did not submit their work on time; and answering students' questions on the material, their homework, and so forth. Not only was it easier and faster for the TAs to handle problems in this way, but the universal availability of e-mail has also extended the role of individual communication with students, which was previously done (if at all) through such cumbersome means as office hours, written notes, or communications in class time. Faculty are also able to communicate directly with students in a way that was not previously possible. However, there were indications in the data that faculty had begun to hand over to their TAs some responsibility for particular areas of communication with students that would not have been feasible before the advent of e-mail. Resolving difficulties with individual students, as well as more general communication to all students in the TAs' groups, seems likely to become an established aspect of the TA role.

CONSULTING ON ISSUES OF COURSE STRUCTURE AND MODES OF PRESENTATION

Their roles as consultants took TAs and coaches beyond the boundaries of more traditional role functions. From their particular vantage points, the TAs and coaches offered ongoing formative evaluation of fundamental aspects of the innovations that they served. Where faculty solicited and made use of this input, TAs first developed a sense that their ongoing collegial critique was helping to make the innovation work, or work better, and then undertook this as a professional responsibility. However, more than that, TAs and coaches showed clear signs of actively seeking to address some of issues of course structure and presentation that they identified, whether individually, alongside faculty, or as a group. These evidences of critique and responsibility for fundamental aspects of the course drew the TAs and coaches into a deeper level of collegial responsibility for student learning than is traditionally open to them.

Some of the matters that TAs and coaches discussed with their faculty were detailed implementation issues that would be of limited interest to innovators at large. However, they also discussed the nature of, and possible solutions to, a set of issues that may be seen as critical to many, perhaps most, innovations. Broadly, these include the structural conditions that enable or constrain innovation, the organizational coherence of new courses, the balance between breadth and depth of content coverage, and the quality of preparation that these courses offer for future disciplinary work. Faculty who are participants, supporters, skeptics, or critics debate these same issues when considering the role and value of innovative courses. What is particularly useful about contributions to these debates made by the TAs and coaches is that they are grounded in independent, direct observation of both the innovative and the traditional classes for which they have worked. TAs and coaches felt free to share their thinking about what enabled innovations to work optimally, where faculty had explicitly and regularly invited them to do so and where they had weekly opportunities to meet and discuss course issues, both with and without faculty participation. Where these conditions are in place, TAs seem likely to develop a consulting function that extends beyond feedback on particular aspects of their own work to expressions of opinion and advice about the broader factors shaping the character of an innovation and its chances of success. As several of the participating faculty attested, they valued this higher level of engagement by their TAs and coaches both as personal support and as contributions to faculty's thinking about the further development of their innovations.

With the exception of lab work where TAs working in more conventional classes may give feedback on the efficacy of particular labs and help faculty to improve them, TAs have not traditionally been collaboratively engaged with faculty in course development, implementation, and refinement. However, in each initiative, I found the TAs and coaches acting as generators of ideas and strategies in support of substantive areas of the courses. In the following sections, I describe specific examples of these contributions.

Advising on Course Approach and Materials

The modular chemistry data offer good examples of TAs actively advising faculty on the approach, content, and format of course materials—in this instance, the module handbooks. The TAs were aware that some modules had received more testing and revision than others. They shared with their faculty their critique and offered suggestions that they hoped would be communicated back to the module authors. As indicated in their evaluative comments in chapter 4, some TAs saw it as an open question as to whether, by using the modular approach, students could build a knowledge structure from which they could approach new questions and unfamiliar areas of knowledge. They questioned whether the open-ended character of the modules would work for students who were not accustomed to abstract thinking, and they advocated more guidance, more buildup by short mental steps, and some changes in handbook layout to increase clarity. They also highlighted problems in logical flow, insufficient guidance for certain activities, mistakes in problems, and other errata:

> TA 1: Some of the modules are getting close to finished and are almost ready to be published. Others are at all different stages of development, so I think we can make a contribution as to how they finally come out by passing on what we notice through our prof.

> TA 2: Yeah, because sometimes you find incomplete trains of thought. The idea stops all of a sudden, and you're like, "Where did they mean to go with this?" Because, there I am trying to explain it to the students, and I can't because they don't completely explain where they want the students to go with the experiment.

> TA 1: And we've pointed out some of the questions at the end of the lab reports that you can't ask yet because they haven't explained some of the things the students would need to know first to answer them.

The TAs' editorial suggestions again reference the need for all developers of new learning materials to make the conceptual framework of the course and its logical sequence patent to students.

Two more TAs discussed the questions posed to students by the module authors and advised on their utility for the level of students to which they were addressed:

> TA 1: As I first looked through the modules, I thought, "Wow! These are really good questions!" But as I worked with the students, I could see that the point of some of them was going right over their heads. Because they don't have a real intuitive feel for chemistry yet. And some of them are written in such an open-ended way that there was a whole spectrum of answers that you could give. You could really cop out and answer, "Yup" for some of 'em!

> TA 2: Exactly. For some of them, my first thought was "This is a real insightful question." Then my second thought was "But I don't think they're going to get it."

> TA 1: I'd actually like us to sit down with [Professor X] now that we've gone through two modules and go through the handbooks giving feedback on what range of responses we got to each question. I think we could help to rework some of them so that students at our level could really get into them.

Again, pitching new materials at an appropriate level for each stage in the conceptual development of the course is a generic issue for innovative classes and their TAs.

Advice on "Signposting" Issues

One fundamental issue of course structure and presentation on which the TAs and coaches offered advice may be regarded as being central to all classroom innovations that involve new materials and methods. I briefly reference this idea in chapters 4 and 5 under the label "signposting." We first discovered this issue and its consequences for the success of classroom innovations in our work as formative evaluators for modular chemistry. In our first round of interviews with students who had experienced modules, it became evident that a serious barrier to student learning by new methods was insufficient attention to signposting in module design and implementation. Based on the evidence from those interview data, the issue may be broadly stated thus: In rethinking the sequencing, emphasis, and presentation methods for the concepts that define their modules, the authors are, in effect, creating story lines that are intended to take students on particular intellectual journeys. The hypothesis that underwrites the chemistry modules and many other classroom innovations is that, by taking such journeys, students will gain mastery of key ideas, understand the conceptual linkages that connect them, and learn how to apply them in a variety of new situations. Faculty may also want students to cumulatively build their own conceptual frameworks. To achieve these goals, the story line used by faculty to present their course materials has to be made clear to students by signposting its structure, sequencing, major features, and linkages. Students who experienced earlier versions of chemistry modules expressed their need to know what stage their knowledge had reached at any time during the progression of the module—that is, to develop a sense of direction, progression, and cumulative mastery. As one student explained it to her interviewer, "I want to know where I am now, how I got here from where we started, and where we are going with all of this."

The need for signposts—written, verbal, demonstrated, and oft repeated— is fundamental to the achievement of course learning goals but may not be met in many classes, whether innovative or traditional. Indeed, this may be seen as a generic problem for all teachers, although it may go unidentified as such in more traditional lecture-style teaching. The desire to meet this learning need is also a strong motivator for innovation: faculty may attempt reforms precisely because they observe that students compartmentalize, and then forget, pieces of knowledge learned for tests and thus fail to develop a coherent body of knowledge to carry forward and build on. However, it is easier for faculty to identify these needs than to meet them. In the early years of chemistry module development, the authors, testers, and evaluators identified, discussed, and then worked to address the challenge of shaping their modular materials into coherent story lines and signposting their constituent elements as they tried out the new materials in class. The outcomes of these efforts were discussed in interviews with samples of students who experienced the later modules, with participating faculty who reflected on their classroom ex-periments, and with their TAs whose observations and ideas are represented here.

In all three innovations, TAs and coaches commented on the nature and significance of the signposting problems they encountered. In each initiative, signposting issues were differently manifested, although the students' basic need for structure and direction was the same. In the astronomy course, the students experienced difficulties in making sense of the large amounts of in-formation to which they were exposed and placing pieces of information into a conceptual framework where the relative importance of particular concepts was clear to them. By the later stage of modular chemistry (when their TAs were interviewed) the story lines of the individual modules had al-ready been the overt focus of a process of collegial discussion and editing. However, there still remained difficulties for students in working effectively with a larger-than-accustomed variety of reading sources and in linking the particular set of modules chosen by the teacher into a coherent syllabus. The Berkeley initiative stands somewhat in contrast because the innovators had no power to change the selection, emphases, or presentation of materials in the lectures and labs. An important part of the intervention was, in effect, to structure the TA sessions so as to provide the kinds of signposts that would allow students to get the most out of the unchanged lecture and labs.

The observations of the TAs and coaches on the need for signposting closely matched those of the original student interviewees. They reported that their students needed to understand how the ideas that they were now learning connected with what they had already learned, where these ideas were heading, and how this body of knowledge was constructed. Where the links that connected one piece of the story to another were missing or ob-scure, TAs and coaches advised faculty of these gaps and suggested ways to address them. As illustrated, they also worked to make the story more co-herent for their students.

Although concerns about insufficient signposting were expressed by TAs and coaches working in all three initiatives, the Interactive Astronomy course provided the clearest example of coaches acting as consultants to faculty on signposting problems and doing what one coach described as "repair work" with students. This arose partly because Interactive Astronomy afforded the undergraduate coaches an active role in course development and partly be-cause the innovator was a single individual who began to develop his course without the benefit of a collaborative, information-sharing faculty network. In this respect, Interactive Astronomy may be more typical of science edu-cation reforms than the other two initiatives. The astronomy coaches de-scribed the signposting issues manifested in their class in terms of student difficulties in developing a coherent hierarchical framework of ideas from the hypertext and lecture:

Coach 1: It's all flying off the top of his head, and to someone who knows some-thing about the material, it's very exciting. But the students are like, "Do I write that down? Is this important?" I think if there's going to be formal lecture time, then it needs to be more structured. And an outline up front would be good so they know what's going to be talked about and how things fit together. Then they can organize their thoughts in their notes.

Coach 2: But now it just seems like free-falling.

Coach 3: Teachers who teach like that are very, very difficult to learn from be-cause it's difficult to filter out what's important. I've had teachers very similar—just in regular classes. And, in one way, it's encouraging and fantastic that pro-fessors are so enthusiastic about what they are doing. But it needs some restraint to focus it and impart to the students what is really, really critical.

Coach 2: I think you have to make it clear when you are lecturing—telling things that you know—and when you and the students are discussing some of those ideas. You can't assume that students understand the difference straight off.

The astronomy coaches advised their professor that, if the intent of his lec-ture was to draw together materials from several sources and get the students to understand the connections, it was especially important for the lecture to have a clear structure that tied ideas together. Not only did the coaches ad-vise their professor of this learning need, but they also worked to meet it themselves:

He had a lot of different expectations for how things were gonna work, and he couldn't actually know how that was going to work out without actually expe-riencing them. He expected the kids to come up with their own challenging questions and expected that we would be pushing them to be more question-ing. And that never happened. It didn't pan out that way. So, the job responsi-bilities he laid out for us at the start actually evolved into a basic responsibility to help students get a handle on the wider picture and put all this fascinating stuff into a structure and sequence that made sense to them.

They advised their professor of their students' need for lectures and tests that focused on key ideas and distinguished what was important from what was ancillary. In what they (but not necessarily the students) identified as re-lated ideas, coaches noted the absence of vital steps that would allow stu-dents to put information gathered from the hypertext into a conceptual framework. They offered advice on selecting materials for lecture discus-sions and on giving students more context for their learning:

Coach 1: He will start like at the broadest plane, and then he'll zoom in on this little tiny thing and miss everything on the continuum in between.

Coach 2: And he'll skip way over there.

Coach 3: Then he's like all the way on the other side of the world talking about something else. Then he'll make a generalized statement. So, there's this inconsistent depth and breadth, and I can see how the students are incredibly confused on what level they're supposed to focus their understanding at.

Coach 2: Right, because they're looking for their cue from the lecture, and they don't know how to read it.

Coach 1: They don't develop an understanding of how this or that fits into the big puzzle. We discussed this with him recently at one of our meetings.

Coach 3: We told him that it would be good for him to spend his time after the quiz dealing with one related chunk of issues and only talk about one main thing.

Coach 1: I am sure he has difficulty knowing what size chunk to focus on. And our students don't know how big that chunk is in relation to everything else.

Coach 3: I think the discussion session is a great idea—getting people to talk about astronomy—but he needs some way to make sure the students are taking home what he wants them to take home. So, more structure, and more explaining that this is what we talked about today and this is why it's important.

They then proceeded to brainstorm what might be done to address aspects of the problem:

Coach 2: I think it might be incredibly worthwhile to pay a grad student to spend the summer reading the hypertext and making an outline of core material with chapters and subheadings. That way, the student could download single pages and see how what they're looking at relates to other things.

Coach 1: If they could get the relationship of where the information they are looking at fits into other things in the class . . . I appreciate it would be hard to do, but it needs someone who knows the material and has a good editor's eye to go through it and bring out the structure of what's there.

They also described their own efforts to provide conceptual patches when the story line that connected elements in the materials was incomplete or obscure to their students:

What the students expect from us in which weeks and what we expect of ourselves in that time has to be clear. And we have to help them make sense of this knowledge and why this course is set up the way it is.

Sometimes it's not clear enough in the way it's laid out. And we have to give it more explanation. If the professor worked at that more, we'd have less of that kind of connecting work to do, and it would save the students some grief.

Modular chemistry TAs advised faculty who want their students to use the Internet as an informational source to give good guidelines by which to focus their searches on relevant areas of information:

TA 1: I suggested that they help students narrow down their web searches. It's hard to go searching for "fats"—you come up with just a million matches. You obviously can't check every one, or you're going to be doing it for weeks.

TA 2: We said to him, if they are going to send the students to the Internet, they need to write in some guidance about where they should go searching and why.

TA 1: We think they could add that without too much trouble.

Modular TAs advised that signposting was also needed in the labs. By linking some of the smaller individual lab activities, students would be enabled to see how they were conceptually linked. It would also help to overcome students' traditional resistance to making full use of their lab time: where there were multiple, apparently disconnected activities to be done, students were (as already discussed) apt to develop the theory that "the faculty are just finding ways to keep us here."

To faculty who were making a one- or two-semester course out of several modules, their TAs advised faculty to place more emphasis on the connections between modules. As students learned concepts in the context of particular applications, TAs thought that there was a risk that students would not be able to extract generalized principles and apply them to other situations. In one institution, the TAs noticed that students were more comfortable with the modular approach in the second of a two-semester series. The TAs advised that it was worth building on this inclination by working at getting students to see their growing body of knowledge as being interconnected:

TA 1: In the second semester, you could really see that they were making the connection between the lectures and the labs.

TA 2: And all the complaining had pretty well subsided. They came in just ready to go again.

TA 1: So we thought it was a good opportunity to set up some discussions that got them to link some of the ideas that they learned last semester in the different environment modules. You don't always connect the dots straight away, and we don't want them to just forget what they learned.

TA 2: And that's the whole point. We want them to really build up what they know, not just learn it and put it aside.

TA 1: So we suggested some discussion topics, and we have started figuring out with [Professor X] when to do them.

This conversation (again) points to the TAs' sense of responsibility for, and investment in, their students' learning and their assumption that it is truly part of their job to work with faculty to figure out resolutions to course structure issues. It also illustrates an important TA observation made in chapter 5, that student resistance to innovative forms of learning tends to fade as students get accustomed to using them and see their own progress.

Another important aspect of signposting is enabling students to make optimal use of course materials. These may include texts used for reference as well as basic information, other reference volumes, journal articles, handbooks (such as those used in the chemistry modules), and online sources. In a web-based course such as Interactive Astronomy, where the amount of information available is vast, coaches advised their professor that students need a guide or map to help them cluster and connect the detailed information that they amass:

> Coach 1: I think that both the strength and weakness of a web-based course is that you have unlimited access to information.
>
> Coach 2: It's hard to know what's important, and I have sometimes noticed students having trouble piecing the details together. They can understand the discussion questions individually, but they can't always understand how all these questions fit into the bigger picture. They need to know the agenda.
>
> Coach 1: We suggested to him that he give them a week-by-week schedule that tells them what they should focus on now, where they're going next, and what they should end up knowing.

In a broader sense, signposting involves setting the content of the class within its structural and pedagogical context so that students know where they are going. The coaches advised their professor to set the direction and tone of the class right from the outset by explaining the approach and structure of the class, laying out what is expected of students, and giving an overall guide (both electronic and verbal) whereby to navigate course content and source materials:[1]

> I think that goes for any class that the first two weeks are totally critical as to what the students are going to do for the rest of the semester. You know, you can use the horse analogy—if you let it eat in the first two minutes of your ride, it's gonna eat it's way through the rest of the ride. So I think you have to convey the structure, establish some consistency, let them know what's expected and how they are going to go about learning in this particular class. And, if we have fun at the same time, then people will get into the swing of it and be excited to come to class.

Coaches observed that some early student resistance to the course was triggered by a failure to adequately clarify at the outset the nature of the class and its structural dimensions. For this class, they thought that it was particularly important for students to have a clear guide to the sources of materials they would use—both online and written—and how they were to use them. Without this guidance, coaches warned that they were set up for confrontations with students who subsequently discovered how the class worked. Based on their experience, their advice was that the class would work best if students received a detailed guide to course features and activities that was regularly updated. The coaches did not place all of the responsibility for making preparations for the next class on the professor but saw a role for themselves in this work, both as individuals and as a group:

> Coach 1: I think he does a good job of explaining that they are going to be taking an active part in their own education, but I think we need to do a better job about being clearer and more straightforward at the beginning of the semester about how the course is going to be run—just how every part of the class is going to work, what they are going to be learning about, and how they will do that.

> Coach 2: And when we come back in August, I want to ensure that the labs are ready and all the software is up and running perfectly—all tested and no flaws. And I want all the aspects of the course to be hammered out before the students come in, so they can be explained right from the beginning.

> Coach 1: That way, they can see where it's all going and what's the point of each activity.

The coaches advised that the philosophy of the course has to be part of this initial briefing because students need to understand the rationale for the expectation that they undertake more responsibility for their own learning and why the class places greater emphasis on hands-on activities and less on lecturing. Both coaches and the modular chemistry TAs thought that an explanatory introduction was important in any class but thought it particularly critical in innovative classes. Some of the coaches also decided that they should lay out their expectations for members of their learning groups:

> Next semester, I'm going to have a syllabus, and it's going to have what I expect of the students and the way we'll be working, and I'm gonna hand that out the first day. That's what I want because otherwise we waste a lot of time that we could spend clarifying issues and asking more questions.

In the chemistry modules, as already indicated, a considerable amount of work had already been done on the story lines of each individual module before this set of interviews with the TAs was conducted. Thus, the modular chemistry TAs identified and offered advice about a residual set of signposting problems with particular modular handbooks, difficulties caused by students' unfamiliarity with learning from multiple sources, and the broader issue of linking several modules together within a single semester such that they addressed linked sets of concepts whose relationships became patent to the students. Aspects of each of these issues have wider relevance for other innovative courses and their TAs. Both their local and broader implications are discussed in the following section.

Enabling Student Learning from Multiple Sources

A central issue of these and many other classroom innovations is how best to enable students to draw on and synthesize material from a variety of sources. TAs identified this as an issue with signposting implications, discussed how faculty might address the challenge, and devised strategies to meet the needs of their own student groups. Modular TAs described the difficulties of students who were unaccustomed to the mixture of narrative, discussion, activities, questions, and examples that they encountered in their modular handbooks. They were unfamiliar with the process of cross-referencing ideas encountered in one source with those found in others—in this case, relating materials in the modular handbooks with parallel material in their textbooks or journal articles. Students also found it difficult to track the key ideas and needed the TAs' help in learning how to work with multiple source materials:

> They had difficulty extracting the important material out of the real-world stuff. Like, these students need to have a list of definitions or a bolded word here and there to show them what the fundamentals are. They don't know how to do that on their own yet. And I can see from the older modules that the writers have realized it's important to write the modules that way to guide students—kinda teaching them how to read to extract the most important parts.

Broadly, TAs approved the faculty's intent of teaching students to work from a variety of sources and commented on their own and the faculty's efforts to show students how to do this:

> The issue is to tie it all together. You know, to actually point people to the pieces that are going to help them explain something. I take my copy to class all the time so we can look things up together, and they get comfortable with that.

Where a textbook was used for reference, TAs reported that it was not a problem for students to move around within a text so long as the connections with the class material were made clear. Some classes were given a written syllabus with cross-referenced items that connected passages in the modular handbook to articles and particular textbook pages—for example, good explanatory sections or sample problems:

> The cross-referencing guide they got at the beginning helps a lot. And I suggested that they get it laminated. Many of the class are freshmen who are not used to using a reference book. It's not something everybody comes out of high school knowing, so they could have a hard time navigating the modules without that extra help to learn how to use several sources together.

Where students were given directions on where to find further explanation of modular material in their texts, TAs reported that students had fewer problems working with their text as a source of reference:

The professors have gone through it and directly related the information in the modules to the text pages and other information. It's laid out well enough. The students don't seem to have too much trouble finding their way around

Some TAs showed their students how to link the modular handbook to the text by developing their own cross-referencing systems:

I showed my group how to take little sticky notes and mark each section of the module with the corresponding pages in their text. Then they know where to go. They soon catch on.

Because of the break with single texts in favor of multiple resources that are a feature of many classroom innovations, learning how best to help students work with multiple source materials and advising faculty on adjustments that enable this strategy are likely to be a regular feature of TA work in many innovative classes.

Advice on Other Issues of Course Structure

Among the modular chemistry TAs and Interactive Astronomy coaches, attention to signposting was the most often discussed issue of design and implementation. However, the TAs and coaches also offered reflections and suggestions to faculty on a number of other fundamental aspects of course structure and coherence that they saw as bearing on student learning. Some aspects of course structure are determined by the departmental and institutional conditions within which new courses must operate; others reflect organizational decisions by the innovators. The Berkeley initiative and modular chemistry, when taught at a research university, provided the sharpest examples of innovations operating in limiting circumstances. TAs identified a number of factors as barriers to effective implementation of innovations, of which large class size was seen as the most constraining:

There was an effort to get the students to construct the knowledge in their own minds. And it did not work for a number of reasons. One was that many of them didn't have sufficient chemistry background. Another was that they are freshmen and don't have sufficient intellectual background to do that. Most of all, the class was simply too big. We told them—there's too many people in the lab groups and not enough time to interact with the TAs and with their peers to construct that knowledge for themselves. They simply didn't have the tools, the time, or the structure in order to do that. To me that was what made the modules difficult to teach and difficult to learn from.

They're thrown into a situation where there's five hundred people and TAs teaching it for the first time. And we just can't compete with class overwhelm. I had a couple of guys that had AP chemistry, and they bombed my class. I couldn't really explain it except that I guess it happens everywhere with the big classes. A better ratio of students to teachers would help.

TAs and coaches explained why class size matters and what is lost when a small innovative class increases in size. They identified the main negative effects of large classes as losses in continuity, interaction in learning, and active student engagement with the course—all of which they valued as aspects of the particular innovations for which they worked:

> Interaction is very important, and I don't know if you could really achieve it because of the class size. Interaction is very hard in a big class.

> Continuity is very important, and in smaller groups, it has a chance. A smaller group is much more effective for interaction. Students feel they develop a relationship with the instructor and a relationship with the material because they get to talk about it directly. I've TAed for classes of equally large size, but in this lab the groups were almost twenty students. It's in the lab that you get a chance to go into that interactive style as opposed to lecturing them. But it's so much easier to interact with ten students than twenty. You get to know them. You remember the last question that they asked you and where they may have gotten stuck. I would typically go round the room, and, with the smaller number, you get a sense of guiding the whole room and where each person is at. As the number increases, there's just some point at which you lose out, and every time you speak to a person again, you have to reacquaint yourself with how far along they've gotten.

A group of coaches who had worked in the course at an early stage commented on the decline in effectiveness of the professor's interactive whole-class sessions as student numbers rose. They also described the negative impact of the size and type of room that is required to accommodate a large class, including a reversal to some of the disengaged student behavior (which I describe in chapter 5) as being normative in many large classes. The teacher in this class, and also those in the very large modular chemistry class at the research university, had tried, by the use of cordless microphones, to enable whole-class discussion and short interactive activities followed by reporting. In neither case did the TAs and coaches feel that these strategies worked. Passing around the cordless microphone proved cumbersome; it was also intimidating to some students, and slowed down the discussion:

> Coach 1: It's way too big. The whole philosophy behind the discussion questions is interaction—you just can't interest with a group that big. And now you're in a big lecture hall, and you're trying to work with hand-around microphones. The mike is a big disadvantage.

> Coach 2: Yep. Because it's clunky.

> Coach 1: And it raises a lot of intimidation.

Coach 3: Right. It's more like a performance.

Coach 2: Exactly. I mean, I would have been petrified to stand up and talk in front of a class of two hundred.

From their experience of working for the course in both a small and a larger form, the same group of expert coaches explained how and why size affects interaction and student engagement:

Coach 1: When we were in the little room with no more than seventy-five people, they were interacting way more.

Coach 2: They paid attention.

Coach 3: This other room is kind of a dungeon that works for lectures because people who care go and sit up front and learn. The people who don't, sit in the back and fail. But for this kind of class, it really doesn't work.

Coach 3: It's just the proximity of a smaller group in a smaller room that allows the class discussion to work.

Coach 1: And now we've got the problems you get in all big classes—people who continually talk, people that fall asleep, people that do other work and don't pay attention.

Coach 2: In the little classroom there were just six rows, and you were aware of everyone in the room. It was quite intimate, and people got a lot out of the discussions.

Coach 1: It was easier to understand everything because the prof was right there, and while we were going through the discussion questions, he was an immediate resource.

Coach 2: So, it's not just the numeric jump that matters. It's the big drop in the quality of the experience of learning. Where he used to be speaking directly to students in the audience and trying to engage them in dialogue, now he often has to cut off his answers and shorten the discussions to move on to the next question.

Both TAs and coaches offered estimates of the numeric limits within which active and interactive teaching methods will work. These are somewhat relative because, across the set of institutions within which the TAs and coaches were working, what they defined as a "large" class varied from one hundred to over one thousand students. However, what seemed to matter was not the upper limit of the class but the size beyond which it became difficult to use class time for direct conversational contact between students and their professors, TAs, or coaches, and with each other:

I think we're breaking the class down into about twenty per group with about sixty students total. I think it's very feasible to get everyone involved with those numbers.

TA at the research university: I think that the problem with the modules was just the class size—not anything else. It meant a lack of effective interaction. I mean, they tried really hard to make it interactive, but in a class like that, interaction is critical and I don't know if you could ever achieve it with several hundreds in the class.

Across the institutional sample, TAs and coaches estimated that the upper limit for running a class with whole-group interactive sessions was approximately seventy to eighty students, with lab groups of ten to fifteen and recitation sections up to about twenty. Chemistry faculty interviewees who had worked in innovative mode with classes of different sizes offered eighty as the approximate upper limit for whole-class discussions, although some reported that they had managed to do question and answer, discussion, and student presentation sessions with as many as 120 students.

The astronomy coaches noted that innovators may be pressured by their departments to scale up their method for a much larger class once the initial experiment seems to be working:

Coach 1: Like he said, he's going to bigger groups in the fall.

Coach 2: It's pretty much decided that they're going to register 150 students. So, he'll hire more coaches, but our groups are gonna have to get bigger too.

Coach 3: And the computers will have to be shared more.

Interviewer: Has your professor asked your opinion about the change?

Coach 2: We talked a bit at last week's meeting. But it seemed like its departmental logistics. Nothing he can do.

Coach 3: Yeah. It's just how it's gonna be.

This set of observations on the issues that class size can raise for innovative courses again reflect the degree to which the TAs and coaches saw themselves as being actively engaged with the faculty in experimental teaching work. In their discussions among themselves, and in the suggestions they offer to faculty, the tone of their remarks is collegial and contains embedded assumptions that their feedback is of potential value and is likely to be received in that light. The TAs are neither "grumbling" nor "complaining" about things over which they feel no sense of control. Rather, they actively seek to critique, explain, and suggest, and they perceive these contributions as being useful. They also express a sympathetic collegial view of their faculty's constraints.

The TAs also offered warnings that reflected their sense of engagement and collegial concerns for the success of the innovation. For example, structural constraints on the effectiveness of innovations can, in the view of TAs, be exacerbated when faculty perpetuate normative practices that are dysfunctional to their innovation. This contingency arose in one state university where a group of faculty decided to interleave chemistry modules with more traditional content and teaching methods. The TAs warned that the effectiveness of their work was compromised for want of sufficient commonality in their selection of content, method of teaching, and timing of presentation to students. These faculty had not yet figured out how to keep students more or less evenly prepared each week so that, in labs and recitations, the TAs could work with their student groups on broadly the same new material. TAs saw the problem as historic and structural on the one hand but, on the other, as a problem that could be surmounted by purposive conversation and collective effort:

> TA 1: There are four sections now. So we get sets of students, each of whom has been taught by a different person.

> TA 2: That's a huge problem. [Professor X] taught this, but [Professor Y] didn't.

> TA 3: And they all teach it differently. Even when they are working on the same material, they approach it differently.

> TA 2: I'm always asking the prof, "Have you covered this in class yet?" Our students are all from different sections and have different professors, but they all have to be ready to take a standard test. So all the professors have to get them to such and such a point by the test date.

> TA 3: And it plays hell with the labs. Sometimes my students have met the materials and are prepared, and sometimes they aren't.

> TA 1: And some of them are asking the rest, "Do y'all know anything about Lewis structures?" [*laughing*].

> TA 2: We did the global warming module all together, but some of them hadn't had Lewis structures beforehand.

> TA 1: And we have been trying to figure out if there's a way for each of us only to get students from one teacher. But there are serious timing problems against that.

Having laid out the problem, they undertake to encourage their faculty to take collective action to solve it:

> TA 2: So it comes back to how we persuade the faculty to teach the same material at the same time in something like similar ways.

> TA 3: In synch.

> TA 1: More in harness.

> TA 2: We need them to talk to each other and think about how to do that.

The TAs clearly saw it as their business to canvas their faculty to address a serious structural difficulty that was affecting students' learning. They saw it as being appropriate to offer respectful criticism and to take an active role in figuring out possible solutions. Their attitude is, thus, both proactive and collegial.

Modular chemistry TAs at the research university discussed a similar situation. Several faculty taught different sections of lecture and lab as a way of coping with a large class. However, there was insufficient collaboration to ensure that the whole class moved forward together in what they had learned. These course disjunctions were further compounded by wide variations in the content and method of recitation sections run by TAs. Some TAs advised that the resulting lack of coherence and continuity undermined the chances of success for the introduction of modules. Indeed, it is this kind of structural (and cultural) difficulty in schools with large introductory science classes that the Berkeley initiative was developed, in part, to address. Again, the TAs advised that the problem was not insuperable if faculty were willing to discuss it:

TA 1: The students are suffering from trying to piece together the different materials they are getting from different teachers and then from their TAs. They need continuity, not this disjointed hit-and-miss coverage.

TA 2: And the module teachers know this is an issue. We've talked to them about it, and I know they wring their hands over it. But they seem sort of frozen out by their colleagues—best I can tell.

TA 3: I don't get it. It's not that hard to fix. They just have to talk about it and agree what they will teach and when and what we should do for them as backup.

TA 2: But I think they are too hung up on doing their own thing in the classroom, so . . .

TA 1: Perhaps they just can't let go of that.

TA 3: I think it's a great big control issue with them [*laughing*].

Constraints on Faculty Collaboration and Their Consequences

The issue that these TAs raise for the wider reform community is that even innovators may have difficulty in letting go of long-standing habits—in this case, reluctance to discuss and align aspects of their teaching and testing strategies with those of other departmental faculty. This issue was discussed by participating modular chemistry faculty in interviews. It also arose from discussions with the evaluator about why volunteer faculty groups who had attempted to develop common testing methods across different modular classes had largely failed in this effort. Innovators who had surmounted this socialized inner constraint continued to report difficulty in engaging colleagues in conversations about generating shared solutions to structural problems that constrained the effectiveness of their teaching.

Their TAs did not necessarily understand why it was apparently so hard for faculty to collaborate to set up a common teaching strategy for their new course, discuss the details with them in advance, and allow them to start the semester in an organized manner. Without understanding the process of socialized normative constraints that tend to make faculty view teaching as a highly private and independent affair, they saw resolution of shared class planning in simple organizational terms:

> TA 1: I think that, two weeks before the semester starts, the professors need to go into hibernation and spend some time together thinking it out, planning it, explaining to each other how it should work, and then discussing it with us. Like, with the four of us, they need to be ready to say, "We'll walk into the first class, and I'll be talking about this, and then we'll do the computer stuff, and then the group activity, and then we move into full groups in the first lab." And so on.

> TA 2: Yeah, and this takes a lot of thinking and working out. And we *all* need to be in on the discussion to figure out the details.

The undergraduate coaches who had yet to develop a sense of their teaching as a private form of activity were agreed that it was important for them to agree to act consistently with each other in the ways in which they conducted their groups:

> Coach 1: I think it's really important for us to be consistent between teams.

> Coach 2: Yeah, that's really critical for the students.

> Coach 3: Before you ever get to meet them—while you are still training as coaches—you have to pool together what you know and take decisions together about what the groups should do next.

> Coach 1: And agree on what it's worth doing next time.

> Coach 2: Yeah, otherwise it's just individualized. You might feel more good about doing it that way, but your students will suffer.

These observations stand in contrast to those of some of the Berkeley graduate students (discussed in chapter 4) who resisted a shared approach to their work with student groups on the grounds that it limited their professional freedom to teach as they saw fit. The differences between faculty and graduate student TAs on the one hand and undergraduate TAs and coaches on the other may largely be explained in terms of the norms of professional socialization already developed by the former and lack of awareness of those norms among the latter. However, the collaborative approach to course problems taken by the TAs and coaches suggests that the freedom offered by innovative courses to comment, suggest, and brainstorm solutions is developing a new set of collaborative attitudes toward teaching in this generation. This can set a trend for the greater engagement of TAs in fundamental aspects of course development. It also socializes a new generation of college teachers into a less private, more collegial approach to their teaching work.

Composition, Coherence, and Consistency of Course Materials

Some structural difficulties arise from the context within which innovations must operate. Others (as illustrated) are created by counterproductive, if normative, patterns of response to structural problems, particularly those arising from management of large classes. The TAs and coaches commented on structural issues that arose from the choices made by innovators. For example, an important issue for modular chemistry teachers was whether one or two modules could successfully be embedded in a class that was largely taught in a traditional way. Except where a single module was placed at the end of the course as a culminating experience, modular TAs advised their faculty not to attempt a mix-and-match approach. Students became confused when they returned to a lecture format after working in an active, interactive mode for several modular weeks, and they began to question what was the "right" way to learn chemistry:

> TA 1: This is our second modular semester, and there are definitely some difficulties for the students when you take a module and put it somewhere in a more traditional class. And it doesn't much matter where you put it, it still creates difficulties because the structure of the class wasn't built for it. There are going to be some disjunctions.

> TA 2: We've told our professors how much better it is this time. They took four modules and put them together to make a whole semester. Having run through this once, we began to rethink how we set up the class and the labs so that it makes a completely planned semester.

A group of modular TAs in another institution similarly endorsed the principle of consistency in the pedagogical approach used in the course from start to finish:

> TA 1: It should be all or nothing. Start off that way and do the whole class by module.

> TA 2: Make it modular the whole way through.

TA 1: Exactly. And advertise it that way up front so the students can make a free choice and know what they're getting into.

TA 3: It's no good starting out with a good module like "Fats" and getting them all interested in applying what they know in everyday life, and then ducking back into the same old lectures. If the modular way is good, it should be consistently good.

TA 1: 'Cause otherwise, students doubt it's the right way to learn even when they learned a lot and enjoyed it.

TA 2: Maybe the profs are afraid of being too radical too soon.

TA 3: They shouldn't be. If they seem confident, the students are more likely to go with it.

Interviewer: Did you talk to them about this?

TA 1: Oh yes. We really encouraged them to think all-modular next semester.

The same advice was offered to faculty in both interview rounds by some of the students who had experienced modular classes. The TAs' advice may also apply to novice innovators who introduce new material and methods into their courses in a tentative, partial way. TAs advised that this may not work well if students become confused about what is the "right" way to learn in this course. Their observations in the modular classes suggest that faculty do not need to be overtentative: as indicated earlier, modular TAs reported that student resistance fell sharply toward the end of all-modular semesters and was insignificant at the start of a second consecutive all-modular semester. In the preceding set of quotations, again, we note that the TAs are comfortable with giving strong advice about a central issue of course approach and structure. They support their faculty and seem quite confident that their suggestions will be taken into account.

The issue of how best to use new materials and methods to construct a coherent new course is another generic issue for classroom innovations. With much to choose from, the innovator has to select materials and activities that can be organized in a way that addresses a chosen set of learning goals. As some TAs observed, this means avoiding the temptation to let the syllabus expand into interesting related areas. Letting the course content drift creates signposting difficulties for students who lose the threads that should tie course ideas together. One head TA advised his professor thus:

> I think I would just say to [Professor X], "Choose your goals carefully for a given semester; stick with that set and don't stray into other areas." I think we tried to tackle material that was outside the scope. It was still introductory, but it wasn't within what the catalogue description said the class was about. So that needs to be thought through carefully because, although sometimes, we thought, "Now that would make a great lab," we were actually writing a lab for another course.

We have to be willing to say, "Well, we may have to lay aside that lab for this class and find one that has real synergy with the rest of the material."

A related issue is balancing the desire of innovating faculty to build some flexibility into their experimental syllabus with what the TAs and coaches saw as the students' need for a structure, coherence, and consistency. While they understood that innovation requires adjustment in light of feedback, they advised that making spontaneous changes in the course structure provokes student anxiety and protest:

> TA: At the beginning, you could easily introduce the modules, talk about what was expected of them [the students], introduce them to the computer system so they'd be prepared to get started. Once you have the structure laid out for them, then you could be flexible about which module we're gonna teach next, or if we need an extra week for a module, take it and make adjustments. I think flexibility is good. I've been in far too many overstuffed classes where the rush to get to the next item on the syllabus interfered with whatever you were trying to learn right now. But you still need the building blocks in place.

> Coach: Developing the curriculum while you're teaching it allows flexibility, but it introduces instability and anxiety—and then revolt! I think you need to keep an open, flexible mind, but you need much of the structure laid out beforehand— like you build in four labs but have eight ready, so as we see different things being learned and responded to, you can choose which lab comes next.

Meeting the students' need for coherence and consistency in the presentation of new materials is, again, part of designing a well-signposted course. The examples offered suggest that TAs have a constant part to play in signaling course disjunctions that limit student learning.

"Coverage" and Pace

A commonly experienced form of difficulty for innovative science faculty in selecting course materials is that of letting go of a strongly internalized and deeply felt moral responsibility to "cover" a sufficient amount of the disciplinary canon. What is deemed "sufficient" may arise from a concern to adequately prepare students for subsequent classes in a sequence, for work in a related major, or for professional entrance examinations. It may also be a response to an embedded, though not overtly articulated or research-based, theory that students should serially revisit particular concepts over the first few semesters of a science major in order to build up an understanding over time. These beliefs and imperatives may explain the practice common among science faculty of providing broad surveys of disciplinary concepts. To address all of the topics necessitates a fast pace and shallow treatment of any particular item. The issue of how to resolve the problem of "coverage"

in innovative classes has been widely discussed among the science education reform community (Seymour 2001). It was viewed as a key issue to be
resolved by the module authors and testers. It was also evident in interviews
with module teachers and their departmental colleagues, either as a focus for
concern or as a source of objection to using modules. Some student interviewees also expressed the belief that there was a defined body of chemistry
that they were supposed to know and that without sufficient coverage in
early courses, they would later find themselves at a disadvantage. TAs were
well aware of this common student fear:

> When I took one of the early modular courses, actually my primary fear wasn't
> whether I would retain what we had learned—which is something I should
> have been more concerned about—but that we wouldn't get enough of what-
> ever it was that we were supposed to know. And, of course, I had no idea what
> that might look like, except that it seemed expected that you crash through
> masses of material in a big fat textbook.

The modular chemistry TAs had discovered the issue for themselves, as
learners and from what they observed in their students:

> TA 1: I think that if you don't get something in a regular intro class, you are likely
> to come back to it in another class, and you go over it again and learn it a bit
> more.
>
> Interviewer: Do you find that chemistry teachers go over materials that you were
> already taught in an earlier class?
>
> TA 2: Yeah. They all do that.
>
> TA 3: Yeah, pretty much that's how it's done.
>
> TA 1: There's a kind of habit of revisiting things you just skimmed over in an ear-
> lier class—usually real fast [*laughing*].
>
> TA 2: One thing I like about the modules is that the things they focus on are
> done in some depth so the kids walk away to the next class understanding them
> better than we did.
>
> TA 3: I agree. I can see that there's a lot to be said for doing it more slowly and
> going for depth.

Treating fewer topics in depth was a feature of the modular approach that
TAs saw as being particularly beneficial. Some thought this worked better
than the way that they had been taught and reassured their faculty by citing
its advantages to their students and themselves:

> TA 1: And I think it is true that we have got through less than we would have
> got in a normal intro class. But I think the things that we covered, both the stu-
> dents and I understood better. I got really curious about how the ozone hole

formed, and now I can explain it to someone, which is not something I could have done before.

TA 2: That's right. And I think because we worked in the modular format, I understand some concepts that I didn't really get a hold of in the earlier classes. But it did mean we covered less . . .

TA 3: Stuff! [*laughing*]

TA 3: I think our profs were a bit worried about this. And I told them that the ozone module had really opened up our minds to environmental chemistry—me and the students—and I wasn't really worried about getting the basic chemistry behind it. I think we got a good grip on that, and I think we will all remember it. But talking to my students, I could see it was also giving us all something about what chemistry is all about.

TA 2: And what you can do with it that's important in the world.

These TAs gave their faculty encouragement in support of their approach—encouragement that was grounded in the TAs' own experience and that of their students. As noted in a prior example, sometimes the TAs see it as being appropriate to their role to warn of a problem and explain its sources; here they give collegial support based on their observations.

Highly related to the issues of course material selection and the introduction of greater depth into lower-level courses is the challenge of setting an appropriate pace for the course. Modular TAs in particular advised that the modules worked best when the teachers gave sufficient time to a topic to discover the pace at which their students could move and whether they were pitching the material at the right level. Each module covered a lot of conceptual ground, and TAs advised creating sufficient dwell time for students to get the most out of it:

TA 1: They had three assignments due every week and three lectures to go to, plus labs and office hours. I mean, it was a constant on-the-go thing for them. They were always doing chemistry stuff! But they didn't have enough time to sit and absorb the information—really synthesize and internalize it. There was too much busy work that got in the way.

TA 2: I know. Maybe we should have a stronger sense of humility about how much time we're asking of students, given all their other classes too. You don't have to bludgeon them. I mean, that's one of the things that's wrong with traditional classes, and it's one good reason why we are doing modules. I think you can let chemistry sort of speak for itself more. If they have more time to think and talk about it, it will come.

Some faculty attempted five modules in a semester, which their TAs reported to be counterproductive—three or four seemed about right to them.

They argued for enough time in lab or recitation to spend with the students in going over matters that caused them difficulty:

> We didn't give long enough to the lab and the discussion, and we ended up cutting the discussion short, and we didn't get to the problems and were scuttling to do the lab reports. If something matters, I think we should give it enough time.

> Why go to all this trouble to do modules if you are going to rush students through them? It defeats the purpose. I think learning on the run is kinda a bad habit we've all gotten into.

TAs valued minilectures where the teacher dealt with conceptual difficulties as they arose by interrupting other activities, bringing all the students together, and devoting short periods of class time to this single topic. They also advised that students needed more time to do modular exams that contain open-ended questions and require students to write or to use material in contexts other than those in which they had learned them—a requirement that students often referred to in interviews as "stretching":

> TA 1: They could have done the exams better if they had more time. They are mostly freshmen, and they only know how to do one sort of science exam.

> TA 2: They needed time to learn *how* to do it as well as to do it well. There are some really thoughtful questions, but what's the point if they don't have time to think about them. What's the big rush?

One of the concerns bearing on innovating faculty as they decided how much breadth they could relinquish in favor of greater depth was whether those students who wanted to enter graduate or medical school after graduation would be adequately prepared for the Graduate Record Examinations (GRE) and Medical College Admissions Test (MCAT). TAs who offered advice on this issue confirmed that this fear circulated among students, often without their knowing what the character of the examination itself would be:

> TA 1: A lot of people are taking this class because they want to take the MCATs, and what they think they need is learning equations and stuff like that. But I don't think they know much about what those exams are actually like.

> TA 2: I think actually they will be well prepared. I mean one of the sections just involves writing.

> TA 1: I'm premed, and I know that there's an interdisciplinary approach in that exam, and the modules help with that.

> TA 2: I don't think anyone is very well prepared for the MCATs after most gen chem courses. But I think this course gives them a good foundation. Most of what they need comes in Organic, and you get a whole year of that.

> TA 1: But that doesn't stop them panicking!

Interviewer: Some of the premeds seem worried about the MCATs—whether this modular course will prepare them well enough.

TA 1: Oh they'll be fine for the MCATs.

TA 2: Yeah, it will be just fine. This richer, cross-disciplinary approach is actually just what they need for the MCATs. It's just that they don't know enough to know that yet.

TA 1: And they run on rumor and swap bad information!

All of the TAs and coaches, including those who expressed reservations about the approach that their faculty were using, offered feedback via the interviewer on aspects of the innovations. As indicated in table 7.1, 74 percent of them indicated that they were actively sharing their observations, insights, warnings, advice, and encouragement with faculty.[2] This is illustrated in many of the examples included in this chapter. Many of the speakers made it clear that they were discussing course issues with each other and were taking their collective suggestions to the faculty. Thus, the TAs and coaches' potential as consultants may be seen as a constant. As indicated earlier, the factors that turn this potential into active engagement in the course as working consultants are as follows:

- A clear message that faculty want their ongoing feedback. This needs to be offered as an invitation at the outset and regularly repeated.
- The establishment of regular meetings in which concerns can be discussed and suggestions proposed. Meetings may sometimes include the faculty and sometimes involve only the TAs.
- An open, nondefensive attitude by faculty toward critique that models for their teaching assistants how collegial, professional discussion is conducted.
- Evidence of changes in the course that reflect the teaching assistants' advice and also their students' feedback that the TAs convey to faculty.[3]

Knowing that their faculty pay serious regard to their observations and advice, and are ready to act upon it, is key in securing the trust and active engagement of both students and teaching assistants as consultants to the innovation. The practical implications for classroom innovators (and faculty at large) of establishing this tone are discussed in more detail in the chapter 10.

COLLABORATIVE ENGAGEMENT

Many of the TAs and coaches developed a level of engagement in the innovation for which they were working that may be described as being professional and collegial. To varying degrees, these teaching assistants shouldered responsibility for student learning alongside their faculty and with each other. They thought creatively about their teaching role and devised strategies for their own spheres of work that supported innovation goals. They also played an active role in getting students to learn more independently and interactively, contributed to the resolution of problems, and dealt directly with aspects of student resistance. As discussed in the previous section, many TAs and coaches acted as course consultants in that they offered critique, information, and suggestions to their faculty and discussed problems and their resolutions with both faculty and peers. They discussed improvements that they and their faculty could make in subsequent semesters and how best to transmit methods that had worked to incoming teaching assistants. Some had already worked in the innovative course for a second semester; some were planning further engagements with the course. This high level of collaboration arose because these TAs and coaches came to see themselves as partners in the enterprise—an identification that was reinforced where faculty took their ideas seriously and treated them with collegial courtesy.

Ownership and Responsibility

The primary shift on which all of these contributions hinged was one of attitude—from an incoming expectation of servicing the class under faculty direction to a sense of ownership in its success. Internalizing the idea that faculty valued their contributions and needed their help in making the innovation work prompted a sense of responsibility for the course and to their students that extended well beyond what faculty normally expect from their teaching assistants. This sense of responsibility was largely embedded in teaching assistants' observations about concrete issues and was expressed only occasionally as an abstract statement, as in the following declarations by a Berkeley TA and a modular chemistry TA:

I think it's always the professor's responsibility to make sure that students learn. Our professors clearly see it that way, although there's many faculty that don't take this on and put all the responsibility on the students. But, by extension, I think it's the TA's job too. That means that professors need to make sure that their TAs really understand the material well and learn different ways to get it across so that they can help the students understand it.

What mattered most to me was whether the students were learning the fundamentals of chemistry that they needed to take away from the class. I mean, for me, that's what really mattered, and I've tried to put most of my energy into ensuring that. You can't walk away from that. If they don't understand key ideas, I blame myself, and I have to think of ways to make it happen.

Expressions of a sense of responsibility to enable student learning and find ways to address course problems were offered by individual TAs in all three initiatives. However, the liveliest examples came from the Interactive Astronomy initiative, where the combination of a course with unresolved structural issues (more so than either the Berkeley initiative or modular chemistry), the openness of the professor to assistance in resolving these, and a weekly forum for collegial debate seemed to promote engagement and feelings of ownership among the coaches. The evidence for this does not lie in statements about their work but is embedded in their discussions about how to handle particular problems. In the following example, the coaches show their commitment to encouraging students to break with passive learning habits. They clearly do not find this easy but, over two semesters and in face of some student resistance, were dogged in pursuit of this goal:

Coach 1: A big thing was that they just wouldn't read the material—"Just tell us the basics." And we were saying, "No. You have to read the paper. We are only talking about four pages."

Coach 2: They just cling to the old, passive ways of learning. They just hate to read and write. And some of them never get over that.

Coach 3: They still have to be pulled and pushed into doing their work. And it's five o'clock on a Sunday afternoon, and the deadline for the entire semester is six PM. And I can see that such a person is online and still hasn't answered their question. "Do I have to pull your teeth to get you to participate?"

Coach 1: The answer is "Yes we do!"

Coach 2: And I tell them, "You're sitting at this keyboard that's connected to every possible piece of information you could ever desire, you know, but not once in my coaxings did you do a Yahoo! search on this . . ."

Coach 1: It's exasperating. But the professor is right. He wants them to go and learn something for themselves—to go and find it. And it's our job to push and prod them into doing that.

Coach 2: Actually, they are better this semester. I think we might be getting somewhere.

Coach 3: I hope so. Some days I feel like the road warrior!

In another example, the coaches discussed their sense of responsibility for students who were at risk of failing the course:

Coach 1: For some students, once they get into that rut, it just gets worse and worse and you can never dig them out of it.

Coach 2: You can never recover once you, like, don't care, and your grades are low, so "What's the point?"

Coach 3: That's the thing. We've gotta keep people from falling into that.

Coach 1: Yes, I think so.

As already discussed in the section on signposting, some of the coaches decided to save students from unproductive learning habits by laying out the ground rules for their learning groups at the start of the semester:

> I'm going to have a syllabus, and it's going to have the rules I expect and what's gonna happen in the group. And I'll hand it out the first day so they'll know exactly what's expected. Letting them sit at the computer and find their answers in group is a waste of all our time. They can do that at home. What's valuable is when they're working in a group, discussing the answers. And that happens too rarely. So, I'm determined to change that.

They discussed other reasons to establish a consistent pattern both for group activities and grading, made these their concern, and encouraged their professor not to change course rules in midcourse:

> Coach 1: There's something about the question setup which keeps people separate unless you work very hard at putting them together.

> Coach 2: I think it's the TAs' fault. I think my biggest mistake is not having laid out what I expect for my students. And the same thing goes for the professor, you know. Changing things in the middle is very bad—deciding halfway through to take off points for this or that. People have already made bad habits, so the syllabus needs to be drafted to set up the way it's gonna be and it stays that way.

> Coach 3: Also I think it's really important for the TAs to be consistent among themselves so you don't have one group claiming that their TA doesn't make them do something that their group has to do. We need to draw up a syllabus for the learning teams that's classwide and that lays out how the group work is to be done and what the grading system is.

> Coach 1: And you're right. If they are not getting engaged, then a lot of it is our fault. Then it's really hard because teams get set in their ways, and lifting them out of that is difficult.

The point of these examples is not whether and how the coaches resolved these particular issues but their clear assumption that shaping student learning behavior was a responsibility that they shared with the professor and each other.

The closest parallel to this level of ownership and responsibility described in the literature may be that offered in two discussions of the developmental stages of TAs in conventional classes by Nyquist and colleagues (Nyquist and Wulff 1996; Nyquist and Sprague 1998). The first two stages more clearly refer to the TAs' apprenticeship in traditional support roles. First, there is the senior learner, who is primarily concerned about self-survival and students' perceptions of him or her as a person. Next, is the colleague in training, who is concerned with how to lecture or discuss the subject matter and is more detached from students. However, the third and highest level observed in their studies—namely, the junior colleague who is concerned with students' learning and is engaged yet professional with students—equates fairly well with that noted among the coaches and TAs. Nyquist and Wulff (1996, 21) explain the developmental stages that they observe:

> At first, beginning teachers are likely to express a preponderance of self-concerns. . . . Following their survival concerns, beginning teachers then typically move to wonder about what methods they should be employing with students. Can I lecture effectively? Can I lead a class discussion? Can I maintain discipline? Will I be able to grade papers, construct tests? The last phase of aspiring teachers' concerns, after they feel somewhat competent in their interactions with students, is concern for impact on the student. Only then will they begin to wrestle with questions about how much students are learning or why students apparently cannot demonstrate on tests what they seem to understand in discussions or how they can get students more engaged in learning the material.

As is clear from the foregoing examples, a significant subset of these coaches and TAs had already reached the level of engagement and professional responsibility of junior colleagues.

As I have already indicated, a major determinant of teaching assistants' readiness to assume a high level of responsibility for the course and to actively seek answers to class problems is their cumulative experience of faculty who encourage, acknowledge, and draw on ideas that they or their students generate. The open communication and sense of being taken seriously also contributed to coaches taking responsibility for how well the students learned:

> You know, I blame myself for that because I just didn't get around to making up good questions. Overall the project went well, though it took them a while to understand exactly what they were doing, and at the end I had to do some prodding. But I knew where it was lacking. They needed something to help them see what it meant. That's what's key. And that was my failing, I should have put some questions at the end of the homework, or I could have set some discussion questions so they would start to think about what they'd got and what it all meant.

Kirk and Todd-Mancillas (1991) offer a similar, but crucially different, finding from a study of TAs in conventional classes. These TAs judged their professional competence by the extent to which their students demonstrated that "learning" had taken place. However, unlike the coaches who were supported in their professional growth by their professor, and who sought to address what they identified as their shortcomings without losing confidence, the TAs in the Kirk and Todd-Mancillas study doubted their qualifications and abilities as instructors when their students failed to show that they had learned. How faculty responded to their TAs' feedback was clearly critical in shaping their level of engagement. In the following example, the professor responded positively to a suggestion made by the students through their coaches. The coaches applauded both his response and its outcome:

> Coach 1: He's come to every group in rotation. And it was team five that instigated that. They asked me to ask him, and we took the idea to our weekly meeting. And I think it's become really important just to know that the professor is connected and that he cares how they are learning.
>
> Coach 2: The way the course is with the discussion-and-answer system, they need to learn to feel comfortable with talking to him. He's an authority figure, but at the same time, he understands that they don't know everything so they need to be comfortable telling when something doesn't make sense. So, his coming and talking with them helps them do that, and he learns something about what they find it hard to understand, and maybe why. So it's been a success.
>
> Coach 1: I agree. It's important.

In another example, the professor agreed to let the coaches try out their suggested solution to a common large-class problem. They were pleased with the outcome and that they had been encouraged to try the method:

> Coach 1: The teams began by sitting in the same places in the lecture—just wherever they sat on the first day. So what happened is that the groups at the front got very active and always wanted to answer the first question, and the people in the back just slacked off. So we suggested that we rotate the teams.
>
> Coach 2: Our prof really does have a knack for—I mean, he enjoys the exchanges. He gets excited about it, which makes the students excited about it too. So, the people in the front can see this excitement and feel the energy and get drawn in. But the people in the back don't get that.
>
> Coach 3: Right, and we could see that there was like a learned helplessness in the back, so . . .
>
> Coach 1: So, we suggested that we kept moving the groups in a circle round the room. Each week they moved round one place.
>
> Coach 2: We did that, and it seemed to work pretty well. And the prof was pleased with it.
>
> Coach 3: Yeah. We actually facilitated the rotation ourselves, and I thought it worked great.

Coach 1: And it goes back to what we were saying about laying down ground rules. We start out by telling them that this is what we are gonna do and sticking with it.

Coach 2: And I bet, if we start out this way, we won't have to facilitate it after a week or so. They'll get into a pattern and start doing it themselves.

As people who had taken ownership of the course learning goals, these coaches saw the importance of the same process emerging among their students. As noted earlier, students who took responsibility for working productively together were observed to be the ones getting the most out of the class:

When you set the working rules right at the start of the class, the students pick it up, and they start doing it themselves. And then it's even better because it seems like, the more ownership they take, the more they get out of it. Like I've got some people in my groups who are awesome. They've decided they want to get the most out of this, and they go above and beyond what we ask in every way. . . . They have bonded into like little subgroups that work great together and help each other out. They are doing a lot of stuff that I wish the whole group could do.

Fostering Interaction

As is evident in the examples presented throughout this and the previous chapter, the TAs and coaches who expressed a sense of shared responsibility for achievement of class goals were also thinking creatively about their own role as teaching assistants in innovative classes. This includes realizations that their central role is to facilitate student learning and that the main methods by which they do this are by fostering interaction with students and between students. As this modular chemistry TA observed,

It's hard for some of the undergraduates to get it into their heads—"So, if you're not teaching and the professor's not lecturing, who's teaching me?" They are thinking about who should be teaching them, not "How do I learn?"—which is a very different way of looking at things. And I'm responsible for helping them learn for themselves. But they also need someone that can help them make the linkages and clarify things when they get stuck. Part of that comes from effective group work and part from their discussions with me. And I think that getting them to use both resources well is an essential piece of my job.

Improving student interaction was an aspect of their classes where many TAs and coaches believed that they could make a key contribution. They described their own efforts at fostering student engagement in their small-group work, in labs, in office hours, and in whole-class sessions. The following three examples were offered by the Berkeley TAs:

TA 1: So I tried to sit every time in a different place. And I'd purposely sit next to someone who never talked to me.

TA 2: Yeah. Same here.

TA 3: It was quite hard to do because I always had to think about it, do it consciously, and yet make it seem natural. And they may not want to talk.

TA 1: [*Expressing exasperation*] Well, I don't know what you can do because they have to come to you in order for you to help them.

TA 2: Work your room. You work your room.

TA 3: Yeah. During the lab.

TA 1: Okay. You're right. Working your lab is really important.

TA 3: Totally.

TA 2: Going round and talking to people who don't talk to you. Talk to the people who don't come to office hours. That's key. Because those are four whole hours during the week that you have access to them. And, if they don't come to class and they don't come to office hours, that's where you can talk to them one on one.

I think there are certain things in general chemistry, like structures, where they should spend the time in group work figuring it out together and some time on the board actually doing it together. Definitely. Instead of just hearing it. I've found it makes a big difference if they hear it first, then I get them into a group, get them talking about it and then trying things out together on the board.

One of the modular chemistry TAs discussed her role in reaching out to students who are slow to participate:

[Professor X] gives them problems or whatever, and what I'll do is go round the table and find out who is having problems. So we make a start on something. But I'll have everybody help with that. And there are those shy kids that just want to absorb it, and I won't let them do that. You have to take an active role in your own education, or you're not going to get anything out of it. So I'll ask them, "Now, how do we balance this equation? Do you think this is right?" And then I ask them to say why it's right or not. They often don't like it to start with, but I persist and I notice that they get more willing to say, "Hey. Wait a second. That's wrong."

They discussed the pros and cons of "calling on" students as a way to keep them engaged in larger classes and how it might be made to work:

TA 1: I know she [the professor] had difficulty engaging some of the people in the middle and back of the class, because we've talked about that.

TA 2: And it's not easy to figure out how to get them involved. I think we have all tried singling people out. That keeps people alert, but sometimes you can really offend people.

TA 1: There isn't an easy answer

TA 3: It might work if people knew they were going to be asked a particular question. Maybe that would relieve some of the anxiety of getting randomly called on, and maybe the answer would be better.

TA 2: Some people get miffed if they are ready and then don't get asked.

TA 1: But that's always going to be a problem with a class this big. No way around that.

The astronomy coaches and their professor came up with a different strategy for getting students to offer answers to the professor's questions in class—they threw candy:

Coach 1: In the big class session, if they answered a question—right or wrong—we tossed them a piece of candy.

Coach 2: Yeah. When they raised their hand—whether they got it or not. The candy was really for raising their hand.

Coach 3: And it worked. It broke the ice and got them used to the idea that, in this class, we talk to each other. The first discussion session should be fun. Once the ice is broken, you can start getting more serious.

Coach 2: I think doing something like this is important in a class where you want people to be ready to speak up and discuss things. We didn't do it every time, but now and then we would have another candy-throwing session, and everyone just woke up.

In their group work, TAs and coaches sought creative ways to open up discussion and engage students in teaching each other. A commonly used strategy across all three initiatives was to charge the group with the goal that "no one leaves until you all can explain this":

That's a very good strategy. Nobody gets out of here until everyone understands it. They may chafe at the idea to begin with, but they soon learn how valuable it is to them be able to explain something to someone else until they get it.

Some of the modular chemistry faculty modeled this method in class, and their TAs picked it up; other TAs learned it in training or discussion sessions; some discovered it from other sources or figured it out for themselves.

As described in chapter 3, many TAs and coaches described working interactively with students as an intrinsic pleasure and saw learning to do it effectively as one of the main gains of working for an innovative class. The following affirmations were offered by TAs in modular chemistry and the Berkeley initiative:

> The very best thing? I enjoyed the interaction with the students in the labs. I enjoyed walking round the lab and making sure they were all up to speed, understanding what they were doing, and knew where they were heading. I liked stirring up some productive conversations about what they were seeing.

> I think the very best thing was the interaction with the students, especially the groups who came to my open office hours. I ran into a student this semester, and she thanked me over and over again. She said she got so much out of those sessions and that gave me even more pleasure to know that what we did together had helped her learn.

Curriculum Development and Testing

A limited number of teaching assistants were given the opportunity to work on curriculum development. For example, as already described, in modular chemistry and the Berkeley initiative, TAs helped their faculty to troubleshoot, adapt, and refine new labs. This kind of activity, and the level of trust and collegial effort that it engendered, reinforced the TAs' sense of investment in the course and its outcomes. In another example, one of the head TAs working for Interactive Astronomy described the process of designing, testing, and refining a set of labs with the coaches:

> It was quite challenging because I had to make a good many assumptions about how this material would be received. And I got some valuable feedback from the undergraduate coaches who had worked in the class the year before. They told me if the material was too advanced or if I'd put too much into it or made the lab too long. The coaches encouraged me to try the labs out on them first, and so I got two rounds of great feedback before the students saw the material. By the time I showed the material to the prof, I think it had improved significantly. And, working back and forth with them gave me a chance to pilot what I was doing. And I was learning a great deal about my own teaching. I know I got more feedback than I had in traditional classes.

The capacity and willingness of TAs to work together on aspects of course development and testing have (as yet) been little explored in the literature. However, the indications in these data suggest this as another potential aspect of an enhanced TA role. Classroom innovators might consider making greater use of their teaching assistants' interest and abilities in this activity.

Consolidating and Transmitting Their Own Contribution

In the interviews, TAs and coaches who had come to see themselves as enablers of learning reflected creatively and critically on their work with students. They also discussed difficulties and their resolution with each other and with the professors and wanted to pass on to the next group of teaching assistants some of what they had learned. This can be seen as evidence of longer-term investment in the products of their work that lifts their overall role to a more professional level. For example, toward the end of their semester, the coaches reviewed their activities, began to plan for the next semester, and thought about how to transmit what they had learned:

Coach 1: I think it would be useful if we got together just to design how learning teams should work and our roles in them in light of what we now know.

Coach 2: Because if these things are allowed to develop individually, they don't have the same impact and something you have argued about and agreed upon.

Coach 3: Then we could draft our combined ideas and discuss it with the professor. I think what we need to come out of this is a learning team syllabus.

Coach 1: When he hires some new coaches, it would be really valuable for them to get some hands-on training, and that should include the syllabus that we have worked out with him.

Coach 3: Yeah, because just now, there's really no real training, and we've learned that it doesn't work to have new people jumping in and making things up as they go along. It means that every group is running differently.

Coach 2: And that's something we want to avoid next time.

Coach 1: Once everyone is oriented and the groups are working in sync, we could discuss any variations. It's still an experiment, and we don't have it all figured out, but we've learned a lot about what doesn't work and should build on that.

One of the modular chemistry TA groups was thinking along similar lines:

TA 1: It would be really good if we could work together the summer before the class was taught. We could do some curriculum development work together, and we'd be well prepared before the class began.

TA 2: Even if it was just one week—an intensive start-up week—that would be very valuable for training the new TAs and a good rethink for those of us that stay on.

TA 3: I think we could easily go through three of the modules and plan out our parts. We've learned a lot this semester, and I hate not to carry that forward.

TA 2: It would get us all up to speed on material that is unfamiliar and allow us to work through the labs together.

TA 1: And we could try out some of the teaching activities on each other—sort of like a workshop.

These examples, again, illustrate these TAs' sense of ownership in the future of the course and an emergent professionalism in their concern to see future TAs and coaches build on the lessons that they had learned.

SUMMARY

I have highlighted the willingness and ability of many TAs and coaches to shoulder responsibility for student learning alongside faculty and with each other. Over the course of the last two chapters, I have also sought to illustrate how the TAs' critical feedback as course consultants, active involvement as troubleshooters, collaboration in addressing fundamental aspects of course innovation, as well as their enhancement of formal role duties in light of new course learning objectives all combine to lift their overall working role to a level that greatly transcends the traditional roles of teaching assistants.

In many ways, a key contribution of TAs who support the goals of their classroom innovation is that of "making it work." This may be a considerable contribution in situations where (as I have illustrated) innovators have not yet figured out many of the operational details by which their student learning objectives are to be implemented. However, this is also likely to remain a permanent aspect of TA work in innovative courses. This is partly because innovative faculty are likely to continue to develop new ideas and draw colleagues into working with new methods. Furthermore, each new class of students has to be enabled to learn in new ways, let go of passive attitudes and behaviors that constrain learning, and take more responsibility for their own learning.

As I indicated in the previous chapter, the three factors that TAs and coaches saw as having encouraged them to expand their working role in the ways I have described were professional preparation, regular meetings with each other and with the faculty, and the experience of faculty openness to critique and suggestion. As also previously mentioned, no teaching assistant in this sample experienced all three, but many reported two. More formal preparation and support were the most advocated and least experienced of these variables, and a collegial faculty attitude was seen by TAs as the single most significant factor in prompting a high degree of engagement in the innovation.

I do not argue that teaching assistants working in more conventional settings do not, or cannot, make comparable contributions to their courses. Indeed, as I have indicated throughout the narrative, both faculty accounts and some other studies comment on such instances. However, what may occur in the particular constellation of circumstances that characterize innovative undergraduate science classes is that this potential is more apt to be realized and that both the value and the possible scope of an enlarged TAs' contribution will become clear.

Finally, I should make it clear that these observations by a sample of 110 TAs do not stand alone. As I have indicated at points throughout this account, the interviews with the forty-two TAs working with modular chemistry courses were one part of a much larger, comparative, and longitudinal interview study with undergraduates who were (and were not) experiencing early- and late-stage modular courses. These data are further complemented by a body of interviews with chemistry faculty who used the modules and with a sample of their colleagues who did not. Through all of these bodies of evidence, we became aware that innovations that shift the focus from faculty teaching to student learning fundamentally change the ways in which students, faculty, and TAs respond to course goals and relate to each other. More is demanded of each group than its members expect of themselves in more conventional courses, and changes in attitudes toward learning, once made, are not easily revoked. People who have experienced the benefits of particular changes for themselves simply cannot return to a state of not knowing. As with our faculty interviewees who experienced the challenges of innovation and some measure of success in addressing them, I predict that the changes in thinking and beliefs about teaching and learning that these TAs and coaches experienced are likely to be permanent.

In the following chapter, I explore some differences in the responses of undergraduate and graduate TAs to the challenges of working in innovative courses.

NOTES

1. Karasz, Reynolds, and Wall (1997) found that students were concerned about the disparities they found between the course lecture and innovative recitations and felt as if they were attending two distinct classes. Karasz reports that this confusion was more derived from students' expectations of a "rehash" of lecture material in recitation sections than from students' problems with the active learning methods that had been introduced into the recitations. Karasz's finding is consistent with the views of the astronomy coaches that professors who attempt to make the small-group work of their TAs more active or project oriented should make a special effort from the outset to explain the purpose and nature of such changes to the undergraduates.

2. Faculty in the Teaching Teams Program at the University of Arizona valued as being constructive the feedback they received from undergraduate TAs during their weekly meetings. Faculty reported gaining information from their undergraduate TAs that they did not get from students (Larson et al. 2001; Stover et al. 2001).

3. Stoecker and colleagues (1993) found that sociology TAs at the University of Toledo acted as intermediaries who amplified their students' perspectives to the professor and translated the professor's thoughts back to the students.

9

The Relative Contributions of Undergraduate and Graduate Teaching Assistants

In this chapter, I compare and contrast the ways in which undergraduate and graduate TAs working in these innovative classes perceived their work roles and responded to them. As I shall argue, differences in the academic level and circumstances of the two groups, their prior experience as TAs or tutors, and their perceptions of the advantages and disadvantages of the position have the capacity to profoundly affect the manner in which they responded to their new work roles.

The data from all three initiatives highlight the potential of TAs to be useful, even critical, partners in enabling these innovations to work well. This potential, which I have sought to explore and illustrate throughout this volume, is all the more remarkable because 57 percent of all of the participating TAs and coaches were undergraduates.[1] In the case of modular chemistry, the high proportion (66 percent) of undergraduate TAs reflects the nature of the institutional sample—namely, four liberal arts colleges, two state universities, and one research university. However, the proportions of undergraduates in both the Berkeley and the Interactive Astronomy initiatives (26 percent and 92 percent, respectively) were the result of deliberate faculty choices. Some of the Berkeley undergraduate TAs had studied under the innovating professors in modular chemistry classes. They were recruited both for their interest and for their experience in the pedagogical methods used in the new initiative. In Interactive Astronomy, the use of undergraduates was a central feature of the course design, with a different role designated for the graduate head TAs.[2]

The undergraduates employed in the three initiatives varied from each other by academic level and disciplinary knowledge. All of the modular chemistry and Berkeley undergraduate TAs were junior and senior chemistry majors. By contrast, although some of the coaches were juniors in astronomy or other science and engineering majors, most were sophomores who were recruited largely for their interest and success in prior astronomy classes.

A review of the data presented in chapters 6 and 7 on how TAs and coaches operationally defined their work roles reveals that undergraduates undertook some aspects of traditional TA roles that are often part of graduate TA work. As with their graduate colleagues, they extended their formal work roles and developed new ones to meet the challenges presented by new course methods.

FACILITATION OF LEARNING

The graduate and undergraduate TAs were comparable, both in the work they did and how they approached it, and this was especially marked in their facilitation of student learning. Across the innovative courses, most TAs saw this as their central responsibility and approached it largely by fostering all forms of interaction (student–student, student–TA, and student–professor). This was most evident in their group work with students where undergraduate TAs and coaches showed themselves to be as able as graduate TAs to organize and run groups and to establish and monitor their cohesion, morale, and effectiveness.

Taking responsibility for student learning also involved monitoring students' progress, intervening to avert failure, motivating students to seek timely help, addressing unproductive student learning methods, and advising faculty on areas of students' intellectual confusion and its causes. As I argue in the previous chapter, an important facet of TAs' consulting activities was alerting faculty to learning difficulties created by selection, level, and pacing of class materials and by structural or conceptual disjunctions in course design. Until these were addressed, both undergraduate and graduate TAs did "repair work" in which they applied conceptual patches to a disjointed course storyline. However, this aspect of the work was more difficult for undergraduates who worked with less background in the discipline.

The astronomy coaches, as a group, were the least prepared in disciplinary knowledge across the three initiatives. As indicated, some were majors, but most were not. As all of the undergraduate TAs working in modular chemistry classes and in the Berkeley initiative were chemistry majors, the astronomy coaches' experience makes the best case for what undergraduates with more limited disciplinary knowledge can accomplish as learning facilitators. The coaches knew more astronomy than did class members but not necessarily much more. However, they shared a strong interest in learning the subject and were ready to explore alongside their students what they did not know.

Undergraduate TAs were able to articulate the extent of their responsibilities in facilitating student learning. They were clear that their job was not to "lecture" or "teach" but to enable, encourage, motivate, and explain and to generate discussions in which undergraduates helped each other to understand ideas and their relationships. They also drew on their own understanding of why undergraduates find some ideas hard to grasp. In the following sample, two coaches explain the essence of their learning facilitation work and how it differs from traditional TA work:

> Coach 1: I hate recitations in the big science classes—with the TA standing up there lecturing. You have no clue if what they are telling you is right. And often they have no clue about how to teach. I would never choose one of those classes if I could avoid it.
>
> Coach 2: See, that's the thing. We are not asked to teach per se, and I think that's good.
>
> Interviewer: So what is your job as you see it?
>
> Coach 2: I think we're there to manage and encourage and motivate . . .
>
> Coach 1: And generate discussions about the material . . .
>
> Coach 2: And be a peer who can help them find things—like a resource provider.
>
> Coach 1: And help them understand. I find that if I can read it and understand it myself, I can explain it to someone else. But I'm not a teacher. I'm definitely not there to lecture.

"Explaining" comes rather close to "teaching," but neither the coaches nor other undergraduate TAs saw themselves as authorities who could draw on a bank of superior knowledge or supply additional information as graduate students should be able to do. As one modular undergraduate TA explained it,

> I think as long as we keep that perspective that we're not the teacher, then it takes away that level of accountability for information that we can't provide. I can't lecture.

Instead, they grappled with the same material along with, or a little ahead of, their students and found a variety of ways to express, interpret, illustrate, and restate what they all had read. By doing this, they were often able to clarify things that their students were unsure about:

> Coach: I was happy to read the hypertext along with my students. And I am quite capable of reading and learning the same way that they are, so I was able to answer the questions they had on that basis. Having a little bit of authority, just knowing a bit more than them, having more expertise in finding material,

and seeing what was information more and less important so you could help them. Those were actually enough.

Berkeley undergraduate TA: I can explain things better than I used to because, when my students had trouble with something, I would go read up on it and try to explain it to them. I don't think it's necessary for us to know as much as a grad student would in order to meet these needs.

The coaches got group members to pool their emergent knowledge and develop a common understanding by discussing the material. Because they knew a little more than their groups or learned more quickly than many of their students, they also knew enough of the material to challenge their group members:

Like a sports coach, you are suppose to make things happen—I mean, I've gotten on my group to move and do things. And every once in a while, I'll ask than a tough question.

The coaches also modeled the ways in which the professor wanted the students to learn, and exemplified the message that learning together is an effective way to learn:

You're just a little bit ahead and you know a bit more. And you're maybe learning on your own—and that's more than they are used to—someone reading and figuring it out for themselves. You're a role model in that way.

Stoecker and colleagues (1993, 335) also report that TAs are able to model critical thinking by questioning the instructor, helping to "produce a more collective learning process, emphasize the role of experience in learning, integrate thought with experience, and empower students."

Undergraduate TAs expressed awareness of the advantages and limitations of their effectiveness in enabling student learning. Being similar in age and in their understanding of shared perspectives and problems can be an asset, and undergraduates TAs thought that this gave them some advantages over graduate students. They highlighted their better understanding of why students find certain things hard to understand—an awareness that arises from their own, more recent struggles with difficult conceptual material. As one Berkeley undergraduate TA explained it,

I was asked to return as a TA again—I like interacting with the students. And I can see a lot of their frustrations that I had when I was at their stage. I just think I can help them a lot more than the grad TAs because of that.

Eby (2000) also found that undergraduate TAs were able to explain students' problems by sympathetic reference to what it is like to be first-year students with limited experience by which to navigate early college classes. Eby also reports that, because these TAs are much closer to the students than are faculty, they are also more aware of conceptual difficulties that students commonly experience and how easy it is to misperceive the intellectual level at which many incoming undergraduates can work.

Undergraduate TAs also understood the sources as well as the consequences of counterproductive attitudes and behaviors that supported poor learning methods or constrained their students from seeking help with academic difficulties. As I discuss in chapter 5, many undergraduate TAs clearly understood why students might cling to ineffectual learning formulae or prefer passive learning methods. Along with graduate students, they were able to draw distinctions between genuine student learning difficulties with new pedagogies and resistance arising from other sources.

Undergraduate TAs saw themselves as being more approachable and thus more helpful to students with questions and concerns than were some professors who seemed aloof, intimidating, or less able to establish rapport with students. One of the head TAs commented, "I always notice how well the coaches are able to establish rapport with their peers and to get their discussions working well." Undergraduate TAs are aware of how younger students think and feel. Not only are they empathetic, they are also seen as empathetic by their students:

> Maybe it's easier for them than having someone who is older. They feel like they can ask me questions or come to me with concerns and problems.

Both Murray (2001) and Jacobs (2002) also found that students valued undergraduate TAs because they were "close to them in age and therefore understood their experiences and concerns" (Jacobs 2002, 45).

Students may perceive graduate students as being hard to approach. Indeed, some of the Berkeley undergraduate TAs wondered if they (perhaps unconsciously) cultivated a detached professional demeanor:

> And professors are intimidating, and grad students can be intimidating as well. I think they could be practicing for future use [*laughing*]. Some people carry that "keep out" air about them. You don't want to walk down the hall and say "Hello" when you meet them. They see their undergraduates but they just walk on by. That scares students. But they don't necessarily know that.

Undergraduate TAs also understood that not all students are as assertive as they might need to be in getting their academic needs met. As one undergraduate TA in a modular chemistry class reported,

> I don't have any problems making connections with some of the professors who seem so very far away, but I know some of my student do. I can help them out, but at the same time, I can encourage them to go and ask for what they need.

Although coaches reported some initial skepticism among their students that undergraduate peers could meet their learning needs, by the end of the course the student interviews revealed a high degree of acceptance and appreciation of the value of their coaches' work. The ease with which undergraduates are accepted in a learning facilitation role is likely to be dependent on the institutional context. Both the astronomy coaches and the undergraduate TAs in the Berkeley initiative were operating in research universities where their use was more unusual. In the modular chemistry classes in the liberal arts colleges and state university, students are long accustomed to having other undergraduates perform a variety of academic support functions, such as assistants in their classes and labs, as tutors, and (in some schools) as "student instructors."[3]

Undergraduate TAs and coaches discussed limitations on their capacity and effectiveness as learning facilitators and how these might be addressed. First, they were clear in their understanding that, although they try to explain things that their students found obscure, they could not, ultimately, be accountable for student comprehension. In modular chemistry, the handbooks give structured guidance to a body of knowledge for both the TAs and their students. The Berkeley worksheets perform the same function, with weekly meetings to clarify areas of possible difficulty and informational backup from the course coordinator. However, undergraduate TAs looked mainly to their professors to deliver information and act as the authority in instances of student confusion; they were wary of putting themselves into a situation where they might give incorrect information. The astronomy coaches who worked with less-structured sources of reference and with the least disciplinary preparation also looked to their head TA as a knowledge resource. They recommended adding several more graduate students in that role. From their own experiences in defining an incompletely prestructured role, they advised that the relative roles and responsibilities of two tiers of TAs should be made clear to all:

> There's a need for some people who have a depth of knowledge—who can actually explain and clarify, and make linkages in ideas. You wouldn't need to assign them to particular groups—they could be more roving and keep open office hours so people could get to see them and be available by e-mail. The prof needs to make these formal TA positions and explain to the students how to use them, so they would know that the TAs would be there every class and would always know what the prof is doing and what he is trying to get over in each session. They should bring to the job a good solid understanding and be ready to teach in these more clarifying ways to small groups and individual students.

One of the head TAs concurred with this coaches' view. The coaching system working well on whole, but more backup was needed to answer knowledge questions:

I know it was useful for me to be there when there was a question that out-stripped their knowledge—such as the explanation of a concept that may have been beyond them.

The head TA offered the suggestion that, in interactive classes with a strong group emphasis in institutions where both undergraduate and gradu-ates are available, an optimal arrangement may be a balance of undergradu-ate and graduate TAs with some division of responsibility and activities:

> I think the best situation would be where you have a smaller number of grad students who could help develop the curriculum and who could answer stu-dents' questions at a deeper level. But, for much of it, running the learning teams, the undergrad coaches were invaluable once they were able to estab-lish a good level of rapport—being close to peers. And the undergraduate coaches got such a lot out of it. I'd like to see more professors use them in these ways.

Thus, the area in which the capacities and practice of graduate and un-dergraduate TAs diverge the most is in the nature and level of individual ac-ademic support they can offer to students. Some of the Berkeley undergrad-uate TAs who worked alongside graduate TAs suggested that the students' needs could be better met if the graduate TAs took on an additional formal function as a knowledge resource for students. They could offer open office hours and answer e-mail questions to help students when they get stuck.

In the case of the liberal arts colleges where there were no graduate stu-dents to act as knowledge resources, it was apparent in student interviews that, although students appreciated the help of the undergraduate TAs, they also saw the high degree of availability in their course professors as being crucial in meeting their learning needs. In these schools, the students ex-pected, and seemed to get, a much higher degree of academic and personal dialogue with their faculty than was evident in the research universities. The astronomy coaches who worked in a research university could have been augmented by a small number of graduate students but were, by the pro-fessor's choice, restricted to just one head TA per course. In this circum-stance, the unusually high degree of accessibility of this professor to his stu-dents was seen by the coaches as a critical factor in ensuring student comprehension:

> I think they understand that, since we're undergraduates, we don't know as much as a grad would. And I tell 'em, "Hey, you should ask the prof that ques-tion." He's totally open to that—and that's critical if you are not going to have grad students for backup to the coaches.

In the liberal arts colleges where moderate or small class sizes are tradi-tional, the direct availability of faculty to their students is treated largely as a given. However, in research universities, it is hard to replicate this situation. As described in chapter 7, the Interactive Astronomy class grew from around 70 students to approximately 150. The coaches who experienced this change pointed to losses in the interactive quality of the class as its size increased. Among these was the limited ability of their professor and a single head TA to deal with students' questions about the material. The professor was still open for student questions, but the task of answering them all became more than he could deal with directly. The coaches warned that, in the enlarged class, more complex student learning needs could not be met by the existing setup. Some students became so disheartened that they would not approach the professor or would not do so soon enough. The coaches stepped in to prevent losing students altogether, but they looked for more graduate students to fill this gap:

> I think the biggest frustration for students is wanting someone to explain the links we just made or needing to hear it in another way so they can really get a hold of it. That's a real need. We try to meet it, but it can be more than we can handle. You are aware that, if they can't get it from you, then it really sinks some people. They can get to a stage where they are so demoralized that they don't ask, don't know that that's an okay thing to do, or don't ask soon enough. With a class this size, you just have to get a group of graduate students to back up what we and the prof can do.

Thus, both undergraduate TAs and coaches pointed to the need for authoritative intellectual support to augment their work as learning facilitators. They articulated a need for, and appreciation of, structured material resources with weekly meetings to discuss them and for direct student access to the course professors, course coordinators, head TA, and graduate TAs. How these needs could best be met, however, depended on institutional traditions and resources as well as class sizes.

LABORATORY ROLES

Undergraduates performed the same learning facilitation role as graduate TAs in their supervisory and support work with students in the lab. In modular chemistry and in the Berkeley initiative this role was partly traditional—TAs helped to set up labs, then circulated to assist student lab groups. However, the modular chemistry labs were open-ended in character, and all TAs helped students collect and analyze data from experiments whose outcomes were variable. They also helped to troubleshoot practical problems that arose with new labs, made computer applications work, and dealt with student anxiety and resistance to the uncertainties (and full length) of authentic lab work.

Some graduate students and head TAs went further. They helped to develop and test new labs, advised on setting student activities at an appropriate level of difficulty, designed related computer exercises, and initiated prelab sessions. However, some undergraduate TAs in modular chemistry classes similarly assisted faculty in the lab-testing and refinement process and were active in giving feedback on how well they worked with students. The unfinished nature of some lab experiments, procedures, or activities for both modular chemistry and Interactive Astronomy labs at the start of the initiative offered some TAs—both graduate and undergraduate—a professional development opportunity to work on aspects of course design or implementation and gain management skills. One of the graduate head TAs for Interactive Astronomy described this role expansion as follows:

> It was a very interesting experience because it called on a whole different set of skills than being a TA in the past. I had to learn people management skills in order to interact with the coaches and try to get them to do things for me. And that was in a different way than I have interacted with undergraduates before. And I also had to work with our programmer. That involved taking the science we wanted the students to learn in the lab and describing to him something that was feasible in HTML code so that he could work on it. However, my main duty was to develop the lab exercises. The learning teams sometimes worked on discussion questions or projects, but we also had some lab exercises. The prof laid out the ideas and it was my job to expand them and make them tangible. Curriculum development for new labs is very challenging, and it's usually the job of a tenured professor. A beginning graduate student would have been very inappropriate for this new course. I hadn't done this before—just given some assistance in updating a standard lab manual. And I considered this a much better preparation for teaching my own first course than all of the lab sections I had ever taught. And it should almost be created as an additional, separate kind of experience for grad students

These graduate TAs were clearly working in a responsible and collaborative mode that demanded a creative response to an evolving course curriculum:

> It was a bit chaotic in that we had to deal with the new format because of the increased class size and the number of meetings we could accommodate. So we were playing it by ear how many labs we could fit in. I invented a couple of them right from scratch.

In chapter 10, I offer a further example of collaborative graduate-with-undergraduate TA work in developing, testing, and refining new labs.

These accounts contrast with the finding offered by the Teaching Teams Program at the University of Arizona (Larson et al. 2001; Stover et al. 2001; Wood et al. 2001) that, when faculty use undergraduate TAs, some graduate

TAs may be displaced from their traditional teaching roles and may find their role reduced to holding office hours and grading. As was evidenced in the Teaching Teams Program and in several instances across the initiatives included in this study, innovative courses can (as shown earlier) offer graduate TAs professional development opportunities that include working to develop and refine new pedagogies, student mentoring, course development, and interdisciplinary teaching. There also seems to be professional development potential for both levels of students in contributing to lab design, testing, refinement, and management.

LEARNING ASSESSMENT

In their work related to tests, quizzes, and grading, again, much of the work done by undergraduate and graduate TAs was similar. More traditional types of work included grading, reconciling grading systems, posting and keeping track of grades, addressing student issues with assignments and grades, and dealing with students who submitted late work. New aspects of the TAs' assessment role focused on encouraging students to use assignments, tests, and test preparation as essential parts of their learning. TAs at both levels expanded their role as learning facilitators into this area of work and sought to improve both student preparation and performance. They helped students prepare by teaching them how to study in meaningful ways for questions and problems that could not be answered by rote learning. After tests, they used group time to discuss the questions, explore alternative ways to approach them, and clear up misperceptions. They also offered their professors feedback on the effectiveness of particular course assessments. Where the work of graduates and undergraduate TAs diverged was in the writing of quizzes and the development of ideas for projects in which graduate TAs were more often engaged (though not exclusively so) than undergraduate TAs.

DELEGATED AUTHORITY

The roles and capacities of graduate and undergraduate TAs become more differentiated in exercising authority with their students. For all TAs, facilitating learning by active and interactive methods involved finding appropriate ways to use delegated authority and bring personal and moral pressure to bear. These were needed to deal with student resistance to the course approach or methods, problems with attendance, and failure to produce work on time or contribute appropriately to the work of the group. With respect to maintaining good order, undergraduates TAs showed an ability to develop, and put into effect, policies to establish consistency across their groups and to support each other in enforcing them. They took individual and collective initiative in dealing with problematic student behavior in their groups, such as nonattendance and poor participation, and, as I illustrate in chapter 6, sometimes they tackled disciplinary problems in class, such as disruptive or disengaged behavior and cheating in quizzes and tests.

However, both the undergraduate TAs themselves and some of their graduate colleagues commented on the greater struggle of undergraduates to establish and maintain their authority in appropriate ways. They described the kinds of help they needed from faculty to prepare for this aspect of their role. More than do graduate TAs, undergraduates need faculty to convey to students their role, responsibilities, and powers, as well as their professors' intention to support their TAs in exercising these. Exercising delegated authority provokes more anxiety for undergraduates than for graduates. They need preparation and guidance in how to use their authority and avoid the dangers of overreacting to breeches of rules on the one hand and being over-friendly or giving in to students on the other. Some undergraduate TAs and coaches managed to resolve these problems more easily than others and establish a good working tone:

> I'm a peer, but they do know that I have that authority if they're like late to class—that I'm not going to accept that. They do understand that.

> I have other classes with my own students, and that's worked out to be quite cool. They know I'm the coach here, but we sit together in this class and get the work done and sometimes talk about what we have to do for our other classes.

As one of the head astronomy TAs observed,

> Sometimes it was hard for them to set the right level of authority. And that's something a grad student could take more for granted. But when they got that straight, I think the relationship with the students was very valuable. The main thing is to give them some preparation and support in how to set the tone right from the start and how to deal with contingencies as they arise.

Accounts by undergraduate TAs (discussed in chapter 6) illustrate how they were able to overcome initial disciplinary difficulties. Their accounts also stress the extra help that undergraduates need from faculty by way of structure, guidance, and backup in order to operate at par with graduate TAs.

LEVELS OF TA ENGAGEMENT

The manner by which TAs are recruited into TA positions distinguishes all of the undergraduates from the graduates in ways that have bearing for their relative levels of engagement and support for innovative classes. In contrast with graduate students, many undergraduate TAs and all of the coaches were invited to become TAs. Some got the job without any previous experience because they had done well in a previous class. Some were offered a job because of their previous experience as TAs, because the professor thought that they showed promise, or because a colleague had recommended them. This modular chemistry TA was selected because she had struggled through her initial academic difficulties to a good performance level. She thought the professor appreciated that she would understand why other students found certain ideas difficult to understand:

> In last year's chemistry classes, I started off the year kinda rough and then did better and better throughout the year and ended up with the second-highest score. She gave me the "most improved" award for making the most progress through the year. When she asked for anyone that wanted to be a TA, I applied and she gave it to me.

Undergraduate TAs are often "repeaters," who are pleased when asked to do the job for a second or third time:

> We've done it a couple of times because he asked us, "Please do it again." This year, they just asked all of us to think about doing it again.

As described in chapter 7, more experienced TAs and coaches were often invested in preserving ideas and practices that they had developed and that worked well by passing them on to the next group of TAs.

As indicated earlier, undergraduate modular chemistry TAs were mostly juniors and seniors in chemistry majors, and many of them had taken more conventional courses in their first two years in the major. However, almost half (twelve of twenty-eight) of these TAs had taken an earlier version of the modular classes. They described this experience as a strong motivator to work as a TA in a modular class—to which, some added, that they especially wished to work with this professor. Some of the Berkeley TAs (both undergraduate and master's students) had also taken modular chemistry classes and were encouraged to become TAs by the innovating professors. All of these students reported good experiences in those courses, knew what was involved, and were inspired to become TAs in the innovative courses. Some TAs were also motivated by the expectation that both the preparation they would receive and their work with students would consolidate their own knowledge:

> While I did well in the same course last semester, I thought it might help reinforce some ideas—be a good review for me. And it does actually do that.

By contrast, wanting to be a TA to deepen their own understanding was a motivating factor that was not mentioned by *any* of the graduate TAs in the Berkeley interviews.

In the liberal arts schools, the state university, and the junior college included in the modular chemistry sample, undergraduate TAs were aware that their work was a valuable commodity because there were either no graduate students or only a limited supply of them available to fill all course support roles. They knew that faculty depended on their help and sometimes had difficulty in getting enough people to fill their TA positions:

> I'm a senior, and I'm filling in a gap for lack of personnel. We do this a lot at this university. Faculty always tell you just how important the senior undergraduates are here.

> I became a TA because they were short of people and my schedule allowed for it. I took general chem in my freshman year, and I thought it would be fun to make the whole circle. And they are very short because people just can't fit it in. Scheduling conflicts mostly—all of us who are science majors have labs in the afternoon.

> They always need people to do this. They're always short. There's about ten labs to man so that's twenty TAs right there. They have a hard enough time getting TAs for the labs. They have to beg and plead.

This kind of awareness clearly contributes to the good self-concept and social status of undergraduates who act as TAs and adds to their sense of making a valued contribution.

Interestingly, the modular faculty interviewed in these institutions reported they did not have difficulty in filling their available undergraduate TA positions. They were mostly able to find enough volunteers from among students who had taken their modular classes.

It was a matter of debate among undergraduates TAs and some of the graduate students who worked alongside them as to whether those TAs without experience were working at a disadvantage. It was clear that some faculty chose inexperienced undergraduates because they seemed to discern in them natural capacities, such as an ability to explain, ask questions, be curious, interact with a group, show leadership, and handle authority. In the view of one head TA, experience helped the coaches at the outset in setting up the group's work, handling administrative tasks, and dealing with computing and other technical aspects of the course. However, this graduate TA did not think that it correlated with their effectiveness as group leaders, which may be grounded in some degree of natural aptitude:

> We had a mixture of experienced coaches and novices, and how well they did was surprisingly uncorrelated with their experience. The first week, we had a

lot of administrative stuff, plus a great deal of computing, technical details to get worked out, sort of getting everyone into the system. And for that, the correlation between effectiveness and experience was very strong. The experienced coaches were much more effective. However, when it came to the meaty part of the work—being a good learning coach for their teams, I found it seemed to have much more to do with almost their innate ability to interact, how they could assist people—get them to see things. Some of the new people were very effective—more so than some of the students who had done it once or twice before.

There appear to be other advantages, however, in retaining some TAs from a current class to work in the next class, such as helping to orient new TAs and advise them on practical details. Some TAs who had kept in touch with each other over the break or summer believed that this had increased their sense of camaraderie and made them more eager to keep the continuity of their collaborative work going. Having had experience at a similar level (for instance, in knowing how to run a lab) was seen as making a huge difference to effectiveness:

> As far as running a lab section's concerned. I felt much more comfortable. I was pulled in very late to teach this, and so I missed the first training session. But I'm a junior, and I've taught twice before. So being a TA at this stage isn't quite as traumatic as first time out. I didn't feel worried about who was looking to me and who wasn't. 'Cause for one thing, I knew that the students were much more distracted in the first week or so of class than I was.

CONTRASTS AND THEIR CONSEQUENCES IN THE SITUATIONS OF UNDERGRADUATE AND GRADUATE TAS

Both the educational stage and circumstances of recruitment distinguish graduate from undergraduate TAs in ways that have significance for the ways that they approached their working role. For an undergraduate, becoming a TA brings a number of benefits that may seem less significant to a graduate student doing the same work. It offers a good opportunity to revisit and deepen their understanding of disciplinary knowledge. In these innovative classes, faculty gave undergraduate TAs considerable responsibility for organizing student learning. They also reported the work to be intrinsically interesting—more so than other on-campus work options available to them:

> He told us a little bit about the class, and I was sort of intrigued. I wanted, you know, to participate. I haven't found any other campus job that is so interesting.

> Some semesters I have taken on an overload as a TA because there's a shortfall in the research funds and the extra money is good. But that's not it. So long as

you can manage, the main thing is the work itself, and I am very enthusiastic about TA-ing, especially in these new classes where you learn so much of your craft as a teacher.

Undergraduates reported that the pay compared favorably with other on-campus work options, and some institutions also offered credit. The position also enhances an undergraduate's résumé.

When the circumstances of their recruitment and the intrinsic and extrinsic benefits of the work are added together, it becomes clearer why undergraduates who work as TAs—especially those who work in innovative classes—show generally high levels of engagement with, and support for, their work and for the goals of the course. Undergraduates gain status by doing this work for which they were recruited and recommended. They are apt to feel "chosen," even special, and the faculty for whom they work tend to reinforce this by praise and encouragement. The work itself is interesting and well paying, and the undergraduate TAs see themselves as deepening their disciplinary knowledge and learning valuable professional skills. As I have illustrated, they may also get a first experience of what it is like to work collegially with faculty, graduate students, and together as peers—all of which tend to encourage young people to treat what they are doing seriously. This seems to be true even in institutions without graduate students because innovating teachers seek out students with experience with the innovation or those who show the requisite interest and aptitude. It is especially true (as in the Berkeley initiative) where undergraduates successfully compete with graduate students for positions that offer equal status.

By contrast (as I discuss in chapter 4), new graduate students are often assigned to work for particular courses without being given the choice of alternative courses. They may find it difficult to arrange a transfer out of courses whose goals and methods they find that they do not like. In the Berkeley initiative, two-thirds of the thirty-one graduate student TAs were first-year students without prior TA or tutoring experience. Indeed, many, perhaps most, graduate TAs in introductory classes at large universities are apt to be similarly placed. As they take up their TA position, new graduate students are coping with the strains of making the intellectual, practical, and emotional transition into graduate school. As the innovating faculty observed, inexperienced graduate TAs suffer from the burden of being expected to know more than perhaps they do. Graduate TAs may feel constrained to keep to themselves any sense of inadequacy they may have about suddenly becoming "experts" for an introductory class. This situation is less troubling to undergraduate TAs who can be more open about what they do not yet understand without loss of face to faculty and peers. More senior graduate students who are already engaged in their doctoral research may take on TA work by default—because research assistantships are in short supply or because they have to complete so many semesters as TAs as part of their program. They may or may not have some choice about the course for which they work. Unlike the undergraduates, the pay is often less attractive than that offered to research assistants.

This said, many graduate students in these studies were clearly happy to work as TAs in these courses because they were interested in teaching as a professional option; wanted to build their teaching skills; were interested in learning more about educational research, theories, and methods; and were attracted by the innovative approach of particular faculty. However, these positively motivated TAs, along with those who are more instrumental or reluctant in their attachment to the work, described conflicts of time and commitment imposed by the dominance of research over teaching in most departments. Pressures from their research advisors and other departmental members could discourage them from spending more than a perfunctory amount of time and energy in their teaching work, and they may be sanctioned if their involvement in teaching interferes with progress in their research or is thought to do so by their research advisors.

These traditional deterrents to active engagement in teaching work among graduate students may be further compounded by the requirements of innovative classes. Faculty may ask for more of their time and mental effort than TAs consider compatible with sustaining their research time tables. Also, as I have illustrated, when innovating faculty ask graduate students to forego some of what they have come to see as markers of emergent professional status in order to facilitate learning as part of an collegial, inquiring community of learners, the response is sometimes anger, revolt, even sabotage. Among the few traditional perquisites to graduate students of a culturally devalued job have been the assumed "right" to teach their recitation or lab sections in whatever manner they deem appropriate and to act as a disciplinary authority for their groups of undergraduate students. Thus, the new work role offered to graduate TAs per se can be perceived by them as one of reduced status and professional autonomy. This can be further eroded if undergraduate TAs are given the same role, status, and respect with no complementary opportunity for professional development at a level commensurate with graduate students' greater knowledge and skills. Graduate TAs may also feel less secure in their status than when working in traditional classes where the structured distancing between them and their students make it easier to establish their authority than in interactive classes with more open discourse.

All of this is intended to clarify a critical distinction between undergraduate and graduate TAs who work for innovative science classes—that undergraduates have a great deal to gain and little to risk by their engagement. It is therefore understandable that many undergraduate TAs and coaches responded so positively to the innovating faculty and to their work roles. By contrast, TA appointments in science courses are traditionally regarded by graduate students as less prestigious, and carry less potential for professional advancement, than research assistantships. Working as a TA in an innovative science course may also be seen as adding an additional layer of risk or loss of status, depending how both the student and their research advisor view its opportunities for professional growth versus its demands on their time and energy. In chapter 3, I illustrate how a sharp perception of these risks and losses fed the strongly expressed resistance of a small but vocal number of graduate TA dissenters. Some graduate TAs experience role losses when faculty use undergraduate TAs alongside graduate TAs. Rather than embracing new responsibilities—such as mentoring undergraduate TAs, designing and leading group activities, or introducing new projects and technology into the curriculum—some graduate TAs at the University of Arizona felt displaced from their traditional teaching functions and reduced to a residual role of holding office hours and grading (Larson et al. 2001; Stover et al. 2001; Wood et al. 2001).

This said, it is quite remarkable that so many of the graduate students in this study rose to the challenges of their new roles and defined their experiences in terms of personal and professional gains. Experienced graduate students often found engagement in classroom innovations more rewarding than traditional forms of TA work. As I describe in chapter 3, graduate TAs reported gains in knowledge and understanding (both in their disciplines and in education theory, research, and practice) and gains in skills in a variety of teaching methods. They found their teaching and mentoring work inherently interesting and rewarding and were encouraged to see its career possibilities. The latter was especially important for a subset of graduate students who had strongly felt, but sometimes covertly held, longer-term interests in teaching as some facet of their future working lives. A few were also offered opportunities for course development or interdisciplinary teaching. The capacity of graduate students to respond creatively, professionally, and collegially to these opportunities is amply illustrated in previous chapters.

Whether graduate TAs make these gains and build these capabilities depends, however, even more than it does for undergraduates, on the adequacy of the educational preparation and support that faculty build into their program and on the collegial and reciprocally respectful relationships that graduate TAs are enabled to build with the innovating faculty. For all of the reasons that I have summarized in this chapter, faculty innovators who ask a great deal of their graduate TAs need to be sensitive to their constraints and concerns and how these vary at different stages in their graduate school careers. At several points in this book, I highlight the building of trust between and among faculty and their TAs as perhaps the most critical element in securing the success and longevity of course innovations—especially those that depend on active TA engagement. A sense of mutual trust is important to all TAs, but, given the more vulnerable situation of graduate students, its importance is even greater for them.

In the following two chapters, I discuss the professional development needs of TAs who work in innovative STEM courses and the factors that foster their collegial engagement.

NOTES

1. Refer to the project and data set descriptions in chapter 2.

2. There was just one graduate student with the title "head TA" working with each iteration of the astronomy course.

3. In contrast to traditional tutoring services, where tutors respond to random individual student needs, student instructors tutor undergraduates who are having academic difficulties in a directed, structured program. The student instructors' work is based on lesson plans that are closely coordinated with the teaching in particular courses. Some departments in two of the liberal arts institutions included in the sample offered these services in parallel to the tutoring system.

10

Professional Development for Teaching Assistants

All teaching assistants need educational preparation and ongoing support for the roles that they are asked to play. However, not all receive it, and the forms of preparation that are provided may or may not adequately meet TAs' needs. In innovative classes where much of the role is unfamiliar, formal arrangements for the professional development of TAs become a necessity. The literature on what is usually referred to as "TA training" (and to a lesser degree, ongoing support or overall professional development) forms a substantial portion of all literature on TAs. In the first part of this chapter, I review what is known about the extent and quality of TA preparation and support in both conventional and innovative classes from research and evaluation studies and also from scholarly articles that discuss TAs' preparation needs. I have omitted from the review any articles that describe particular programs without offering evidence from program evaluation. Throughout the following account, I substitute "educational preparation and support" or "professional development" for "training," as the latter connotes a lower level of skills and knowledge than is actually required for TA work. As TAs are also involved in the process of becoming professionals—a process that continues throughout their careers—their educational preparation is one important part of their overall professional development. The second half of the chapter discusses the TAs' and coaches' definitions of their professional development needs and how well the innovators in these three initiatives meet them.

THE HISTORY OF PROFESSIONAL DEVELOPMENT
FOR TEACHING ASSISTANTS

The need to prepare TAs for their duties was first mooted in the 1930s, and it continued to be proposed throughout the following decades. However, in a historical review, Nyquist, Abbott, and Wulff (1989) comment on the slow progress of universities to provide formal professional development for teaching assistants. Their assessment is corroborated by Chism (1998b), who reports that, prior to the 1960s, most universities did not recognize the need to prepare TAs for their teaching responsibilities. Finally, in 1986, the issue of what universities should provide by way of preparation was discussed at the first national conference on TA issues held in that year. In the following years, universities began to offer TA teaching preparation (often through orientation programs) as part of an effort to improve the quality of undergraduate education (Nyquist, Abbott, and Wulff 1989; Chism 1998b).

Over the last two decades, several factors have combined to promote the perception that the professional development of TAs is important. These include the accelerated increase of content knowledge in every discipline, the increased diversity of the student body, and dissemination of theory and research in cognitive psychology and pedagogy (Nyquist, Abbott, and Wulff 1989). Bomotti (1994, 388) strongly suggests that the education of TAs should "move beyond the current focus on orientation and training programs." Although the term "TA training" continues to be used, by the late 1990s the research literature begins to describe the preparation of TAs in terms of "professional development." Its proposed goals include support by the academic community to meet TAs' evolving needs as teaching professionals that would extend beyond graduate school into their early faculty career, enable TAs to become self-reflective practitioners, and help to develop research-grounded conceptual frameworks for their teaching practice (Chism 1998a). Nyquist and colleagues (1989) argue that professional development for TAs should go beyond pedagogical preparation in order to address all aspects of graduate school life that bear upon their current and future teaching work.

Notwithstanding scholarly clarifications of what may be needed, the available research indicates that most institutions and disciplines either do not offer formal preparation programs for their TAs or offer programs that are informal or limited in scope. Although the STEM disciplines are major employers of TAs in their large introductory classes, Shannon, Twale, and Moore (1998) found that TAs in science, mathematics, and engineering were the least likely to receive training. In Bomotti's study (1994) of eight disciplines, including the sciences and mathematics, only 45.3 percent of TAs at a premier research university had ever attended a teaching workshop or taken a formal education class. Rushin and colleagues (1997) found that 49 percent of all universities with biology graduate programs did not require formal preparation for TAs, only 22 percent offered presemester workshops that were required or strongly recommended, and only 14 percent required teaching seminars during the academic year. White (1993) found that only 45 percent of engineering graduate schools have a structured preparation program for TAs and that this most commonly consists of a one-day orientation emphasizing policies and procedures. Lack of, or limited, formal training is also common in other disciplines. For example, in a study at the University of Maryland, Ford (1993) found that 42 percent of TAs working in arts and humanities classes received no training before they began teaching their own courses. Similarly, Savage and Sharpe (1998) found that less than half of all research universities with physical education graduate programs had any form of formal graduate TA training.

In addition, where preparation is offered, as White (1993) found, it is often limited in scope. In their study of twenty-nine departments at a major Southern research university, Shannon, Twale, and Moore (1998) found that the preparation for 57 percent of TAs consisted of one-day workshops that covered policies and procedures and offered general advice about teaching or dealing with common problems; 55 percent of TAs also received departmental training, which varied from a single meeting to a week-long program. Tang and Sandell's national study (2000) of engineering schools found that, where teaching topics were included in TA preparation programs, they were limited to lecturing, grading, and reviews of teaching and learning styles. Less than one-third of engineering graduate schools addressed any of the cultural issues that bear upon the work of graduate students, although several researchers have found these to be important components of professional development (Tang and Sandell 2000). Rushin and colleagues (1997, 90) conclude, "Even when there is some formal structure in the [graduate TA] training program such as workshops, seminars and courses, these experiences are often brief and follow-up activities are loosely defined or nonexistent." The 2000 National Doctoral Program Survey (2001) reported that only 51 percent of life science students, 58 percent of physical science students, and 57 percent of engineering students believed that they had received adequate training and experience for a teaching career.

A small number of studies document the concerns of teaching assistants about underpreparation for their work and its consequences.[1] In a study at a public research institution, 31 percent of TAs thought that they had received both inadequate preparation and insufficient information before they began their teaching assignments (Duba-Biedermann 1993). The result is that TAs often feel anxious, overwhelmed, unsupported, and frustrated (Lumsden 1993; Hendrix 1995; McManus 2002). Their descriptions of the personal consequences of underpreparation include feeling "bewildered," "frustrated," and "apprehensive"; being a "nervous wreck"; and being prone to "a lot of anxiety" in a "scary" situation (Worthen 1992). By contrast, Prieto and Altmaier (1994) found that TAs who received what they saw as adequate preparation at the University of Iowa had significantly higher sense of self-efficacy than those who were not well prepared for their work.

THE NATURE OF AVAILABLE PROGRAMS OF EDUCATIONAL PREPARATION

Across institutions and departments that offer formal programs of educational preparation for their TAs, programs are of several different types. Some consist of a single element. Others include several of the following common elements: general, universitywide, presemester orientation; departmental, presemester orientation; one- or two-credit courses in pedagogical methods; or, more rarely, role modeling and mentoring.

The most common form of preparation for TAs across all disciplines entails a generic one- or two-day workshop that is held before the start of the academic year and that provides a general orientation consisting largely of information on university policies and procedures (Lumsden 1993; Poole and Sebolt 1993; White 1993; Main 1994; Druger 1997; Nurrenbern, Mickiewicz, and Francisco 1999; Hollar, Carlson, and Spencer 2000; Tang and Sandell 2000; University of California, Los Angeles 2000; Hedengren 2001; McManus 2002; Luft et al. 2004). A few generic institutional orientation programs also include information about teaching effectiveness and skills, and some offer hands-on practice exercises that allow TAs to try out different teaching techniques (Main 1994; Nurrenbern, Mickiewicz, and Francisco 1999).

In some institutions, general university orientations are complemented by one-to-three-day content-specific departmental workshops (Lawson, Rissing, and Faeth 1990; Lumsden 1993; Main 1994; Druger 1997; Tang and Sandell 2000; French and Russell 2002; Luft et al. 2004). The scope of departmental programs is highly variable (Main 1994; Shannon, Twale, and Moore 1998). At one end of the spectrum, they are restricted to informing TAs about departmental policies and procedures. At the other, thinly represented end, they offer seminars on educational philosophies; learning and teaching styles; course goals; teaching in diverse classrooms; classroom management; practical exercises; and workbooks with readings, videotaping, and critique (Wagener 1991; Lumsden 1993; Hollar, Carlson, and Spencer 2000).

A small number of institutions offer semester-long courses on pedagogy for credit. Although few in numbers, these courses offer a useful mix of educational theory and research, pedagogical practice, learning assessment, practice, and critique (Darling and Earhart 1990; Wagener 1991; Etkina 2000; Robinson 2000; Sundberg et al. 2000). Some universities also offer professional development seminars throughout the semester (Druger 1997; University of California, Los Angeles 2000; McManus 2002), and one university offers a year-long professional development program (Stoecker et al. 1993). The Center for the Advancement of Engineering Education fosters growth in pedagogical understanding through its innovative Teaching Portfolio Program (Linse et al. 2004). Another program, out of the Center for the Integration of Research, Teaching, and Learning (CIRTL), partners graduate students with faculty mentors to address teaching challenges for which neither know the answers (see www.cirtl.net). A more common type of ongoing TA preparation is English-language instruction for international TAs (Tanner, Selfe, and Wiegand 1993; Druger 1997).

When role modeling is included in programs of preparation for TAs who teach, experienced TAs are asked to help novices. In preterm workshops, they share their knowledge and experience and provide peer support (Darling and Earhart 1990; Lumsden 1993; Hollar, Carlson, and Spencer 2000; Tang and Sandell 2000). Some preterm programs facilitate community building between more- and less-experienced TAs through discussion sessions (Winternitz and Davis 2000) or social events (Poole and Sebolt 1993). A few programs also build in observation and critique of recitations and lab sections taught by peers (Murray 2001; Robinson 2000), experienced TAs (Tanner, Selfe, and Wiegand 1993), or faculty (Wagener 1991).

Mentoring, monitoring, and evaluation are also built into a small number of programs that match TAs with faculty mentors, who provide individual supervision, guidance, evaluation, and feedback (Wagener 1991; Main 1994; Etkina 2000; Streveler and King 2000; Winternitz and Davis 2000). This apprenticeship-style of preparation may also include co-teaching with a faculty mentor (Main 1994; Streveler and King 2000). However, the most common types of mentoring are much more informal: TAs are expected to seek out the course instructor to discuss issues as they arise. Verbal or written evaluation of TAs' teaching may be given once or twice during the course, based on observations by the faculty member, a course supervisor, or fellow TAs. These sometimes include videotaping of the TA's work with students (Darling and Earhart 1990; Wagener 1991; Poole and Sebolt 1993; White 1993; Main 1994). However, the most common form of feedback on the TAs' work comes from the end-of-term evaluations by students.

Notwithstanding the importance of TAs in supporting student lab work in the bench sciences, Rushin and colleagues (1997) report from their study of biology departments that only 14 percent offer their TAs formal courses in biology lab instruction. More commonly, faculty who teach courses that include labs supervised by TAs hold weekly meetings to demonstrate, practice, or discuss the upcoming week's lab experiment. Sundberg and Armstrong (1993) found that 88 percent of universities depend exclusively on weekly meetings to prepare their TAs for work in biology classes and labs.

Studies of the Effectiveness of TA Preparation Programs for Conventionally Taught Classes

Although the literature offers many descriptive accounts of particular programs, there is little evaluation data that explore their effectiveness in meeting the preparation needs of TAs or show their effectiveness in student learning outcomes. Reviews of research on the effectiveness of TA preparation programs conducted prior to the 1990s report limited information from well-designed formal evaluation work (Carroll 1980; Levinson-Rose and Menges 1981; Abbott, Wulff, and Szego 1989). Nyquist, Abbott, and Wulff (1989, 13) describe the main problems with this earlier work as poor research design, or success criteria that depend either on student ratings of TAs or on measures of TA satisfaction with their preparation.

In their review of findings from thirteen evaluation studies—each of which included a control group and/or a pre- and posttest design—Abbot, Wulff, and Szego (1989) identified the components of TA preparation that were significantly related to TA teaching effectiveness. These were as follows: providing TAs with student ratings of their work as the course progressed; consultation or interpretation of the ratings with faculty; self-evaluation; and consultation with an education specialist based on videotapes of the TAs' teaching work. Other important outcomes were increases in TAs' disciplinary knowledge and in their awareness of findings from learning research. In a later review, Rushin and colleagues (1997) reported a study based on end-of-term student evaluations: At the University of Missouri, positive student evaluations of TA effectiveness increased from 71 percent to 87 percent following the inception of required biology TA preparation that included both university-wide and departmental pre-course training that emphasized pedagogy. This group of evaluation studies focused on TAs who actually taught students and not on TAs who performed different functions. Nyquist, Abbott, and Wulff (1989) argued the need for studies that explore program effects on the professional development of TAs and on the learning of the undergraduates they served. This call was rarely heeded during the 1990s. In her recent review of the research, Chism (1998a) found that most TA preparation programs continued to measure their success in terms of TA satisfaction: TAs generally gave high ratings to their preparation programs, but, again, she faults evaluation studies that offer little information about the programs' impact on TA teaching or on student learning.

It is clear from this synopsis of research and evaluation studies, and by the judgment of scholars in this field, that academe has not yet widely accepted either the importance of appropriate professional development for their TAs or the importance of well-designed evaluations of those programs that they offer. Instead, the academy is portrayed as holding to its "traditional assumption that knowledge of subject matter is a necessary and sufficient condition for being a university faculty member" (Nyquist and Sprague 1998, 63) and, by implication, for the professional preparation of the future professorate. Since few TAs experienced inquiry-based learning in their own undergraduate education (Lawson, Rissing, and Faeth 1990), and as most TAs believe that lecturing is the most effective pedagogical method, it is not surprising that many TAs resist adoption of alternative pedagogies—either initially or indefinitely. In a study of TAs in mathematics, McGivney-Burelle and colleagues (2001) found that, prior to receiving educational preparation, TAs largely viewed the attributes of "effective instruction" as being knowledgeable in the subject matter, delivering well-organized lectures that stimulate student interest, grading fairly and returning work promptly, being available to students seeking help, and knowing students' names. McGivney-Burelle and colleagues also reported that many TAs believed that students learn by "solving problems on their own." The authors argue that, unless TAs are exposed to knowledge, education, and experience in active, interactive, supportive, collaborative, constructivist, and inquiry-based learning, they will teach much as they were taught. It is therefore critical for the success of innovations in undergraduate educational reform that are based on some combination of these pedagogies that the TAs receive professional education in their theoretical basis and use.[2]

Meeting the Preparation Needs of TAs Working in Innovative Classes

Researchers point to the expanded preparation needs of TAs in light of a growing national focus on the improvement of teaching and learning in higher education. Drawing on her review of TA preparation literature, Chism (1998a) argues that the well-prepared TA will increasingly need not only a deep understanding of their own discipline but also an appreciation of interdisciplinary connections and the application of knowledge; skill in using interactive and team-based pedagogies; an understanding of how students learn; knowledge of instructional design and assessment techniques; an appreciation of what promotes diversity; and facility with interpersonal interactions. Other researchers have made similar recommendations. Effective programs should include both content knowledge and pedagogical strategies (Shannon, Twale, and Moore 1998; Luft et al. 2004), model the type of learning that TAs are expected to facilitate, and give TAs practice and support in learning to use different pedagogical methods (Shannon, Twale, and Moore 1998; Nurrenbern, Mickiewicz, and Francisco 1999). Developing the ability to be reflective about their teaching practice is also cited as a valuable component of TA preparation (Druger 1997; Chism 1998a; Nyquist and Sprague 1998; Luo, Bellows, and Grady 2000). As Feldman and colleagues

(1996, 22) explain, "It is through this heightened awareness of one's work that practice can be enhanced by experimenting with alternative methods and ideas."

Studies of educational programs that are specifically designed to prepare TAs for innovative classes indicate that their content varies significantly from conventional TA preparation:

- More precourse workshops and semester-based courses are offered that place emphasis on pedagogy (Lawson, Rissing, and Faeth 1990; Lawrenz et al. 1992; Hammrich 1994, 1996; Nurrenbern, Mickiewicz, and Francisco 1999; Etkina 2000; Robinson 2000; McGivney-Burelle et al. 2001; Murray 2001; Sarquis et al. 2001; French and Russell 2002).

- Workshop or course teachers often model their teaching methods while TAs who play the role of students who are actively engaged in their own learning (Lawson, Rissing, and Faeth 1990; Lawrenz et al. 1992; Hammrich 1996; Etkina 2000; Hollar, Carlson, and Spencer 2000; Robinson 2000; McGivney-Burelle et al. 2001; Sarquis et al. 2001; French and Russell 2002; McManus 2002).

- TAs are encouraged to define their role as facilitators, research advisors, coaches, or research mentors rather than as primary sources of students' knowledge (Courter and Millar 1995; Courter et al. 1996; Millar et al. 1995; Alexander et al. 1996; Millar et al. 1997; Nurrenbern, Mickiewicz, and Francisco 1999; Streveler and King 2000; Larson et al. 2001; Stover et al. 2001; Sarquis et al. 2001; Streveler 2001; Wood et al. 2001; French and Russell 2002).

- Collegial meetings that include discussion of pedagogy are held at least weekly throughout the course (Lawson, Rissing, and Faeth 1990; Wagener 1991; Lawrenz et al. 1992; Hammrich 1994; Nurrenbern, Mickiewicz, and Francisco 1999; Trautwein 1999; Robinson 2000; Streveler and King 2000; Murray 2001; Sarquis et al. 2001; Stover et al. 2001; French and Russell 2002).

- Innovative course instructors more actively mentor TAs through role modeling, discussion, observation, and feedback (Etkina 2000; Robinson 2000; Streveler and King 2000; Sarquis et al. 2001).

- TAs' thoughts, feelings, perceptions, concerns, ideas, and feedback to the faculty are treated as relevant matters for discussion (Eby and Gilbert 2000; Stover et al. 2001).

- TA preparation may include reading articles on pedagogy (Etkina 2000; Winternitz and Davis 2000).

Some of these content items are encountered again later in a discussion of studies of ongoing TA support.

Studies of the Effectiveness of TA Preparation Programs for Innovative Classes

As already discussed, a review of recent literature reveals a continuing lack of evaluation work on the effectiveness of TA preparation programs for conventionally taught science that uses appropriate criteria for success. However, the need to evaluate innovative courses has stimulated a small number of evaluation studies that explore the effectiveness of TA preparation for innovative work using outcome measures that reflect course goals. McManus (2002) asked a sample of experienced and alumni TAs working in an innovative oceanography course to rate the importance of elements in a precourse program. They stressed the importance of learning how to use active learning methods, lecture to small classes, and lead discussions. The TAs sought more help in learning how to engage and motivate students, help them learn, and manage their classrooms. In a second example, physics TAs in a peer-observation training program valued most of the feedback that they received from faculty who observed their interactions with students. They credited their preparation program with improvements in their skills of student interaction and self-observation and and in their self-confidence as teachers.

Another small group of studies focused on program success in (1) changing TAs' beliefs about learning and their teaching practice in relation to innovative course learning goals and (2) securing their support for the course approach. French and Russell (2002) used pre- and posttests to study the perceptions of biology TAs whose training included precourse orientation and weekly meetings where issues arising from the inquiry-based course methods were discussed. The TAs' perceptions about the nature of their role changed over time: novices initially saw themselves as presenters of information; experienced TAs were more apt to support the inquiry-style methods of the course and view their role as facilitating or guiding student learning. Hammrich (1996) found that securing both TA buy-in to the approach of an innovative course and a good understanding of the theory and methods that it employs are not easy to achieve. Her study explored changes in attitudes of twenty-five biology TAs who prepared for a course based on inquiry, cooperative learning, and discovery-based methods. The TAs attended a precourse workshop on course content and pedagogy. They also learned about cognition and discussed the nature and sources of student misconceptions. Hammrich reports that TAs made only partial shifts in favor of the course's approach to teaching and learning. Her pre- and posttests revealed only partial understanding and acceptance of the theories of cognitive change and pedagogical methods used in the course. Half of the TAs continued to see student understanding as a matter of "automatic transmission or absorption of scientific knowledge" and did not come to see learning as "an active process of interpreting information and constructing understanding" (8). Robinson (2000), who observed TAs attending a half-semester course on active learning in chemistry labs, found that an initial lack of skill and disinclination to adopt the new methods could be surmounted for some TAs by continued encouragement, while others continued to resist. Lawrenz's evaluation (1992) of physics TAs' preparation at Purdue University entailed two ninety-minute meetings held each week to discuss course content and pedagogy. First-year TAs expressed uncertainty about how to facilitate cooperative problem solving in their recitations, although they found doing this easier in the labs. Many TAs were also unsure of the value of using these methods. After receiving more focused training, the following year's TAs were more supportive of inquiry-based learning and problem solving and demonstrated more expertise in each. Students were also more engaged and more satisfied with their learning in the second year.

Even when innovators succeed in changing TA perceptions about the value of pedagogical innovations, their use of more traditional teaching practices may persist. The effectiveness of a mandatory course in pedagogy for mathematics TAs at the University of Connecticut was evaluated by data collected from TAs by interviews, journal entries, responses to questions on class topics, and classroom observation of teaching (McGivney-Burelle et al. 2001). As a result of their training, TA perceptions about the teaching practices of effective instructors shifted toward support for collaborative learning, greater focus on facilitating conceptual understanding, and more self-reflection about their work. However, McGivney and colleagues' observations of the TAs' teaching behavior indicated that they continued to use traditional teaching methods. They argue that this discrepancy results partly from the strength of institutional and cultural attitudes supporting traditional forms of teaching and learning and partly because too few faculty actually model new methods of teaching so that TAs can see how they work in practice and how students respond.

Four other studies have investigated changes in TAs working in innovative courses where the faculty employed some combination of observing TA behavior in the classroom with feedback and discussion, modeling new pedagogy co-teaching, and regular meetings to discuss pedagogical issues. Etkina (2000) documents her own work as an innovating physics professor who modeled for TAs the switch from lecturing to question, answer, and discussion in class; demonstrated how to anticipate and address conceptual difficulties; and discussed with TAs how to structure a class based on student learning objectives. She reports on the issues raised by her TAs. These included difficulties in understanding that every class session had its own learning goals; that, for effective learning, students needed to work at an appropriate pace, with time for absorption of new knowledge; and that TAs could enable learning by identifying the fundamental issues that underlay their students' questions. In a study of engineering TAs who co-taught with an instructor and met regularly to discuss pedagogical issues, Streveler and King (2000) reported that TAs demonstrated greater understanding of the learning process and its variation among learners. In addition, students developed a greater self-reliance as learners and an enhanced ability to work collaboratively.

Lawson, Rissing, and Faeth (1990) studied the impact on biology TAs of an intensive three-day precourse workshop in which they learned new teaching methods by faculty role modeling. The workshop also focused on "levels of reasoning, reasoning patterns, the psychological process of self-regulation, and learning cycle instructional methods" (345–46). The TAs were provided with an instructional guide, and they attended two-hour weekly meetings that included inquiry-mode role playing, discussion of methods used, and issues that arose during the prior week. Although the TAs were initially reluctant to teach in the active-learning mode, Lawson reports increased support for these methods and considerable improvements in their skills in using them by the end of the semester. The intensity and scope of both the TAs' precourse preparation and weekly meetings may be an important factor in the success of this program.

In one of the few studies to employ trial and control groups, Nurrenbern and colleagues' study (Nurrenbern, Mickiewicz, and Wulff 1999) of TAs for an innovative chemistry course found that the preparation experiences of the trial TAs produced a number of outcomes that were less evident in the control group. While both groups attended precourse sessions on active learning, the trial TAs prepared learning materials for their recitations, used active-learning techniques, and discussed issues of pedagogy at weekly meetings with their faculty supervisors. Their faculty reported that it took four to five weeks before most TAs expressed commitment to the new methods and that some TAs resisted using them throughout the course. Questionnaire data from TAs in both the both the trial and control groups rated the departmental orientation as effective in providing them with teaching skills. However, trial-group TAs credited the support of the innovating faculty and staff for improvements in their teaching skills, described their recitations as being enjoyable (while control group TAs more often reported that "time dragged"), found that collaborative work had enabled them to approach problems in a variety of ways, and to become more skilled at evaluating the effects of different teaching strategies. Students also rated trial TAs significantly higher than they did the control group TAs on overall performance; on their preparation, understanding of material, clarity of explanation; and on helping students to develop critical thinking and problem-solving skills.

Accounts of programs designed to prepare TAs for work in innovative science courses, and evaluation work on their efficacy, are promising in a number of ways. The process of rethinking course goals in terms of student-learning outcomes appears to have prompted course designers to think about preparation in terms of what they need TAs to know and what TAs should be able and ready to do in order to meet student learning goals. "Readiness," which includes active support for course philosophy and methods, is portrayed as something that cannot be taken for granted, may be difficult to achieve, and that course designers must address in their program curricula. At the same time, the course innovators' need to demonstrate to colleagues, institutions, and program funders that their course can improve student learning and have other measurable benefits has prompted a more rigorous approach to the design, execution, and evaluation of TA preparation programs that serve these initiatives. This small group of studies of TA preparation in innovative courses offers some exemplars in methods and measurement for the evaluation of TA preparation programs that can also benefit more conventionally taught science courses.

Studies of Ongoing Support for Teaching Assistants

Whether in conventional or innovative courses, researchers have increasingly called for more ongoing support for teaching assistants throughout their teaching experience, largely in the form of weekly meetings and mentoring (Duba-Biedermann 1993; Poole and Sebolt 1993; Hendrix 1995; Nyquist and Wulff 1996; Druger 1997; Chism 1998b; Savage and Sharpe 1998; Shannon, Twale, and Moore 1998). Druger (1997) argues that TAs need on-the-job mentoring, the opportunity to practice, feedback and reinforcement, and regular discussion with faculty supervisors and other TAs. Worthen (1992) found that TAs value ongoing support and report that it increases their confidence. Graduate TAs in STEM fields at the University of Wisconsin, Madison, expressed a need for firsthand observation and performance feedback on their teaching strategies and practices, help in trying new activities, opportunities for critical self-reflection, and practice with new pedagogical methods (Millar, Clifford, and Connolly 2004). The reality is that most TAs complete an orientation program and are then left to cope on their own. Feedback from 341 graduate assistants from a random-sample survey at a public research institution indicated that only 41 percent received regular feedback during the term; of those, only 59 percent reported the feedback as being helpful (Duba-Biedermann 1993).

In a rare controlled study that used student performance as well as student ratings of TAs' impact as outcome measures, Hampton and Reiser (2002) examined the effects of feedback and consultation on thirty-seven TAs who were teaching computer literacy and introductory chemistry lab courses. Half of the TAs who were randomly assigned to the treatment group received initial consultation, midterm student feedback, observation, a second consultation based on both feedback and observation, and a final observation and review. Students rated the trial-treatment TAs significantly higher than they did the control TAs on usage of the instructional activities and their overall teaching effectiveness. Significant differences were also found in the final-exam scores of students whose TAs were in the trial group.

Bomotti (1994, 389) goes further in clarifying the TAs' need for professional development within supportive, collaborative relationships with faculty. From a study of 191 TAs working in multiple disciplines, including science and mathematics, she concludes that the most critical factor in improving the quality of undergraduate instruction is developing "a teaching-oriented, collaborative relationship between TAs and the supervisors." The supervisors should offer "information and feedback to TAs that is immediately useful in the classroom. They need someone to answer questions as they arise in the context of actual teaching and help them solve immediate problems." Kirk and Todd-Mancillas (1991) come to a similar conclusion in their study of TAs in nine departments. They found that one quarter of the "turning points" that affected TAs' sense of similarity, belonging, and membership with their department related to "the importance of supportive interpersonal relationships with peers and faculty" (417). These researchers were among the first to identify the importance of developing a collaborative working relationship among TAs and between TAs and faculty. I discuss in some detail in chapters 7, 8, and 9 the significance of collegiality evident in the data from the three innovations included in this study.

Nyquist and Wulff (1996) discuss the broader professional development needs of TAs that can only be met by support over time. These include the need to develop professional independence: beginning graduate students are "very enamored with the scholars with whom they have come to work" and "depend heavily on their supervisors."

> [Faculty] are held in high esteem, often emulated, and quite frequently quoted and imitated. As maturity comes, however, so does a time of dissociating from authority figures. To develop a sense of self and confidence in their own ability, graduate students must break away from supervisors to establish separateness and, eventually, independence. (23)

Through a process of continued engagement and support, TAs move "to the final stage of joining of a community of professionals that will establish mature, collegial relationships where all viewpoints are prized and sought after" (23). Like other researchers, Nyquist and Wulff recommend regularly scheduled meetings, observation by supervisor, and frequent feedback for both senior learners and colleagues in training.

Although the longer-term need for professional development has been advocated by the preceding group of scholars, formal or regular feedback (except for end-of-course evaluations by students) is rare for the majority of TAs.

As already indicated, preparation is typically assumed to be complete after the preterm orientation. There are, however, a handful of exceptions to this general picture that suggest what forms effective ongoing professional development for TAs can take: (1) Some departments actively facilitate supportive relationships among TAs or between faculty and TAs. (2) Some active-learning TA training courses provide support for half or all of the school term. (3) Some faculty (especially those who teach science) set up formal weekly meetings to discuss progress and problems in implementing aspects of the course and in using particular forms of pedagogy. The available literature, both on the need for these types of ongoing support and on the efforts to meet these needs, are discussed in the following sections.

Formal and Informal Mentoring

In more conventional courses, a number of studies report that faculty often fail to provide effective communication, management, or supervision of their TAs' work, and leadership of the teaching team (Duba-Biedermann 1993). Anderson and Swazey (1998) report that interactions between faculty supervisors and their TAs were limited in scope and duration, and Bashford (1996) found that faculty rarely gave guidance on how to teach effectively and thought it difficult to give their TAs useful feedback on their teaching work. This situation was compounded because the TAs did not receive professional development in the use of constructive criticism. TAs are usually more comfortable seeking information and receiving advice either from their peers (Staton and Darling 1989; Duba-Biedermann 1993) or from younger members of faculty (Worthen 1992). As I indicated earlier, the TAs' peer relationships are often their greatest source of information, support, and camaraderie (Worthen 1992; Anderson and Swazey 1998), and TAs tend to use these as their main reference groups unless course faculty are proactive in giving guidance and soliciting feedback. TAs give each other information about aspects of their role, norms of appropriate behavior, departmental rules and procedures, and available resources. Staton and Darling (1989) note that peers also share their concerns and discuss ideas for solving problems. They also note that international teaching assistants seek information and advice from other international teaching assistants rather than from U.S. TAs. McManus (2002) records that, apart from the normative experience of faculty inattention to their TAs' need for guidance and support, TAs are also reluctant to seek advice from faculty because they are afraid to seem incompetent.

Some universities have begun to address the undermet need for formal and informal mentoring for TAs by encouraging the development of ongoing supportive relationships that pair new and experienced TAs in formal mentoring relationships (Murray 2001; McManus 2002). Peer learning and building a supportive community of experienced and novice TAs are built into preparation programs by a number of methods: experienced TAs teach preterm workshops and share their knowledge and experience with novices (Darling and Earhart 1990; Lumsden 1993; Hollar, Carlson, and Spencer 2000; Tang and Sandell 2000); discussion sessions are set up (Winternitz and Davis 2000); or social time is built into preparation programs (Poole and Sebolt 1993). Only a small number of programs match TAs with faculty mentors for interactive supervision, guidance, evaluation, or feedback (Wagener 1991; Main 1994; Courter et al. 1996; Courter and Millar 1995; Etkina 2000; Streveler and King 2000; Winternitz and Davis 2000; Larson et al. 2001; Stover et al. 2001; Wood et al. 2001; Manogue and Krane 2003).

Thus far, most formal attempts to provide ongoing mentoring depend on developing peer relationships. However, this inevitably limits professional growth to the collective experience of TAs and shapes their professional development in conservative directions. The failure of most programs to address the preparation and support of TAs through collegial working relationships with faculty represents a missed opportunity. However, as already indicated, science education innovators have begun to rethink TA preparation in light of new demands on their TAs in serving revised student-learning objectives. Three studies report that innovative course instructors mentor their TAs through role modeling, discussion, observation, and feedback (Etkina 2000; Robinson 2000; Streveler and King 2000; Sarquis et al. 2001), and a fourth study documents innovative faculty treating TAs' perceptions, concerns, ideas, and feedback as relevant matters for discussion (Eby and Gilbert 2000; Stover et al. 2001).

Continuing Formal Education in Pedagogy

Compared with faculty teaching courses in a conventional manner, and departments in general, faculty who design and teach innovative courses are also more likely to offer their TAs formal classes in educational theory and pedagogical methods that are concurrent with TAs' teaching assignments. They are also more likely to provide continuing support for their TAs (Robinson 2000; Streveler and King 2000). Some courses that support innovative pedagogy by emphasizing active learning include TA classroom observation and feedback (Darling and Earhart 1990; Robinson 2000; Sundberg et al. 2000); some include role modeling by experienced TAs or faculty and TA critiques of their observations (Wagener 1991; Etkina 2000; Robinson 2000).

Weekly Meetings

Formal weekly meetings to prepare their TAs for recitations or labs most often occur in traditional science classes where TAs lead students through lab experiments. However, in innovative courses, faculty often institute weekly meetings with their TAs to discuss class subject matter and pedagogy (Lawson, Rissing, and Faeth 1990; Millar et al. 1997; Robinson 2000). Researchers report that their agendas include elements of new learning (for example, theories of conceptual change, alternative pedagogies and problem-solving strategies, approaches to inquiry-based or cooperative learning) and discussion of emergent issues and alternative practical strategies, for example, how to address students' common conceptual misconceptions, how and when to pose questions to students, or what constitutes acceptable student hypotheses (Lawson, Rissing, and Faeth 1990; Wagener 1991; Lawrenz et al. 1992; Hammrich 1994; Nurrenbern, Mickiewicz, and Francisco 1999; Trautwein 1999; Robinson 2000; Streveler and King 2000; Murray 2001; Sarquis et al. 2001; Stover et al. 2001; French and Russell 2002). Nurrenbern, Mickiewicz, and Francisco (1999) report that faculty–TA meetings in innovative courses are characterized by collegial discussion of between one and three hours and that staff may also be invited to take part. Central agenda items are TA concerns, observations, and suggestions about course content; discussion of pedagogical strategies; and implementation issues (Eby and Gilbert 2000; Robinson 2000; Stover et al. 2001). Role playing is sometimes used to introduce new activities and predict student responses (Sundberg et al. 2000); and, in innovative science courses, where faculty often conduct their own labs, they model for TAs the modes of teaching and learning to be used. Weekly meetings held after classes and labs offer the opportunity to discuss emergent issues, such as "what sorts of questions to pose, when to pose them, and when to introduce new terms" (Lawson, Rissing, and Faeth 1990, 346). TAs may also discuss acceptable and unacceptable hypotheses that students might propose (French and Russell 2002), learn how to help students deal with common misconceptions, and enable them to make mistakes and learn from them (Sundberg et al. 2000). As with the Berkeley initiative, faculty may provide TAs with guide sheets that summarize lab objectives and offer background information and tips on how to increase student learning (Lawson, Rissing, and Faeth 1990). TAs report varying degrees of benefit from weekly meetings, depending on their character and mode of conduct. For example, when the agenda does not address TA needs, meetings may be seen as a burden to attend (Worthen 1992). As Nurrenberg and colleagues (1999) note, when meetings effectively address the TAs' need to improve their teaching skills, the improvement becomes evident to others. Nurrenbern and colleagues report that the Purdue University chemistry TAs who participated in these sessions were rated significantly higher than the control group on overall performance, preparedness, understanding of material, clarity of explanation, and in encouraging the development of thinking and problem-solving skills in their students.

Studies that evaluate weekly meetings are, as yet, rare. In a study in which TAs estimated the value of optional weekly meetings in a conventionally taught speech communications course, those TAs who attended described the meetings as being initially beneficial but a burden over time because the agenda did not address their needs (Worthen 1992). Studies that include evaluation of the effects of weekly meetings in innovative courses are rare. In a study of chemistry TAs at Purdue University, the TAs valued the support that weekly meetings provided and credited them as a source of improvements in their teaching skills that a TA control group did not demonstrate (Nurrenbern, Mickiewicz, and Francisco 1999). The meeting attenders were also rated significantly higher than the control group on overall performance, preparedness, understanding of material, clarity of explanation, and in encouraging the development of thinking and problem-solving skills in their students.

Thus, for all types of TA preparation and support, as well as for the broader aspects of their professional socialization discussed earlier, it would seem that course innovation prompts more rethinking of TA preparation because of the critical role that TAs play in meeting revised student learning goals. As innovative courses proliferate, we may expect to see more examples of active partnerships developing between faculty and their TAs in these courses. After so many decades of limited attention to the education and support of TAs in more conventional undergraduate courses, it seems likely that the community of innovating faculty may provide both the impetus and the models for more comprehensive forms of professional development for the future university teachers. The innovative faculty also appear to be leading the way in setting up well-designed evaluation studies of their programs' effectiveness based on appropriate criteria, such as impact on TAs' beliefs and practices and consequences for student learning in alignment with course learning goals.

In the balance of this chapter, I describe and discuss the nature of the education and support needs of the TAs and coaches working in the three initiatives discussed in this volume. Special attention is given to weekly meetings; learning pedagogical skills; and TA evaluation of the degree to which faculty met their preparation, support, and longer-term professional development needs. The TAs' and coaches' estimates of what more would be needed to make them optimally effective partners are also discussed.

PREPARATION, SUPPORT, AND OTHER ASPECTS OF PROFESSIONAL DEVELOPMENT IN THE THREE INITIATIVES

The three initiatives vary considerably in their approach to TA preparation. The Berkeley initiative is grounded in a specially designed TA education program. Indeed, success of the initiative depends on the effectiveness of its TA preparation and support methods. The chemistry modules, by contrast, are offered in different types of institutions—some that traditionally employ graduate or undergraduate TAs and some that do not. The chemistry module handbooks do not (as yet) discuss ways to make use of TAs in modular teaching. However, we found that, across the seven institutions in the modular chemistry sample, those faculty who worked with TAs had improvised a range of formal and informal provisions for their education and support. The lone innovator who developed and taught Interactive Astronomy was in the process of discovering what kinds of provisions for TA role support were needed, and why.

As with many other aspects of these classroom innovations, the TAs and coaches were highly articulate about what they needed to sustain what, to most of them, were unfamiliar roles. Across the three data sets, 87 of the 110 TAs and coaches (79 percent) offered 170 observations on educational preparation and professional support issues. Of these, the largest group of observations (64 percent across all three initiatives) referenced what TAs and coaches identified as their education and support needs and the degrees to which they were met. Appreciation for aspects of the teaching preparation and support received accounted for another 31 percent, and complaints about what was offered totaled 6 percent. Thus, as in many other areas of the TA data set, the TAs emerged as a rich source of guidance to faculty about what needs to be done to make their innovations work optimally. These are described in the second half of this chapter.

What TAs Needed to Know at the Outset and on an Ongoing Basis

The primary need of all TAs was for clear, up-front information about the nature of the course for which they were to work. Meeting this need was important whether or not TAs could choose the courses for which they worked. In some departments, TAs are assigned to particular classes, with little choice for either faculty or potential TAs:

> I had no choice about the class. I was just assigned to it. It was a bit of a shock, but it happened to other people too.

This situation can become uncomfortable where a student either does not like the course approach or develops an unfortunate work relationship with the teacher, and neither can change the TA's assignment. This problem arose at three institutions in our sample, where it seriously compromised the innovation by unsettling undergraduates and other TAs and undermining faculty credibility with both. In most schools, students have some choice about the classes in which they work, and faculty can interview prospective TAs. In either situation, TAs saw it as being vital that they be offered advance information about the pedagogical approach that the faculty teaching the class intended to use.

> I had no idea about the modules. I didn't really know anything about the job until the first week, and I was very surprised. I was glad of a friend who had worked with [the faculty] on modules the previous semester, and he explained some of it to me. But I had no clue what it was all about.

> I felt more comfortable with the approach later in the semester, but it took me quite a while to see where they were going with the modules.

The TAs also advocated that any TA who was assigned to an innovative class, but who expressed a preference to work in a more traditional class, should be supported in finding an alternative position.

TAs also need to know from the outset what their role will entail. Because all of these classes were unlike anything that most of the TAs had encountered, they needed the working structure of the class to be laid out in some detail, along with what they were expected to contribute and how they were to do this:

> When I took the job, since I'd taken the class, I thought I would understand how it was structured. So, it was definitely a shock for me—to have it all so different. I've just been so used to the textbook format. It's not that I don't like the modules—actually I do now—but I needed more help up front to understand what they were trying to accomplish and how I fitted into that.

This was relatively easy to accomplish with the chemistry modules where student activities, course content, and methods of assessment are laid out in both faculty and student handbooks. However, these still need to be explained, and TAs need opportunities to ask questions and discuss how these aspects of the class will operate in practice. Where the course structure and methods are still being developed and refined, TAs found it especially hard to understand the dimensions of their role and how to operate effectively:

> When we started off, it was fairly unorganized, and we got the impression that they were writing pieces of the modules and handing them to us a week later. And things like that obviously happen quite a bit in classes from what I've seen. However in an experimental class, it's probably not the best way to do it. They might have been more successful if they had started a year later and planned everything out fully—which is overkill for a normal classroom, but I think would have been very useful. That way they could have gone through everything with us right from the start.

More experienced TAs noted that although many traditional faculty also work "off the cuff," they are nevertheless operating within familiar parameters.

Some TAs found their faculty's initial explanations of the nature of the course, and definitions of the TA's role, too cursory and urged that these not be skimped:

> They gave us the module and said, "This is what the students have to read before they come to class." And that was about it. It wasn't specific enough.

The third kind of information that TAs need is explanation of the nature of the course content and where it differs from courses with which they are more familiar. At the outset, TAs need to know their teachers' broader purposes for student learning; how the semester will be structured; and how labs, reading materials, tests, and other forms of learning assessments will be used:

> For any experimental semester, the ducks all need to be lined up. In a regular classroom where the system is established and the students are familiar with it, we all kinda know what to do. But this is a different game. We need much more guidance. They should hand out a syllabus on the first day that's fairly detailed—week by week at least.

> We didn't get the big picture. They essentially gave us the books and said, "This is what the course is going to be. This is what all of the labs are." Maybe a summary of each lab would be good. I needed more of a road map so I'm less confused going into my first day and what his expectations of me are. Then I can focus more on how I'm going to work with the materials and be effective.

> They didn't really make it very clear at the beginning what was going on with the different modules. They explained some of their motivations for wanting to do the first one but never told us that there were going to be other ones following it or how they connected. And the transition into the next module was a little weird because we didn't really know what to expect.

Lack of clarity on these issues by the faculty was seen as being unfair and unreasonable:

> We were dropped in at the deep end without much preparation. And, after that, we learned about the materials in spits and starts.

It also made it difficult for TAs to give their students good signposts:

> It was kind of being introduced to the structure as we went along. As a TA, that was a difficult situation because the students were looking to you in the labs to explain where we were going with this.

The last speaker references the need to meet students' expectations of their TAs as their main personal resort in understanding class materials and the nature of the work required of them. Without clear direction both at the outset and on a continuing basis, TAs felt underprepared to meet those needs and, thus, insecure in their role. They expressed concerns about their credibility with students:

> We'd read a sheet about the lab in advance, and we'd seen a little demo, but the procedure was only so clear. And you'd come into the lab, and a lot of it was really unknown. And the students would ask you a question, and you had never done this lab, and you didn't really know the equipment. So, answering questions off the top of your head was really tough.

> I think the worst thing was being caught in a lecture, and the teacher asks the students a question, and you're kinda guessing where they were going with it.

Knowing what levels of preparation (e.g., in mathematics and chemistry), interest, and motivation that students bring to any class is useful information for both teachers and TAs. However, in innovative classes, TAs thought it particularly important to discover the composition of their sections early in the class and to use the information to structure groups, decide how to pitch ideas, and select examples for students from particular groups of majors:

> I mean, you can't put all of your attention on the weaker students and neglect the stronger ones. It was just hard to find middle ground. I had people who were completely lost all the way to people who didn't pay attention because, I guess, they knew it. So, that was my biggest problem—knowing what range of students I had and figuring out where to pitch the session.

> I didn't know what level of preparation some students had, but I learned right at problem set number one, and then in the quiz—they both came in the second week. I would like to have known more about them at the start.

Some TAs expressed their willingness to help their professors determine the range of preparation among their students, and one group had experience of one way to do this:

> TA 1: The professors did a pretty good job of telling us what we should expect about the students' level of chemistry knowledge, but not how much math they came in with.

> TA 2: Yeah, I didn't figure out that out until most of the way through. And that bears a lot on what chemistry you can explain to them.

> TA 3: You should pass out a sheet on the first day: "What's your name, your e-mail, how much chemistry and math have you had." Then you know. I've got six people with AP chem, two sophomores who tried this last year, and whole bunch of people who don't know what's going on.

Chapter 10

TA 1: We did that last year, and it worked out well. We found some people had groups who had no chemistry. I had half who had AP or several years of chemistry, so I could step it up and make it more interesting to them.

TA 2: I've done that on my own, and I found it very valuable.

TA 3: And it can change your approach. If I have mostly premeds, I am not going to give engineering examples. I'll try to tailor it more to their interests.

This is another example of the TAs' willingness to work with faculty to brainstorm ways to meet particular needs and to try out solutions for themselves.

TAs clearly needed as much advance information as faculty could offer as to what students would experience in the innovative classes, how they were likely to respond, and what strategies they and the teacher could use in order to deal with whatever difficulties could be foreseen with these new modes of learning. TAs also looked for information on an ongoing basis. Wherever possible, TAs requested that information be offered to them in writing. They described eight major areas of need that, taken together, outline key elements in a curriculum for TA preparation. Each of these is discussed in turn.

Curriculum Emphasis

TAs wanted faculty to clarify on a weekly basis what they had done with the students in class and what they wanted TAs to focus on in their follow-up sessions with their students:

I'm always asking him, "Have you covered this in class yet?" It's worse because my group are all from different sections with different professors. They just have to get them to the standard test by a certain date. It really hit when we're doing the global warming module and I found some of my group didn't know anything about Lewis's structures.

There's not enough time for us to explain things, so we need to know what they should know and not to have to second-guess the professors and what they are trying to achieve.

Weekly meetings were an important feature of the Berkeley initiative. Their purposes were to give feedback and discuss the previous week's worksheet activities and labs, to review the content and methods of the worksheet for the coming week, and to work through the week's lab experiments with the discussion coordinator. Reviewing content was found to be important because the innovating faculty discovered at an early stage that they could not take it for granted that all TAs had a good understanding of the concepts to be explored in any week. Going through the worksheets allowed TAs (as well as their undergraduates) to improve their mastery of concepts. TAs found it useful when meetings had the same format each week. TAs who supported the innovation's objectives agreed that having a weekly meeting was key in bringing "quality control" and uniformity to TA teaching across the group:

> I would say, overall, that it's helpful to have the meetings. In the classes I have taught before, there were no formal organizing meetings. TAs would sort of be on their own in terms of what they wanted to do and . . . some people would not do a very good job of covering the material. . . . At least the worksheets can give you somewhat of a minimum [level of quality]. . . . It's a good idea, in general.

As indicated earlier, TAs saw it as being optimal that they sit in on classes so that they could know what students experience, what they should understand, and what they find difficult:

> We were required to sit with them in lecture. And it was very easy to see what they were having difficulty with. Sometimes they were very intent and they'd ask questions; and sometimes they were scratching their heads and had no clue at all. You could tell by just sitting in lecture what they were getting. It also meant I got to know my students better. Just being there was good, I think.

The chemistry modules are apt to move fairly quickly into content areas that are new or less familiar to TAs, especially to undergraduates:

> We didn't get enough background information. We've never studied this stuff, so we often didn't understand from our own learning the question that was posed to the students. So the problems were often beyond what we were capable of doing, and trying to help the students work through them was just a nightmare.

Attending class with their students enabled TAs to learn unfamiliar aspects of the innovative course content and consolidated their understanding of more familiar material. It also modeled the innovative teacher's pedagogy, how discussions and small-group activities can be set up and run, and how multiple reading sources can be used in conjunction with the text. Where class attendance is not possible, weekly meetings with the TAs may include, as a regular agenda item, bringing TAs up to speed with class and lab content and making linkages between the two.

Learning Assessments

As tests in new-style classes could be radically different from familiar forms of assessment, TAs wanted to be briefed in advance about the nature, purpose, format, structure, and timing of tests in order to help students prepare for them appropriately:

> We should have some information on the exams before they are given out. We don't have to see the problems, and we don't want to bias the students, but knowing the type of problem and the format in which they will be asked is important. Like we recently got quantitative exams, which is not what they've been teaching to. The first exam surprised everybody—including us. The second was closer to what they've been emphasizing in class, but it was still not a good match with the materials. And we don't know how to help the students prepare.

As well as learning how to prepare students more effectively, they were also interested in contributing ideas for the quizzes or exams:

> They weren't terribly consistent about getting out to us what kinds of topics were going to be on the exams. And if we had a better notion of what the structure and the content of the exams would be, we could certainly have helped them more with that.

Because of the unfamiliarity of the material, TAs often felt uncertain that they understood the point of particular test questions and feared that they would mislead the students unless the professors explained what they were looking for in students' answers:

> I felt in the dark about these ungraded class quizzes until the very end of the term, when I guess they eventually listened to us. But they wouldn't tell us what the answers were at all. The students were supposed to come to our office hours and get help in reasoning through the questions, but there were occasions where I came up with the wrong answer, and I didn't know it until two or three weeks later. Details of the chemistry or the way the question was worded were unclear to me, and I would end up giving my students bad guidance.

Handling Questions

TAs sought guidance in dealing with questions to which they did not know the answers and reassurance that it was "okay not to know everything":

> It happens more with modules. We start talking about something, and they are now used to asking questions—they ask a lot of questions—and just get straight to something I don't understand [*laughing*].

> Even if it should be obvious to them that one of the answers is right, it's not necessarily obvious to us, because there are gray areas. And the more discrepancy between what your TAs and your students know, the more it's going to be a problem. So they should come out and tell us what they see as the right ap-

proach, and at least we can argue about it a bit. Again, it's this communication thing.

As indicated earlier, it was important to TAs to observe how their professors fielded questions for which they had no ready answers.

Advance Knowledge of Discussion Questions

TAs needed to know in advance what questions the teacher was going to ask TA-led groups to discuss, so they could prepare for them. Similarly, in a course such as one based on modules where faculty stress students' discovering things for themselves, TAs needed to understand why this matters and how to make it work:

> She wanted the students to discover things and be able to ask us things like how they could start on a question, but not to give away the answer. I don't actually remember her telling us not to give them the answer, but she definitely teaches us to point them in the right direction by asking them questions.

Disciplinary Responsibilities

TAs sought guidelines and situation-specific advice and support in handling disciplinary problems, such as what to do when students failed to hand in work or were absent from labs or groups. This guidance was particularly important to undergraduate TAs, but all TAs wanted guidelines and procedures within which to work.

Preparation for New Labs

Receiving sufficient information and training to work effectively in unfamiliar labs, both at the outset and throughout the course, was the most urgent and strongly expressed informational need of modular TAs. This need was also identified by the Berkeley TAs who saw it as being well met. The modular TAs wanted to spend time learning new labs, understanding how they worked, identifying predictable problems, and figuring out how they could be addressed. Prelab sessions were seen as one way in which some of these needs could be addressed:

> I think the prelab is a really good idea because it gives me a chance to catch up—get some reading done—just in case I need to review some of the basics, because if you don't use the stuff, you tend to forget it. They are good for the students too because it gives them a chance to ask questions right at the beginning instead of waiting until they get to the lab. And they can ask their question before the whole class, and the whole class learns from the answer.

Given the discovery orientation of the chemistry modules, TAs wanted to discuss how to give students useful exploratory leads without giving away answers. They also needed to know what students had done in class by way of preparation for each lab and what they could be expected to understand. Although (as illustrated earlier) some modular teachers were lauded by their TAs for the good lab preparation they received, there was wide variation in the extent and quality of this aspect of their preparation. Eight modular TAs who reported insufficient briefing about the nature of the labs and their lab role thought that they entered labs "knowing as little or as much as the students." They were frustrated at feeling incompetent and being unable to help confused students:

> We seemed to be using fairly advanced techniques right away. I didn't know how they wanted us to do these, and they didn't explain it to us. They just assumed we knew what this procedure was and how to perform it. It was incredibly frustrating.

> I was handed the lab manual five minutes before the lab started, so I'm sitting there reading, trying to catch up and figure out what the students would need to do.

> It seemed like the first couple of labs were just thrown in. She wrote points about what the lab was to be on the board, and then the students had to discuss as an entire lab section how they were going to do this. I guess that was early on, but it was very intimidating for me because I had to answer their questions, but I was working very much in the dark.

Some of these experiences were clearly a consequence of faculty trying out labs before they were fully ready to use them. Some TAs reported that the lab preparation improved as faculty gained familiarity with the new labs, provided them with advance materials, and discussed with them each lab's objectives and methods. However, their experience is a reminder of the frontline status of TAs in innovative classes and the stresses that they bear when faculty underplan or work overspontaneously.

The Role and Significance of Weekly Meetings

Both the astronomy coaches and the Berkeley TAs experienced regular weekly meetings. In the case of the Berkeley initiative, this was a structural feature of the innovation that proved critical to its functioning. Thus, many basic needs were routinely met for these two groups—receiving course information, giving and receiving feedback and support, troubleshooting problems (labs, technical issues, grading, disciplinary matters, test preparation, "fit" issues, etc.), and discussing the work for the week ahead. The Berkeley TAs found it especially useful to spend time on material that students found difficult. This group also received some background in the research on learning and different pedagogical methods and would have liked more of this. Their negative observations referenced specific aspects of the meetings (e.g., meeting length, needing more guidance to resolve problems) that might be improved, and the organizers made adjustments in light of these. However, only the small number of TAs who were opposed to the idea of using common teaching methods across sections queried the value of weekly meetings.

Across the modular chemistry sample, nineteen TAs discussed the importance of regular meetings largely as an undermet need. Five described aspects of meetings with the other TAs and their professor and explained why they valued this arrangement; the other fourteen wanted to see regular preparation meetings instituted and explained why this would be useful. There was strong agreement across this group that meetings should be both regular—preferably weekly—and formal. Both TAs working in large institutions with large classes and those working in small schools with small classes were in agreement on this point. However, some TAs had received no regular formal training. This group worked in smaller schools where, because casual contact with professors was fairly high, faculty might think they were giving adequate guidance and support. This group had initially received some orientation in the principles on which the course was built and the nature or use of class materials. However, beyond that, they described an informal, haphazard pattern of interaction with faculty about class-management issues. What they lacked was a detailed understanding of how they were to work with their students in discussion, activity, or lab groups as the course progressed. Those who met with their professor or other TAs on an irregular basis reported that these meetings quickly became focused on problem solving rather than planning. Clearly, even where TAs and faculty relate in a friendly, informal way, TAs still need regular sessions to receive help and discuss class issues.

Some modular TAs described casual encounters with their professors that had no pattern or agenda. As at most smaller schools in our sample, TAs knew and liked the professors for whom they worked and felt uncomfortable about complaining or suggesting a more formal arrangement:

> They give us the modules ahead of time, and we are expected to read them and be prepared, but they don't really plan it together with us. At least [Dr. X] will sit down with me and sort of go over what we're doing and ask if I have any questions. Maybe they just don't have the time to come and meet with us. I sometimes go back to him and ask, "What do you want the students to get out of this?"

> I don't feel like I'm well informed about what's going on because there's no communication about what we're doing the next day sometimes. Every once in

a while we'll have a meeting, but I think we could be better informed and better prepared. I'd like a session once a week so we could get together and go over the lesson plans so we could do some prior preparation for the class.

Sometimes, he'll just happen to meet me in the corridor, and we will have an interesting conversation about how it's going. And he's a great guy and a good teacher. But it's really not enough help to make sure I'm doing what I need to make this class work right.

Both the chemistry and the astronomy TAs had definite ideas about the preferred agenda for weekly meetings. They needed to plan the week ahead—to hear explanation of what content, student activities, and tests were planned for the coming week; what the teacher would emphasize in class; what class–lab connections the teacher wished to stress; and what the TAs were to focus on in their work with students. They also wanted to offer their faculty detailed feedback on how the previous week's work had gone—how students had responded to the activities; how well they had done in labs, in recitation or discussion sections, and on graded work; and what seemed to cause them difficulty. They wished to discuss these issues with the teacher and the other TAs and to offer suggestions about how to make particular activities work better:

The TA meetings were good because the professor was somewhat out of touch with the students—just because it was such a large class. And the meeting helped the professor know what students were struggling with and how we could correct this in the coming lecture.

TAs also liked to take an active role in designing activities, quiz questions, and handouts for their students and planning group work. They wanted practical instruction and guidance in the pedagogical techniques that were stressed in the course and that they were asked to use, and they appreciated feedback on how their own teaching methods were working. Some information about the theoretical underpinning of the pedagogy of the class was also welcome. Spending part of the meeting time on their own—that is, without the professor—was advocated by the TAs who had experienced it:

We spend an hour, but we split it in two, and that's useful because there are some issues that we don't feel comfortable bringing up in front of the professor. It's also important to do that because we can talk as peers and figure out how to deal with some things without involving the teacher. We get help from one another and give support in how to deal with something. Someone takes notes, so we gather together all of the issues that we have to talk to him about before he gets to the meeting. We didn't do this at the beginning, but we've found it stops the meeting from getting scattered.

TAs also appreciated a formal agenda circulated by e-mail before the meeting, to which any TA could make a contribution. Those TAs who could not make a particular meeting needed some mechanism for catching up on information missed and issues discussed, and, in one class, the TAs wrote and circulated minutes of their sessions.

Learning Pedagogical Skills

Across the three initiatives, twenty-seven TAs spoke about their need for information and preparation in the teaching methods that they were expected to use in their innovative classes. Eight TAs spoke in positive terms about the assistance they had received, and nineteen described their unmet needs. TAs working in these active and interactive classes needed practical help to understand how to work with students in each area of contact. This included their interactive work in recitation or discussion sections, small groups and labs, supporting students in computer-based work, and assistance to students during office hours. The kinds of help that TAs thought that they needed in order to use the innovative pedagogy effectively were broadly of three kinds:

- Practical guidance and modeling of teaching methods
- Regular opportunities to discuss problems that arose in their teaching and student support work and to get help in resolving them
- Feedback on their teaching and support work

Requests for help in using interactive methods were most strongly expressed by those who had not taught before:

> I'm new to teaching, and the two hardest things are not taking it to a level they can understand or, when they say they don't understand, coming up with some little analogies or something to help them. I guess that comes with experience, but I could use some help with it also.

However, many TAs found themselves struggling to help their students understand ideas that they found difficult and to address ideas at an appropriate level:

> Maybe it's a right- and left-brained thing. Some people see it the way I do, but others see things differently. And I need to learn how to relate to them both. Right now I don't have the knowledge or skills to do that.

> Sometimes I find it hard to explain things to them. When they saw the demo last week, they thought it was way cool, but they didn't understand why it happened. And I had to explain. Some students picked it up pretty well, but not

others—maybe because of me—I just didn't know how to approach it so they could understand.

TAs who received some guidance on particular teaching methods enjoyed the experience and looked for more:

> I went to a team-teaching seminar in the lunch hour last semester. And she did a fantastic job. I often feel it would be tremendous if they could just explain to us some of the ways to explain things so that students would get it. There's an education school here, so there's got to be people who could teach us how to do this.

Those who got sessions on how to teach from their faculty found a number of things useful—explanations and demonstrations of how to use particular methods and activities, advice about teaching behaviors to avoid, information about theories and research that underpin active and interactive learning, worksheets to use in group sessions, examples and applications to help convey difficult concepts, and both peer and teacher critiques of their teaching. They also appreciated handouts that summarized this information.

TAs found peer discussions that focused on particular teaching and group-management issues particularly helpful—for example, how to be aware of, and avoid, gender bias:

> One evening we got into the issue of gender equality on the science classroom. That was a very fruitful discussion. And there were a couple of really gems of conversation that came out of those sessions.

These discussions were seen as most effective when linked with feedback on their own teaching:

> It came up because of something we saw on the tape. There were three guys and three women sitting around a table talking with their TA. The TA was talking to the men, and one of the women piped up and said something, and he didn't hear it or respond to it. He just kept talking the other way. And he was totally oblivious that he had done that. So it was a good way to start the discussion, "Does this happen? Am I guilty of the same thing?" It's a good thing to bring into consciousness and talk about.

Videotaping of TAs in action with their student groups was reported in two innovative classes in our sample. The TAs who experienced videotaped critiques of their work thought this worked best when

- TAs were filmed at work with their students:

  > There's a real value to seeing yourself at work. Like, I didn't realize how bad I was until I saw myself on tape—twice! We got into some really good dis-

cussions after seeing ourselves working with the students. We all had things we wanted to talk about. Those were the things that were most helpful about those sessions.

- When the taping was done by someone with the knowledge and skills to discuss the tape with the TA after the class:

The guy who videotaped me—I think he was from the ed school—he was very helpful. We talked about my game plan before the class, and then we went over the tape for about an hour afterwards. He said things like, "Why don't you slow down for your students? I liked the way that you followed up on that question." That was very useful.

- The subsequent discussion focused on particular themes illustrated in the tapes (e.g., pace, fielding questions, stimulating discussion, board work, keeping students' attention):

We saw some clips where you might think, "I really like the way this person explained a topic," or "That was cleverly done." Things like keeping the class under control, keeping peoples' attention.

Videotaped feedback sessions worked less well where

- TAs filmed each other or TAs role played their teaching with other TAs acting as surrogate students:

The first time they taped us teaching to a bunch of other TAs who were pretending to ask questions, and that was not terribly useful—everyone was heckling! Videotaping us working with a real group was much more useful because you could look at yourself in front of the students and see that this person needs to work on their board work or whatever.

- The exercise was repeated too often—three or four sessions of shared extracts and discussions focused on particular issues were thought to be sufficient:

You need to do this enough to flush out the issues that we all need to pay attention to, but not everyone's tape has to be seen. That gets too much repetition. You can look at your own tape and see some of the things we discussed right there.

- Discussion of the taped material ranged across too many issues in any one session.

However, all of the TAs who had worked with video critique thought the combination of taping and focused discussion was a good way to learn how effectively they were teaching and to see how their students were responding:

> The discussions after taping were particularly good. I think they helped us figure out what kinds of issues each of us had and also what was going on in our sections—whether the students were understanding us. Very helpful.

As well as needing help to develop their teaching skills, TAs needed preparation in some specific aspects of their role. In innovations that employ computers in class, lab, projects, or assessments, TAs needed early preparation in the systems or software used so that they could help their students and troubleshoot technical difficulties. As indicated in the previous section, they needed a practice run with new labs. For small-group work especially, TAs requested some hands-on modeling of methods, sessions on group dynamics, addressing variations in levels of student contributions, handling disciplinary problems, and implementing the grading policy. Finally, with respect to office hours, the TAs wanted help with the problem also commonly reported by faculty—how to motivate students to come to see them. They wanted to discuss how best to help those students who did attend.

In this chapter, I have pointed to models for TA educational preparation, support, and ongoing professional development that are emerging in evaluation studies of classroom innovations and in discussion articles by scholars who study them. From the TA data in the three initiatives, I have also demonstrated the TAs' need for formal preparation and support—even in small departments with an informal communication style between TAs and faculty. Programs need to begin before the start of each course and to continue throughout them. TAs clarified their needs for full course information, educational knowledge and skills, and opportunities to give and receive feedback to their faculty and to each other in weekly meetings. The data also include strong indications of the capacity and willingness of TAs to be active as troubleshooters for the course—a capacity they seek to extend through appropriate forms of education and mentoring.

NOTES

1. One source of ongoing research on this topic is the Center for the Integration of Research, Teaching, and Learning (CIRTL), a National Science Foundation Center for Learning and Teaching (see www.cirtl.net).
2. This is a fundamental tenet of CIRTL.

11

Fostering Collegial Engagement among Teaching Assistants Working in Innovative Courses

It is clear that classroom innovators who work with TAs have much to gain by soliciting and reinforcing their active engagement.[1] Without their TAs' readiness to address day-to-day practical issues, including student problems with new forms of learning, it would be hard for those faculty who work with larger classes that require the help of teaching assistants to succeed in implementing their new courses. As indicated in the chapter 4 discussion of TAs' negative course evaluations, an innovative course's chances of success are at risk if innovators fail to persuade skeptical TAs to give a new course a fair trial. Both TAs who express vocal opposition to an innovation and those who covertly fail to carry out the tasks requested of them can seriously undermine the willingness of students to try new forms of learning, the morale of other TAs, and that of the innovators themselves. As already illustrated, there is also much to be lost by failing to tap into the potential for creative collaboration that TAs can bring to their work and, conversely, a great deal to gain by doing so. A combination of collegiality in faculty and peer relationships, the opportunity to give regular feedback and to discuss ways to resolve problems, and a preparation program relevant to the new pedagogy were found to be major factors in TAs' active support for innovative class goals. Conversely, faculty's failure to establish open communication and a collaborative working relationship with TAs dissipates their goodwill. Our data clearly show that if faculty succeed in setting and maintaining a collegial, collaborative tone from the outset, TAs are willing to argue the value of the innovation to undergraduates and engage in making it work.

TA experiences with collegiality were not uniform within each initiative: they varied among institutions in modular chemistry, changed over time in the Berkeley initiative, and were greater among the more experienced novice coaches in Interactive Astronomy. However, a broad view of the importance of collegiality and collaboration can be gained by first looking at the two innovations working largely or exclusively with undergraduate TAs and coaches. Of all sixty-eight TAs and coaches working in modular chemistry and Interactive Astronomy (of whom fifty-two were undergraduates), sixty-one raised the issue of collegiality as a factor in their attitudes toward the innovation. Of these, forty-six had, to varying degrees, worked with their faculty in collegial, collaborative ways, with open communication and a sense that their contributions were valued. Another thirteen were disappointed because they had hoped to work more collegially with their faculty. They described missed opportunities for collaborative effort and loss of morale when faculty either failed to meet their need to discuss aspects of the course or seemed to undervalue their contributions.

The picture for the Berkeley initiative changed over time, and the issue of collegiality is one factor that distinguishes the earlier and later sets of interviews. In interviews with a first cohort of seventeen TAs, it was evident that many of them did not think that they were treated collegially by some or all of the course faculty. No positive statements about these relationships were offered, and eight TAs felt poorly informed about course content or direction, complained of insufficient contact with the lecture professor, or believed that the professors had little confidence in them. Those who were more supportive of the innovation described problems in the TA–faculty relationship as an important factor in the reluctance of other TAs to use the worksheets as the innovators wished. After learning this, the worksheet designers and their coordinator made a strong effort in subsequent semesters to address this issue. In interviews with a second cohort eighteen months later, the twenty-five TAs were asked to comment on the degree of collegiality they had experienced. None of these interviewees reported any problems in their working relationships with the innovation organizers, and eighteen specifically commented on their collegial nature.[2]

Across the three initiatives, TAs and coaches in different institutions and classes described the impact of their working relationships with faculty on the scope and quality of their work. These observations often arose out of discussions of other, often more concrete issues—for example, their needs for preparation and support and how well these were met, how particular implementation problems were addressed, their estimates of the value or likely success of the innovation, and what they liked or disliked about the job. These observations were gathered together and are summarized in this chapter.

REPORTS OF COLLEGIALITY AND ITS IMPACT

In its simplest form, collegiality was described in TA statements of appreciation for faculty who listened to them respectfully as people with something valuable to contribute:

> I really feel that he listens. I don't feel like I'm on the same intellectual level as him, but he doesn't treat us like he's holier than thou. He welcomes all our feedback, our ideas for the class. He says it's really helpful to him hearing us each review our week's experiences.

In a more complex form, collegiality arose from a deliberate faculty effort to draw their TAs into an open-ended conversation in which class issues could be aired and resolved. This appeared to work best where the conversations began before the start of the semester and continued throughout. TAs applauded faculty who did not dominate these conversations or use them as part of an effort to sell a predetermined package but who were patently open to TAs' contributions. Two modular chemistry TA described how their faculty set up an orientation meeting two weeks before the start of the semester:

> TA 1: They explained the idea behind the course in some detail and told us why they were using the modules and some of the research about why this is a good way to teach. We learned a bit more about that in later meetings. Sometimes we learned about a new teaching method before they used it—like the jigsaw groups.
>
> TA 2: Yeah, that was very interesting. We tried it out first to see how it worked. It made it easier to explain it to the students.
>
> TA 1: And get them doing it.
>
> TA 2: And they went over the whole shape of the semester—which modules we were going to do and a bit about each of them. Then we took a close look at "Fats"—that was the first one we did.
>
> TA 1: They had done it once before, so they explained how they wanted us to work with the students and some of the things that had come up—there were some things that they needed to fix or just change. And they asked us to help them work things out—you know, to tell them things that we noticed and how the students were doing. . . .
>
> TA 2: Like what they found hard to understand.
>
> TA 1: And our suggestions. They really wanted those. They asked us every week, "So, how did that go? What's working? What's a problem?"
>
> TA 2: And when we told them, you knew they were glad to have the information. It helped them figure out how to adjust things as we went along.

TA 1: I felt we were really useful to them in getting the course shaped up, and they let us know that.

TA 2: Yeah. You really felt you were working right along with them, and we were helping to make this course work really well.

TA 1: Yeah. It was a really good feeling.

Those TAs who had experienced creative, collegial discussions found them enjoyable, useful, and intellectually stimulating. Once established, these conversations tended to continue outside of formal meetings, where they had the effect of encouraging TAs to treat each other seriously as colleagues:

We had some fine discussions with the supervisors. Those were very good. But we also had some really good discussions just among ourselves. We talked about the logistics of how to present things in the modules and brainstormed some concrete examples we could use. I think we have become good friends very much because of these discussions outside of the TA meetings. It's often just spontaneous, but it's very worthwhile in terms of how we approach our job.

Where faculty cultivated an open relationship, TAs felt more confident about offering honest feedback on how aspects of the pedagogy were working and how students were responding and in acting as a conduit for students views:

Modular TA: We have meetings every Monday, and from our office hours and the labs, we can always tell her what the students were having trouble with in the previous week. She wants us to be honest and give her details. I really like that. It makes me feel that I am really contributing to the class.

Coach 1: The weekly meeting was a forum to voice students' opinions also. Like, they said, "He's not really preparing us for the kind of quiz he's setting, and we don't know where to focus our reading." So I brought that up, and some of the others said how their students were responding to the quizzes.

Coach 2: And he would go round and check the progress with each team and see what everyone thought.

Coach 3: Right. And when there were concerns, you would bring it up, and he was glad to have the information. He wanted to know everything because, if there was a problem, he wanted to try to fix it. He wanted to know if they were understanding the big picture. I think it was helping him decide what he would do in lectures.

TAs who experienced this level of collegiality enjoyed the sense that their input made a useful contribution to the success of the class and took pride in their work:

Like we said at the beginning, it helps us if faculty take us into their confidence and treat us somewhat as equals so we can give them good feedback and do a good job for them with the students.

Another element in developing a sense of co-ownership of the class was the experience of being given real responsibilities, along with guidelines about how to use them and backup in difficult or complex situations. For example, one professor gave his TAs leeway in establishing and implementing a disciplinary policy for their small groups in matters such as members' absence or failure to hand in work. Finding that the professor backed up decisions based on the TAs' policy and was ready to step in to enforce it if necessary increased both their confidence and their sense of investment in the class. In a second example described earlier,[3] a professor divided up management responsibilities for student lab projects between herself and her small group of TAs. She worked alongside them as a colleague among colleagues and helped them out as needed. Her TAs reported that they felt accountable for their students' learning: "It was our job to make it work." Their initial feelings of inadequacy were replaced with a sense of professional growth: "It really makes you rise up to the job." Being given real responsibilities and feeling like valued colleagues contributed to the strong sense of trust that permeated this faculty–TA relationship. TAs who experienced this appreciated the freedom and responsibility that they received from their professors, felt trusted to "work stuff out," and spoke of it as a privilege. A group of astronomy coaches described their experience thus:

> Coach 1: I think one of the neatest things about being a TA in this course is just how much freedom has been given to us.
>
> Coach 2: Yeah, especially as we're not grad students; we're undergraduates.
>
> Coach 1: I mean, it's a privilege. And it's hard sometimes to know how to do it, but we've been able to work stuff out pretty well.
>
> Coach 2: Yeah. He really makes you feel like a partner—like you he really trusts you to do a good job.

Mutual trust is a critical dimension of collegial rapport. In on-site interviews, where we encountered the most extensive examples of trust in working relationships, these included not only the faculty innovators and their TAs but also their students and noninnovator faculty colleagues. The faculty in four of the modular chemistry classes and in Interactive Astronomy had built up a culture of trust and open communication with their TAs and coaches that was immediately apparent to the interviewers. The TAs' and coaches' descriptions of working relationships in these five classes show how mutual trust arose from cumulative shared experiences of faculty who gave them guided responsibility, respect, and support and who responded attentively to their suggestions and critique.

A high level of trust in their faculty was a major source of the good disposition of these TAs toward class goals and their role in achieving them. Their engagement was marked by an open and constant flow of interaction with the faculty and among themselves and by expressions of ownership in the course. Where TAs and coaches saw their professors using their ideas, their sense of ownership was reinforced. They also saw this as an important factor in spreading their own sense of trust and engagement to their students:

> Coach 1: I mean, a lot of the improvements that have been made have come from us—like changing the lecture.

> Coach 2: And from us relaying ideas from the students. Like my team had an idea that would allow the teams better file access. I told the prof. He said it was a good idea. I told the web guy, and he implemented it. So, that's one of the cool things about this course.

> Coach 1: The students thought it was pretty cool, and they were like, sweet! And you know, the more stuff that keeps getting fixed, I think they got happier.

TAs reporting a trusting relationship with their faculty expressed confidence that their feedback could, if necessary, be critical and communicated without fear of reproof:

> TA 1: I tell [Dr. A] what I think all the time.

> TA 2: Yeah, and last semester, [Dr. B] always asked me what I thought.

> TA 1: Now that [Dr. A] is on sick leave, [Dr. C] talks back and forth to me. He's the same way—he's open to anything.

> TA 2: He asks us a lot of questions.

> TA 1: And the two lab profs, they are all listening for what you say. You can always tell them what you think, and they want to hear it.

> TA 2: And you don't have to worry if it sounds like bad news.

Building trust is clearly of great practical consequence for the success of innovations. Where teachers and TAs had built up respectful, honest, and open rapport, TAs worked creatively to make their innovation work well. Because they had no hesitation in offering suggestions or taking problems to their professor, faculty benefited from immediate feedback and good ideas from TAs who understood and supported their goals for the class. These experiences also contributed to the TAs' professional development. For example, they learned to take their own and each others' ideas seriously:

Last semester, there was an experiment about acid pollution that didn't work well, so we discussed it with each other and then with the prof. And he agreed with us that we should leave it out this time. Later on, we suggested getting the students to investigate the problem we had been discussing online, then do a survey and write a letter to a newspaper editor. And he was amenable to that. He even assigned 5 percent of the whole course grade to our project.

For this group of TAs and coaches, concern for the welfare of the class was not necessarily limited to this job and the current semester. It also included thinking about how an issue could be addressed in the next semester, when the speaker would no longer be there.

The practical significance of a high-trust atmosphere became dramatically clear during our interviews in one particular department. A modular chemistry teacher became ill and, in midsemester, had to take an immediate and extended leave. A colleague with just a little experience in using the chemistry modules stepped in, and, from that point, he and the TAs ran the class between them, with backup by telephone from their sick colleague:

> Her illness was so sudden, but we all rallied round so [Dr. B] could pick up the class. We showed him how some of the activities worked, and we did more in the prelabs to help him out. It's a big group, so he just tells some of the students to come to the back and work with me while he deals with another group up front. The other day I was checking the work, and no one had it right, so he asked me to do it on the board for them. It was weird standing up there with them asking me questions, but he trusted me to do it.

In interviews with the students, and both of the class faculty as well as with the TAs, it was remarkable to find how little disturbance this sudden change in teachers had created among the students. They understood the situation and were remarkably patient while the new teaching team figured out how to proceed. There was no discernable student resistance to learning in unfamiliar ways nor protest at this midcourse disruption. This was not achieved in isolation but reflected the culture of this institution. Other departmental faculty, the chair, and two administrators who were interviewed as part of the wider study were also highly aware of the high-trust atmosphere in which they worked. They regarded collegiality at every level as something that they deliberately and continuously cultivated.

Another example in which a high level of collegiality and trust between faculty and TAs benefited the innovation was achieved in far less promising circumstances. As part of their preparation to co-teach modules for the first time in a multisectioned introductory chemistry course, five chemistry faculty at a state university asked the modular chemistry organizers (i.e., ChemConnections) to offer a summer workshop on their campus. They invited faculty from their department and from neighboring schools to attend, plus the eight

TAs who were to help with the modular course in the fall semester. The workshop organizer later said that he should, perhaps, have set up some activities or sessions specifically for the TAs. His omission was, however, serendipitous as the TAs joined in all of the hands-on sessions alongside faculty. When interviewed toward the end of the first modular classes in late fall, they exhibited a high level of active engagement with the course, the faculty, the students, and each other. They spoke about the importance of being invited to the workshop and described the enthusiasm of the workshop presenters as being infectious. They also explained that seeing how the presenters worked together had enabled them to see why it was worth the extra effort to teach this way and how they could do this themselves:

> From the workshops, you could see that this way of teaching is the way many people will be teaching chemistry five years from now. We have to think in terms of team coordination with the TAs and professors as well as the students. You can't teach and learn this stuff well just all on your own.

Working together in the workshop set up a pattern of collegial effort among these faculty and TAs that was modeled for them by the workshop presenters. It also secured TA buy-in for the goals of the modular course, which they conveyed directly to their students:

> We have to explain to the students that we are not going to pressure you to take the initiative. You have to take it yourself. You have to ask questions like "What is my car producing? How much carbon dioxide is coming out?" It's hard to get across unless you use some kind of team teaching—which is why the workshop was so good. There were five people, and we watched how they all helped each other out. So now, when the prof teaches, we three are all out there among the class. We have to be there, hands-on, and ready to explain it to them, work with them. So, I think the class has to become like a workshop.

Attending the workshops as equals also contributed to the TAs' sense of co-responsibility with faculty for the success of the course. What is striking about the following conversation is, first, that the TAs clearly felt as comfortable and as entitled as their faculty to offer some constructive criticism to the workshop team. Furthermore, the rationale for their critique was rooted in the assumption that it was part of *their* job to help students to understand why they were using the new approach. In a less-collegial context, TAs might reasonably have left to faculty the job of explaining the modular idea to their students:

> TA 1: Some of the authors of the modules came here to talk with us, and all of us TAs went along. And the modular faculty actually performed pieces of three different modules. And it was good—very well run. They did have some glitches with the computers, but it didn't really matter.

TA 2: And they were really enthusiastic about the modular idea of teaching. They conveyed that very clearly.

TA 3: I agree. Although I think they need to do a better job of explaining what modules actually are. That needs to be better addressed, because that's something we have to explain to the students; otherwise, when you start teaching the modules, they are at a loss.

TA 1: Yeah, you have to explain to them how it's different, what you are trying to do and why we are exposing them to this new kind of thing—what's involved. As we were going to be doing that, we could have used more help from the workshop in how to explain the approach to students.

Following the workshop, the collaboration between the five teachers and their eight TAs continued as they prepared for the large modular class. This was not usual practice in this department but grew directly out of the energy and interest generated by the workshop. The TAs advocated keeping this going in subsequent summers so that TAs and faculty could learn together how best to prepare themselves:

We should go on preparing the summer before with the teachers and the TAs, so we get into the flow together. Both we and our teachers are highly compromised by the fact that we never learned that way ourselves, so we have to practice it together. We all have to be there to do that.

As in other contexts where the sense of collegial co-responsibility for the class was high, these TAs treated unresolved class problems as a shared concern. As illustrated in the following two examples, they discussed among themselves how best to resolve them:

TA 1: If you charge ten or twelve bucks for a module, and there's four of them plus a textbook, it's a problem for our students. They are not well-off.

TA 2: I think they could pay like seven bucks, and then if we could get one of the secretaries to, like, scan the modules in so they would all be on the net. I mean, if the publisher would allow that.

TA 3: Yeah, you might have to promise to erase it.

TA 1: But it could be like a library resource, you know, with a site license. That would work.

TA 1: And my students were really taken aback that they had to look at some stuff they had never seen before. And I explained it to them right at the start: "This is a new thing that we're trying. So, from now till next week, you need to look at your handout, look at the CD-ROM and these websites, and follow what your handbook says to read." And, at first, I don't think there were many that did. They were sort of surprised and shocked when they came into the class.

TA 2: In this school, particularly, there's a need to motivate students, to sell them on learning.

TA 3: Yeah, you really have to get them a reason to understand why they should be reading and going through their notes before they come into class. You really can't take it for granted; otherwise, it's not going to work. You really have to get that through to them.

As these two samples illustrate, this group of TAs had no hesitation in treating class problems as "theirs." As well as offering suggestions to the class coordinator, they also sought to work out solutions with each other and initiated improvements that fell within their province:

TA 1: I don't know what you guys think about this, but I'd like to put back a quiz at the beginning of each lab period again. I know it seems like it goes against the modular way of teaching—you know, making them do a test as they walk in—but we need to do something until we learn better how to motivate them to read ahead of time.

TA 2: No, I think it's okay to do that because the head of science who came to the workshop, she said they did that at her two-year college.

TA 1: Because I really have a problem when they come to every lab period, and they're not prepared. They just want to follow the procedure from the book. So, I would really like to have a quiz.

TA 3: You'd have to tell them up front that we are going to do this, so it's fair and square. But it would be okay if we did that.

TA 2: I agree. Let's try it.

The reference to the "head of science" from a neighboring college who attended this workshop again indicates that the TAs regarded all of the workshop attenders as colleagues. Their sense of shared collegial responsibility for the success of the class and their active thinking about how to improve it also extended to the developers of the modular materials.

TA 1: I'd like to see the people who are writing the modules give us more support. We need more figures we can make slides out of, and maybe some video cassettes. It's not very expensive. If you go onto a class to try to explain Lewis structures, it's not really modular if you show the same old book and diagrams that people never understood before—probably never will. So, a small video connecting things about chemistry to real life would make it easier for us.

TA 2: Along the same lines, that CD-ROM is nice. But they could do so much more with animation. If you put the graph from the book on the board, there's nothing dynamic about it that gets them to learn.

TA 3: And they need to be really dynamic, really graphic so that they remember. I can't remember a single graph that anyone ever put on a board. Man, I see some really great stuff out there. I've been reading stuff about how people learn—that they can learn if they can think about a thing. So, that's a good reason to ask for more animation that gets people to think in ways that the old textbook drawings can't.

As this extract illustrates, some TAs were thinking and reading about how learning happens and what is limiting about traditional ways of illustrating concepts. It is also clear that they felt just as comfortable making suggestions (via the interviewer) back to the module developers as they did in giving them to their own faculty.

Assumption of professional responsibility for their students' learning by the group of TAs who attended the precourse workshop was especially important because (as we learned from faculty and the two administrators interviewed) the prevailing student culture on this campus encouraged a habit of minimal effort based on instrumental attitudes focused on grades rather than learning. Indeed, the main reason why five members of the chemistry department had decided to try the modules and had invited the ChemConnections workshop team was that they had been unable to improve student motivation to learn using more traditional teaching methods. Against this background of long-standing difficulties with student learning behavior, it was remarkable that a group of TAs had so actively embraced the task of increasing student responsibility for their own learning. They also believed they were making progress. Asked if, at this late stage in the semester, they were still meeting student resistance to the new mode of learning, they replied:

TA 1: No, it's not a problem now. They have actually stopped grumbling [*laughing*].

TA 2: I think they have come to like it better than the old way. I think for the first time, they understand what they are learning and why.

TA 1: Yeah, that's the key. The modular work actually gets them to see the point of the learning.

TA 3: I'm really pleased with the way it's turned out. We've really made some progress here.

In this case, it was clearly the workshop experience that had set the tone of shared, active responsibility that had carried both the TAs and their faculty through the semester. Their workshop experience gave the TAs an understanding of why and how the modules might work for their challenging student population. It also prompted a process of planning and troubleshooting with their faculty that began before the semester and continued throughout it. Another positive factor in this situation was the work of the course coordinator who had a strong interest in active and interactive learning. He persuaded his four colleagues, department chair, and dean that teaching introductory chemistry with modules was a promising and viable way to address their apparently intractable problems with poorly motivated students. It was his belief in a collective approach to this shared problem that drew the TAs into the teaching team and helped to maintain them there.

As indicated earlier, the combined effect of being treated with collegial respect and being challenged to undertake, and be responsible for, aspects of student learning within a supportive, mentoring relationship had a powerful impact on the TAs' sense of identity and accountability as young professionals. Rising to the challenge of being trusted to work as partners in pursuit of the course goals was, in the accounts of those TAs who experienced it, a critical experience in their professional development and self-esteem. It is one of the strongest findings of this study that the exercise of collegiality and the building of mutual trust through open communication play a powerful role in determining how willing and active TAs will become and in enabling their optimal functioning in innovative classes.

THE CONSEQUENCES OF FAILURE TO MEET
TA EXPECTATIONS OF COLLEGIALITY

Thirteen TAs interviewed at four different schools described how failure to meet their expectations of collegial engagement had undermined their goodwill toward the faculty and the innovations—an outcome that greatly reduced their effectiveness. At the outset, these TAs had expected to contribute ideas and feedback to their professors and wanted to know that what they had offered was valued and useful. TAs in three different classes expressed their disappointment as follows:

TA 1: There was a kind of condescending attitude toward our personal interactions while we were looking for a more collegial dialogue.

TA 2: I agree. It was very disappointing.

Not only have we all taken this course recently, but half of us have taught other classes, so we should have some valid feedback that they could accept.

We've gotten together just twice, and I've given him feedback about the students. But after that, nothing really changed, even though he says he wants the feedback.

As is illustrated in the last observation, where faculty had neglected their TAs' need for regular two-way conversations in which they could debrief the previous week's activities and plan ahead, both their morale and the effectiveness of their contributions were reduced:

> There's no communication about what we're doing the next day sometimes. Every once in a while it will be there, but we could be better informed, and he could be better prepared.

A second example, originally presented in chapter 6, involves a discussion of grading work. A different TA in the same class discussed the incident in light of its demoralizing effect on TAs:

> We felt kept in the dark over grading, and there was a whole hullabaloo among us about homework grading. The students were assigned ten lengthy homework sets that the TAs were told to grade every week. And you could easily spend hours grading them. But the students hardly looked at them when you'd give them back because they were worth very little towards the final grade. But we weren't told that. We thought these homeworks were much more important for the grade than they actually were, and we spent four or five hours each on something that should have taken us half an hour.

As already indicated, formal weekly team meetings can meet many TA needs. However, as is illustrated in the following exchange, their effectiveness is shaped by their agenda and by the character of communication that is established:

> TA 1: We had our meetings every week, but there wasn't a lot of two-way communication.
>
> TA 2: Yeah, it wasn't very productive in that, sometimes, they wouldn't listen to our feedback, and there wasn't necessarily any action taken on what we told them. I'm not saying that they ignored us, but there just wasn't a two-way conversation.
>
> TA 3: And there was another thing—the instructors seemed very defensive about what they took as criticism.
>
> TA 1: I also thought they had a condescending attitude towards the students. But we were trying to explain why some of them found the ideas hard.
>
> TA 2: I guess what we are saying is we needed to be listened to a bit more like colleagues.
>
> TA 1: Yeah. That's what we needed more of.

Some TAs were disgruntled, even angry, where their contributions at meetings seemed unwelcome and their suggestions went unheeded. They experienced insufficient or unsatisfactory communication as a professional rebuff.

However, TAs who lacked regular meetings by which to gain information, discuss problems, or offer feedback were even more dis-spirited:

> I don't really know what the other teachers would think about trying to meet every week. I mean, I've talked to [Professor X] about it, and she's aware there's a problem. But she's not going to be here next year, and I don't know how much she's saying to the other faculty—people who actually have a say.

> I don't talk to [Professor A] very often. I probably never talk to [Professor B]. I've just talked to [Professor C] a few times—just random conversations. But I do think we are underused. Maybe some feedback to them weekly—even a few minutes together every other week would help. Though, actually, an hour's what we really need. And I feel it's like affected my attitude for the job that I don't have much contact with the professors—which isn't for lack of trying.

> They had weekly meetings—the faculty—but we didn't get invited to them. So, I'm just a hired help. I'm like a second helping hand if they need me. I'd like more of a role in lab—to help more with instructing the students. But I'm just there to answer questions, and their attitude seems to be that I should be able to pick up what I need to know from reading the material myself.

Some of these TAs presented themselves as being solitary, underused, and disappointed. One described herself as "just a worker bee plodding away at my job."

By default, the TAs in one course had organized their own discussion and planning group, but they wished the professors would attend:

> I'd like to see more TA influence in this class. I would like the professors to sit in on a TA session—which just happened once. And then the professor could see what the TAs are struggling with and what the students are struggling with too. That one time they came was helpful.

Insufficient initial briefing and discussion, and lack of regular open communication (or its poor quality), set in motion a process in which those TAs who saw their work as being undervalued experienced a slump in morale and developed feelings of resentment:

> I needed to be brought on board before we got started about the way this class was going to be taught. I think that not getting that from the beginning just made me start to resent this new way we were going to present it.

> TA 1: When we said we didn't think the students were getting this, I think they felt that was a slam about how they were trying to teach the course.

> TAs 2 and 3: Yeah. Uh huh. That's right.

> TA 1: They were giving us new topics to talk about in discussion in addition to all the things that came up in the lecture. We told them we thought it was too

much information and we couldn't get it across to everyone. You either need to discuss more of it in lecture or give us more discussion time. And they weren't really hearing any of that. It's the issue of taking you fully into their confidence and listening to what you have to say, and acting on it, rather than just hearing it and letting it go.

In a focus group, four TAs described how their initial interest in the class, and the possibilities of their role in it, had been dashed.

TA 1: I think, at the beginning, we were all very excited about the new class.

TAs 2, 3, and 4: Uh-huh. Yeah. That's right.

TA 1: Because we thought they would be listening to us and we would have a part in shaping the class. So I think a lot of us were disappointed that, although we did give feedback, it didn't actually affect the shape of the class. If they had not said, "This is how we are going to teach it" and not invited our feedback, everybody would have been fine with that. But we were set up to expect that they wanted to hear what we could contribute.

TA 2: That's right. We could have helped them a lot.

TA resentment was exacerbated where they had come to perceive faculty's overtures of collegial consultation as being insincere:

At our TA meetings, they would say, "What do you think about this?" And they would let us respond, but they wouldn't really take any of our answers in.

I felt it was a bit dishonest that we were told we could offer them suggestions. But then they weren't implemented on many occasions. So, I'd rather know that they were going to treat the TAs that way. And that's fine. I just wanted to have it straight from the beginning. That's maybe just me, but I feel I've been dealing with resentment all the way through.

The faculty referenced in this discussion as a disappointment to their TAs might be surprised to see themselves thus characterized. They may believe that they made a good effort to work in a consultative or collaborative way with their TAs—perhaps more than is customary. We have no way of knowing, and know of no work that can clarify, how TAs in more traditional classes evaluate their working relationships with faculty. However, becoming a TA for an innovative class clearly raises expectations of collaboration that can backfire on innovators when these expectations are unmet. In interviews and discussions with faculty at all of the schools in this sample, faculty were clearly aware when TAs seemed disengaged or were surly, confrontational, or noncompliant. However, they were often unsure of the causes of the problem. As outlined in the section on negative TA evaluations in chapter 4, some TA disaffection arose directly from a clash of perspectives about the value of the innovation and its perceived implications for student learning or for the TAs' role and status. However, the difficulties presented in this discussion are less fundamental and far more easily addressed.

A CASE OF MIXED REPORTS ON
COLLEGIALITY AND CHANGE OVER TIME

As indicated at the beginning of this chapter, the Berkeley faculty who organized the worksheet sessions and the related program of TA education and support drew on information from the formative evaluation to rebuild TA collaboration over a relatively short period. The outcome was a marked improvement in TA engagement and support for the innovation. In the second interview round, conducted eighteen months after the first, none of the twenty-five TAs interviewed reported problems in their working relationships with the innovation organizers or with the course coordinator, and ten specifically commented on their collegial character.[4] These improvements did not, however, extend to their relationships with the two professors who were responsible for the largely unchanged lectures and labs in this very large class. The relationship between TAs and these two professors was, as in the first interview round, reported to be distant, and offered few opportunities for interaction. TAs reported regular contact with the innovation organizers, especially with the lab coordinator—with whom they unanimously reported positive collegial relationships. The following two excerpts illustrate the differences that TAs perceived in the quality of interactions with the innovators and with the regular course faculty and how they interpreted these:

Interviewer: Your contact is with the coordinator.

TA 1: Yes.

Interviewer: And whom else?

TA 2: I see [Professor X and Professor Y].[5]

Interviewer: And are those collegial relationships? Do they treat you respectfully and thoughtfully?

TA 1: Oh yeah! The lab coordinator does. She definitely treats us well.

Interviewer: And is that important? I mean, I'm getting the impression that it is.

TA 2: Oh yeah! Yes, of course. You know, she cares what we tell her. She definitely cares. And it's nice to know that she does.

Interviewer: Even though you don't have much contact with the lecture professors, do you feel treated like a colleague?

TA 1: No.

TA 2: No . . . they're the grand magnificent lecturer, and we're in the labs. And I think our students realize that we have some power, but very little . . .

TA 1: [Professor A] is just basically absent, which I can understand.

TA 2: Right. But [Professor B's] kind of in between. I feel like he's there, but I don't really feel like he necessarily respects the opinions of the TAs all the time.[6]

TA 1: Right . . . he can be a little dismissive.

TA 2: I feel like he's very dismissive.

TA 1: He just showed up, just for the grading rubric thing. He was the one that showed us how to do it.

TA 2: There was a training on how to use the grading rubric. And he just showed up for ten minutes and showed us. . . . But he can make comments that are sort of a little snide.

Interviewer: Does that matter? How do you feel about that? Would it be good if people were more collegial with you?

TA 1: I think it's kind of an all-or-nothing thing. I feel no problem with [Professor A] being absent, and the lab coordinator is great because she's always there.

TA 2: Right.

TA 1: But when you have someone like [Professor B], who's sometimes involved and sometimes not, it's very annoying that we've worked with him all semester, I've worked with him in small groups several times. He still has no idea who I am. And that bothers me.

TA 2: Yeah.

Improvements in working relationships with the innovating faculty (if not with the regular faculty) that were evident in the second set of interviews were qualified, however, because TAs were evenly divided as to whether they had sufficient opportunity to give feedback on their worksheet sessions, how open the innovation organizers were to receiving it, and how comfortable they were in doing this. By contrast, those TAs who saw changes made to the worksheets that reflected their feedback described faculty as being open and receptive:

TA 1: If I have a question about the worksheet, I will bring it to the people that have written the worksheet, or just prior to lab meeting, anytime.

Interviewer: Yes. Are they responsive, do they listen?

TA 2: Yes they do . . . they definitely do. . . . There's been specific things that I either didn't like—the conceptual way of doing it or even the worksheet's point—and I have been given the response that "Oh, yes. There's a committee of us that make these questions, and I didn't agree with that one either"—or things along those lines. So, feedback is definitely well received.

However, the other half thought that formal opportunities to discuss issues arising from their work were limited or that faculty were insufficiently open to hearing their views. Some of these TAs perceived faculty as dismissing their difficulties in using particular worksheets as criticisms of the approach rather than as implementation problems:

> Interviewer: Do you feel comfortable about telling faculty about how well things are working or not working?
>
> TA: Not really, because it seems that this is the way they want you to teach it, and if you say, "Well, I don't think this is working," they say, "Okay. So here's tips on how you can integrate the worksheet better in your classroom." And that really doesn't address the issue that I'm experiencing in teaching this particular worksheet. . . . I don't feel like the faculty's advice helped any. . . . And if I say, "I don't think this is addressing enough topics," the answer that I get back is "Well sure it is, you're just not teaching it right" or something like that.

As this extract conveys, although the TA wants to discuss problems in teaching particular worksheets, the innovator also picks up that the TA is not entirely comfortable with the overall approach and that some of the TA's teaching problems derive from that uncertainty.

This mixed pattern of improvement in attaining collegial working relationships and meeting the Berkeley TAs' need to discuss their progress and problems may be explained on the one hand by the faculty's overt efforts to be open and available to their TAs and, on the other, by a change in the character of the weekly meetings. At the time of the first interviews, these included some lectures on education theory and research in support of the new pedagogy and some hands-on sessions on teaching by active and interactive methods. The innovators also gave time for feedback on student responses to the previous week's worksheets as well as preparation for the coming week. In the second interviews, the weekly meetings were described by TAs as being focused on instructing them on how to prepare for the coming week (for example, the lab experiments) and reviewing details of class administration. TAs apparently received less guidance in how to teach using the worksheets. While some TAs offered opinions or advice about the worksheets or other aspects of the course, it did not seem to them that a formal objective of the weekly meetings was to provide them with this opportunity. As the interviews were with two completely different groups of TAs, those interviewed in the second round were unaware of this change. However, as was described in chapter 5, across all three initiatives, TAs reacted to what they identified as missing by asking for both more teaching preparation and more formative feedback sessions:

It's not that they're not receptive, but there hasn't really been any forum for that at our meetings—for giving them detailed feedback on how the worksheets are working out in practice.

It is unclear why this change occurred: it seems to have been less the result of a conscious decision and more a case of paying insufficient attention to TA preparation and debriefing needs. These observations by TAs again illustrate how faculty openness to TA feedback and ideas, and a regular formal opportunity to express them, is a vital component in achieving the creative collaboration of TAs. Although the innovating faculty had clearly made progress in this direction, the process was incomplete.

The Berkeley example underscores what faculty need to do in order to convince teaching assistants to support innovation goals, to secure their active collegial effort to make the innovation work as intended, to sustain their morale, and to build their professional confidence and expertise. To create these desirable outcomes, the most important actions that faculty can take appear to be

- setting from the outset, and maintaining throughout the semester, a collegial, respectful tone in all encounters with TAs;
- holding orientation sessions before the start of the semester in which the philosophy, goals, and methods are discussed, the TAs' role is clarified, and the faculty and TAs begin to plan activities together;
- establishing regular formal meetings throughout the semester that offer TAs explanation and demonstration of unfamiliar pedagogy and content, as well as opportunities to raise problems and discuss ways to address them;
- giving TAs real responsibilities, guidance in how to exercise them, and supporting TAs in difficult situations;
- offering open communication that models collegial, professional behavior;
- treating TAs' concerns, critique, and suggestions as valued contributions and actively responding to them.

As the evidence presented in this discussion suggests, these elements operate as a coherent package: insufficient attention to key elements throws doubt on the faculty's sincerity and limits the development of trust. The positive but qualified shift in TA cooperation in the Berkeley initiative makes this point. By a making a conscious effort, the innovation organizers were able to significantly improve their working relationships with their TAs. However, this was limited by the continued disengagement of the noninnovating faculty and by their failure to meet the TAs' expressed need for a regular formal opportunity to give feedback and discuss progress in an open, collegial way.

The strong message to innovators and, indeed, to all faculty who would like to employ their teaching assistants to optimal effect, is clear. It is embedded in the testimony of those TAs and coaches who reported collegiality and trust in their working relationships with faculty. By extending to them a level of courtesy, communication, and respect that is appropriate among colleagues and by approaching the implementation of innovation as a collaborative endeavor, these faculty created and sustained in their TAs and coaches a sense of ownership in the course, accountability for student learning, good morale, professional development, and creative engagement in support of their course goals. These favorable outcomes seem well worth the faculty thought and effort that it took to create them.

NOTES

1. A promising program that seeks to foster collegial relationships between faculty and TAs comes out of the Center for the Integration of Research, Teaching, and Learning (CIRTL), a National Science Foundation Center for Learning and Teaching (see www.cirtl.net). A core component of the CIRTL program involves internships where graduate students partner with faculty mentors to address a teaching challenge for which neither know the answer.

2. See Weise (2001, 2003).

3. See the discussion on TAs' gains in teaching skills and insights into teaching in chapter 4, beginning on page 30.

4. The levels of TA engagement and support early and later in the development of the initiative are recorded in Weise's two evaluation reports (2001, 2003).

5. These are the faculty innovators.

6. Professor A, the lecture professor, was often away from the university on academic business; Professor B was in charge of the lab course.

12

Conclusions

SUMMARY OF KEY FINDINGS

I began this account with the observations of high-ability undergraduates in conventionally taught science and math classes in our 1997 study (Seymour and Hewitt 1997) at seven institutions. In that study, 84 percent of the undergraduates testified to the critical role played by their TAs in enabling their learning—even their survival—in their intended SME major. This finding strongly contradicts faculty mythology that places some portion of blame on TAs for the loss of students from introductory SME classes. The undergraduates also commented on some of the difficulties that constrained the effectiveness of otherwise helpful TAs—notably, inadequate preparation for their teaching work. In their accounts of unsatisfactory experiences with faculty teaching, the undergraduates also drew our attention to the cultural ambivalence of many SME faculty toward the teaching aspects of their professional role. Undergraduates saw this ambivalence as encouraging negative or indifferent attitudes toward teaching in some graduate TAs and making it harder for graduate students who enjoyed teaching to invest too much time and effort into their TA work. It also had a dampening effect on the career aspirations of undergraduates interested in teaching. These problems and their causes proved to be important themes in the three evaluation studies that are drawn on for this volume. However, the undergraduate learners' strong testimony as to the value of their TAs is amply corroborated in the TAs' own accounts.

The formative evaluation of these three initiatives offered a unique opportunity to discover what TAs would both gain and contribute when some of the limitations of conventionally taught classes were addressed and when

TAs were encouraged to be more active partners in course teaching, assessment, and curriculum development. The invitation to discuss, critique, and offer feedback that was inherent in the innovative contexts of their work encouraged the TAs to analyze and creatively respond to many dimensions of their experiences. In chapter 3, the TAs explain in detail how they benefited from their engagement in innovative classes. They describe gains in disciplinary knowledge and in their depth of understanding, insights into teaching, improved teaching skills, appreciation of the intrinsic pleasures of teaching, and the personal and professional value of participating in innovative forms of teaching and learning.

The TAs are also clear about what they need to meet the expectations of the innovating faculty and to do a good job. Many TAs emerged from their experiences with a strong awareness of the professional implications and possibilities of teaching and, therefore, of their need for a comprehensive program of professional development. Their suggestions about its content, based on experience-grounded identification of their needs, constitute a working blueprint for the design of such programs. In descriptions of their preparation and support needs, and in their critique of what was provided by the innovating faculty, they closely follow the models for professional development advocated in the small body of literature on classroom innovations that I discuss in chapter 9.

TAs also argued that, regardless of the size of institutions and the degree of openness, informality, and accessibility of faculty, they needed formal educational preparation. Casual and occasional meetings with their faculty were never enough. They sought a program of preparation that would begin before the start of each course and be continuous throughout. Its curriculum would include early and full information about the course approach, sessions on education methods and research, skill development and critique, and opportunities to exchange feedback with faculty and each other in weekly meetings. They looked for ongoing education, support, and mentoring in developing their teaching and communication skills, as well as more opportunities to engage in aspects of curriculum development.

The TAs' evaluative observations presented in chapter 4 offer insights and advice about the nature of the task involved in developing active, interactive, and discovery-focused courses, including some commonly encountered challenges. Across the three initiatives, positive evaluative observations were 44 percent of all evaluative comments, with some variation among the three initiatives; another 28 percent were qualified positives in which TAs who largely approved their initiative's approach offered critique and practical suggestions intended to improve its effectiveness. Overall, negative evaluations were of similar proportions (28 percent). The TAs' evaluative observations, which are of value both to innovating faculty and to those who favor more traditional teaching approaches, operate at several levels. At the simplest level, we learn what teaching and learning strategies, in the TAs' experience, work better or worse. Notably, we hear the TAs' consensus as to the powerful contributions to student learning made by small-group activities and other forms of discourse and interaction. At a more complex level, the TAs explained how and why attention to particular course design features is essential to success. Notable among these is the alignment (or "fit") of course elements with each other—especially class presentations, lab work, course materials, and assessments. This element was identified as critical to the intellectual coherence of the course and, thereby, to effective student learning. The TAs also explained how attention to the framing and directional "signposting" of concepts and their interconnections is needed if students are to master key ideas, understand conceptual linkages, build their own conceptual frameworks, and apply concepts in a variety of new situations.

In their positive evaluative comments, TAs offered evidence of improvements that they observed in students' understanding and learning retention and that they credited to both the overall class approach and the specific class attributes—notably, a wide range of small-group activities, opportunities for discussion, writing, and oral presentation. From their own group work with students, TAs reported student progress in asking fundamental questions, explaining and debating ideas, and talking about class material with each other. They saw each of these contributing to better learning retention. They observed that, looking back over the semester, students often expressed pleasure in how much they had learned—especially those who confessed to anxiety about taking a hard science class. Whether students were intending science or nonscience majors, TAs were clear that those who gained most were those who were willing to actively engage with the class approach. They also cited particular gains in learning from the innovative labs, including learning to think about experiments to address open-ended questions, collecting and analyzing their own data, making estimates, and explaining data trends. The most important observed gain, however, was students' increased understanding of the conceptual relationships between ideas presented in class and the hands-on activities of the labs.

TAs also credited some portion of improvements in student learning to the innovating faculty's success in changing student attitudes, the most important of which is a shift toward greater responsibility for their own learning. Many TAs explained that improving both attitudes toward learning and the students' methods of learning were critical factors in improving their actual learning.Why it is important and sometimes difficult to make these changes is explained in the TAs' descriptions (discussed in chapter 5) of the instrumental learning attitudes and behaviors, and of the formulaic habits of learning, that many students bring to introductory science classes, whether or not these are conventionally taught. Their observations can be used to explain why students may resist assumption of responsibility for their own learning and why, in both innovative and conventionally taught classes, faculty experience frustration in face of student disengagement. The negative responses of some students to the challenges posed to them by innovating faculty throw light on the causes of student resistance to learning in traditional as well as innovative classes. Indeed, the TAs' analysis identifies the need to address students' counterproductive approaches to learning as a central teaching challenge for themselves and for all faculty.

At the analytic level (rather than at the level of individual TA's awareness) I found what I think may be an important difference in the nature of the evidence and argument upon which TAs drew in reaching judgments about aspects of the courses or their overall approaches. It was notable that the opinions of TAs who expressed greater openness to the innovator's approach, or support for it, were based on their observations of student responses to new learning methods rather than on their beliefs about how introductory science classes "should" be taught. This was true even when TAs with pro-innovation views expressed reservations about some aspects of course implementation. By contrast, the opinions of TAs who gave negative evaluations (also discussed in chapter 4) were more often grounded in fundamental objections to the philosophy that informed the class design. Negative evaluations were often expressed in terms of strong beliefs about what was appropriate and attainable in introductory science classes, particular perceptions of the nature of science and science learning, and a sense of orthodoxy that some TAs derived from prior teaching and learning experiences. Far fewer negatively expressed criticisms and concerns were based on observations of student performance than were those expressed in positive and mixed evaluations. Objections of principle were also rooted in TA perceptions of their rights and status as apprentice teachers—perceptions that were acquired in the process of professional socialization. Where faculty innovators required particular common approaches to the TA's teaching role, some TAs saw this expectation as undercutting the perceived prerogative of all teachers, including TAs, to teach as they saw fit.

Because negative evaluations tended to be derived from beliefs that may be deeply felt, they are inherently more difficult for innovating faculty to address than are pragmatic concerns about implementation. A small number of vocal dissenters were seen to have a disproportionately large impact on the morale and effectiveness of both faculty and TAs and on the level of student buy-in to the course approach. As I discuss in chapter 4, the power of disgruntled TAs to create anxieties and dissention among their undergraduates was evident both in this study and in prior work.[1] The good news is, first, that strong dissent was found in only a small minority of the sample and, second, that this is not an impasse. A dramatic shift of opinion in favor of the goals of the innovation and its common approach to TA teaching methods was evident between the first and second interview rounds in the Berkeley

TA education initiative. It was accomplished by the course organizers' paying active attention to TAs' specific concerns—in short, by treating TAs as colleagues and consultants. This positive change, based on direct feedback from TAs' meetings and from the formative evaluator, underscores the value of both regular meetings and of formative evaluation per se.

I also draw attention to the value of "mixed reviews" because they are a rich source of practical advice to faculty on aspects of the course that TAs see as being in need of adjustment. These come largely from TAs who are well disposed to the course approach. They include observations on how well aspects of the course design or implementation are working, issues that have been neglected or need attention, factors that limit success, explanations of situations where a strategy works better or worse, and advice on what shifts of strategy could improve effectiveness. Half of the mixed evaluations addressed issues arising directly from the design, structure, or approach of the innovation. These included issues of course structure and alignment, the level at which newly conceived content is presented to students, and the volume of work demanded of them. Most of this group of mixed observations reference generic problems for curriculum developers. The other large category of mixed comments (21 percent) alerts innovators to greater demands in time and effort that innovative courses tend to make of their TAs—demands that are increased where TAs do "repair work" to deal with unresolved course problems. The nature of the TAs' positive and mixed evaluations, taken together, strongly point to a theme that I have stressed and illustrated throughout this volume—namely, the potential of TAs as collegial commentators on faculty's innovative teaching work and enablers of course success.

The data also revealed the TAs to be good diagnosticians of the different types of problems that students commonly encounter in innovative science courses. These are discussed in chapter 5. Notably, they distinguish between students' resistance to new learning approaches and their learning difficulties related to the unfamiliar demands of the innovative class. They define these as different phenomena with different origins that require different remedies. The TAs' portrayal of learned attitudes and behaviors that inhibit active student engagement with their own learning is built from many observations of particular facets of the syndrome. No single TA laid out all of its elements or used them to formulate an explanatory model. However, the composite picture that emerges is clear. TAs collectively explained many of their students' problems and protests as arising from inadequacies in their preparation as learners that become exposed by the demands made on them by innovative college science classes. The methods of the innovative teachers thwart a set of expectations and habits that amount to a formula for learning science that is heavily reliant on memorization, performance of mathematical or lab tasks without necessarily understanding their meaning, and a focus on grades rather than on learning processes or outcomes. The formulaic approach is learned in high school or earlier but may remain undisturbed or be reinforced in other college science classes. Because formulaic learning methods may produce good grades for students over a period of years, they are apt to acquire, in the perception of students, the character of an implicit contract with their teachers. Resistance to faculty teaching methods in traditional or nontraditional science classes may be viewed as an effort to draw faculty attention to an assumed contract that is not, in the students' view, being upheld.

Although TAs are not unsympathetic to their students' dilemma in being asked to break with familiar methods of study, TAs distinguish between these problems and what they treat as more legitimate difficulties when students actually try to adopt new learning methods. Observations of this type focus partly on disparities in students' academic preparation. Poor preparation included, for many students, limited experience with learning through independent reading, reading from multiple sources, and writing as a way to learn and to consolidate and express understanding. The TAs worked to help students acquire these capabilities and unlearn their minimalist attitudes toward reading and writing. TAs also expressed sympathetic understanding for the vulnerabilities of first-year students, especially their anxieties about learning in ways that appear to be taking risks with their grades and letting go of performance-focused learning methods. They also stress the responsibility of innovators to structure the intellectual journey they expect students to take in ways that allow the learners to see where new pieces of knowledge fit with what they already know. Sharing understandings about the sources of both students' resistance to new learning methods and their difficulties in adapting to them was seen as an essential element to be incorporated into the TA professional development program of any innovative course.

The data from all three initiatives highlight the potential of TAs to be useful, even critical, partners in enabling these innovations to work well. This potential, which I have sought to explore and illustrate, is all the more remarkable because 57 percent of all of the participating TAs and coaches were undergraduates. As I discuss in chapter 9, the competence and skills of graduate and undergraduate TAs appear to be highly comparable, especially in their facilitation of student learning. Most TAs saw this as their central responsibility and approached it largely by fostering all forms of interaction (student–student, student–TA, and student–professor). This was most evident in their group work where undergraduate TAs showed themselves to be as able as graduate TAs to organize and run groups and to establish and monitor their cohesion, morale, and effectiveness. Undergraduate TAs were clear that their job was not to "lecture" or "teach" but to enable, encourage, motivate, and explain, and to generate discussions in which undergraduates helped each other to understand ideas and their relationships. They also drew upon their own understanding of why undergraduates find some ideas hard to grasp. Undergraduate TAs discussed limitations on their capacity and effectiveness as learning facilitators. Although they tried to explain things that their students found obscure, they could not ultimately be accountable for student comprehension. Beyond the course materials, they looked to either the faculty or, where available, head TAs and graduate TAs to be the students' ultimate knowledge resource.

Many of graduate students in these innovative courses were clearly effective in, and committed to, their TAs roles. However, in chapter 9, I offer the caveat that their engagement with innovative courses has different significance for them than for undergraduate TAs and can place strains on them that undergraduates do not experience. Undergraduates gain status by doing this work for which they are often recruited and recommended. They are apt to feel special, and the faculty for whom they work reinforce this by praise and encouragement. They find the work intrinsically interesting and comparatively well paying and see themselves as deepening their disciplinary knowledge and learning valuable professional skills. They may also get a first experience of what it is like to work collegially with faculty, graduate students, and together as peers.

By contrast, new graduate students commonly do not choose to work for particular courses but are assigned to them. They are often first-year students without teaching experience who are coping with the transition into graduate school. They suffer from the burden of being expected to know more than perhaps they do and often struggle with a sense of inadequacy about being "experts" for their students. This situation is less troubling to undergraduate TAs who can be open about what they do not yet understand without loss of face. More senior graduate students may take on TA work by default—for example, because research assistantships are in short supply—and (unlike the undergraduate TAs) find the pay less attractive than that offered to research assistants.

The critical distinction between undergraduate and graduate TAs who work for innovative science classes is that undergraduates have a great deal to gain, and little to risk, by their engagement. It is therefore understandable that many undergraduate TAs and coaches responded so positively. By contrast, graduate TAs see their appointments in science courses as being less prestigious and as carrying less potential for professional advancement than research assistantships. Working as a TA in an innovative science course adds an additional layer of risk and loss of status, depending on how both the student and their research advisor view its opportunities for professional growth versus its demands on the student's time and energy.

Many graduate students enjoyed working as TAs in these courses because they were interested in teaching as a professional option; wanted to build their teaching skills; were interested in learning more about educational research, theories, and methods; or were attracted by the innovative approach of particular faculty. However, these positively motivated TAs, along with those who were more instrumental or reluctant in their attachment to the work, described conflicts of time and commitment imposed by the dominance of research over teaching in most departments. This said, it is quite remarkable that so many of the graduate students in this study rose to the challenges of their new roles and defined their experiences in terms of personal and professional gains. Experienced graduate students often found engagement in classroom innovations more rewarding than traditional forms of TA work. They reported gains in knowledge and understanding (both in their disciplines and in education theory, research, and practice) and gains in skills in a variety of teaching methods. They found their teaching and mentoring work inherently interesting and rewarding and were encouraged to see its career possibilities. A few were also offered (and others sought) opportunities for course development or interdisciplinary teaching.

Working for these innovative courses was seen by the TAs as requiring more time and effort than teaching in a more traditionally taught course. Across the three initiatives, this extra work included keeping abreast of (and sometimes helping to develop) new class and lab materials, learning to work with new forms of student activities and types of assessment, dealing with student responses to these, and helping to resolve implementation problems. TAs who were enjoying the work and seeing its value to students did not necessarily complain about the extra work. However, they suggested ways to use their time more efficiently.

While some formal responsibilities are the same as those in conventional courses, as I discuss in chapters 6 and 7, it was a strong finding that TAs expanded and enhanced these tasks in order to serve new course goals. This was partly instigated by the innovators, but it was also an inventive voluntary response by the TAs themselves. TAs' accounts of their work referenced five traditional role responsibilities. Three of these involve interactive work with students—namely, work in small groups, laboratory support roles, and academic support for students (largely in office hours). The fourth involves some degree of responsibility for grading and test setting; and the fifth, some exercise of delegated responsibility. The ways in which TAs were expected to perform these functions were somewhat prescribed by the innovating faculty or the course design. However, the data strongly indicate that TAs were engaged in an organic process of interpreting and expanding on these formal responsibilities in response to course and student needs.

The process of TA improvisation did not expand the overall TA role in random directions. Indeed, the process of role redefinition was remarkably consistent. Three forms of behavior and attitudes emerged as a response to the challenges of meeting course goals, faculty expectations, and class logistics.

These shaped the ways in which the TAs and coaches defined the boundaries of their work and approached their responsibilities. Expressed in behavioral terms, TA assistants became

- Creative troubleshooters, who spotted and addressed day-to-day problems, sought to resolve those that lay within their skills and knowledge, and alerted faculty to difficulties that they alone could address
- Consultants, who offered faculty feedback, analysis, and advice that was grounded in their experiences
- Collegial collaborators, who shouldered responsibility for student learning alongside the faculty and with each other, took ownership of their work, and thought creatively about facilitating learning in their interactions with students

Across the initiatives, these three forms of responses to working in innovative courses emerged partly as a consequence of TAs seeking to implement course goals in situations where the teachers' methods were still in flux and unforeseen issues arose day-to-day. They were also a response to fundamental changes in teaching and learning relationships that are apt to be a predictable and ongoing part of even well-developed innovations. All of these innovations essentially redefine what it means to be teachers, learners, and teaching assistants.

As I discuss in chapter 7, individual TAs and coaches varied in the degree to which they responded to the challenges of working in innovative classes by infusing their more traditional responsibilities with troubleshooting, consulting, and collegial behaviors and attitudes. Similarly, not all TAs and coaches extended their role by undertaking new responsibilities that reflected these three forms of engagement, nor did they do so to the same degree. Developing collegial, collaborative working relationships with the professor and with each other, and a sense of responsibility for student learning and the success of the innovative class, was the highest level on a spectrum of work-role extensions. However, taking the three initiatives together, approximately 84 percent of the TAs (92 out of the 110 interviewees) offered observations on what they were doing and how they were thinking about their work in which it was evident that (to varying degrees) they were voluntarily extending the limits of their formal responsibilities.

The same three dimensions of troubleshooting, consultation, and collaborative engagement are evident in the ways in which teaching assistants voluntarily extended the overall scope of their formal role responsibilities in ways that help to make these innovations work or work better. As I argue in chapter 7, these are not changes in defined, formal areas of responsibility. They are, rather, a set of attitudes and behaviors that lift the total role of the TA to a higher level of professionalism, engagement, and responsibility. This shift is prompted, in part, because innovative faculty both ask more and receive more from their TAs than they might in more conventional faculty–TA relationships in more conventional courses. Both direct and implied invitations by faculty to contribute provoked an active response from the TAs. The level of collegial engagement that I have documented points to the TAs' potential to play a greater formative and collaborative role in course development and implementation than has been traditionally part of their remit. What I have sought to present is a picture of faculty and TAs' reinventing together what the TA role can become.

As I have illustrated in chapter 4, in my discussion of the sources and consequences of TA resistance to working in these innovative contexts, and also in chapters 6 and 7, where I describe the extent to which TAs can go to in become engaged colleagues, there is clearly much to be gained by drawing TAs into creative collaboration with faculty and each other. There is also much to be lost in failing to do so. Critical elements in securing TA trust and engagement are collegiality in faculty and peer relationships, regular opportunities to give feedback and discuss ways to address problems, and an appropriate and adequate program of professional development.

As I describe in chapter 10, a high level of trust in their faculty characterized the attitudes of TAs who were highly committed to enabling achievement of course goals. Their engagement was marked by an open and constant flow of interaction with the faculty and among themselves and by expressions of ownership in the course and the success of its students. TAs who came to see themselves as colleagues described faculty as listening to them respectfully and treating them as people with something valuable to contribute. At its most effective, collegiality arose from deliberate faculty efforts to establish and maintain an open-ended conversation with their TAs in which they felt confident in offering honest feedback. TAs who had experienced collegial discussions found them enjoyable, useful, and intellectually stimulating. The experience bonded TAs to the endeavor in emotionally supportive and intellectually creative ways.

Building trust with and among TAs is clearly of great practical, as well as intrinsic, value to innovative course teachers. Where faculty and TAs had built up respectful, honest, and open rapport, TAs worked creatively to make the course work well. Because they had no hesitation in offering suggestions or raising problems, faculty benefited from ideas and immediate feedback from TAs who understood and sought to enable the course goals. I have offered examples of how collegiality and a high level of mutual trust both were and were not achieved in particular contexts and with what consequences for course success. The strong message to all faculty who would like to employ their TAs to best effect is that, by extending to them the level of courtesy, open-ended communication, and respect that is the ideal for all colleagues, faculty may instill in TAs a sense of collaboration and ownership that is as beneficial to the professional development of the TAs as it is to good outcomes for the course. This is likely to be as true for conventionally taught courses as it is for those using innovative pedagogies.

THE POSSIBILITIES AND REWARDS OF CHANGE

This study has thrown into sharp focus the potential of this large population of young scholars in graduate and undergraduate programs to contribute far more to the education of undergraduates than has been expected hitherto. Both in the research literature and in these data, there are sharp contrasts between the preparation and employment of TAs in conventional classroom work and that of those working in innovative classes. The indications of TA potential afforded by studies of classroom innovators such as this one highlight a gross loss of human capacity on a nationwide scale when TAs are a highly used workforce but remain underemployed, undereducated, and undervalued. Although these data were drawn from innovative science courses, this message applies equally to more traditional classes and to all disciplines. The potential for teaching assistants—both graduate and undergraduate—to become professional partners in enabling and supporting student learning has barely been explored.

We therefore owe a debt of thanks to those science faculty who, in their innovative classroom and lab work, have begun to explore this potential. However, it is not yet clear that the science education reform community at large has investigated the possibilities of making TAs—graduate or undergraduate—active partners in their creative work. In their rethinking and development of new forms of teaching and learning, the growing circles of faculty innovators around the country have a special opportunity to make teaching assistants a critical force in their work, and a duty to share the results of their experiments through their workshops, writing, evaluation work, and communication networks. Enlisting the active engagement of TAs in facilitating active and interactive learning will enhance the growing nationwide effort to improve the quality and effectiveness of undergraduate education in the STEM disciplines. This collective effort seeks thereby to improve recruitment and retention in these majors, increase the participation of students of color and women of all races and ethnicities, and make a working understanding of mathematics and science accessible to all students. One may also hope that the discoveries of the classroom innovators will also encourage more traditionally minded members of faculty, their departments, and their institutions to rethink the professional education and educational deployment of TAs.

There is a second, wider challenge that the more effective engagement of TAs in STEM undergraduate education can also address. The nation is struggling to recover from its failure in recent decades to "challenge more of our finest young people to consider teaching as a career."[2] It is currently scrambling to meet the shortfall in qualified, well-prepared public secondary school science and mathematics teachers by a variety of accelerated, emergency ("alternative certification") programs. Despite the emergency efforts underway in many states—and despite major programs such as the Statewide Systemic Initiatives, sponsored by the National Science Foundation—we still cannot fill these vacancies with discipline-qualified teachers.[3]

An important cultural cause of these difficulties has been a historical decline in the perceived value of teaching as a career at every educational level. In *Talking about Leaving* (Seymour and Hewitt 1997), we report that approximately 20 percent of current and former SME majors in our sample expressed an interest in science or mathematics teaching at various levels. By senior year, active career interests in teaching had dwindled to 6.6 percent. Students described their teaching interests in a manner that we labeled "deviant ambitions" because they saw their aspirations as being disapproved and overtly discouraged, both by faculty and by other significant people in their lives. Most did not declare or discuss their teaching aspirations with faculty because of an implied message that, should they do so, they would be taken less seriously as aspiring scientists. Likewise, in some institutions in the present sample, this finding was echoed in the accounts of both undergraduate and graduate TAs who expressed an interest in teaching.

In recent periods of economic downturn, more young people have discovered teaching as a career option. However, this trend has not spread significantly into the sciences. The STEM academic community bears considerable responsibility for this state of affairs. As funded research has evolved into its present dominant place in universities, there has been a commensurate decline in departmental (and, thus, faculty) emphasis both on teaching within the academy and in promoting teaching as a career for its most promising graduates. As this and our earlier work attest, undergraduate and graduate students feel discouraged from seriously considering teaching as a career and from preparing for it through TA experience. The tenure system also discourages and underrewards faculty (and, thus, graduate students) who seek to pursue their teaching roles as serious professional responsibilities. As one consequence, we are now losing from faculty ranks those late-stage graduate students and pretenured faculty (often women) who see teaching as an important part of their career aspirations.[4] It is this situation that prompted Ernest Boyer (1990) to propose ways to rethink the academic rewards and tenure criteria so as to accommodate educational scholarship.

In light of the findings offered throughout this book, I propose that rethinking the roles and professional development of teaching assistants offers a nationally available opportunity to break the cycles that have simultaneously diluted the quality of undergraduate STEM education and constrained the building of a discipline-educated teaching force in science and mathematics that is adequate to national needs. It lies well within our capacity to once more make our universities and colleges a premier source of well-educated, skilled, and motivated teachers. It will require of us both an openness to learn from the work of innovating faculty and their TAs and the exercise of our collective will.

NOTES

1. See Gutwill-Wise (2001).

2. President William Clinton, State of the Union Address, 1997, available at www.thisnation.com/library/sotu/1997bc.html (accessed April 26, 2005).

3. Accounts of this growing shortage begin in the early 1990s (Choy et al. 1993; Weiss, Matti, and Smith, 1994; Shugart and Hounshell 1995; Kahle 1996; Henke et al. 1996; Shields, Corcoran, and Zucker 1994).

4. This process and its effects have, most recently, been documented in Yu Xie and K. A. Shauman's *Women in Science: Career Processes and Outcomes* (2003). It is also the topic of an ongoing study in my own research group, Ethnography and Evaluation Research at the University of Colorado at Boulder, as part of our research and evaluation support for LEAP, a National Science Foundation–funded ADVANCE grant.

References

Abbott, R., D. Wulff, and C. Szego. 1989. Review of research on TA training. *New Directions for Teaching and Learning (Teaching Assistant Training in the 1990s)* 39:111–23.

Alexander, B., D. Penberthy, S. Millar, and E. Standifer. 1996. *Formative feedback report: Important issues in the TA experience in courses or programs involving active learning reform initiatives. A joint report of the Freshmen Learning Community Program (FLCP) and the Chem 110 adaptation evaluations.* Madison: University of Wisconsin, LEAD Center.

Allen, G., J. Weldman, and L. Folk. 2001. Looking beyond the valley: A five-year case study of a course. *Innovative Higher Education* 26 (2): 103–19.

Anderson, M., and J. Swazey. 1998. Reflections on the graduate student experience: An overview. *New Directions for Higher Education* 26:3–13.

Bashford, B. 1996. Pedagogy and intellectual work. Annual meeting of the Conference on College Composition and Communication, March 27–30, Milwaukee, Wisc. ERIC Database document ED403578, www.eric.ed.gov.

Bomotti, S. 1994. Teaching assistant attitudes toward college teaching. *Review of Higher Education* 17:371–93.

Boyer, E. 1990. *Scholarship reconsidered: Priorities of the professorate.* Princeton, N.J.: Princeton University Press.

Carroll, J. 1980. Effect of training programs for university teaching assistants: A review of empirical research. *Journal of Higher Education* 51:167–83.

Chism, Nancy Van Note. 1998a. Evaluating TA programs. In *The professional development of graduate teaching assistants,* ed. M. Marincovich, J. Prostko, and F. Stout, 249–62. Bolton, Mass.: Anker.

———. 1998b. Preparing graduate students to teach: Past, present, and future. In *The professional development of graduate teaching assistants,* ed. M. Marincovich, J. Prostko, and F. Stout, 1–17. Bolton, Mass.: Anker.

Choy, S., R. Henke, M. Alt, E. Medrich, and S. Bobbitt. 1993. *Schools and staffing in the United States: A statistical profile, 1990–1991.* NCES 93-146. Washington, D.C.: National Center for Education Statistics.

Courter, S., L. Lyons, S. Millar, and A. Bailey. 1996. Student outcomes and experiences in a freshman engineering design course. In *American Society for Engineering Education annual conference proceedings.* Washington, D.C.: American Society for Engineering Education.

Courter, S., and S. Millar. 1995. *Final evaluation report: Pilot of first-year design course 1994–95 "Introduction to Engineering."* Madison: University of Wisconsin, LEAD Center.

Cox, M. 2001. Student-faculty partnerships to develop teaching and enhance learning. In *Student-assisted teaching: A guide to faculty-student teamwork,* ed. J. Miller, J. Groccia, and M. Miller, 168–71. Bolton, Mass.: Anker.

Darling, C., and E. Earhart. 1990. A model for preparing graduate students as educators. *Family Relations* 39:341–48.

Druger, M. 1997. Preparing the next generation of college science teachers. *Journal of College Science Teaching* 26:424–27.

Duba-Biedermann, L. 1993. Graduate assistant development: Problems of role ambiguity and faculty supervision. In *The TA experience: Preparing for multiple roles,* ed. K. Lewis, 7–13. Stillwater, Okla.: New Forums Press.

Eby, K., and P. Gilbert. 2000. Implementing new pedagogical models: Using undergraduate teaching assistants in a violence and gender learning community. *Innovative Higher Education* 25:127–42.

Etkina, E. 2000. Helping graduate assistants teach physics: Problems and solutions. *Journal of Graduate Teaching Assistant Development* 7:123–37.

Feldman, A., M. Alibrandi, E. Capifali, D. Floyd, J. Gabriel, M. Mera, B. Henriques, and J. Lucey. 1996. Looking at ourselves look at ourselves: An action research self-study of doctoral students' roles in teacher education programs. Annual meeting of the American Educational Research Association, April 8–12, New York.

Ford, W. 1993. Identification and validation of training needs for teaching assistants. In *The TA experience: Preparing for multiple roles,* ed. K. Lewis, 25–36. Stillwater, Okla.: New Forums Press.

French, D., and C. Russell. 2002. Do graduate teaching assistants benefit from teaching inquiry-based laboratories? *Bioscience* 52:1036–41.

Freyberg, M., and E. Ponarin. 1993. Resocializing teachers: Effects of graduate programs on teaching assistants. *Teaching Sociology* 21:140–47.

Gutwill-Wise, J. 2001. The impact of active and context-based learning in introductory chemistry courses: An early evaluation of the modular approach. *Journal of Chemical Education* 78:684–90.

Hagedorn, L., H. Moon, D. Buchanan, E. Shockman, and M. Jackson. 2000. *Cooperative learning and unity: The perspectives of faculty, students, and TAs.* ERIC Database document ED443853, www.eric.ed.gov.

Hammrich, P. 1994. Learning to teach: Teaching assistants conception changes about science teaching. National Conference on College Teaching and Learning, April 1994, Jacksonville, Fla.

———. 1996. *Biology graduate teaching assistant's conceptions about the nature of teaching.* ERIC Database document ED401155, www.eric.ed.gov.

Hampton, S., and R. Reiser. 2002. From theory to practice: Using an instructional theory to provide feedback and consultation to improve college teaching, learning and motivation. Annual meeting of the American Educational Research Association, April 1–5, New Orleans, La.

Hatch, D., and C. Farris. 1989. Helping TAs use active learning strategies. *New Directions for Teaching and Learning (Teaching Assistant Training in the 1990s)* 39:89–96.

Hedengren, E. 2001. TA training across the curriculum: Covert catalyst for change. Fifth National Writing across the Curriculum Conference, May 31–June 2, 2001. Bloomington, Ind.

Hendrix, K. 1995. Preparing graduate teaching assistants (GTAs) to effectively teach the basic course. Annual meeting of the Southern States Communication Association, April 5–9, New Orleans, La.

Henke, R., S. Choy, S. Geis, and S. Broughman. 1996. *Schools and staffing in the United States, a statistical profile, 1993–1994.* NCES 96-124. Washington, DC: National Center for Education Statistics.

Hesse, D. 1993. Teachers as students, reflecting resistance. *College Composition and Communication* 44:224–31.

Hollar, K., V. Carlson, and P. Spencer. 2000. 1 + 1 = 3: Unanticipated benefits of a co-facilitation model for training teaching assistants. *Journal of Graduate Teaching Assistant Development* 7:173–81.

Jacobs, W. 2002. Using lower-division development education students as teaching assistants. *Research and Teaching in Developmental Education* 19:41–48.

Kahle, J. 1996. Why teach? In *Teacher preparation in science, mathematics, engineering, and technology: Review and analysis of the NSF workshop, November 6–8, 1994,* ed. S. Millar and B. Alexander. Washington, D.C.: National Institute for Science Education.

Karasz, H., P. Reynolds, and M. Wall. 1997. *New models for teaching assistants: The research mentor project.* ERIC Database document ED416511, www.eric.ed.gov.

Kirk, D., and W. Todd-Mancillas. 1991. Turning points in graduate student socialization: Implications for recruiting future faculty. *Review of Higher Education* 14:407–22.

Larson, H., R. Mencke, S. Tollefson, E. Harrison, and E. Berman. 2001. The Teaching Teams Program: A "just-in-time" model for peer assistance. In *Student-assisted teaching: A guide to faculty-student teamwork,* ed. J. Miller, J. Groccia and S. Miller, 27–33. Bolton, Mass.: Anker.

Lawrenz, F., P. Heller, R. Keith, and K. Heller. 1992. Training the teaching assistant. *Journal of College Science Teaching* 22:106–9.

Lawson, A. 2000. Managing the inquiry classroom: Problems and solutions. *American Biology Teacher* 62:641–48.

Lawson, A., S. Rissing, and S. Faeth. 1990. An inquiry approach to nonmajors biology: A big picture, active approach for long-term learning. *Journal of College Science Teaching* 19 (6): 340–46.

Levinson-Rose, J., and R. Menges. 1981. Improving college teaching: A critical review of research. *Review of Educational Research* 51:403–34.

Linse, A., J. Turns, J. Yellin, and T. Van DeGrift. 2004. Preparing future engineering faculty: Initial outcomes of an innovative teaching portfolio program. In *American*

Society for Engineering Education annual conference and exposition proceedings. Washington, D.C.: American Society for Engineering Education.

Luft, J., J. Kurdziel, G. Roehrig, and J. Turner. 2004. Growing a garden without water: Graduate teaching assistants in introductory science laboratories at a doctoral/research university. *Journal of Research in Science Teaching* 41 (3): 211–33.

Lumsden, A. 1993. Training graduate students to teach. *American Biology Teacher* 55:233–36.

Luo, J., L. Bellows, and M. Grady. 2000. Classroom management issues for teaching assistants. *Research in Higher Education* 41:353–83.

Luo, J., M. Grady, and L. Bellows. 2001. Instructional issues for teaching assistants. *Innovative Higher Education* 25:209–30.

Main, E. 1994. *Teaching Assistant Training and Teaching Opportunity (TATTO) Program.* Washington, D.C.: U.S. Department of Education, Office of Educational Research and Improvement. ERIC Database document ED416758, www.eric.ed.gov.

Manogue, C., and K. Krane. 2003. Paradigms in physics: Restructuring the upper level. *Physics Today* 56 (9): 53–58.

Mazur, E. 1997. *Peer instruction.* Upper Saddle River, N.J.: Prentice-Hall.

McDowell, E. 1993. An exploratory study of GTAs' attitudes toward aspects of teaching and teaching style. Annual meeting of the Speech Communication Association, November 18–21, Miami Beach, Fla.

McGinnis, J. 1991. Behavior and attitude of science education graduate assistants: A case study. Annual meeting of the National Association for Research in Science Teaching, April 7–10, Lake Geneva, Wisc.

McGivney-Burelle, J., T. DeFranco, C. Vinsonhaler, and K. Santucci. 2001. Building bridges: Improving the teaching practices of TAs in the mathematics department. *Journal of Graduate Teaching Assistant Development* 8:55–63.

McManus, D. 2002. Developing a teaching assistant preparation program in the School of Oceanography, University of Washington. *Journal of Geoscience Education* 50:158–68.

Menges, R., and W. Rando. 1989. What are your assumptions? Improving instruction by examining theories. *College Teaching* 37:54–60.

Millar, S., B. Alexander, H. Lewis, and J. Levin. 1995. *Final evaluation report on the pilot Wisconsin Emerging Scholars Program, 1993–1994.* Madison: University of Wisconsin, LEAD Center.

Millar, S., M. Clifford, and M. Connolly. 2004. *Needs assessment study: Professional development in teaching at the University of Wisconsin-Madison.* Madison, Wisc.: Center for the Integration of Research, Teaching, and Learning.

Millar, S., S. Priest, D. Penberthy, S. Kosciuk, and L. Squire. 1997. *Formative feedback report: Chemistry 103, new traditions: Revitalizing the curriculum.* Madison: University of Wisconsin, LEAD Center.

Murray, M. 2001. Students: Managing to learn. Teachers: learning to manage. In *Student-assisted teaching: A guide to faculty-student teamwork*, ed. J. Miller, J. Groccia, and M. Miller, 50–55. Bolton, Mass.: Anker.

National Center for Education Statistics. 2000. *National postsecondary student aid study, 1999–2000.* Washington, D.C.: National Center for Education Statistics.

National Doctoral Program Survey. 2001. *The 2000 national doctoral program survey*, http://survey.nagps.org (accessed April 15, 2005).

Nurrenbern, S., J. Mickiewicz, and J. Francisco. 1999. The impact of continuous instructional development on graduate and undergraduate students. *Journal of Chemical Education* 76:114–19.

Nyquist, J., R. Abbott, and D. Wulff. 1989. The challenge of TA training in the 1990s. *New Directions for Teaching and Learning (Teaching Assistant Training in the 1990s)* 39:7–14.

Nyquist, J., and J. Sprague. 1998. Thinking developmentally about TAs. In *The professional development of graduate teaching assistants*, ed. M. Marincovich, J. Prostko and F. Stout, 61–88. Bolton, Mass.: Anker.

Nyquist, J., and D. Wulff. 1996. *Working effectively with graduate assistants.* Thousand Oaks, Calif.: Sage.

Penberthy, D., and S. Millar. 2002. The "hand-off" as a flawed approach to disseminating innovation: Lessons from chemistry. *Innovative Higher Education* 26 (4): 251–70.

Peterson, E. 1990. Helping TAs teach holistically. *Anthropology and Education Quarterly* 21:179–85.

Pickering, M. 1978. Provocative opinion: How to win friends and motivate teaching assistants. *Journal of Chemical Education* 55:511–12.

Poole, J., and D. Sebolt. 1993. Effectiveness of a teaching support program from the TA perspective. In *The TA experience: Preparing for multiple roles*, ed. K. Lewis, 319–25. Stillwater, Okla.: New Forums Press.

Prieto, L., and E. Altmaier. 1994. The relationship of prior training and previous teaching experience to self-efficacy among graduate teaching assistants. *Research in Higher Education* 35:481–97.

Robinson, J. 2000. New teaching assistants facilitate active learning in chemistry laboratories: Promoting teaching assistant learning through formative assessment and peer review. *Journal of Graduate Teaching Assistant Development* 7:147–62.

Rushin, J., J. De Saix, A. Lumsden, D. Streubel, G. Summers, and C. Benson. 1997. Graduate teaching assistant training: A basis for improvement of college biology teaching and faculty development. *American Biology Teacher* 59:86–90.

Sarquis, J., L. Dixon, D. Gosser, J. Kampmeier, V. Roth, V. Strozak, and P. Varma-Nelson. 2001. The workshop project: Peer-led team learning in chemistry. In *Student-assisted teaching: A guide to faculty-student teamwork*, ed. J. Miller, J. Groccia, and M. Miller, 150–55. Bolton, Mass.: Anker.

Savage, M., and T. Sharpe. 1998. Demonstrating the need for formal graduate student training in effective teaching practices. *Physical Education* 55:130–37.

Seymour, E. 2001. Tracking the process of change in U.S. undergraduate education in science, mathematics, engineering, and technology. *Science Education* 86:79–105.

Seymour, E., and N. Hewitt. 1997. *Talking about leaving: Why undergraduates leave the sciences.* Boulder, Colo.: Westview Press.

Seymour, E., A. Hunter, S. Laursen, and T. DeAntoni. 2004. Establishing the benefits of research experiences for undergraduates in the sciences: First findings from a three-year study. *Science Education* 88 (4): 493–534.

Seymour, E., L. Pedersen-Gallegos, S. Laursen, and D. Weise. n.d. Responses of students to chemistry classroom innovation: The case of modular chemistry. Ethnography and Evaluation Research, Center to Advance Research and Teaching in the Social Sciences, University of Colorado, Boulder.

Shannon, D., D. Twale, and M. Moore. 1998. TA teaching effectiveness: The impact of training and teaching experience. *Journal of Higher Education* 69:440–66.

Shields, P., T. Corcoran, and A. Zucker. 1994. *Evaluation of the National Science Foundation's Statewide Systemic Initiatives (SSI) Program: First year report,* vol. 1, *Technical report.* Menlo Park, Calif.: Stanford Research Institute. ERIC Database document ED376047, www.eric.ed.gov.

Shugart, S., and P. Hounshell. 1995. Subject matter competence and the recruitment and retention of secondary science teachers. *Journal of Research in Science Teaching* 32 (1): 63–70.

Staton, A., and A. Darling. 1989. Socialization of teaching assistants. *New Directions for Teaching and Learning (Teaching Assistant Training in the 1990s)* 39:15–22.

Stoecker, R., M. Schmidbauer, J. Mullin, and M. Young. 1993. Integrating writing and the teaching assistant to enhance critical pedagogy. *Teaching Sociology* 21:332–40.

Stover, L., K. Story, A. Skousen, C. Jacks, H. Logan, and B. Bush. 2001. The Teaching Teams Program: Empowering undergraduates in a student-centered research university. In *Student-assisted teaching: A guide to faculty-student teamwork,* ed. J. Miller, J. Groccia, and M. Miller, 98–102. Bolton, Mass.: Anker.

Streveler, R. 2001. Academic Excellence workshops: Boosting success in technical courses. In *Student-assisted teaching: A guide to faculty-student teamwork,* ed. J. Miller, J. Groccia, and M. Miller, 98–102. Bolton, Mass.: Anker.

Streveler, R., and R. King. 2000. Facilitating open-ended problem solving: Training engineering TAs to facilitate open-ended problem solving. *Journal of Graduate Teaching Assistant Development* 7:139–46.

Sundberg, M., and J. Armstrong. 1993. The status of laboratory instruction for introductory biology in U.S. Universities. *American Biology Teacher* 55:144–46.

Sundberg, M., J. Armstrong, M. Dini, and E. Wischusen. 2000. Some practical tips for instituting investigative biology laboratories. *Journal of College Science Teaching* 29:353–59.

Tang, L., and K. Sandell. 2000. Going beyond the basic communication issues: New pedagogical training of international TAs in SMET fields at two Ohio universities. *Journal of Graduate Teaching Assistant Development* 7:163–72.

Tanner, M., S. Selfe, and D. Wiegand. 1993. The balanced equation to training chemistry ITAs. *Innovative Higher Education* 17:165–81.

Trautwein, S. 1999. From teaching assistant to educator: Beginning steps on the professional path. *Journal of Graduate Teaching Assistant Development* 7:19–26.

Twale, D., D. Shannon, and M. Moore. 1997. NGTA and IGTA training and experience comparisons between self-ratings and undergraduate student evaluations. *Innovative Higher Education* 22:61–77.

University of California, Los Angeles. 2000. *Assessment of the general education cluster course experience: A pilot program of the College of Letters and Science. Year one of a five year study: The student perspective, the graduate student instructor perspective, the faculty perspective.* Los Angeles: College of Letters and Science, University of California.

Wagener, U. 1991. Changing the culture of teaching: Mathematics at Indiana, Chicago, and Harvard. *Change* 23:28–37.

Weise, D. 2001. *The pedagogical initiative with general chemistry teaching assistants at UC Berkeley, Spring 2001: A formative evaluation.* Boulder, Colo.: Ethnography and Evaluation Research, Center to Advance Research and Teaching in the Social Sciences, University of Colorado.

———. 2003. *Educating teaching assistants in new models for teaching and learning at the University of California, Berkeley. Second part of a formative evaluation: Qualitative analysis of second-round interviews with teaching assistants to a large introductory chemistry course.* Boulder, Colo.: Ethnography and Evaluation Research, Center to Advance Research and Teaching in the Social Sciences, University of Colorado.

Weiss, I., M. Matti, and P. Smith. 1994. *Report of the 1993 national survey of science and mathematics.* Chapel Hill, N.C.: Horizon Research.

White, L. 1993. Future engineering faculty: An assessment of engineering TAs. In *The TA experience: Preparing for multiple roles*, ed. K. Lewis, 339–46. Stillwater, Okla.: New Forums Press.

Winternitz, T., and W. Davis. 2000. Lessons learned during five years of the UC Davis program in college teaching. *Journal of Graduate Teaching Assistant Development* 7:69–75.

Wood, D., J. Hart, S. Tollefson, D. DeToro, and J. Libarkin. 2001. The Teaching Teams Program: Transforming the role of the graduate teaching assistant. In *Student-assisted teaching: A guide to faculty-student teamwork*, ed. J. Miller, J. Groccia, and M. Miller, 34–39. Bolton, Mass.: Anker.

Worthen, T. 1992. The frustrated GTA: A qualitative investigation identifying the needs within the graduate teaching experience. Annual meeting of the Speech Communication Association, October 29–November 1, Chicago.

Xie, Y., and K. Shauman. 2003. *Women in science: Career processes and outcomes.* Boston: Harvard University Press.

Index

About the Author

Elaine Seymour is a sociologist who, since 1989, has been director of Ethnography and Evaluation Research at the University of Colorado, Boulder. She is a British American whose education and career have been conducted on both sides of the Atlantic. Her research group, which includes both social and physical scientists, explores education and career issues in science, mathematics, and engineering. Elaine has served both as an evaluator and as an advisory board member for many initiatives that seek to improve quality and access in science education. The issues of women in science and engineering have been a special focus, and in 2002 Elaine received Women in Engineering Programs and Advocates Network's Betty Vetter Award for Research in recognition of this work. Her best-known book may be *Talking about Leaving: Why Undergraduates Leave the Sciences* (1997), coauthored with Nancy M. Hewitt. Her interest in teaching assistants that resulted in this book arose from Ethnography and Evaluation Research's evaluation work with groups of classroom innovators in chemistry and astronomy. Data from these and other studies of innovation in science education also inform Elaine's ongoing work on the sources and nature of change and resistance to change. Her efforts to find learning assessments that serve new science learning objectives and pedagogy resulted in her codevelopment of the online Field-Tested Learning Assessment Guide (FLAG) and a widely used online instrument, Student Assessment of their Learning Gains (SALG). She and her research group have recently coauthored a series of articles based on their groundbreaking study of undergraduate research from the perspectives of students and faculty over time. This work explores the benefits and costs of undergraduate research and the processes by which these are generated.